Bernard Ward

The holy gospel according to Saint Luke

Bernard Ward

The holy gospel according to Saint Luke

ISBN/EAN: 9783337282318

Printed in Europe, USA, Canada, Australia, Japan

Cover: Foto ©Thomas Meinert / pixelio.de

More available books at **www.hansebooks.com**

ST. EDMUND'S COLLEGE SERIES OF SCRIPTURE HANDBOOKS.

THE HOLY GOSPEL
ACCORDING TO
SAINT LUKE

WITH INTRODUCTION AND NOTES

BY THE
RIGHT REV. MONSIGNOR WARD
PRESIDENT OF ST. EDMUND'S COLLEGE

LONDON
CATHOLIC TRUTH SOCIETY
69 SOUTHWARK BRIDGE ROAD, S.E. ;
245 BROMPTON ROAD, S.W. ; 22 PATERNOSTER ROW, E.C.
1897

PREFACE.

THE present Commentary has been designed in the first instance for the students of St. Edmund's College. The privilege of affiliation to the University of Cambridge makes it necessary that our upper classes, or "College" Division, should be presented for the Higher Local Examination, in which Scripture is an important subject. The arrangements now made by the University authorities ensure that students from our Colleges studying Scripture shall not be at any disadvantage compared with other candidates. At the same time, the standard to be attained is a high one. The notes and Introduction have accordingly been made fuller than would be necessary for the ordinary Local Examinations, whether Senior or Junior, of either Oxford or Cambridge. To render the work more complete for its purpose, an Introduction has been prefixed dealing with the characteristics of the Gospel of St. Luke and kindred subjects. Further, in order that it may suitably find a place in the series of simple but adequate Commentaries projected some years since by the Catholic Truth Society, some pages have been added, dealing with the original texts, the Vulgate, and the Douay Version. Thus it is hoped that the use of the book will not be limited to candidates for any particular examination.

The three maps issued herewith have been specially prepared. The plan of the Temple is published by the kind permission of Lieut.-Colonel C. M. Watson, R.E.,

C.M.G., and is taken from the plans prepared by him for the *Palestine Exploration Fund*. He wishes it to be understood that it is not to be considered final, for many points are not yet known with certainty: see his article in the quarterly statement of the *Palestine Exploration Fund* for January, 1896.

It is proposed to continue the series as the needs of the Examinations require. The work for next year, together with the Gospel of St. Luke, includes the Second Epistle to the Corinthians. This will be edited by Mr. R. D. Byles, B.A., late scholar of Balliol College, Oxford, now a master at St. Edmund's. The Gospel of St. Mark is in preparation by our former Vice-President, the Rev. Edmond Nolan, now of Trinity College and St. Edmund House, Cambridge. The Gospel of St. John will be ready for 1899, and will be edited by the Rev. John McIntyre, D.D., Professor of Scripture at St. Mary's College, Oscott. Should the series be completed, it is intended to issue an Introductory Volume, in which the articles on the Greek Text, the Vulgate, and the Douay Version printed in this book will naturally find their place; as well as articles on Inspiration and other matters suitable for those beginning the study of Scripture.

My best thanks are due to Mr. B. F. C. Costelloe, M.A., for the great trouble he has taken with the MS. and for his valued counsel and assistance. Many changes have been made at his suggestion, and some parts almost rewritten. I am also indebted to Mr. Alfred Herbert, M.A., one of our Masters, and to Mr. James Britten, K.S.G., Honorary Secretary of the Catholic Truth Society. And I must also express my warmest thanks to the Rev. John McIntyre, who has kindly undertaken the office of censor.

St. Edmund's College,   BERNARD WARD.
   Feast of St. Luke, 1897.

It may be well to mention that at the time that this series was set on foot, the Catholic Manuals, edited by Rev. Sydney Smith, S.J., had not been announced as in preparation.

CONTENTS.

I. INTRODUCTION—

                                                                             PAGE

    CHAPTER I.—LIFE OF ST. LUKE   .   ix

    CHAPTER II.—TEXT OF THE GOSPEL.

        (1) The Original Text   .   xii
        (2) The Vulgate . .   xvi
        (3) The Douay Version   xxviii

    CHAPTER III.—CONTENTS OF THE GOSPEL.

        (1) Circumstances of Composition . xliv
        (2) Characteristics of the Gospel . . xlvii
        (3) Harmony with the other Three
            Gospels lvii
        (4) Analysis of the Gospel . . lxii

II. TEXT AND NOTES   1–283

III. MAPS—

    The Holy Land in the time of our Saviour *Frontispiece*
    The Temple of Jerusalem   .   1
    Plan of Jerusalem .   .   221

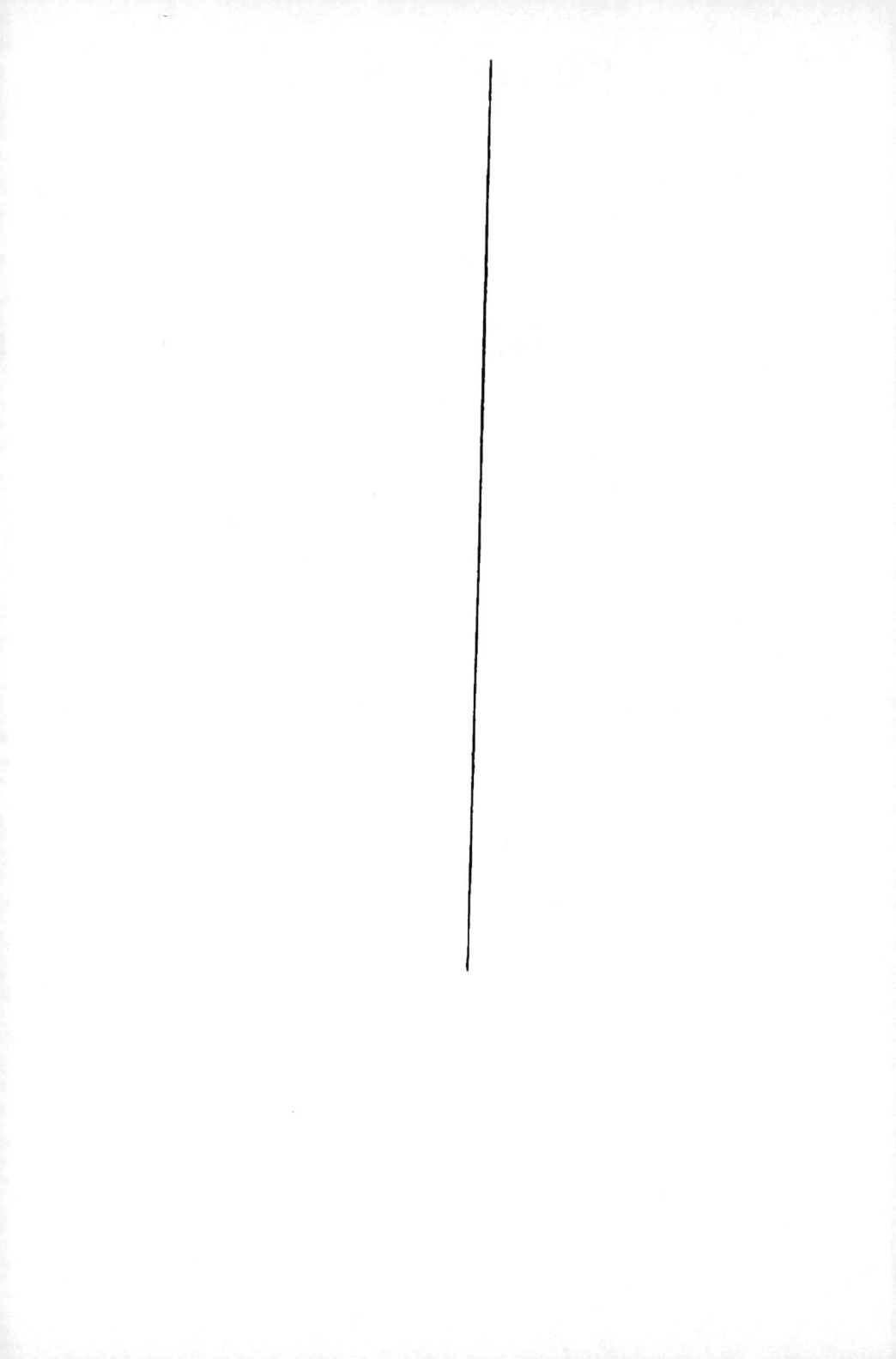

INTRODUCTION

CHAPTER I.

LIFE OF ST. LUKE.

THE sources of information from which to write a Life of St. Luke are at best scanty. They consist of (1) some deductions which can be made from his own writings: (2) a few chance allusions in the epistles of St. Paul; and (3) some early traditions quoted by the Fathers. The first two sources are very meagre. St. Luke tells us nothing about himself directly. Most of our information comes from the fact that he uses the first person plural in some parts of the Acts of the Apostles, thereby denoting that he took part in the events there described, while in the greater part of that work he uses the third person, showing that he took no part, but learnt them from others. The allusions to him in St. Paul are only three in number, and tell us little more than that St. Luke was with him at those particular times. The third source is more prolific, but also less trustworthy. A number of traditions have existed at various times, many of them contradictory, others of very small worth. A few only are ancient and reliable.

It is tolerably certain that St. Luke was a native of Antioch. Alban Butler considers it probable that he was one of the Hellenists, or Grecian Jews, of whom there were very many at Antioch; but the language used by St.

Paul (Col. iv. 11, 14) seems decisive against this view, for he expressly places him in another class than those "of the circumcision." It is quite probable, however, that he had been a proselyte to Judaism, which would account for his familiarity with the Septuagint version of the Scriptures, from which all his quotations are taken. By profession he was a physician, as we learn from St. Paul (Col. iv. 14), and though it is said that physicians did not always belong to the upper classes, it is evident from his style of writing that St. Luke was a man of education and refinement. He is also said to have been skilled in painting. Several pictures of our Lady still extant are attributed to him, one being at St. Mary Major's in Rome, and others at Bologna and Florence. The tradition is said to date back to the sixth century.

It is fairly certain that St. Luke never saw our Lord. This appears from his own statement at the beginning of his Gospel, to the effect that he had to consult others who were eyewitnesses, for an authentic account of what he wrote about, and it is confirmed by tradition. It is true that St. Epiphanius thinks that he was one of the seventy-two disciples, but this probably rests in the first instance on no further evidence than the fact that he alone records their mission; and the suggestion, also sometimes made, that he was one of the two disciples at Emmaus, is probably of similar origin. If, then, he became a Christian after the death of our Lord, it must have been at the preaching of one of the apostles. Both St. Peter and St. Paul preached at various times at Antioch, and the fact of St. Luke having become a companion of the latter has led some to believe that he was one of his converts. In any case, there is no doubt that St. Paul's influence over him was very great, and that they were greatly attached to one another.

The first time that we can trace St. Luke's movements with certainty is during St. Paul's second missionary journey, when he was setting out from Troas to Macedonia. At this stage in the Acts (xvi. 10 *seq.*) St. Luke suddenly uses the first person plural, thus showing that he took part in what is narrated. From that time onwards he seems to have been always either with St. Paul, or working under his direction in the different churches which he had founded. When St. Paul left Philippi, the third person is used again (xvii. 1), showing that St. Luke stayed there at least for a time, and he was there again when St. Paul returned seven years later. On the journey to Jerusalem they travelled together (Acts xx., xxi.), and during St. Paul's two years' imprisonment at Cæsarea (Acts xxiv.-xxvi.) St. Luke was with him. It was very probably at this period that he wrote his Gospel and part of the Acts (see *infra*), but the latter was certainly not completed at that time, as it contains an account of St. Paul's journey to Rome, and his shipwreck off Malta. In describing these, St. Luke again uses the first person plural, showing that he took part in them himself. The book of the Acts ends with St. Paul's arrival in Rome and his first imprisonment there, which lasted two years: a church now stands on the traditional site of his prison in the Via Lata. Though he was confined there and could not himself go out, others were allowed free access to him, and he continued his preaching to them (Acts xxviii. 30, 31). At the end of two years, as his accusers did not appear, he was set free. St. Luke evidently continued with him afterwards, for he was still in St. Paul's company during his second imprisonment and within a few months of his death, when his other friends had all forsaken him (2 Tim. iv. 6, 11). There seems no reason to doubt that he was with his master till the end.

About St. Luke's later history we have only tradition to guide us. It seems probable that he preached in Galatia, Dalmatia, and elsewhere. The tradition of his having been martyred is almost certainly correct: and though the place and manner of his death are not exactly known, there seems some reason for believing that he died in Greece.

CHAPTER II.

TEXT OF THE GOSPEL.

(1) THE ORIGINAL TEXT.

St. Luke wrote his Gospel in Greek. Nothing, however, is known of the original autograph. Indeed we have no trace of a single original autograph of any part of the New Testament. They seem to have perished in very early times, for it has been pointed out that in the controversies towards the close of the second century, much often turned on a disputed reading, and had any of the original autographs been extant at that date, they would certainly have been appealed to. Possibly the explanation is to be sought partly in the vividness of the oral traditions, which survived for several generations after the death of the Apostles, and obscured the necessity and critical value of the written records in their actual handwriting. It is not till the latter part of the second century—some sixty or seventy years after the death of St. John—that we find definite allusions to the Gospels and citations from them for controversial purposes. Irenæus (d. A.D. 203), Tertullian (d. about A.D. 220), and Clement of Alexandria (d. A.D. 220), are among the earliest Fathers who allude definitely to St. Luke's Gospel. It is mentioned by name in the earliest canon known, which has come down to us through the celebrated Muratorian fragment, and which is referred to the date A.D. 180. Another source of very early knowledge of St. Luke is the so-called Gospel of the heretic Marcion. The date of this is about 140 A.D. His work was, in fact, only a very mutilated edition of St. Luke's, in which the greater part of the first four chapters was omitted, and the remainder altered and interpolated to suit his doctrines.

Though the originals perished early, and though the full critical value of the Gospel manuscripts was not realized, it must not be supposed that they were looked on as valueless. There is evidence to show that many copies were made of part or the whole of the Gospels, and also of the Epistles, for devotional use, both public and private. The multiplication of sacred books led to their being made a special object for persecution, and one of the signs of apostasy was the surrender of them to the hands of the pagans. Those who did so were in consequence called *traditores*, with which we may compare our word *traitor*. It appears that very many copies were destroyed in this way, which will in some degree account for the fact that none dating back to the days of persecution are now extant. The earliest manuscript of the Gospel which we now possess forms part of what is known as the *Codex*, or *Manuscript*, which is in the Vatican Library at Rome, and dates back to some period in the fourth century. Another, the Sinaitic Codex, discovered during the last half-century, is almost as old.

The important manuscripts of the original text of the New Testament are of two kinds, called respectively *Uncials* and *Cursives*. The former are written throughout in capital letters; the latter in ordinary running hand. All the oldest manuscripts are Uncials; but the Cursives are far more numerous. Thus no Uncial is later than the eleventh century; no Cursive earlier than the ninth. On the other hand, there are only about a hundred Uncials, but more than 2,500 Cursives. Many of these latter are of not much value, being of comparatively recent date; and many of the Uncials contain very little text; while very few of either Uncials or Cursives contain the whole New Testament.

There are five chief Uncial manuscripts, dating between the fourth and sixth centuries. The following is a list. The letter after each is that by which it is distinguished for reference, according to a commonly adopted system; though it should be added that these apply only to the Gospels, and a different division is made for the Epistles and Apocalypse.

Codex Vaticanus (B), which has probably been in the Vatican Library in Rome since its establishment, about A.D. 1450, is the oldest and most valuable of all the Uncial manuscripts. It dates back at least to some part of the fourth century. Tischendorf places it about the middle of it, and Dr. Tregelles adds, "How much older it may be, we have no means of determining." The last eleven verses of St. Mark's Gospel, half of the Epistle to the Hebrews, the Pastoral Epistles and the Apocalypse are wanting; or rather were added in the fifteenth century. The rest of the New Testament is complete. Each page has three columns of text, which is written in the usual Uncial form, in continuous capitals and without divisions between the words. There were originally neither breathings nor accents, though these have since been added. The only punctuation consists of occasional intervals in the text. There are also divisions into paragraphs or chapters, according to a method not found elsewhere except in one single palimpsest MS. of a fragment of St. Luke. According to this method of division, all St. Paul's Epistles appear as one long work in ninety-three paragraphs.

Codex Sinaiticus (א), discovered comparatively recently (1859) by Tischendorf, in the Convent on Mount Sinai, and now kept at St. Petersburg. It is almost, but probably not quite, as old as the Codex Vaticanus, and contains the whole New Testament, written in four columns to a page, in much the same style as the Vatican MS.

Codex Alexandrinus (A), presented to Charles I. by the Schismatical Patriarch of Constantinople in 1628, and now in the British Museum. It dates from the fifth century. Most of the Gospel of St. Matthew is wanting, but the rest of the New Testament is almost complete.

Codex Ephraemi (C), in the Paris Library. This is a "palimpsest" MS. The original text was effaced as far as possible in the twelfth century, and the parchment used to receive the works of Ephraem the Syrian: hence the name now given to the Codex. Although it apparently includes all the New Testament, not much more than half of it is decipherable. The original writing belongs to the fifth century. In the sixteenth it was at Florence, and was brought thence to Paris by Catharine de Medici.

Codex Bezae (D), so called because it was presented by Beza to the University Library at Cambridge, where it now is. Beza himself found it in the monastery of St. Irenæus at Lyons, A.D. 1562. In some respects it is the most remarkable of all the Uncials. It is in Greek and Latin, and though dating only from the sixth century—more than a hundred years after St. Jerome's time—the Latin does not agree with what is now known as the Vulgate, but with that of the older Latin versions. It contains the four Gospels and Acts, and a part of the Catholic Epistles; but there are many verses wanting, and many very curious interpolations and glosses, especially in the Acts.

Besides these five chief Uncials, there are many others of considerable value, twenty-one of which have the Gospels complete. The value of the Uncials varies very much. In some instances there is evidence of their having been copied from very early MSS., and in that case they become of the highest importance. There are also a number of *lectionaria*, both Uncial and Cursive, containing selected portions of the New Testament for liturgical use.

In order to arrive at the true text of the Gospels, much work is necessary in collating the various manuscripts and examining the evidence of early versions and quotations from the Fathers so far as they bear on the discrepancies of these manuscripts. Origen (d. A.D. 254), who may perhaps be styled the earliest textual critic, testifies that even in his day there were various readings in different copies, which he described as arising " partly from the carelessness of individual scribes, partly from the wicked daring of some in correcting what is written, partly also from those who add or remove what seems good to them in the process of correction." Textual criticism has made great progress of recent years, and it is now said that the number of discrepancies actually observed in the various manuscripts, including Uncials and Cursives, amounts to over 120,000. Though this number sounds very large, yet when we consider how easily mistakes may occur in the mere copying of so long a work, and when we remember how often it has been copied and recopied (for very many of the intervening copies have been lost or destroyed), and then add the corrections hazarded in many cases, as Origen says, when the reading appeared difficult, the number may be accounted for without supposing any serious or deliberate corruption of the text.

The process of textual correction has been now reduced to an accurate science. The various manuscripts are not regarded as so many isolated authorities; but the gradual change in the text is worked into a sort of evolution on fixed principles, so that each MS. fits into its place as a link of a chain reaching from the Apostolic original to the modern printed text. Certain canons are applied throughout to test the validity of the reasoning, and also to ascertain the relative value of the different manuscripts. The result of the latter has been to show the immense superiority of the Vatican Codex in this respect over all others. Nevertheless, it is evidently not correct in every case, and its readings must be tested by the same rules as those of other manuscripts. As a result of all this investigation, it is said that, apart altogether from the Church's authority, the exact reading of seven-eighths of the New Testament has been critically ascertained with absolute certainty; and that of the remaining eighth part, the true reading may be determined in so many cases with a probability amounting to moral certainty, that the part in which there is substantial difference of opinion among scholars amounts to less than one-thousandth of the whole.[1] It need hardly be said that there is no other work of such antiquity of which we have a tithe of this certainty or completeness.

(2) THE VULGATE.

i. *Ancient Latin Versions.*

From very early ages versions of the original text were prepared in different languages. The first one is said to have been that of St. John's Gospel and of the Acts of the

---

[1] See article on Textual Criticism by Rev. J. O. Murray, M.A., in the *Cambridge Companion to the Bible*, p. 75.

Apostles which were translated into Hebrew. It is also said that parts of the New Testament were translated by those who were opposed to the Christians, to warn the Jews against Christianity. Among the early Christian versions may be mentioned, besides the Latin ones, those in Syriac, of which the *Peshito*, or *Common*, dates back to the third, or some think even to the latter part of the second century; the Egyptian, some of which are of almost equal antiquity; the Gothic (a language akin to English) of Bishop Ulfilas, belonging to the fourth century; and the Armenian and Æthiopic of the fifth century.[1] But the earliest of all were in Latin, and to them we shall confine our remarks, as these lead up to the well-known Vulgate version, which is the only one formally approved by the Church as authentic.

The Latin versions date back probably almost to Apostolic times. St. Augustine says (*Doctr. Christ.*, ii. 11) that "in the earliest ages of the faith, every one who got a Greek MS. into his hands, and thought he had some little acquaintance with each tongue, ventured to translate." It does not, of course, follow from this that many, or any, of these translators made a Latin version of the whole, or even a considerable part of the New Testament. It may, however, be taken as certain that such a version existed in the second century, and it was in all probability the work of many different authors. It may, in fact, easily have been the result of the joint labours of some of the early translators to whom St. Augustine alludes. This version, which is called the *Vetus Latina*, was current in Africa in the time of Tertullian, who gives an account of the character of its text. St. Cyprian (d. A.D. 258) also gives extracts from it.

As to the history of the *Vetus Latina*, critics are not agreed. In the years 1832-3, Cardinal Wiseman, then

---

[1] The versions which make up the celebrated Hexapla of Origen do not concern us here, as they were exclusively of the Old Testament. The six columns were supposed to be arranged in order of their nearness to the original: (1) Hebrew, (2) Hebrew in Greek letters, (3) Aquila, (4) Symmachus, (5) Septuagint, (6) Theodotion.

Rector of the English College in Rome, published a series of articles in the *Catholic Magazine*,[1] in which he maintained that it was purely African in origin, and that all other early Latin versions were merely recensions or revisions of it. He supposed that some of these were made in Italy, and that there was a particular one in use there, called in consequence the *Itala*. St. Augustine is well known to allude to a version by that name, and it was inferred that he became acquainted with it during his sojourn at Milan. In favour of Wiseman's contention, it may certainly be urged that the need of a Latin version would have been felt among the African Christians, who all spoke Latin, more than in Rome, where Greek was largely current; and the whole theory found at the time wide acceptance among those best qualified to judge. Of late years further investigation has tended to throw doubt on at least part of it. It has been said that the supposed Africanisms, on which great stress had been laid, have been most, if not all, paralleled from authors undoubtedly unaffected by African influences. Many modern scholars, however, even if they reject Wiseman's view as to its place of origin, freely admit the existence in early times of one chief Latin version from which all others took their rise; and believe that while individual verses or groups of verses may have been often retranslated from the Greek, no other complete version was made at that time.

ii. *Labours of St. Jerome.*

Although we admit that there was one chief Latin version of the Gospels, there is no doubt that from a very early date changes and modifications made their appearance in great numbers, introduced, as St. Jerome says, "by false transcriptions, clumsy correction, and careless interpolations," so that by his time he asserts that there were "almost as many forms of text as copies." The synoptical Gospels suffered especially in this manner,

---

[1] The articles were afterwards reprinted, with additions, among his essays.

INTRODUCTION

the omissions of one being often supplied by interpolations from another. By the latter half of the fourth century the evil had assumed such proportions that it was felt on all sides that something must be done to remedy it. The only way to do this was to produce an amended text by comparing the different versions with each other and with the Greek originals, and correcting the one by the other. To this task, at the request of Pope Damasus, St. Jerome addressed himself in the year A.D. 383.

St. Jerome was peculiarily fitted for undertaking the work. Born at Stridon, in Dalmatia, in the year A.D. 329, he lived to the age of ninety, and was a student, with little intermission, throughout his life. Though he did not begin the study of Hebrew till he was middle-aged, he nevertheless acquired a sufficient knowledge of it to produce a rendering of the Old Testament from the original, the faithfulness of which as a translation has never been questioned.

We are here concerned, however, not with St. Jerome's translation of the Old Testament, but with that of the New. This stands on a different footing in two ways. In the first place, while the translation of the Old Testament was undertaken by him spontaneously, that of the New was made, as stated, at the request of Pope Damasus, in order to supply a pressing need of the Church, and hence must be considered to have had from the first a high ecclesiastical authority. In the second place it was not, strictly speaking, a new translation at all, but rather a revision of an existing one. It is true that he wrote with the original Greek before him, and any amendment he made was based on it. But in very many cases, when the sense was not affected, he allowed the old rendering to remain, though it was not such as he would himself have chosen. This he did for the obvious purpose of avoiding offence by needless change. Hence the greater part of his work consisted in the removal of interpolations and corruptions, much of which could be, and was, done by a systematic comparison of different copies of the Latin. It is needless to point out that this was a far less laborious undertaking than producing a new translation throughout, and St. Jerome's work on the New Testament occupied fewer months than the other took years.

Besides the New Testament it appears that St. Jerome, while in Rome, likewise revised other parts of the Bible, by the aid of the Greek of the Septuagint. Most of his revision has, however, perished. The most important part remaining is the Psalter, which was used by the Church for many centuries, and is known as the "Roman Psalter." Later on, during his stay at Bethlehem, he produced a second revision of the Psalter, using this time the Hexapla text of Origen. This revision is now known as the "Gallican Psalter," from its having been adopted almost immediately throughout Gaul. Both of these revisions must be again carefully distinguished from the translation from the original Hebrew, which formed part of his great work on the Old Testament. So far as the Psalms are concerned, this version never found its way into either Breviary or Missal—a fact due to motives of convenience; for the Psalms being in such continual use, it was practically impossible to make so considerable a change as would have been involved. For similar reasons the "Gallican Psalter" has been likewise retained in the Vulgate.

From a critical point of view the value of St. Jerome's revision of the Gospels can hardly be over-estimated, affording as it does, in innumerable instances, evidence of the readings of early Greek texts, which have long since perished. For the newest part, consisting of the passages retranslated by St. Jerome himself, is almost, if not quite, as old as the Vatican Codex, and a very large part is retained from the *Vetus Latina*, which was at least two centuries older. And to this we must add that, as he himself tells us, he consulted many Greek texts, some of which were then very old, and all of them older than any we now possess. These were themselves often imperfect, and contained errors of copyists or of other kinds; but such errors naturally proceeded on a different plan from those in the Latin versions, so that it was possible to correct both by mutual comparison. And such mutual comparison acquires much additional weight through having been made by so discriminating and scholarly a critic as St. Jerome. It thus follows that when the Vulgate reading of any particular passage can be certainly ascertained, it is at least equal, and often much superior, in critical value to that of the best MSS. now extant.

iii. *Later History of the Vulgate.*

The new version of St. Jerome was not adopted very readily at first. There was a natural prejudice against innovation, and in favour of the familiar version to which the people were accustomed. Gradually, however, as new generations sprang up, its intrinsic merits gained for it general acceptance, first in one country and then in another. Before the close of the fifth century it was in use throughout Gaul, and a hundred years later St. Gregory the Great (d. A.D. 604) stated officially that the new version was admitted by the Apostolic See equally with the old. By that time, indeed, Africa stood alone in adhering exclusively to the old version, and after the lapse of another century, the use of St. Jerome's was almost universal. The name Vulgate, signifying the common edition, by which it is now known, had been used by St. Jerome himself, not as applied to his own version, but to the one then in common use—either the Septuagint or the old Latin translation of it. The term seems to have been used as applying to the old Latin so late as the time of the learned Friar Roger Bacon (1214-1292): and St. Jerome's is commonly alluded to by the Latin Fathers as "our version." The application of the term Vulgate to it seems to have come about gradually, as it became more and more the one received version. The term was finally stereotyped in its present sense by the decree of the Council of Trent, in which the St. Jerome version is styled "Vetus et vulgata editio, quæ longo tot sæculorum usu in ipsa Ecclesia probata est."

The circumstances of the gradual introduction of the new version, and its existence in many places side by side with the old, produced as a necessary consequence a gradual corruption of the text. Mixed texts made their appearance, and gradually old and new became so interwoven that it became difficult in many instances to ascertain what was St. Jerome's actual text. For this reason several revisions were attempted. One of the chief of these was due to Charlemagne, who entrusted the work to Alcuin about the beginning of the ninth century. Other revisions were made by Theodulf of Orleans about the same time, by Lanfranc, Archbishop of Canterbury, in the eleventh century, and by Abbot Stephen II. and Cardinal Nicolaus in the twelfth. In the thirteenth century, books of *Correctoria* were produced by the Dominicans and Franciscans and others, in which the various readings were discussed. Nothing further of importance happened till the whole state of texts and books was revolutionized by the invention of the art of printing. The very first book to issue from a printing press was an edition of the Vulgate, which was brought out at Mayence about A.D. 1455. Other editions soon followed, and when the Council of Trent began its sittings (A.D. 1545) copies were easily procurable.

By the time that the Vulgate was printed one important development had taken place in the text. This was the fixed division into chapters, which has now become permanent. Since very early days there had been some method of dividing the text, at least by marginal letters, and all the chief Uncial manuscripts have some such arrangement, designed for purposes of reference. The Vatican Codex has a system of its own. Most of the others are divided on a plan invented by Eusebius of Cæsarea in the fourth century. Later on, different copyists had different methods of arranging the text into *capitula*, or headings, and in some cases into verses. Thus, for example, in Charlemagne's revision of the Vulgate, St. Luke's Gospel is divided into 73 chapters and 3,800 verses, as against 24 chapters and 1,151 verses in the editions now in use. There was, however, no uniformity observed, and hence the facilities for reference were very inadequate.

The present division into chapters was due in the first

INTRODUCTION. xxiii

instance to Stephen Langton, Archbishop of Canterbury (A.D. 1207-1228), and was accepted by Cardinal Hugh de Cher (A.D. 1240). When it had once been adopted for the printed editions of the Vulgate, it passed into other versions in different languages, and gradually gained universal acceptance.

The further division of each chapter into verses soon followed. The Latin version of Pagninus was divided in this way, but the verses were much longer than those now in use. The present division is due to Henri Etienne, better known by the Latinised form of the name, Stephanus, or Stephens, one of a celebrated firm of French printers, who accomplished the whole work on his journey to Lyons A.D. 1551, in which year his edition appeared. The arrangement which he made was adopted everywhere in all subsequent editions, and its uniform acceptance has given it special advantages in facilitating reference. In some cases the sense becomes somewhat obscured, as in Luke ix. 7, 8, or 30, 31, where the verses change in the middle of a sentence. This, perhaps, could hardly have been avoided without introducing abnormally long verses here and there. It is difficult, however, to make excuse for the divisions of the chapters, coming, as they often do, at unsuitable places. This is particularly noticeable in St. Luke's Gospel. In several cases new and important sections begin in the middle of chapters ; in others a new chapter begins between verses closely connected in sense. Examples of the former are, iv. 14, vi. 12, ix. 51, xviii. 31 : of the latter, xi. 54 and xii. 1, xix. 48 and xx. 1, xx. 47 and xxi. 1.

But although it would appear that the points of division could in some cases have been better chosen, it must be admitted that *any* division into chapters must injure the resemblance between our version and the original composition of the evangelist. In the R.V. an attempt has been made to meet the case by numbering the chapters and verses in the margin, and dividing the text into paragraphs. A somewhat similar arrangement has been adopted in the modern Paragraph Bibles, and the consecutiveness between adjacent verses makes the narrative run more smoothly; but the division into paragraphs is open to much the same objection as that into chapters, except only that they are better chosen. A somewhat similar arrangement has been adopted in this book, but the paragraphs have been arranged in harmony with the chapters, so that no paragraph extends into two different chapters.

At the Council of Trent (1545-1563) the Vulgate was, for the first time, formally declared to be the Church's authentic version. The doctrinal bearing of the decree involves questions of some difficulty and delicacy; but the disciplinary part is plain enough. From the date of the Council, the Vulgate has been the only Latin version allowed to be used in the churches at public ecclesiastical offices. Up to that time the Psalms in the Roman Breviary had all been taken from the so-called "Roman Psalter." During the Pontificate of Pius V., in conformity with the Tridentine decree, this was changed, and the "Gallican Psalter" was adopted, as it had already been in the Vulgate. In the Ambrosian Breviary (used throughout the diocese of Milan to this day) and in at least one part of our own—the Invitatory at Matins—the earlier version has been retained. In the Missal all the Epistles and Gospels had for a long while been taken from the Vulgate; but in some of the tracts where portions of the Psalms occur—e.g., in that of Palm Sunday, taken from Ps. xxi.—the Roman Psalter is still adhered to. It is easy, therefore, to compare the two versions. It will be found that the difference between them is not great, and is much less than that between either and St. Jerome's translation from the Hebrew: see the instances given at the end of this article.

The Tridentine decree naturally led to the further question, What *was* the text of the Vulgate? St. Jerome's originals had perished long since, and, for reasons already stated, the various early copies differed considerably from one another. The Council accordingly enacted that a corrected edition should be prepared as soon as possible, which was to be the Church's authentic version. There were many critical and other difficulties in the way of carrying out this decree, and although the Board appointed continued its sittings for many years, it seemed as though the difficulties would prove insuperable. Pope Sixtus V., however, on his accession in 1585, took the matter vigorously in hand and carried it through. A Board was formed under the presidency of Cardinal Caraffa, and within five years the edition saw the light. Opinions as to its merits are divided. Pope Sixtus had himself revised and corrected the proof-sheets, and it is said that many of his emendations were faulty, while others agreed ill with the lines on which the editors had worked. But it was meant to be a final text, and was prefaced by the celebrated ordinance known by its first words "*Eternus ille*," prescribing its use in the Missal and all liturgical books, as well as "in all public and private discussion, reading, preaching, and explanation," and prohibiting the further publication of alternative readings.

In the same year in which the work appeared, however, Pope Sixtus died; and his stringent laws were never put into full operation. A further revision was, in fact, immediately put in hand, and carried through with such dispatch, that notwithstanding the delays due to the successive deaths of Popes Gregory XIV. and Innocent IX., it was nevertheless published before the end of the year 1592. This was the first year of the pontificate of Clement VIII., and the edition is known as the Clementine. The Preface was by Cardinal Bellarmine, and one of those who had taken a leading part in the revision was our English Cardinal Allen, the founder of Douay College, at that time residing in Rome. The text is known to differ in many places from St. Jerome's original, and the revisors admit that in some cases they knowingly allowed passages to remain when critically they should have been changed, in order to avoid giving offence, or for other reasons. There are no doubt many other passages where corruptions have found their way in beyond the power of correction. Though not perfect, it is, however, probably as nearly so as any other text that has been produced, or that may hereafter be produced. It really represents the result of the labours of the Papal Commission, which sat some forty years, and included among its members some of the ablest critics of that or any age. It has now held its ground as the Church's authentic version for over three centuries, and will probably continue to do so till the end of time.

The following extracts will give some idea of the relation between the *Vetus Latina* and the *Vulgate*, and likewise between St. Jerome's three versions of the *Psalter*.

I. The Old Latin and the Vulgate.

(MATT. v. 3-18.)

Vetus Latina.[1]

Beati pauperes spiritu, quoniam ipsorum est regnum cœlorum.

Beati misericordes, quoniam ipsis miserebitur Deus.

Beati estis quum ma'edixerint vobis et persecuti vos fuerint et dixerint omne malum adversum vos propter justitiam.
Gaudete et exultate, quoniam merces vestra copiosa est in cœlis; sic enim persecuti sunt prophetas qui fuerunt ante vos patres eorum.

Nolite putare quoniam veni solvere legem aut prophetas: non veni solvere legem aut prophetas sed adimplere. Amen quippe dico vobis, donec transeat cœlum et terra, iota unum aut unus apex non præteribit a lege donec omnia fiant. Cœlum et terra transibunt, verba autem mea non præteribunt.

Vulgate.

Beati pauperes spiritu, quoniam ipsorum est regnum cœlorum.

Beati misericordes, quoniam ipsi misericordiam consequentur.

Beati estis quum maledixerint vobis, et persecuti vos fuerint et dixerint omne malum adversum vos mentientes, propter me:
Gaudete, et exultate, quoniam merces vestra copiosa est in cœlis; sic enim persecuti sunt prophetas, qui fuerunt ante vos.

Nolite putare quoniam veni solvere legem aut prophetas: non veni solvere sed adimplere. Amen quippe dico vobis, donec transeat cœlum et terra, iota unum aut unus apex non præteribit a lege donec omnia fiant.

[1] See Smith's *Dictionary of the Bible*, p. 1697.

II. The Three Versions of the Psalter.

(PSALM XXI.[1])

Gallican Psalter (*Vulgate*).	Roman Psalter.	Translation by St. Jerome from the Hebrew.
Deus, Deus meus, respice in me: quare me dereliquisti? Longe a salute mea verba delictorum meorum.	Deus, Deus meus, respice in me: quare me dereliquisti? Longe a salute mea verba delictorum meorum.	Deus meus, Deus meus, quare dereliquisti me? Longe a salute mea rugitus mei.
Omnes videntes me deriserunt me: locuti sunt labiis et moverunt caput.	Omnes qui videbant me aspernabantur me: locuti sunt labiis et moverunt caput.	Omnes videntes me subsannant me; dimittunt labium, moverunt caput.
Salva me ex ore leonis: et a cornibus unicornium humilitatem meam.	Libera me de ore leonis: et a cornibus unicornium humilitatem meam.	Salva me ex ore leonis, et de cornibus unicornium exaudi me.
Qui timetis Dominum laudate eum: universum semen Jacob glorificate eum.	Qui timetis Dominum laudate eum: universum semen Jacob magnificate eum.	Timentes Dominum laudate eum: omne semen Jacob glorificate eum, et metuite eum universum semen Israel.
Annuntiabitur Domino generatio ventura; et annuntiabunt cœli justitiam ejus populo qui nascetur, quem fecit Dominus.	Annuntiabitur Domino generatio ventura, et annuntiabunt cœli justitiam ejus populo qui nascetur, quem fecit Dominus.	Narrabitur Domino in generatione: venient et annuntiabunt justitiam ejus, populo qui nascetur quem fecit.

[1] This Psalm is numbered xxii. in St. Jerome's third version, which follows the same division as the Hebrew, and therefore agrees with that adopted by the Anglicans.

(3) The Douay Version.[1]

i. *English Versions of the Bible.*

From early ages translations have been made of different parts of Scripture into the vernacular in this country. Venerable Bede finished a version of St. John's Gospel within a few hours of his death. Alfred the Great translated the Psalms, and, it is said, also other parts of the Old Testament. And there are copies still extant of translations, for the most part monastic, which were made both before and after the Norman conquest. It is needless to say that these translations did not circulate largely among the people, not only because the number of those who could read was comparatively small, but also because before the invention of printing every copy had to be made by hand, and was consequently very expensive. But among students and in the monasteries the Scriptures were always studied and reverenced. We read, for example, in the life of St. Edmund, Archbishop of Canterbury (d. A.D. 1242), that throughout his life he was a diligent student of the Scriptures, and that his reverence for them was such that he used to kiss the page before he began to read and after he had finished. In his work, *Speculum Ecclesiæ*, he devotes a chapter to the subject of the Scriptures, the dispositions with which we ought to read them, and the lessons we should learn from them.[2] This may be taken as the ordinary Catholic tradition of his time, namely, the thirteenth century.

Nevertheless, in the time of St. Edmund the Scriptures were seldom read in English. According to Dom Aidan

---

[1] Most of the details of the various editions of the Douay Version are taken from Archdeacon Cotton's *Rhemes and Doway* (Oxford, 1855), which, although written with undisguised animus against the Church, was nevertheless laboriously compiled, and apparently with great accuracy. It should be consulted by those who are interested in a full collation of the various texts. See also an article by Wiseman in the *Dublin Review* of April, 1837, and one by Newman in the *Rambler* of July, 1859, both of which have been reprinted in their volumes of essays respectively.

[2] See *Life of St. Edmund*, by Rev. Wilfrid Wallace, O.S.B., p. 355.

Gasquet,[1] the reason for this is to be sought in the fact that at that time, and even considerably later, the language of the court and of educated people generally, was not English but French, and that while the clergy and religious used the Latin, educated laymen would have used either that or the French; for there were already several versions in that language, as also in Italian, German, and Dutch.

The exact date at which the first English translation of the whole Bible was made is not known, but we have it on the authority of Blessed Thomas More that one existed long before the time of Wycliffe, and was therefore of Catholic origin. There is plenty of evidence to show that copies were in the hands of good and loyal Catholics and used by them with reverence and devotion. The Bible known as Wycliffe's is believed to have been finished about the year 1380. It is tolerably certain that Wycliffe himself had no share in any part of it except the Gospels, and it is doubtful whether he took much personal part even in these. The theory promulgated by him and the Lollards, that the Bible is intended for all, and should be our sole rule of faith, and the controversies to which this gave rise, have given the Bible known by his name an importance which it would not otherwise possess. It is of interest to us at the present day chiefly as being the oldest English version of the entire Bible which is extant. It was translated, not from the originals, but from the Vulgate as it then existed, that is, before the Sixtine and Clementine revisions. The translation is faithful, and free from any sign of controversial bias such as showed itself in some of the versions made during the Reformation.[2]

During the progress of the sixteenth century various versions of the Bible in English were issued by the Reformers. The most famous among these are Tyndale's

---

[1] See his article in the *Dublin Review* for July, 1895. It has recently been reprinted in his work entitled *The Old English Bible*.

[2] Dom Gasquet, indeed, in his essay quoted above, maintains that it is of Catholic and not of Wycliffite origin at all, and that it has been attributed to Wycliffe through error and prejudice.

Bible (1526-36); Coverdale's Bible (1535); Cromwell's, or the "Great Bible" (1539), the second and subsequent editions of which are also known as Cranmer's; the "Geneva Bible" (1560), translated for the most part by the exiled Reformers in the reign of Queen Mary, though not published in England till after her death; and the Bishops' Bible (1568). They were all prepared, not like Wycliffe's from the Vulgate, but from the original Hebrew or Greek; and the art of printing being by this time known, they circulated freely among the people. Though there was much good work in these versions, it was throughout marred by the theological opinions of the translators which led them to pervert many passages in accordance with their views. The Protestants themselves became dissatisfied with them, looking on the text as in many places corrupt. Early in the seventeenth century, therefore, King James I. organized a commission to revise the Bishops' Bible, which was then in use in the Anglican Churches, giving full instructions as to what versions to consult and on what plan to proceed. The result of their labours was the present "Authorised Version" (A.V.), which from a literary point of view has become so justly celebrated. It appeared in the year 1611, and though exceptions may be taken to a rendering here and there, taken as a whole it was distinctly more accurate than any of its predecessors enumerated above. For more than two centuries and a half it held its ground as the standard Anglican version, and will probably always remain the best known. The "Revised Version" (R.V.), published in 1881-5, though embodying the results of modern criticism and research, and correcting many slight mistranslations of the A.V., does not seem likely to supersede it for general use.

ii. *The Douay Bible and Rheims Testament.*

Returning now to the time of the Reformation, it may be said at once that the appearance of so many versions of the Bible in which the text was tampered with, and the theological arguments continually put forth by the Reformers, and based by them on texts of Scripture, rendered it in the highest degree important that a version should be produced by Catholics which could be relied on as authentic, and which could be accompanied by a sufficient number of notes to put the reader on his guard against the misinterpretation of many texts current among Protestants. The two difficulties which stood in the way were want of opportunity for the study required for such an undertaking, and want of means.

The former of these was met by the establishment of the celebrated English College at Douay by Dr. (afterwards Cardinal) Allen in 1568. Thither resorted many of the best scholars of the day, who had adhered to the Catholic faith and been forced to leave England. Hitherto they had been scattered here and there in the Low Countries and elsewhere. One of the chief works they undertook on coming together was the translation of the Bible. Though the result of their labours is known generally as the Douay Version, it was not in actual fact prepared at Douay; for owing to political troubles it was found necessary to quit the dominions of the King of Spain, in which it was then situated, and seek a temporary home elsewhere. A suitable refuge was found at Rheims, and thither the College migrated in 1578, ten years after its foundation. It was intended as only a temporary removal, and so it proved. After fifteen years, in 1593, it was found possible to return to Douay, where the old house had been retained, and where the work of the College was carried on during the next two centuries.

During the stay of the College at Rheims the New Testament was brought out. It bears date 1582. The rest of the Bible did not see the light till twenty-seven years later, when it appeared in two quarto volumes, dated 1609 and 1610. The delay in its appearance was due to want of means, for the translation was completed at the same time as that of the New Testament. Thus it happened that it was published after the return to Douay, and both Old and New Testaments are together known as the Douay Bible, being the work of the Douay Collegians. When the New Testament only is alluded to, it is more commonly called the Rheims Testament, from the place of its origin. It will be observed that the Rheims Testament was published twenty-nine years before the A.V. appeared, and though it is not specified in King James's "Instructions" as one of those to be consulted, is commonly recognized as having had considerable influence on the translators.[1]

In preparing the Rheims Testament the chief share of the work was borne by Dr. Gregory Martin, formerly of St. John's College, Oxford, who prepared the first draft. His text was revised by Dr. Allen, the founder and first president; Thomas Worthington, afterwards third president, Dr. Richard Bristow, and John Reynolds. The notes were chiefly by Dr. Allen, aided by Dr. Bristow and Thomas Worthington. The translation was made, like Wycliffe's, from the Latin Vulgate; but when necessary, duly compared with the Greek and Hebrew originals. The reasons why the translators took the Latin to work from in preference to the Greek and Hebrew are set forth by them in the Preface. They considered that the Greek Manuscripts of the New Testament to which St. Jerome had access were more free from error of reading than those which were then available, and they quoted many Protestant authorities in witness of the accuracy of the rendering in the Vulgate, which in many instances, it was asserted, they themselves had followed in preference to the Greek, when the two disagreed. The editors pointed also to words of the Doctors of the Church in favour of the Vulgate and its formal approbation by the Council of Trent, together with the fact that it had been in use for so many centuries in all liturgy and Church services. The care with which they endeavoured to keep as close as possible to the Latin is best set forth in their own words. In the Preface they speak as follows:—

"This we professe onely, that we have done our endevour with prayer much feare and trembling, lest we should dangerously erre in so sacred, high and divine a worke: that we have done it with all faith, diligence and sinceritie: that

---

[1] See Preface to R.V., i. 2.

we have used no partialitie for the disadvantage of our adversaries, nor no more license than is sufferable in translating of Holy Scriptures: continually keeping ourselves as neere as is possible, to our text to the very wordes and phrases which by long use are made venerable, though to some prophane or delicate eares they may seem more hard and barbarous, as the whole style of Scripture doth lightly to such at the beginning: acknowledging with St. Hierom, that in other writings it is ynough to give in traslation sense for sense, but that in Scriptures, lesse we misse the sense, we must keepe the very wordes."

The desire to keep close to the Latin version, however, led the translators into some obscurities of language ; and much of their translation was, to say the least, not in idiomatic English. The Latin collocation of words was often kept to, especially in the Old Testament, and in some cases the meaning is positively difficult to understand. Many Latin words also, which have no exact English equivalent, were bodily retained. Some of these, such as Pasch, Azymes, Parasceve, Loaves of Proposition, and others, have kept their place in our Bibles to the present day ; but the more extraordinary ones have been struck out long since. Thus, for example, in Phil. ii. 7, we read He "*exinanited* himself" ; in Phil. iv. 10, "you have *reflorished* to care for me"; and in Heb. ix. 28, "Christ was offered once to *exhaust* the sins of many." These three instances were mentioned by the translators in the Preface, and they were defended on the plea that the words in italics cannot be satisfactorily translated and were therefore best left in, so that the reader might ascertain by inquiry the full meaning of them, rather than be led away by an inadequate translation. In one of the subsequent editions, a list of unusual words, with an explanation of their meaning, was given at the end.

No episcopal approbation was attached to the first or subsequent issue of the Rheims Testament, for the good reason that there were, at that time, no bishops in England. An approbation was signed by four professors of theology of the University of Rheims, one of whom was Vicar-General of the Diocese. They duly certified that there was nothing at variance with Catholic doctrine or practice or against the civil rulers; and that it could, therefore, be published with utility. A similar approbation, signed by three professors of theology at Douay, was affixed to the Old Testament on its appearance in 1609.

The Rheims Testament went through four editions in about fifty years. The second one was printed at Antwerp, in 1600; the third, also at Antwerp, in 1621; and the fourth at Rouen, in 1633. Then it was allowed to rest for more than a century. A reprint, called the fifth edition, came out in 1738, which will be mentioned again presently. The place of its publication is not certainly known. In 1788 another reprint appeared, this time at Liverpool, called the sixth edition, and this was the last brought out by Catholics. Several Protestant editions have appeared for controversial purposes, the earlier ones—by Dr. Fulke, and dating from 1589-1633—containing the Douay and Bishops' Versions in parallel columns. The last reprint was a Protestant edition brought out in America, in 1834. The Douay Bible was printed a second time at Rouen, in 1635, but has never been reprinted since.

iii. *Labours of Bishop Challoner.*

The edition of the New Testament of 1738 deserves some attention. If it was printed, as is thought, in London. this fact is an agreeable sign of the gradual change which had come over the country; and after this date, the English Bible was never again printed abroad. It was, however, necessary then and long afterwards, as a matter of precaution, to omit any name of printer or publisher, in consequence of the penal laws still on the statute book, which were liable to be, and from time to time were actually enforced. There were two editors to this edition. One was Rev. Francis Blyth, a Carmelite and a convert; the other Dr. Challoner, afterwards Vicar Apostolic of the London District. The latter had spent some thirty years at Douay College, first as student, then professor of theology, and for the last ten years also vice-president. With the single exception of Alban

Butler, he was by far the most learned Catholic of the eighteenth century in England, and no better editor could have been found. It would seem that his work in preparing this edition brought before him the necessity of a new version, in which the language should be more intelligible and less antiquated; and a few years later he undertook to prepare a revision of the Douay text on his own responsibility. His first edition of the New Testament appeared in 1749, and was quickly followed by the whole Bible the next year, including a second edition of the New Testament, with a certain number—though not a large one—of changes in the text. Two years later, in 1752, he brought out a third edition of the New Testament, with numerous and important changes in both text and notes. This revised text held its ground in the subsequent editions during his lifetime. These consisted of a second edition of the Old Testament in 1763-4, and two more of the New Testament, in 1764 and 1772 respectively. In the last named for the first time the name of the publisher appears, namely, J. Coghlan, the well-known Catholic bookseller of Duke Street. Several other editions have appeared since the author's death, which occurred in 1781.

The appearance of Dr. Challoner's Bible marks an epoch in the history of the English Catholic Scriptures, and his version, though usually with further revision, has formed the basis of all our modern editions of the (so called) Douay Bible. A few words on the nature of the changes he introduced will therefore be in place.

These changes were certainly very considerable. According to Cardinal Newman,[1] they "almost amounted to a new translation"; so that, he says, "it is difficult to avoid the conclusion that at this day the Douay Old Testament no longer exists as a received version of the authorised Vulgate." Cardinal Wiseman, writing more than twenty years earlier,[2] says much the same. "To call it any longer the Douay or Rheimish Version," he writes, "is an abuse of terms. It has been altered and modified till scarcely any

---

[1] *Tracts Theological and Ecclesiastical*, p. 373.
[2] *Essays on Various Subjects*, p. 75.

verse remains as it was originally published." And he adds that "so far as simplicity and energy of style are concerned, the changes are generally for the worse." In support of this statement, he instances passages where Challoner has changed the Latin collocation. Thus in Heb. xiii. 9, where the Rheims Version has "With various and strange doctrines be not led away," which he changed to "Be not carried away with various and strange doctrines." Wiseman admits, however, that Challoner "did well to alter many too decided Latinisms"; and in fact, this was his chief work. Whatever may be said against his version as a whole, it was at least intelligible and written in the language of the day, which can hardly be said of the original Douay. In order to ensure this, Challoner seems to have borrowed largely from the A.V. Newman, indeed, says that his version seems to be quite as much based on that as on the Douay text. "Of course," he says,[1] "there must be a certain resemblance between any two Catholic versions whatever, because they are both translations of the same Vulgate; but this connection between the Douay and Challoner being allowed for, Challoner's version is even nearer to the Protestant than it is to the Douay; nearer, that is, not in grammatical structure, but in phraseology and diction." It will be noted that Newman is here alluding chiefly to the Old Testament. A reference to the extracts at the end of this article will show that a similar criticism can hardly be applied with equal force to the New Testament. But even in the latter, Dr. Challoner undoubtedly made extensive changes, which also usually took the form of approximating to the A.V. In all important texts, however, on which controversies have arisen, he necessarily follows the Rheims Version—as, e.g., in the constant use of the word *penance* for *repentance*. In other places also where there is a well-known diversity of rendering, as for example in Luke xviii. 7, we find him in agreement with it; and this again would follow from the fact of the Vulgate rendering being regarded by Catholics

[1] *Ibid.*, p. 370.

as the only authentic one, so that both the Douay translators and Challoner follow it even where it is practically certain that there is a slight mistranslation: as e.g., in Luke xvi. 22, 23. The phrases which Challoner has adopted from the A.V., are such as would naturally catch the eye and give an appearance of a greater substantial resemblance than in fact exists. An instance may be found in the opening verse of St. Luke's Gospel.[1] At first sight, Challoner's version seems to resemble the A.V.; but on looking into it, we find that in the essential difference— the meaning of the word πεπληροφορημένων (see on i. 1)—he follows the Rheims. In four passages taken at random out of the same Gospel, we find that of twenty-four places where the Rheims differs from the A.V., in fourteen Challoner follows the former: in seven the latter: in the remaining three he gives his own translation.

Two other points in Challoner's revision deserve attention. The first is the change in the proper names. Such names as Jewry, Esay, etc., appear in the Rheims Testament, and for these Dr. Challoner in due course substituted Judea, Isaias, etc. The object was evidently to make the proper names throughout accord with their form in the Vulgate, as had already been done in many cases. Nevertheless, he was not quite consistent, and in some cases where an English form was in common use, he adopted it. Thus, the Rheims has throughout the name *Moyses*; Challoner substituted the common form *Moses*.

The other point to notice is the translation throughout the Rheims Version of *Dominus*, or ὁ Κύριος, by *our* Lord. This is alluded to by the Rheims editors in a note on 1 Tim. vi. "As now we Catholikes must not say *The Lord*, but *Our Lord*; as we say *Our Lady* for his mother, not *The Lady*. Let us keep our forefathers' words and we shal easily keep our old and true faith that we had of the first Christians . . . the very words wil bring us to the faith of our first Apostles and condemne these new apostates' new

---

[1] See the extracts below. The first verse of the modern Catholic version agrees with Challoner.

faith and phrases." Wiseman writes in warm sympathy with this rendering, and quotes in support of it the Syriac version, in which a similar one prevails. But he admits that it is a "departure from accuracy," and this is the more patent from the fact that the version is taken direct from the Latin Vulgate, where the word used is simply "Dominus." It may well be added, that in numerous cases, especially in the Old Testament, the reference is not to Christ at all, but to the God of the Jews: see on Luke x. 1. Yet in many (though by no means all) of these the rendering "*our* Lord" is given in the Douay Bible: see for example Gen. x. 9.

It has been already noticed that Dr. Challoner revised his own translation twice—in his editions of 1750 and 1752. The changes introduced into the former were comparatively slight: those in the latter numbered over two thousand. Charles Butler, who knew the venerable Bishop as an old man, says that these changes were all made to Challoner's dissatisfaction. Dr. Cotton, while questioning this statement,[1] at the same time evidently thinks that they were not for the better, finding especial fault [2] with the change whereby "who" and "which" are throughout replaced by the word "*that*." This he considers an Irish form of speech, and he is of opinion that at least some of the later editions were published in Dublin. Whether this was so or not, it is certain that the latest text, that of 1752, proved the basis of the first really Irish revision of the Rheims Testament, which was brought out soon after Challoner's death. It is known as Dr. Carpenter's Testament,[3] the editor being the Rev. Bernard McMahon. The changes introduced are described by Newman [4] as rendering the text "more colloquial than Challoner's, and sometimes not so English, without being foreign." A few years later, a further revision was made by the same editor, who also brought out the rest of the Bible. This appeared in 1791, with the approbation of Dr. Troy (who had succeeded Dr.

---

[1] *Doway and Rhemes*, p. 50.   [2] *Ibid.*, p. 49, note.
[3] Dr. Carpenter, at whose desire it was undertaken, was then Archbishop of Dublin.
[4] *Tracts Theological and Ecclesiastical*, p. 379.

Carpenter), and is therefore known as Dr. Troy's Bible. The text of the Old Testament and the notes throughout were almost the same as in Dr. Challoner's last editions, but the text of the New Testament was further and very materially changed. The whole Bible was reprinted in 1794, and the New Testament, with some more changes, in 1803 and 1810.

iv. *Modern Editions of the Douay Bible.*

During the first half of the present century many editions of the Douay Bible have been issued in England, with great variety of texts. Haydock's[1] Bible (1811) professes to return to Challoner's text; but in fact in many cases (though by no means universally) it follows Dr. Troy's. Syers's Bible (1811-13) reverts for the most part to Challoner's earlier editions (1749 and 1750), though occasionally it agrees with his third (1752) against the other two. The New Testament issued by the Catholic Bible Society—an association which, after a brief existence, was condemned by Rome in 1816—agrees almost throughout with Challoner's first edition; the New Testament of Dr. Poynter, Vicar Apostolic of the London District, and formerly President of St. Edmund's College, agrees with it exactly. This was several times reprinted. In Dr. Bramston's Bible, however—dated from St. Edmund's College, March 27, 1829—a return was made to Challoner's later (1752) edition, while the New Testament of Dr. (afterwards Cardinal) Wiseman adopted a mixture of two of Dr. Troy's editions (1791 and 1803) and Haydock's.

The Bibles printed in Ireland have approximated more towards uniformity. There have been two chief editions, both of which were stereotyped, and circulate largely at the present day; and most — though not all — of the

---

[1] The editor of this well-known edition, Rev. George Leo Haydock, was one of the last students at Douay College, whence he escaped in 1793, shortly before it was seized by the French Revolutionists. After a year at St. Edmund's College, he completed his education at Crook Hall, the parent of the present Ushaw. Thomas Haydock, the publisher of the edition, was his brother. The Haydocks were an old Catholic Lancashire family: see *Haydock Papers*, by Mr. Joseph Gillow.

other editions printed in Ireland follow one or other of these two. One of them appeared in 1825, with the *imprimatur* of Dr. Murray, Archbishop of Dublin, and is known by his name. The other had the approval of Dr. Denvir, Bishop of Down and Connor, and was first published in 1839. The two editions hardly differ[1] either as regards text or notes. The text of the New Testament is taken from Dr. Challoner's first two editions of 1749 and 1750, but does not agree with either throughout. The notes are those of his third (1752) edition. The text of the Old Testament follows Dr. Troy's Bible, which, so far as the Old Testament is concerned, is almost identical with Dr. Challoner's. Most of the notes of the Old Testament are also those of Challoner.[2]

There is as yet no prospect of absolute uniformity of text among our Catholic Bibles. Cardinal Newman, writing in 1859, mentions four standard texts as current at that time—Dr. Murray's, Dr. Denvir's, Cardinal Wiseman's, and Haydock's. Of late years the issue of the sixpenny New Testament by Burns and Oates has, by its large circulation, tended towards making the text there adopted the standard one. Though it has Cardinal Wiseman's *imprimatur* (1858), the text does not agree with that of his New Testament of 1847, but with Dr. Murray's Bible, and therefore almost exactly also with Dr. Denvir's; but it differs very considerably from Haydock's. It has also the *imprimatur* of Dr. Ilsley, Bishop of Birmingham, dated 1889.[3] The agreement of its text with that of the two chief Irish editions also tends to make it supplant other texts, as Dr. Murray's and Dr. Denvir's Bibles have been issued in cheap form,

---

[1] Dr. Cotton says that they do not differ at all; but a slight variation may be found in John ii. 4, and there may very probably be others.

[2] Besides the versions founded on the Douay and Rheims, there have also been several independent Catholic translations. Among them may be mentioned the New Testament of Dr. Nary, of Dublin, probably printed in Paris (1718); the New Testament of Dr. Witham, President of Douay (1730); the Four Gospels of Dr. Lingard (London. 1836); and the New Testament of Dr. Kenrick (New York, 1849 and 1851).

[3] The latest edition has the *imprimatur* of Cardinal Vaughan.

and now circulate more widely than any other edition in England. The same text has recently been adopted by the Universities of Oxford and Cambridge for use in the special papers printed for Catholic candidates at the Local Examinations. It has, therefore, been employed in this book, and will be adhered to in the other manuals of the same series.

The following passages, taken almost at random from the Gospel of St. Luke, will serve to show the relation between the three versions—the modern Catholic, the original Rheims and the Anglican Authorised. The first named is taken from the text of Dr. Murray and Dr. Denvir; the other two from the original editions, but with the spelling modernised, to facilitate comparison.

i. 1 4.

Original Rheims.	*Modern Catholic.*	*Anglican Authorised.*
1. Because many have gone about to compile a narration of the things that have been accomplished among us :	1. Forasmuch as many have taken in hand to set forth in order a narration of the things that have been accomplished among us ;	1. Forasmuch as many have taken in hand to set forth in order a declaration of those things which are most surely believed among us,
2. According as they have delivered unto us who from the beginning themselves saw and were ministers of the word :	2. According as they have delivered them unto us, who from the beginning were eyewitnesses and ministers of the word :	2. Even as they delivered them unto us, which from the beginning were eyewitnesses and ministers of the word;
3. It seemed good also unto me, having diligently attained to all things from the beginning, to write to thee in order, good Theophilus,	3. It seemed good to me also, having diligently attained to all things from the beginning, to write to thee in order, most excellent Theophilus,	3. It seemed good to me also, having had perfect understanding of things from the very first, to write unto thee in order, most excellent Theophilus,
4. That thou mayest know the verity of those words whereof thou hast been instructed.	4. That thou mayest know the verity of those words in which thou hast been instructed.	4. That thou mightest know the certainty of those things wherein thou hast been instructed.

i. 28–31.

Original Rheims.	*Modern Catholic.*	*Anglican Authorised.*
28. And the Angel being entered in, said unto her, Hail, full of grace, our Lord is with thee: Blessed art thou among women.	28. And the Angel being come in said to her: Hail, full of grace, the Lord is with thee: Blessed art thou among women.	28. And the Angel came in unto her and said, Hail thou that art highly favoured, the Lord is with thee: Blessed art thou among women.
29. Who having heard, was troubled at his saying and thought what manner of salutation this should be.	29. Who having heard, was troubled at his saying and thought with herself what manner of salutation this should be.	29. And when she saw him, she was troubled at his saying and cast in her mind what manner of salutation this should be.
30. And the Angel said to her, Fear not, Mary, for thou hast found grace with God.	30. And the Angel said to her: Fear not, Mary, thou hast found grace with God.	30. And the Angel said unto her, Fear not, Mary, for thou hast found favour with God.
31. Behold thou shalt conceive in thy womb and shalt bear a son: and thou shalt call his name Jesus.	31. Behold thou shalt conceive in thy womb, and shall bring forth a son; and thou shalt call his name Jesus.	31. And behold thou shalt conceive in thy womb and bring forth a son, and shalt call his name Jesus.

ii. 10–14.

10. And the Angel said to them, Fear not: for behold I evangelize to you great joy that shall be to all the people:	10. And the Angel said to them: Fear not: for behold I bring you good tidings of great joy, that shall be to all the people.	10. And the Angel said unto them, Fear not: for behold I bring you good tidings of great joy, which shall be to all people.
11. Because this day is born to you a Saviour which is Christ our Lord, in the city of David.	11. For this day is born to you a Saviour, who is Christ the Lord, in the city of David.	11. For unto you is born this day in the city of David, a Saviour, which is Christ the Lord.
12. And this shall be a sign to you, you shall find the infant swaddled in clothes and laid in a manger.	12. And this shall be a sign unto you. You shall find the infant wrapped in swaddling clothes, and laid in a manger.	12. And this shall be a sign unto you; ye shall find the babe wrapped in swaddling clothes, lying in a manger.

INTRODUCTION.   xliii

Original Rheims.	*Modern Catholic.*	*Anglican Authorised.*
13. And suddenly there was with the Angel a multitude of the heavenly army, praising God and saying,	13. And suddenly there was with the Angel a multitude of the heavenly army, praising God and saying :	13. And suddenly there was with the Angel a multitude of the heavenly host, praising God and saying,
14. Glory in the highest to God : and in earth peace to men of good will.	14. Glory to God in the highest : and on earth peace to men of good will.	14. Glory to God in the highest, and on earth peace, good will towards men.

X. 1–2.

1. And after this, our Lord designed also other seventy-two : and he sent them two and two before his face into every city and place whither himself would come.	1. And after these things, the Lord appointed also other seventy-two : and he sent them two and two before his face into every city and place whither he himself was to come.	1 After these things, the Lord appointed other seventy also, and sent them two and two before his face into every city and place, whither he himself would come.
2. And he said to them, the harvest truly is much : but the workmen few. Desire therefore the Lord of the harvest, that he send workmen into his harvest.	2. And he said to them : The harvest indeed is great, but the labourers are few. Pray ye therefore the Lord of the harvest, that he send labourers into his harvest.	2. Therefore said he unto them, the harvest truly is great, but the labourers are few : pray ye therefore the Lord of the harvest, that he would send forth labourers into his harvest.

xxiii. 35–37.

35. And the people stood expecting, and the princes with them derided him, saying, Others he hath saved, let him save himself, if this be Christ the elect of God.	35. And the people stood beholding, and the rulers with them derided him, saying : He saved others, let him save himself, if he be Christ the elect of God.	35. And the people stood beholding and the rulers also derided him, saying : He saved others, let him save himself, if he be Christ the chosen of God.
36. And the soldiers also mocked him, coming to him and offering him vinegar,	36. And the soldiers also mocked him, coming to him and offering him vinegar :	36. And the soldiers also mocked him, coming to him and offering him vinegar.
37. Saying, If thou be the King of the Jews, save thyself.	37. And saying, If thou be the King of the Jews, save thyself.	37. And saying, If thou be the King of the Jews, save thyself.

CHAPTER III.

CONTENTS OF THE GOSPEL.

(1) Circumstances of Composition.

In order to guide us to a true estimate of the meaning and scope of St. Luke's Gospel, it is first necessary to ascertain the circumstances under which he wrote. These naturally fall into three groups: (*a*) time and place; (*b*) purpose or object; (*c*) language.

(*a*) The traditions as to time and place are numerous, but one which has held its ground for a long time is that it was written at Cæsarea, during St. Paul's imprisonment there, about A.D. 60. This is confirmed by a careful examination of the Gospel, and the Acts of the Apostles, which unanimous and unquestioned tradition, as well as distinct internal evidence, ascribe also to St. Luke. From the very first words of the Acts, it appears that it was written after the Gospel, and hence, if we can assign its date, we shall have a limit of time before which the Gospel was certainly written. The contents of the Acts give us some clue to such limit. The latter half is an account of St. Paul's missionary labours. We know from his Second Epistle to Timothy (iv. 11), that St. Luke remained with him at Rome till the last; yet the treatise on the Acts breaks off abruptly before the end of his first imprisonment, and gives no account of his subsequent labours. It is a natural inference that St. Luke had nothing further to say, because he had brought his account up to the date at which he was writing. And further, the fact that he summarizes the two years which St. Paul spent in his Roman prison in two verses, points to the conclusion that the chief events of that time were familiar to Theophilus and any others for whom the treatise was primarily intended, and therefore did not need recording. Some of these events are known to us from other sources, such, for example, as the visit of Epaphroditus from

Philippi, bearing with him the offerings of the faithful in that city, and the visit of Onesimus, the slave of Philemon of Colossa, which were the occasions of three of St. Paul's Epistles respectively, viz., to the Philippians, to Philemon and the Colossians, the conversion of some of the actual household of Cæsar (Phil. iv. 22), &c. There were no doubt many other equally important events of which we now know nothing. These two years were probably a time of much work for St. Paul, and therefore also for St. Luke, and it is difficult to suppose that he would have found leisure to write the whole of the Acts, much less the Gospel also, at that time. A similar consideration will also furnish us with the probable reason for the Acts having never been finished up to the death of St. Paul. The active and uncertain life of the Apostolate would not easily be compatible with devoting so much time as would be required for examining documents and witnesses, and putting together the information acquired into a regular composition. This would apply to most of the time during which St. Luke was with St. Paul. There is one period to which it would not apply, and that is the two years that they spent at Cæsarea (Acts xxiv.). During that time, though it was arranged that St. Paul should not be kept very strictly, and that his friends —including, therefore, St. Luke—should have access to him (*ibid.*, v. 23), it does not appear that much direct missionary work was done. This time, therefore, would be eminently suitable for writing, and it is natural to conjecture that the Gospel and the greater part of the Acts were written then, and that the latter was finished up to date two years later in Rome.

Such is at least a very old tradition. Nevertheless, there are certain difficulties to be urged against it which cannot be ignored. One of them is connected with Theophilus, to whom the Gospel is addressed. If, as appears probable (see below), he was a Roman, St. Luke would not have come across him till he himself reached Rome. Some have, therefore, supposed that he wrote both Gospel and Acts in Rome about the year 63. Others place them at a later date still—about A.D. 80, after the fall of

Jerusalem; but one of the chief arguments used in favour of this supposition, is the extreme definiteness of the prophecy of the fall, which, it is asserted, points to its having already taken place; and in the mind of a Catholic this argument will, of course, have no weight. Indeed, a similar argument may be urged in the opposite sense; for on another occasion when St. Luke records a prophecy which had already received fulfilment, he does not fail to call attention to the fact: see Acts xi. 28. From his silence as to the fall of Jerusalem, therefore, we may reasonably conclude that it had not yet taken place. On the whole there seems little reason to reject the opinion that the Gospel was written between the years 60 and 63; and that if it was written at Rome, much of the material was gathered during the imprisonment of St. Paul at Cæsarea.

(*b*) The Gospels are not, and do not profess to be, histories. They are rather what we should call biographical notes, intended to serve as a record and explanation of the Redemption. They set before us so much of our Lord's life and teaching as will serve that object. The word Gospel is an abbreviation for God-spel, and is equivalent to " good tidings," as we actually translate it in Luke ii. 10. St. Luke's Gospel is more like a history than any of the others, and gives something of a synopsis of our Lord's life, beginning before His birth, and continuing to His death, resurrection, and ascension. But it is far from a complete account. Many important events, such as the visit of the Magi, the raising of Lazarus, &c., which we know from other sources, are entirely omitted. Throughout his Gospel St. Luke, no less than the other evangelists, was guided by the main object which he had in view, namely, the setting forth of "a narration of the things that have been accomplished amongst us" (i. 1), i.e., of the Redemption, and accordingly he gives the greater part of his attention to the public ministry and teaching of our Lord.

Both the Gospel and the Acts are addressed to one, Theophilus. No certain tradition exists as to who he was, but the title "most excellent" points to his being a man of distinction: see on i. 3. Moreover, whereas throughout the Gospel and Acts geographical explanations are continually given of the different places in Palestine and elsewhere, these suddenly cease when St. Luke comes to speak about places in Italy. Thus we have "a city of Galilee called Nazareth" (i. 26); "into Judea, to the city of David, which is called Bethlehem" (ii. 4); "Capharnaum, a city of Galilee" (iv. 31); "Arimathea, a city of Judea" (xxiii. 51); and other similar passages. In the Acts, in St. Paul's journey to Rome, a geographical note is given on every place till Italy is reached; but Rhegium, Puteoli, Apii Forum, Three Taverns, are mentioned without any additional explanation. We obviously conclude that Theophilus was not a Jew, and that he was a Roman of distinction; but beyond this we cannot go. It is pretty certain, however, that St. Luke had in his mind more than this one reader. It has often been said that he wrote chiefly for Gentiles. This cannot be accepted without some qualification. No doubt Theophilus himself was a Gentile, as St. Luke also was, but the ordinary Church of that date, for whom St. Luke wrote, would have included both Jews and Gentiles, the former as the original nucleus, the latter, in general far more numerous, as subsequent converts, many of whom had reached the Church through the intermediate stage of proselytism to the Jewish religion.

(c) The Jews of the dispersion belonged for the most part to the class we call Hellenists; that is, they spoke Greek, and used the Greek version of the Scriptures, known as the Septuagint; and all the more educated of the Gentiles even in Rome, among whom it appears was Theophilus, were familiar with the Greek language. St. Luke's own native tongue was also Greek, so that it was natural that he should write in that language.

(2) CHARACTERISTICS OF THE GOSPEL.

The chief characteristics of the Gospel may conveniently be classed under three heads: (i.) Those due to the personality of St. Luke; (ii.) those due to the circumstances of his writing and the class of readers for whom his Gospel was primarily intended; (iii.) those not directly traceable to either of these causes.

i. *Characteristics due to the personality of St. Luke.*

(*a*) *Influence of our Lady.* It is an old tradition that St. Luke was acquainted with our Lady, and it is very probably true. In any case, it is certain that the early part of his Gospel is mainly due to her, as no one else would have had the requisite knowledge. For St. Joseph being dead, our Lady alone would have been able to tell the history of the Annunciation and Nativity, and the earlier mysteries of our Lord's life. Again, as both Zachary and Elizabeth must have been dead long before St. Luke became a Christian, it is easiest to suppose that the tradition of the events connected with the birth of St. John Baptist were transmitted through our Lady. The three great Canticles, so characteristic of this Gospel—the *Benedictus*, *Magnificat*, and *Nunc dimittis*—which are recited daily by the clergy at Lauds, Vespers and Compline respectively, must have been obtained by St. Luke directly or indirectly from our Lady.

(*b*) *Influence of St. Paul.* The connection between St. Paul and St. Luke is well known, and has already been commented on. Some have even thought that St. Paul alluded to this Gospel as his own in the Epistle to the Romans (ii. 16). This is not indeed a probable supposition, but the fact that it has been made illustrates the common belief of the close connection between St. Paul and St. Luke. It has been pointed out that each of the four Gospels possesses apostolic authority; for St. Matthew and St. John were themselves apostles, St. Mark wrote at the direction of St. Peter, and St. Luke was influenced by St. Paul. But the influence which St. Paul exerted over St. Luke was different from that which St. Peter exerted over St. Mark, not in degree, but in kind. It is universally admitted that St. Mark's Gospel is to a great extent the work of St. Peter, who directed him throughout, and gave him all the requisite information. St. Luke, on the other hand, did not get his information from St. Paul, but from eyewitnesses, as he himself says. The influence of St. Paul was indirect. Those who have made a careful study of the text tell us that many words and phrases which are characteristic of St. Paul occur frequently in St. Luke. One instance of this is the frequent use of the title "the Lord," as applied to Christ: see on x. 1. The Jews were a monotheistic people, and those who lived in Greek-speaking countries had already been accustomed to the use of this title throughout the Septuagint version as standing for God. St. Paul in more than one text (1 Cor. xii. 3; Phil. ii. 11, &c.) uses it clearly with respect to Christ's Divinity; so that it is a significant fact that St. Luke uses it eleven times in his Gospel, while elsewhere among the synoptic Gospels it occurs only in Mark xvi. 20, which is in the part probably written at a later date than the rest. St. John uses it twice, but he wrote much later, when the doctrine of Christ's Divinity was more clearly apprehended in the Church; and both he and St. Mark restrict its use to Christ *after* the resurrection, when of course His Divinity was more directly in evidence.

Another important example of St. Paul's influence is to be found in St. Luke's account of the institution of the Blessed Eucharist: see on xxii. 19. The close agreement, almost word for word, with the account in the first Epistle to the Corinthians cannot be due to chance. And likewise we cannot suppose it to be a kind of formula which was recognized and in common use. It is probable that some such formula did exist in very early times, and was no doubt the basis of the words used in the Canon of the Mass; but though this resembles St. Luke's account somewhat, they are by no means the same. The only conclusion that seems possible is that St. Luke had heard St. Paul describe the Institution so often that he naturally himself used the same language. This is the more remarkable, as St. Paul had learnt it by special revelation, as he himself tells us, while St. Luke had probably also heard it from eyewitnesses, that is, from some of the apostles.

INTRODUCTION.

It is also noteworthy that St. Paul and St. Luke both tell us of Christ's appearance to St. Peter on Easter Sunday, which the other evangelists omit.

Other facts or teachings of our Lord have been pointed out as common to St. Luke and St. Paul. The student may compare those in the following list, but it will be seen that standing as isolated texts, the similarity is too slight to be of much weight:

St. Luke.		St. Paul.	
	iv. 22.		Col. iv. 6.
	vi. 36.		2 Cor. i. 3.
	vi. 39.		Rom. ii. 19.
	x. 8.		1 Cor. x. 27.
	xi. 41.		Titus i. 15.
	xxi. 36.		Eph. vi. 18.
	xxiv. 46.		Acts xvii. 3.

It is of course true that many of the leading ideas of St. Luke's Gospel, such as the necessity of continual prayer and of thanksgiving, the excellence of the specially Christian virtue of penance, the universality of the Redemption, find expression also in St. Paul's Epistles; but that after all is little more than saying that they both professed one common Christianity. The ideas are not in reality Pauline, but Christian. Nevertheless, in some cases St. Paul's enunciation of them stands prominently forward, especially when he is combatting the Judaizing tendency of some of the early Churches. See also *infra*, § iii.

(*c*) *Physician and Artist.* St. Luke was a physician (Col. iv. 14), and is said to have been also an artist. Traces of both facts are pointed out in his Gospel and in the Acts, though in the former case some technical knowledge is required to appreciate the full force of what is urged. Thus, for example, it is said that the peculiar word ($συνεχομένη$) used of Peter's wife's mother for "taken with" [a fever] is a technical one, and it is not found in the narratives of the same miracle in St. Matthew and St. Mark, but is found again in Acts xxviii. 8 in the same sense. And it is used nowhere else in New Testament Greek. So also the use of the verb $ἰάομαι$ in the active sense (=to heal), and $ἴασις$ in the sense of "healing" appears to be medical rather than ordinary Greek. The verb so used occurs seven times (v. 17, vi. 19, ix. 2, 11, 43, xiv. 4, xxii. 51) in St. Luke's Gospel, and three times (ix. 34,* x. 38, xxviii. 8) in the Acts ; and the noun once in the Gospel (xiii. 32) and twice in the Acts (iv. 22, 30*), but nowhere else in the New Testament. The verb was used as active in the earlier idiom of the Septuagint (as may be seen by the quotations in Luke iv. 18 ; Matt. xiii. 15 ; Acts xxviii. 27); but it is only used in the passive sense by the New Testament writers except St. Luke. It seems to him to have had a special significance as connected with the names of Ἰησοῦς, which he liked to think of as if it meant "the healer," as may be seen by the passages marked above by an asterisk. Other instances usually given illustrating his exact observation of medical facts are the description of our Lord's sweat of blood (xxii. 44), of the "surgical miracle" to Malchus (xxii. 51), of the apostles being "heavy with sleep" during the Transfiguration, and "sleeping for sorrow" during our Lord's agony, and of details of the woman's illness (xiii. 11). And perhaps we may add the careful way in which he distinguishes bodily disease from demoniacal possession (iv. 40, 41, and elsewhere). These things are many of them small in themselves, but their collective evidence is considerable, as identifying the author of both books with the "beloved physician."

The evidences of St. Luke's artistic mind are more numerous, and whether the tradition of his having been a painter is well founded or not, it is evident that he had a habit of minute observation, and a keen perception of artistic situations. His Gospel is graphic throughout, and some of the pictures he draws, though often in very few words, are evidence of his descriptive faculty. Among them may be specially mentioned the Good Shepherd returning with the lost sheep on his shoulders, one of the earliest representations of Christ adopted by Christian art. In the history of our Lord's life we have such incidents as the scene in the Temple at the presentation, the Boy Jesus among the doctors of the law, the scene in the synagogue at Nazareth, the raising of the widow's son at Naim, the home of Martha and Mary, the two disciples with our

Lord at Emmaus, and very many others. Among the parables, or, as many think, true stories, may be named the Good Samaritan, the Prodigal Son, the Pharisee and Publican in the Temple, the Unjust Steward, Dives and Lazarus, &c.

ii. *Characteristics due to the class of readers for whom the Gospel was primarily intended.*

(*a*) *Universality of the Gospel.* It has been pointed out that St. Luke wrote chiefly, but not exclusively, for Gentiles. Hence he gives us the Gospel as preached to both Jew and Gentile side by side. The one great sermon of our Lord which he records in full—the Sermon on the Plain—is one that might well be addressed to a mixed audience such as that of which the Church was composed at the time he wrote. This is equally true whether or not we regard it as identical with the Sermon on the Mount. The only difference is that in the former case the parts inapplicable to such a mixed audience were deliberately omitted by St. Luke, while in the latter case, he advisedly chose a sermon which had, as a fact, been addressed to a mixed audience, in order to suit the purpose he had in view. In our Lord's sermon in the synagogue at Nazareth, a similar idea is prominent, the fact that the prophets of old had been sometimes sent specially to Gentiles, being clearly brought out. See also Simeon's prophecy (ii. 32) that our Lord should be "a light for the revelation of the Gentiles, and the glory of thy people Israel." Then, again, St. Luke is the only one of the synoptists who mentions the Samaritans as the recipients of God's graces and favours: see on ix. 52. Lastly, some of the parables recorded by him bring the same idea into prominence. Such as that of the Good Samaritan, which is peculiar to St. Luke, and illustrates the universality of the outpouring of God's graces; for its meaning is that all men, however different in race and national sympathy, are nevertheless to be considered as "neighbours." In like manner, St. Luke is less concerned than St. Matthew about our

Lord being of the race of Abraham and of David, though he does not fail to note it in its due place, but more with His having a true human nature and being a member of the human family. For this reason, he traces His genealogy not only back to Abraham, as St. Matthew does, but through Abraham back to Adam, who he says "was of God." Among the early parts of his Gospel which are peculiar to himself, may be found descriptions of the events before our Lord's birth, His birth, His life as a child and as a youth of twelve years, and His growth till He was about thirty. And the ceremonies of Purification, Presentation, journey to Jerusalem for the Pasch, are all mentioned as in fulfilment of the law, thereby showing that He was truly **Man.**

(b) *The Gospel of the Poor and the Despised.* The poor and the unfortunate were looked down on by Jew and Gentile alike. The Jews looked on temporal misfortune as a direct chastisement of God: cf. John ix. 2, "Rabbi, who hath sinned, this man or his parents, that he should be born blind?" The pagans looked on the unfortunate as the objects of the malediction of the gods. In the Catholic Church, on the other hand, the poor and the despised in this world are held before us as truly blessed. This was one of the marks of the Church from the beginning, so that many embraced the state of voluntary poverty: cf. Acts ii. 45, iii. 6, iv. 32 *seq.* The Christians for whom St. Luke wrote would have included many who were so poor as to be the objects of "daily ministration"; and he brings this class before us as the objects of our Lord's special solicitude. The text from Isaias with which our Lord opened His sermon at Nazareth, recorded in this Gospel only (iv. 18), is a distinct reference to His special mission to the poor and the outcast: "The Spirit of the Lord is upon me, wherefore he hath anointed me, to preach the gospel to the poor he hath sent me, to heal the contrite of heart: to preach deliverance to the captives, and sight to the blind, to set at liberty them that are bruised," &c. (Isa. lxi. 1, 2). If we turn to the four Beatitudes of the Sermon on the Plain, we find again the blessedness of poverty and temporal misfortune brought forcibly before us, and more so than in the eight Beatitudes of St. Matthew. "Blessed are ye poor," "Blessed are ye that hunger now," "Blessed are ye that weep now," "Blessed shall ye be when men shall hate you," &c. The love of the poor is indeed a special note of Christianity. When St. John the Baptist asked whether our Lord was the Messiah, our Lord gave as one of the signs of His mission, on an equality with the working of miracles, the fact that "To the poor the gospel is preached" (vii. 22). His own example is placed before us in this Gospel in the poverty of the Holy Family, that of the place where He was born, the poor shepherds as His first worshippers, the offering of the poor made for Him in the Temple, the Holy Women ministering to Him in His public life, &c. And among the parables recorded only by St. Luke, we have the Rich Fool, Dives and Lazarus, and the Unjust Steward, all on the proper use of riches. See also xiv. 12-15. Finally, we may notice the parable of the Supper, which is similar to one given by St. Matthew; but the descriptive words, "Bring in hither the poor and the feeble and the blind and the lame," are peculiar to St. Luke.

(c) *The Gospel of Womanhood.* The inferiority of women in Israel is to this day a marked feature in Jewish life. While the man prays each morning, "O Lord I thank Thee that I am not born a woman," the woman on the other hand is taught to say humbly, "O Lord, I thank Thee that Thou hast made me what I am." The inferiority is indicated by the place assigned to women in the synagogue: see on iv. 15. The same characteristic prevails throughout the whole of Oriental, and especially of Semitic, life. In Greek life there was something of the same kind. The wife and mother of earlier days, the matron of Homer for instance, holds a place of far more respect than the type common at Athens in the time of Socrates, Xenophon and Plato, when the wife was less the mistress than the superintendent of the house, who seldom saw visitors, and only rarely issued from home. It has been repeatedly remarked that the office and dignity of our Lady in the Divine economy, which are brought into such prominence in this Gospel, has made such treatment of woman impossible in Christianity. St. Luke lays stress generally on the ministrations of the Holy Women. He brings into greater prominence than any of the other evangelists, the fact that many women followed our Lord from Galilee to Jerusalem; and he alone records their ministrations at an earlier date: see vii. 37 *seq.*, viii. 2, 3, x. 38 *seq.* It may be noted also how many holy women he tells us of. Besides our Lady, he mentions something of St. Elizabeth, Anna the prophetess, Mary Magdalen, Martha, the widow of Naim; and incidentally several others. He alone gives us the account of the sympathy of the Jewish women when our Lord was on His way to Calvary: see xxiii. 27 *seq.* Also, besides the widow of Naim, and Anna the widow, we have the history of the Widow's Mite, the parable of the Importunate Widow, and our Lord's remarks about the miracle of Elias on the widow of Sarepta. With the exception of the history of the widow's mite, which is told also by St. Mark, all are peculiar to St. Luke, and illustrate his tendency to record words of consolation to the most helpless class of mankind.

iii. *Characteristics not directly traceable to either of the above causes.*

(*a*) *The Gospel of Prayer.* St. Luke's Gospel has commonly been called the Gospel of prayer. In it are recorded several parables and sayings of our Lord on the subject of prayer, which do not find a place elsewhere. Thus, after the promulgation of the Lord's Prayer, we find the parable of the Friend at Midnight, with other words of our Lord about the duty of prayer (xi. 1-13); and in another place (xviii. 1-8) the parable of the Unjust Judge enforcing similar lessons. This latter parable is immediately followed by that of the Pharisee and Publican, illustrating what kind of prayer to aim at and what to avoid. See also xxi. 36, where the words about the duty of continual prayer occur only in St. Luke, though the context is common to the three synoptists. A similar advice, to pray under circumstances of trial, is recorded in xxii. 40; but that one is also mentioned by St. Matthew and St. Mark. Besides these sayings of our Lord, His own example is likewise put before us in a very marked manner. Thus St. Luke records that He prayed at His Baptism (iii. 21); after the first great cure of a leper (v. 16); before the Choosing of the Apostles (vi. 12); before the Confession of St. Peter (ix. 18); at the Transfiguration (ix. 29); before the second promulgation of the Lord's Prayer (xi. 1); during the Crucifixion (xxiii. 34); and with His last breath (xxiii. 46). After the Last Supper also St. Luke records (xxiii. 32) that our Lord said He had prayed for St. Peter. All these nine instances are peculiar to St. Luke.

(b) *The Gospel of Thanksgiving.* Prayer and thanksgiving should always go together. Cf. Phil. iv. 6: "Be nothing solicitous: but in everything by prayer and supplication, with thanksgiving, let your petitions be made known to God.' It is natural therefore to find thanksgiving also brought into prominence by St. Luke. Notable instances are the thanksgiving of the shepherds (ii. 20); of the paralytic (v. 25); of the woman healed of her infirmity (xiii. 13); of the blind man of Jericho (xviii. 43); and the story of the cure of the ten lepers, when our Lord reproached the nine who had omitted to return to thank Him (xvii. 12-19). Lastly, the three great Canticles recorded in the first chapter are all canticles of thanksgiving.

(c) *The Gospel of Penance.* The last characteristic to be touched upon is perhaps the most pronounced of all, namely, the prominence given to God's compassion for sinners. We are continually told how our Lord went among sinners, ate with sinners, and the like. In the fifteenth chapter St. Luke tells us how the publicans and sinners, as though by instinct, used to draw near to our Lord; and he proceeds to his three great parables about sinners—the Lost Sheep, the Lost Groat, and the Prodigal Son—only

one of which finds a place elsewhere. So also he records
(xvii. 4) our Lord's instruction about continued forgiveness, if necessary, "seven times a day"; that is, very
often and without limit of number. But the most striking
part is the picture he draws of certain particular peni-
tents, laying stress at the same time on the completeness
with which they were forgiven. Thus the picture of the
sinner, whom we believe to be Mary Magdalen, anointing
our Lord's feet, and our Lord's words to Simon the Pharisee,
"many sins are forgiven her, for she hath loved much," are
given with St. Luke's usual vividness. Hardly less vivid
is his description of the conversion of the penitent thief,
and our Lord's words, "This day shalt thou be with me in
Paradise." These two incidents are related only by St.
Luke. He also draws us pictures of three converted publicans, two of whom—Levi or St. Matthew, and Zaccheus—
were certainly real persons, and the third—the publican who
prayed in the Temple—may very possibly have been.
Then again, although St. Peter's conversion is given by
the other synoptists, St. Luke alone records (xxii. 61)
our Lord's look towards him which produced that conversion. But in truth the greatest penitent of all these was
St. Luke's own father-in-God, with whom he travelled so
long on his missionary journeys, St. Paul himself, whose
conversion he also depicts very graphically in the Acts of
the Apostles.

(3) ON THE HARMONY WITH THE OTHER THREE
GOSPELS.

Having commented on the characteristics of St. Luke's
Gospel, we now proceed to consider its relation to the other
three. The science of gospel harmony is almost as ancient
as the Gospels themselves. The celebrated Diatesseron of
Tatian, which was a harmony of the four Gospels, dates
from the middle of the second century. St. Augustine
(d. A.D. 430) devoted much study to the science, but he
worked on the supposition that St. Matthew's order was
chronological, and accordingly made it the basis of his

harmony. It is now commonly conceded that St. Matthew did *not* follow the order of time, and modern harmonists found their order rather on St. Luke and St. Mark, who in this respect do not differ much from one another. Of recent years the science of gospel harmony has received great attention, and its importance is more generally recognized than formerly. The end aimed at is not merely the reconciling of apparent discrepancies. There is a positive work to be done, and that forms the most important object in view, namely, to put together the four different accounts, and to make them exhibit the life of our Lord and the gradual development of the circumstances which surrounded it, *as a whole*, so that what appear at first as only isolated incidents may be woven together into a complete history. It is obvious that the study of the characteristics of the different periods of our Lord's life, which is necessary in order to determine the true sequence of events related by different evangelists, must lead to a clearer conception of His complete life and work; and likewise that the consideration of the life of each evangelist, and the circumstances and object of his writing, which is most necessary as a foundation for any harmony, will also help towards a better understanding of each individual Gospel.

It becomes at once apparent, as already stated, that the Gospels are not meant as continuous histories: see above, iii. 1 (*b*). From their fragmentary nature two results at once follow. One is the existence of numerous *apparent* discrepancies; the other a large variety of methods of reconciling them. Both are due to our want of knowledge. In order to reconcile different Gospels, we are obliged to have recourse in many cases to pure conjecture. And this method is logically sound, for our object being to show that in case of apparent discrepancies no *necessary* contradictions exist, it is sufficient to show that under one hypothesis or another, both may be simultaneously true. A careful study is, however, needed to determine which hypotheses are admissible, and which more probable, and this leads to a better grasp of the subject itself. In the end, there will always remain a certain number of different harmonies, each with something to be said both for and against it. The strength of different arguments appeals differently to different minds, and it would be idle to expect uniformity in the results arrived at. Much valuable work is, however, done in considering the reasons for or against each system; or in studying the Gospel in conformity with *any* recognized system. Even should we afterwards find that some particular arrangement is undoubtedly false, much excellent work may have been performed in investigating it. It will be well, therefore, to explain what system is adopted in the following pages, not as necessarily in itself the best, but simply that which commends itself to the writer. The student reading any such book for the first time, will do well to accept provisionally the harmony there put forward, till he has acquired sufficient knowledge to form his own independent judgment.

At the outset we have to determine three points: (1) the date of our Lord's birth; (2) the length of His ministry; (3) the date of His death. On the first point see on iii. 1. It is now commonly admitted that our Lord was not born in the year originally supposed, and the year B.C. 4, or rather the end of B.C. 5, is considered the probable date. If this be accepted, we learn also from iii. 23 and John ii. 13 that the "public life" began early in A.D. 27. If we can now determine its length, the date of our Lord's death will follow. This depends chiefly on the interpretation of St. John, who alone mentions the different Paschs of the ministry from which its length can be inferred. Practically much turns on whether the feast of John v. 1 was the Pasch or not. In the former case we have four distinct Paschs (ii. 13, v. 1, vi. 4, xii. 4), and the ministry must have lasted at least three years. In the latter case it need not have lasted much more than two. The full discussion of the question belongs rather to a commentary on St. John than to one on St. Luke. It is sufficient here to remark that if the feast of John v. 1 was not the Pasch, it seems most probable that it was the feast of Purim; and though the ministry *may* in that case have been shorter, it need not necessarily have been so. The feast of Purim was only a few weeks earlier, and there is no special reason why each Pasch should necessarily have been recorded. We shall, therefore, suppose in what follows that our Lord's ministry lasted something over three years, leaving the question of what feast St. John was alluding to undecided. This would make the date of Christ's death A.D. 30.

Many harmonists have found it convenient to mark off our Lord's public life into three divisions, representing respectively the first, second, and third year. We have, however, chosen a slightly different arrangement, depending rather on subject matter than on time,[1] partly because these periods are more definitely marked in St. Luke's Gospel than in any of the others. Owing to the fragmentary nature of the narrative, the points of division do not differ very much from those in the arrangement by time. The references in brackets refer to St. Luke's Gospel.

In the first part of His public life (iv. 14—vi. 11) our Lord appears to have been working as though the new dispensation was to grow out of the old, harmoniously and without conflict. He taught in the synagogues, and worked miracles, as the prophets had done, to authenticate His mission, and went to Jerusalem to keep the feast of the Pasch. There is no reason to doubt that, had the attitude of the Jewish rulers been less hostile, means might have been found in the providence of God, to bring about this gradual engrafting of the Church on the Jewish religion in a peaceable way. From the beginning, however, the hostility showed itself. At its first appearance (John iv. 1) our Lord retired into Galilee, and made His head-quarters at Capharnaum. Apparently it took some time for the opposition of the Pharisees to travel thus far; but eventually it did find its way there, and as soon as it was evident that all chance of agreement with the Jewish rulers was at an end, our Lord took the most decisive step of His whole

---

[1] The division chosen is almost identical with that given by Rev. H. T. Coleridge, S.J., in the *Life of our Life*.

ministry, by choosing the twelve apostles, whom He was to train for the future work of founding the Church. This appears to have been not many weeks after the feast of the Pasch—the second of His ministry—so that the first period would have lasted about fifteen months.

During the second period (vi. 12—ix. 51) our Lord's work centred round the training of the apostles. When preaching to the people He used the form of parables more commonly than before, and at one time almost exclusively, on account of the presence of His enemies, who would thus less easily find anything tangible to accuse Him of; and, apart, He explained everything to the apostles. He ceased His missionary circuits in Galilee, and was no longer to be found regularly at Capharnaum. More than once He even left Galilee altogether. We find Him at one time in the land of the Gerasens; at another towards the confines of Tyre and Sidon; and at the Confession of St. Peter He was so far out as Cæsarea Philippi. The date of this was probably late in the summer, or towards the autumn of the following year, so that the second period of the ministry must have lasted more than a year, and perhaps so much as a year and four months.

Our Lord's teaching changed in character after the confession of St. Peter. In reward for the profession of faith, made in the name of the apostles, He told them plainly for the first time (Matt. xvi. 18) that a new Church was to be founded; and henceforth He preached to them the doctrine of the Cross, of His coming passion and death, and the necessity of His followers suffering for His sake. We may consider this period lasting down to the beginning of our Lord's last journey to Jerusalem (xviii. 30) less than a fortnight before His death; that is, a little more than six months. During the last part of that time must be placed the evangelizing of Judea and Perea: see on ix. 51. Towards the end also the raising of Lazarus took place (John xi.), which led to the chief priests' final determination to put our Lord to death; but which, for reasons which we can only surmise, is omitted from the three earlier Gospels altogether: see on x. 38.

The fourth period (xviii. 31—xxii. 38) covers an interval of only a few days, up to the beginning of our Lord's Passion; but the account of it in St. Luke occupies as much space as some of the earlier periods. It includes our Lord's last conflicts with His enemies, and the final rupture which led to their putting Him to death; and likewise the Last Supper and institution of the Eucharist.

The periods before and after the public life fall naturally into their places: see the Analysis.

Many other points of harmony will be mentioned, so far as seems requisite, in the notes on the text, all being based on the above outline. It may here be noted that the system adopted places the last feast of Dedication, which was between three and four months before our Lord's death, rather earlier in St. Luke's Gospel than has been customary—between chapters x. and xi. The reasons in favour of this arrangement will be stated in their place: see on ix. 51. The difficult questions as to the day and hour of the Crucifixion are also considered under xxii. 1 and xxiii. 44 respectively.

(4) Analysis of the Gospel.

I. Preface. Events preceding the Nativity (chap. i.).
II. Birth, Infancy, Boyhood, and Hidden Life of our Lord (chap. ii.).
III. Preparation for the Ministry. Preaching of St. John Baptist, Baptism of our Lord, His Fasting and Temptations (chap. iii. and chap. iv. 1–13).
IV. Public Ministry. First Period. From the beginning of the Ministry to the Choosing of the Apostles (chap. iv. 14 to chap. vi. 11).
V. Public Ministry. Second Period. From the Choosing of the Apostles to the Confession of St. Peter (chap. vi. 12 to chap. ix. 17).
VI. Public Ministry. Third Period. From the Confession of St. Peter to the Last Journey of our Lord to Jerusalem (chap. ix. 18 to chap. xviii. 30).
VII. Public Ministry. Fourth Period. The Last Journey to Jerusalem to the beginning of the Passion (chap. xviii. 31 to chap. xxii. 38).
VIII. The Passion (chap. xxii. 39 to chap. xxiii. 56).
IX. The Resurrection and Ascension (chap. xxiv.).

The following is an analysis of the contents of each chapter, in accordance with the foregoing division:

§ I. *Events preceding the Nativity.*

Chapter i.
1–4.—Preface.
5–25.—Announcement of the Birth of St. John.
26–38.—The Annunciation.
39–56.—The Visitation. The *Magnificat*.
57–80.—Birth of St. John. The *Benedictus*.

§ II. *Birth, Infancy, Boyhood, and Hidden Life of our Lord.*

Chapter ii.
1–7.—Birth of our Lord.
8–20.—Adoration of the Shepherds.
21–38.—Early ceremonies of our Lord's life. Circumcision, Presentation in the Temple. Purification of the Blessed Virgin Mary. The *Nunc dimittis*.
39–52.—The Hidden Life of our Lord.

§ III. *Preparation for the Ministry.*

Chapter iii.
1–20.—Preaching of St. John Baptist.
21–22.—Baptism of our Lord.
23–38.—The Genealogy.

Chapter iv.
1–13.—The fasting and temptations of our Lord.

§ IV. *Public Ministry. First Period.*

14–30.—Preaching in Galilee. Rejection at Nazareth.
31–44.—The Sabbath at Capharnaum.

Chapter v.
1–11.—Miraculous draught of fishes.
12–16.—Cleansing of a leper.
17–26.—Healing of a paralytic.
27–39.—Call of Levi and the Supper at his House.

Chapter vi.
1–5.—The Disciples in the Cornfields on the Sabbath.
6–11.—Cure of the man with a withered hand.

§ V. *Public Ministry. Second Period.*

12–16.—Choosing of the Twelve Apostles.
17–49.—Sermon on the Plain.

Chapter vii.
1–10.—Cure of the Centurion's Servant.
11–17.—Raising of the Widow's Son.
18–35.—Deputation from St. John Baptist. Christ's Witness to him.

Chapter vii. 36-50.—Supper at the Pharisee's House. Anointing of Christ's Feet.
Chapter viii. 1-3.—Missionary Journeys with the Twelve. The Ministering Women.
 4-8.—Parable of the Sower.
 9-18.—Explanation and Discourse to the Twelve.
 19-21.—The Brethren of our Lord.
 22-26.—The Storm on the Lake.
 27-39.—The Demoniac in the Country of the Gerasens.
 40-56.—Healing of the Woman with an Issue of Blood and Raising the Daughter of Jairus.
Chapter ix. 1-6.—Mission of the Twelve Apostles.
 7-9.—Death of St. John the Baptist.
 10-17.—Feeding of the Five Thousand.

§ VI. *Public Ministry. Third Period.*

Chapter ix. 18-27.—Confession of St. Peter.
 28-36.—The Transfiguration.
 37-50.—The Demoniac Boy.
 51-56.—Preparation for Judean ministry. Journey through Samaria.
 57-62.—Three Applicants for the Apostolate.
Chapter x. 1-16.—Mission of the Seventy-two Disciples.
 17-24.—Return of the Seventy-two.
 25-37.—Parable of the Good Samaritan.
 38-42.—Supper at Bethany.
Chapter xi. 1-4.—The Lord's Prayer.
 5-13.—On Perseverance in Prayer.
 14-36.—Christ among His Enemies.
 37-54.—Dinner with the Pharisee.
Chapter xii. 1-12.—On Pharisaism and the Pharisees.
 13-21.—On Covetousness.
 22-32.—On the Providence of God.
 33-34.—Counsels of Charity.
 35-48.—On Watchfulness.
 49-59.—Other Counsels.
Chapter xiii. 1-9.—Parable of the Fig Tree.
 10-17.—A Sabbath-day Miracle.
 18-21.—The Mustard seed and the Leaven.
 22-30.—On the Difficulty of Salvation.
 31-35.—The Pharisees and Herod.
Chapter xiv. 1-14.—Sabbath-day Meal with the Pharisee.
 15-24.—The Heavenly Banquet.
 25-35.—Conditions for following Christ.
Chapter xv. 1-7.—Parable of the Lost Sheep.
 8-10.—Parable of the Lost Groat.
 11-32.—Parable of the Prodigal Son.

Chapter xvi. 1-13. —Parable of the Unjust Steward.
    14-18.—Warnings to the Pharisees.
    19-31. Dives and Lazarus.
Chapter xvii. 1-10.—Various Teachings of our Lord.
    11-19.—The Ten Lepers.
    20-37.—Further Sayings of our Lord.
Chapter xviii. 1-8.—The Unjust Judge.
    9-14.—The Pharisee and Publican.
    15-17.—Children brought to Christ.
    18-30.—Evangelical Poverty.

§ VII. *Public Ministry. Fourth Period.*

    31-34.—Further Prophecy of the Passion.
    35-43.—The Blind Man of Jericho.
Chapter xix. 1-10.—Our Lord and Zaccheus.
    11-27.—Parable of the Pounds.
    28-48.—Procession of Palms.
Chapter xx. 1-8.—Question from the Sanhedrin.
    9-19.—Parable of the Vineyard and Husbandmen.
    20-26.—Question of the Pharisees and Herodians.
    27-40.—Question of the Sadducees.
    41-47.—Final Rupture with the Jewish Rulers.
Chapter xxi. 1-4.—The Widow's Mite.
    5-38.—Prophecy of the Destruction of Jerusalem and of the Day of Judgment.
Chapter xxii. 1-6.—Treachery of Judas.
    7-13.—Preparation for the Paschal Supper.
    14-38.—The Last Supper.

§ VIII. *The Passion.*

    39-46.—The Agony in the Garden.
    47-53.—The Betrayal.
    54-62.—Denials of St. Peter.
    63-65.—Christ in the House of Caiphas.
    66-71.—Trial before the Sanhedrin.
Chapter xxiii. 1-7.—Christ before Pilate.
    8-12.—Christ before Herod.
    13-25.—Before Pilate the second time.
    26-32.—The Way of the Cross.
    33-38.—The Crucifixion.
    39-43.—The Penitent Thief.
    44-49.—Death of our Lord.
    50-56.—Burial of our Lord.

lxvi   INTRODUCTION.

§ IX. *The Resurrection and Ascension.*

Chapter xxiv. 1-12.—The Resurrection.
       13-32.—The two Disciples going to Emmaus.
       33-49.—Apparitions to the eleven.
       50-53.—The Ascension.

The following parables are given by St. Luke. Those marked with an asterisk are given by him only:

   1. New Cloth on Old Garments and New Wine in old Bottles v. 36-39.
   2. The House built on a Good or Bad Foundation .. vi. 47-49.
   3. Children in the Market-place.. .. .. .. vii. 31-35.
*4. The Two Debtors .. .. vii. 41-43.
   5. The Sower .. .. viii. 4-8.
   6. The Candle under a Vessel .. .. viii. 16.
*7. The Good Samaritan .. .. x. 29-37.
*8. The Friend at Midnight .. .. xi. 5-8.
*9. The Rich Fool .. .. xii. 16-21.
 10. The Faithful and Wise Steward .. .. .. xii. 42-48.
*11. The Barren Fig-tree .. .. xii. 6-9.
 12. The Mustard Seed .. .. xiii. 18-19.
 13. The Leaven .. .. xiii. 20-21.
 14. The Wedding Feast .. .. xiv. 7-12.
 15. The Heavenly Banquet .. .. xiv. 16-24.
 16. The Man building a Tower .. .. xiv. 28-30.
 17. The King going to War .. .. xiv. 31-32.
 18. The Lost Sheep .. .. xv. 3-7.
*19. The Lost Groat .. .. xv. 8-10.
*20. The Prodigal Son .. .. xv. 11-32.
 21. The Unjust Steward .. .. xvi. 1-8.
 22. Dives and Lazarus .. .. xvi. 19-31.
 23. The Servant Ploughing .. .. xvii. 7-10.
*24. The Importunate Widow .. .. xviii. 2-5.
*25. The Pharisee and Publican .. .. xviii. 9-13.
*26. The Pounds .. .. xix. 12-27.
 27. The Vineyard and Husbandmen .. .. .. xx. 9-16.

The following miracles of our Lord are given by St. Luke. Those marked with an asterisk are given by him only:

   1. The Demoniac at Capharnaum .. .. .. iv. 33-35.
   2. Simon's Wife's Mother .. .. iv. 38-39.
*3. The Miraculous Draught of Fishes .. .. .. v. 4-7.
   4. Cleansing of a Leper .. .. v. 12-14.
   5. Healing of the Paralytic .. .. v. 18-25.
   6. The Man with a Withered Hand .. .. .. vi. 6-10.

7. The Servant of the Centurion		vii. 1–10.
*8. The Son of the Widow of Naim		vii. 11–15.
9. Calming of the Wind and Waves		viii. 22–25.
10. The Demoniac in the Land of the Gerasens		viii. 26–33.
11. The Woman with an Issue of Blood		viii. 43–48.
12. Raising of the Daughter of Jairus		viii. 41–56.
13. Feeding of the Five Thousand		ix. 12–17.
14. Cure of the Demoniac after the Transfiguration		ix. 37–42.
15. The Dumb Demoniac		xi. 14.
*16. The Woman with a Spirit of Infirmity		xiii. 11–13.
*17. The Man with the Dropsy		xiv. 2–4.
*18. The Ten Lepers		xvii. 12–14.
19. The Blind Man of Jericho		xviii. 35–43.
*20. Healing of the Ear of Malchus		xxii. 50–51.

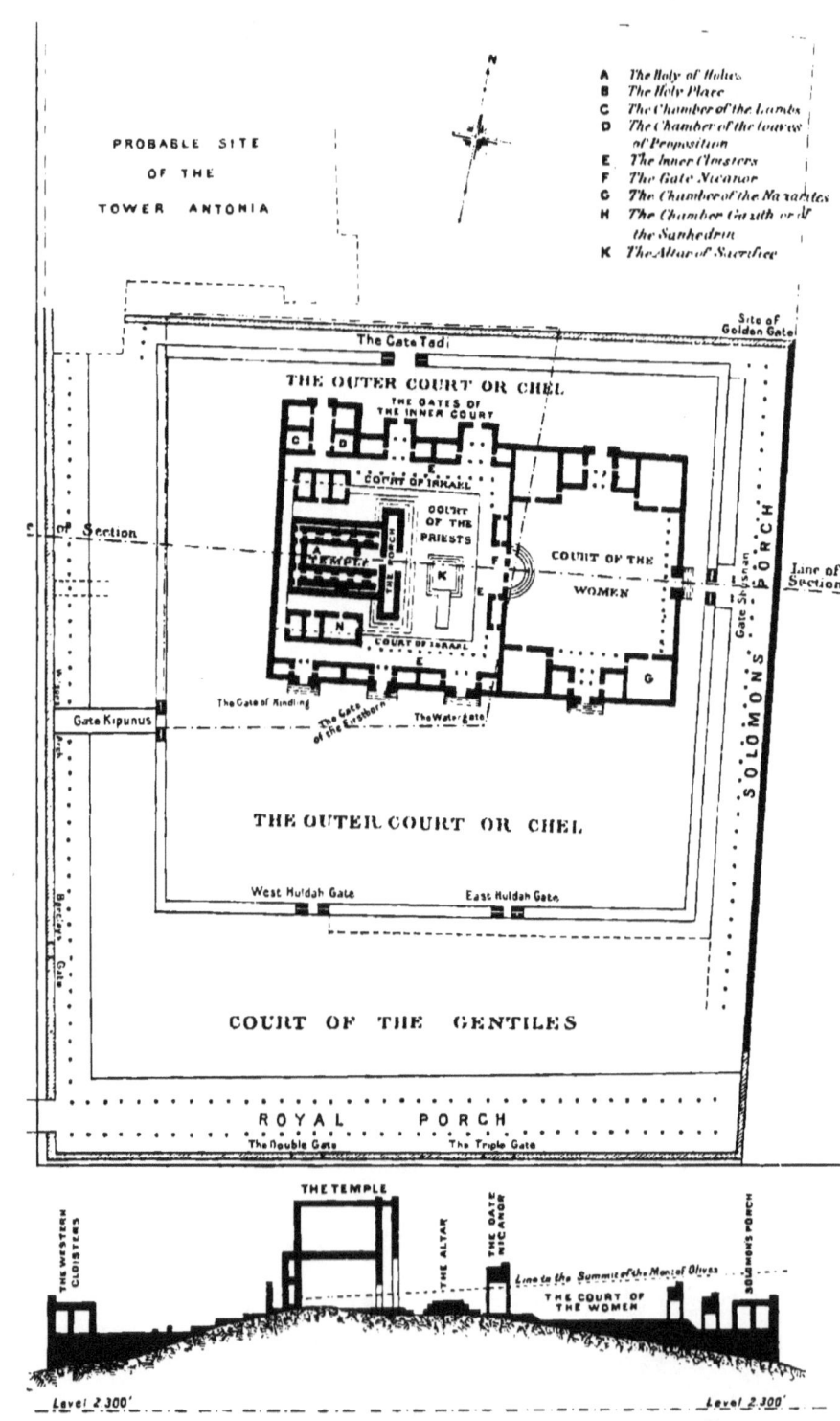

THE HOLY GOSPEL ACCORDING TO SAINT LUKE.

CHAPTER I.

Preface.

(VERS. 1–4.)

FORASMUCH as many have taken in hand to set forth in order a narration of the things that have

1. *Forasmuch as many have taken in hand*, &c. We know far too little about the documents in possession of the Apostolic Church, to do more than guess as to the nature of the works here alluded to. They were not what are now known as the "Apocryphal Gospels," which belong to a later date. And even if they included the Gospels of St. Matthew and St. Mark, which is not at all certain, these would have only made two out of the many. It is obvious that there must have been many well-known descriptions of incidents of our Lord's life current, some of which would have been written, others unwritten; and of the latter, there must have been every grade from those known almost word for word, to those which were comparatively vaguely expressed. It would have been impossible for so many incidents to be independently recorded by the three synoptists, unless they had in some cases used common originals; and those common originals may have been written or oral tradition; but most probably some were written and some were oral. They would have been used week after week by the apostles and others, in the sermons or instructions as to the life and sayings of Christ as the basis of the Christian religion, which formed from the first a part of the liturgy, and were the germ of the Gospel and sermon as we have them. From the identity even of language in large sections of the synoptic Gospels, which do not appear to have been copied one from the other, many have inferred that there was one

"primitive Gospel" (or as the Germans call it "Urevangelion") in the form of a current consecutive account of the ministry of Christ from His baptism to His resurrection, which each of the three synoptists incorporated more or less completely in his text; but the working out of this hypothesis in detail has led to immense variety of theories, to account for various difficulties which beset the problems as to the coincidences and variations of the three documents before us. Perhaps the most consistent view is that some such tradition—written or oral— formed the basis of the Gospel of St. Mark, who added comparatively little separate matter; and that St. Matthew and St. Luke each knew and embodied the same tradition (probably without having the text of St. Mark before them), and each considerable quantities of other information which they incorporated with it. Such a theory will also give a reasonable explanation of the expressions St. Luke uses here. It is not necessary to suppose that each of the accounts of which he speaks was a complete life of our Lord; but they must have been something more than isolated accounts of single incidents, though they may well have been fragmentary—the account of what some particular "witness" had seen, or the story of a period of our Lord's life, such as the Infancy, or the Passion, or the Galilean ministry, or the last months, or the forty days, &c. They seem to have totally disappeared, without leaving any trace behind them: for the Gospels of the Infancy and other Apocryphal Gospels are late and unhistoric; and there is little likelihood that any of them even embodied or used the last authentic accounts. There is mention of a text of "the sayings of Jesus," and some fragments alleged to have belonged to it have just been recovered in Egypt. But even if it were early and authentic, it would not help us much as to the present question, which is one rather of accounts of "doings" than of "sayings." The disappearance of such documents as St. Luke reports is not, however, really strange, since all that they contained of value must obviously have been incorporated in the four Gospels which we now have. And once the Church possessed even the first three Gospels in a written form, and under the authority of Apostolic and sub-Apostolic names, it is evident that they came rapidly to be read in the liturgy everywhere, to the exclusion of all other documents, until St. John's Gospel was added to them; and the four became, as they are called in so early a tract as "The Shepherd of Hermas," the "four supports of the Church." It was probably only after the use of the four, or at least of the three, had become a settled use, that fanciful or heretical teachers either altered them (as in the case of the Syriac Adoptionist text lately discovered on Mount Sinai, and in the case of the well-known Gospel of Marcion), or invented entirely new and apocryphal text (such as the so-called "Gospel of Peter," also lately discovered).

of the things that have been accomplished among us. There is some difference of rendering here. The Greek word πεπληροφορημένων is translated in the A.V. by "surely believed." The R.V. corrects it to "fulfilled," thereby agreeing with our (Douay) version, which is clearly the more correct scholarship.

been accomplished among us; according as they have 2
delivered them unto us, who from the beginning were
eye-witnesses and ministers of the word: it seemed 3
good to me also, having diligently attained to all things
from the beginning, to write to thee, in order, most

2. *Who from the beginning were eye-witnesses.* "The beginning" may mean here not our Lord's birth, but the beginning of the ministry, though the words of *v.* 3 seem to refer to the birth itself. If St. Luke wrote about A.D. 60, many of those who had been "eye-witnesses from the beginning" would have doubtless died; but men of the generation coeval with our Lord would have been between fifty and sixty, and at least some of them would have been living; and if the Blessed Virgin was as young as tradition indicates, some even of her contemporaries might have been alive. There is some reason to infer that Lazarus and Mary Magdalen *were* alive. See on x. 38. The accounts of all these had been "delivered" as by "ministers of the word." This might be either in writing or orally, so far as the words of the text are concerned. But it is possible that St. Luke is referring to the setting forth of these accounts by way of Gospel or sermon in the public worship of the Church—as explained above. The "Ministers of the Word" were not of course confined to the Twelve, but included all who spread the Faith or taught in Jerusalem and the other churches first founded.

3. *It seemed good to me also.* St. Luke here puts his own effort on the same footing as those already written, thus implying that the aim and scope of his narrative was similar to that of the others. This must be partly ascribed to his humility and his unwillingness to put himself forward; for there is little doubt that he was really inspired to aim at something more elaborate and complete than anything, except the Gospels of St. Matthew and St. Mark, which we cannot be sure that he knew, if indeed we were even certain that they had both been written at that time.

having diligently attained to all things from the beginning. This is the qualification on which St. Luke relied for his task—careful study and research; examination of documents and questioning of witnesses. If he put his materials together at Cæsarea, and at the date supposed, he would have been within easy reach of many in Galilee or at Jerusalem or elsewhere who had been witnesses of part of our Lord's ministry. He would have found it specially easy to communicate with the churches of the region where our Lord had preached during the last few months of the ministry, when He was moving in Judea and Perea; and this is just the part which St. Luke gives at greater length than any other.

to write to thee in order. The word καθεξῆς is used by St. Luke on various occasions: see especially Acts xi. 4. The word itself does not necessarily, or even usually, involve the idea of chronological sequence; it only means an orderly narrative. It is true that in the mind of St. Luke, to judge by the abovementioned somewhat similar expression in

4 excellent Theophilus, that thou mayest know the verity of those words in which thou hast been instructed.

the Acts, it would seem that chronological order was a leading idea; but there is no reason to take this too strictly, and in fact needless difficulties have sometimes been created by supposing that sequences in St. Luke must be meant to be chronological, when all the indications of the evidence point the other way. The main outline of his Gospel is admitted by all to be arranged on the basis of time. Individual incidents might well be arranged, nevertheless, in some other way, in order to convey their meaning more definitely, as when a succession of parables on kindred subjects are put together, though delivered on different occasions. And in many cases where the incidents were obtained from different sources, St. Luke might have been himself ignorant of their precise chronological sequence *inter se*, though knowing to which period they were all to be referred: see on ix. 51.

most excellent Theophilus. Reasons have been given in the Introduction for supposing that Theophilus was a Roman. The title κράτιστε implies a man of distinction: cf. Acts xxiii. 26, and xxvi. 25, where the title is applied to the Procurators of Judea. The use of the title here is practically decisive against the supposition that Theophilus is only meant as an ideal name (= "the friend of God"), and not to represent any particular individual—an improbable supposition in any case. It is, however, quite possible, to say the least, that though he was a real person, Theophilus was not his real name. As the name of Lazarus was avoided by the synoptists, and as in the Epistles and Apocalypse it was thought wise to write Babylon for Rome, so there might obviously be reasons why this high-placed Christian should not be named in a document so public as this would become. Such a Christian epithet might well belong to him, as St. Ignatius came to be called Theophorus. We know that there *were* from very early times Romans of the highest station who believed. Such were the Senator Pudens, the convert and protector of St. Peter; Pomponia Graecina, wife of the general who conquered Britain under Claudius, who is supposed to be the foundress of the "Crypt of Lucina" in the Catacombs, that being supposed to be a symbolical or "Christian" name; and T. Flavius Clemens, consul and martyr, who was Domitian's nephew.

4. *That thou mayest know the verity of those words.* The "words" (λόγοι) mean the Gospel, as the "ministers of the word" (*v.* 2) means ministers of the Gospel. Having given his own qualification for the work, St. Luke ends his preface by stating the main object he had in view, which was the instruction of Theophilus. Without doubt, however, he must have had other readers in his mind, and did not wish to limit his work to the benefit of one man. This is the only preface or personal introduction to any of the Gospels. St. John puts a short and somewhat similar personal explanation at the *end* of his Gospel, first (xx. 31) when apparently he had intended it to finish, and then again (xxi. 24) at the conclusion of his supplementary chapter.

Announcement of the Birth of St. John.

(VERS. 5-25.)

There was in the days of Herod the king of Judea, a 5 certain priest named Zachary, of the course of Abia, and his wife was of the daughters of Aaron, and her name

5. *In the days of Herod, the king of Judea.* Herod, commonly known as "the Great," was an Idumean prince. The Idumeans were converts to the Jewish religion, but were not Jews by descent, and Herod was always regarded as a foreign ruler. He owed his position as King of Judea originally to a quarrel between two brothers, Hyrcanus and Aristobulus, who were descended from the Machabees, and who appealed to Pompey (Cn. Pompeius Magnus, friend and afterwards rival of Julius Cæsar) to settle their disputes in the year B.C. 64. Pompey's decision was in favour of Hyrcanus, who was therefore constituted sovereign of Judea, but no longer as an independent prince. He was called *Ethnarch*, and ruled under the authority of the Roman governor of Syria. This was the beginning of the Roman rule over the Jews. Very soon a further step was taken by Julius Cæsar, who united Palestine to the kingdom of Edom, and appointed Antipater, the father of Herod, over the joint kingdom. Herod himself became governor of Judea, and his brother Phasäel governor of Galilee. An insurrection headed by the sons of Aristobulus led to a further rearrangement, and Herod hurried to Rome, where he was formally appointed by the Senate as king, B.C. 37. His kingdom included Judea, Samaria, Galilee, Ituræa, and most of Perea, and more as well. He reigned in all thirty-three years, and died B.C. 4, according to our present reckoning. It thus follows that our Lord was born not later than that year. See *infra*, chap. ii.

a certain priest named Zachary. Of Zachary's antecedents we know nothing. St. Luke only says that he was of the course of Abia. These "courses" were originally twenty-four in number, as instituted by David (1 Paral. xxiv.), and though only four of them returned from the Captivity, these four were again subdivided and the old names of the courses affixed to the subdivisions. The family of Abia was one of those which became extinct, and it was revived out of the four surviving ones; therefore the specification that Zachary belonged to it gives us no information as to his actual descent.

his wife was of the daughters of Aaron, and her name Elizabeth. The name Elizabeth signifies "Oath of God." St. Elizabeth was a cousin of the Blessed Virgin (v. 36), who was of the tribe of Juda. Except in the case of heiresses (Numb. xxxvi.), the members of the various tribes used to intermarry freely. The tribe of the offspring was always reckoned by the male line. Thus St. Elizabeth's relationship to the Blessed Virgin must have been through her mother, who was the sister or near relative of St. Joachim or St. Anne.

6 Elizabeth. And they were both just before God, walking in all the commandments and justifications of the Lord 7 without blame. And they had no son, for that Elizabeth was barren, and they both were well advanced in years. 8 And it came to pass, when he executed the priestly 9 function in the order of his course before God, according to the custom of the priestly office, it was his lot to offer

6. *They were both just before God.* The addition of the words "before God" give to the word "just" its full meaning. Zachary and Elizabeth were not only "just" before men, obeying the law as the Pharisees did, but they had also a true and inward justice before God, who can see the heart.

in all the commandments and justifications. The Greek is ἐν πάσαις ταῖς ἐντολαῖς καὶ δικαιώμασιν. It has been said that the former word has regard to the moral, and the latter to the ceremonial law. If this is so, our rendering is not good, and that of the A.V., "all the commandments and ordinances," is better. It is, however, quite doubtful whether such distinction of meaning was commonly understood by the Jews.

7. *And they had no son.* This was considered a heavy misfortune, because it cut off the chance of fulfilment of the highest ambition of a Jewish woman—to have the Messiah descended from her. It was commonly regarded as a punishment for sin, and hence looked on as a *reproach* (v. 25).

9. *It was his lot to offer incense, going into the temple of the Lord.* St. Luke here means the Temple itself, i.e., the "Holy Place." At the time Herod came to the throne, the Temple buildings were nearly all in ruins, for Pompey when he captured Jerusalem [B.C. 63] slew the priests and desecrated the Holy of Holies. Nevertheless, he left the treasures intact, as also did Herod himself when he took Jerusalem in the year 37 B.C. About the middle of his reign, he conceived a scheme of rebuilding the whole on a very elaborate scale, in order to gain popularity among the Jews. The work was begun in the year 17 B.C. and not finally finished till A.D. 64, which was only six years before it was destroyed. It was thus proceeding all through our Lord's lifetime: cf. John ii. 20. The new Temple was on a much larger scale than the old, and the whole buildings formed a square some 600 feet long in each direction. The different parts were on the side and summit of Mount Moriah, and would have appeared from the city like three terraces, one above the other, connected by flights of steps. In reality, the lowermost area, or Court of the Gentiles, which was a large open space, surrounded the other buildings, which were not in the centre, but towards the north-west. Around the court were porticoes or cloisters, which were a chief architectural feature of Herod's work. The Royal Porch, on the south side, was the most magnificent, and was supported on three rows of columns. On the other three sides

incense, going into the temple of the Lord; and all the 10
multitude of the people was praying without at the hour
of incense. And there appeared to him an Angel of the 11
Lord, standing on the right side of the altar of incense.

there were only two such rows. The cloister on the eastern side was known as Solomon's, and the wall formed part of the fortified wall of the town. The inner buildings were surrounded by a balustrade, on which were inscriptions in Greek and Roman letters, forbidding any Gentile to proceed further. Fourteen steps led up to the second terrace, called the Chel, on which stood the Court of the Women. The gateways were of great architectural splendour: that at the east was probably the one known as the Beautiful (Acts iii. 2). Fifteen more steps led up to the third terrace, on which was the Court of the men of Israel and that of the priests, the former surrounding the latter on three sides. In the forefront of the Priests' Court was the large Altar of Holocausts or Burnt Offerings. In the middle and on the summit of the mountain was the Temple itself, built of white marble, the roof glittering with golden pinnacles, visible from all the city. It occupied the same site as the Temple of Solomon and was built entirely by priests in a year and a half. The interior was divided into three parts: the Vestibule or Porch, the Holy Place, and the Holy of Holies. The Holy Place contained the Altar of Incense in the centre; on the north side stood the table of the Loaves of Proposition, which were renewed weekly; and between the two was the golden seven-branched candlestick. There were two veils, one before the Holy Place and the other, a double one, between it and the Holy of Holies. It was this latter one which was rent at the death of our Lord (Matt. xxvii. 51). No one entered the Holy of Holies but the High Priest, who went in once a year, on the Day of Atonement. There was no longer any Ark of the Covenant; a large stone stood on the place where it should have been, and on this stone the High Priest laid the censer. The Temple was built from east to west, with the Holy of Holies towards Jerusalem: so that if the veils had been removed, the interior would have been visible from the summit of Mount Olivet.

10. *And all the multitude of the people was praying without at the hour of incense.* The ceremony of incense burning took place twice daily. It was the most solemn act performed there with the sole exception of the one day in the year when the High Priest entered the Holy of Holies. There were always people gathered in the Temple at the hour of prayer (cf. Acts iii. 1, 2). The people waited without, while the priest alone entered the Holy Place vested in a white robe and barefooted. At a given signal, he placed the incense on the fire and walked out backwards, so as not to turn his back on the altar. The Levites then intoned the sacred hymn, at the conclusion of which the people dispersed.

11. *There appeared to him an Angel of the Lord.* No doubt the Angel appeared in human form; but the presence of any person in

12 And Zachary seeing him was troubled, and fear fell upon
13 him: but the Angel said to him: Fear not, Zachary, for
thy prayer is heard; and thy wife Elizabeth shall bear thee
14 a son, and thou shalt call his name John; and thou shalt
have joy and gladness, and many shall rejoice in his
15 nativity. For he shall be great before the Lord: and shall
drink no wine nor strong drink; and he shall be filled

the "Holy Place" would at once suggest a vision, as no Jew would be presumptuous enough to enter at the hour of prayer. It was indeed the first time that Zachary himself had been there at that time, for the number of priests was so great that no one priest ever offered incense twice, and many never even once. The sequence was arranged, as stated, by drawing lots.

13. *Fear not, Zachary, for thy prayer is heard.* As devout Jews, Zachary and Elizabeth had no doubt prayed throughout their lives for the blessing of children, and they may easily have continued to do so though all human probability of their obtaining them had passed away. Hence the announcement that their petition was to be granted came as a complete surprise.

14. *And thou shalt have joy and gladness,* &c. The prophecy of the Angel must have been related originally by Zachary himself, and it seems clear that this and many other details of the first two chapters were obtained by St. Luke either from our Lady or from her relatives. See Introduction. In these verses and in others in these chapters (i. 30–38, 42–45, 46–55, 68–79; ii. 29–35) the inspired words are in the form characteristic of Hebrew poetry, such as may be seen in the psalms and in all the canticles. This form of expression was natural to the Hebrews in moments of exaltation. One of its marks is the Oriental delight in clothing a simple idea or fact in splendid language; another is the habit of constructing each verse of the poem by first stating an idea shortly and then re-echoing it with a variation. This verse exhibits both these characteristics. As St. Luke was writing and thinking in Greek, he would never have invented such a poetic form in these passages for himself, and he is evidently therefore using words repeated to him by a Hebrew narrator—perhaps by our Lady herself. It would thus appear that these were not the *ipsissima verba* of the Angel, but only their sense; though it is of course possible that St. Gabriel would have accommodated his style and language to that of the person he was addressing.

15. *And shall drink no wine nor strong drink*, i.e., he shall be a Nazarite. The Nazarites (from *nazar*, to separate) were persons consecrated to God by a special vow, either for a stated period or for life. The vow bound them to avoid every sort of legal defilement, especially that of a dead body; and also to keep two special rules, the one to abstain from all wine and strong drink, the other to let their hair grow as an outward sign of "separation." Three are mentioned in Scripture

with the Holy Ghost even from his mother's womb. And 16
he shall convert many of the children of Israel to the Lord
their God. And he shall go before him in the spirit and 17
power of Elias; that he may turn the hearts of the fathers
unto the children, and the incredulous to the wisdom of
the just, to prepare unto the Lord a perfect people. And 18
Zachary said to the Angel: Whereby shall I know this?
for I am an old man; and my wife is advanced in years.

as having taken the vow for life: Samson, Samuel, and St. John. Tradition says that St. James the Less was one, but our Lord was not (*infra*, vii. 34). The Nazarites were not a sect or a community or even a school of thought. They must not be confounded with the heterodox sect of the Essenes, who also abstained from strong drink and practised other asceticisms, but refused to recognize the Temple worship altogether, and lived a kind of monastic life in the hill country of Judea. The suggestion has sometimes been made that St. John the Baptist had some relation to them, but there is no foundation for it. The Nazarite vow was Mosaic, and was regulated by the rules given in Numbers vi. Many zealous young men seem to have become "Nazarites of days," the usual period being thirty days, though sometimes it was longer. See Amos ii. 11; 1 Machabees iii. 49.

he shall be filled with the Holy Ghost even from his mother's womb. It may be noted that the doctrine of the Trinity was unknown to the Jews, and the expression of the Angel would have had only a vague meaning in the mind of Zachary. By the time St. Luke wrote, however, the Trinity had been preached and the words would have had in the mind of the Evangelist a deeper signification. It is generally supposed that they referred to the sanctification of St. John from original sin, which is therefore believed to have taken place in the womb of St. Elizabeth, and at the moment of the Visitation. See *infra*, on v. 41.

17. *In the spirit and power of Elias.* The comparison between St. John and Elias was also made by our Lord Himself (Matt. xi. 14, xvii. 12, 13; Mark ix. 12).

that he may turn the hearts of the fathers unto the children. These words are from Malachias iv. 6, and refer to the mission of Elias. Hence the Jews expected that he would return to earth before the coming of the Messiah: see Matt. xvii. 10. The words which follow are not a quotation, but rather an amplification of the preceding and its application to the reconciliation of man with man and with God, to prepare the people for the reception of the Messiah.

18. *Whereby shall I know this?* The answer of Zachary was a refusal to submit to believe what was apparently so unlikely. It resembles in tone St. Thomas's words when told of our Lord's Resurrection (John xx. 25), and those of the daughter of Sara (Gen. xviii. 12).

19 And the Angel answering, said to him: I am Gabriel who stand before God; and am sent to speak to thee, and to
20 bring thee these good tidings. And behold thou shalt be dumb, and shalt not be able to speak until the day whereon these things shall come to pass, because thou hast not believed my words, which shall be fulfilled in their time.
21 And the people was waiting for Zachary; and they won-
22 dered that he tarried so long in the temple. And when he came out he could not speak to them, and they understood that he had seen a vision in the temple. And he
23 made signs to them, and remained dumb. And it came to pass, after the days of his office were accomplished, he

19. *I am Gabriel who stand before God.* The name "Gabriel" means "hero of God." His special mission on earth seems to have been the announcements of the Incarnation. See Daniel ix. 21, as well as the two instances in this chapter. The Jews knew of the Angels as God's messengers, as is evident in many instances in Scripture. The Archangel Raphael is mentioned by name in the Book of Tobias (iii. 25, xii. 15). the Archangel Michael and the Archangel Gabriel in the Book of Daniel.

20. *Behold thou shalt be dumb.* The miracle which followed Gabriel's announcement was at once a witness and a punishment. Zachary could no longer doubt after the evidence of his loss of speech, and it was at the same time a punishment for his former incredulity.

21. *They wondered that he tarried so long in the temple.* The interior of the Holy Place was looked upon as so sacred that any unusual delay in the priest's coming out would suggest some possible judgment of God. In the law directing the ceremonies it is implied that any omission or violation thereof would be punished by death (Lev. xvi. 13).

22. *And when he came out he could not speak to them.* It seems to be implied that the people asked what had happened, and that he made signs to them to satisfy their curiosity as far as he could; but he remained dumb, and probably deaf also: see on *v.* 60. The word κωφός implies either deafness or dumbness or both. The same word is used in vii. 22, and where the context shows it to mean *deaf.*

23. *After the days of his office were accomplished.* The period of a ministration was a week—from the evening of one Sabbath to the morning of the next.

he departed to his own house. The home of Zachary and Elizabeth is traditionally asserted to have been Hebron, a fair-sized town about twenty miles south of Jerusalem. Alban Butler accepts this without comment; but it is not a very old tradition, dating not further back than the ninth century, and it is not a probable one, for the language of verse 39 seems hardly consistent with such a well-known town. An old local tradition gives the place as Ain Karim, a village in

vv. 24-27.] ST. LUKE, I. 11

departed to his own house. And after those days, Eliza- 24
beth his wife conceived; and hid herself five months,
saying: Thus hath the Lord dealt with me in the days 25
wherein he hath had regard to take away my reproach
among men.

The Annunciation.

(VERS. 26-38.)

And in the sixth month, the Angel Gabriel was sent from 26
God into a city of Galilee, called Nazareth, to a virgin 27
espoused to a man whose name was Joseph, of the house

the hills near Jerusalem. There were eight sacerdotal cities in the
neighbourhood of Jerusalem, of which Hebron was one; but it is not
certain that the priests serving the Temple (who are said to have
numbered about 20,000) were at this time compelled to live in these
eight cities only.

24. *Elizabeth his wife conceived.* On so unusual an event at her age,
St. Elizabeth would naturally "hide herself"; that is, live in seclusion
and avoid public notice as far as possible. The specified time of five
months is clearly not intended to limit the time of her seclusion, but
to lead up to the events of the sixth month, recorded immediately
afterwards.

26. *Into a city of Galilee.* The district known in our Lord's time by
the name of Galilee was in the North of Palestine, and divided from
Judea by the country of the Samaritans: see on ix. 52. It covered,
roughly, the ancient territories of Issachar, Zabulon, Aser, and Neph-
thali, and was called by Isaias (ix. 1) "Galilee of the Gentiles," from
the number of strangers who resided there. Josephus describes the soil
as rich and well cultivated, and the inhabitants as industrious and war-
like, being trained to arms from their infancy. We know of at least
one occasion when they revolted against Rome, about the year B.C. 4,
in the days of Judas the Gaulonite, a mountaineer in the neighbourhood
of the lake; and many formally refused to take the oath of allegiance to
Augustus, probably at the time of the census. Another disturbance in
which the Galileans were concerned, about A.D. 29, is alluded to in
xiii. 1.

called Nazareth. Nazareth itself was but a small village, little known
and of mean repute (John i. 46). It was prettily situated among the
hills which form the southern ridge of Lebanon.

27. *To a virgin espoused to a man whose name was Joseph.* It was
usual for a couple to be betrothed for a year before the marriage, during
which time the maiden lived in seclusion. Some have thought that it
was during this period that the Annunciation took place; but there are

28 of David; and the virgin's name was Mary. And the Angel being come in, said unto her: Hail, full of grace, the Lord is with thee: Blessed art thou among women.

several difficulties in the way of this supposition. For (1) the Visitation followed immediately on the Annunciation, and seems inconsistent with the strict seclusion which would be observed by our Lady at such a time; and (2) the marriage would not have been solemnized till after her return, and thus our Lord would have been born within six months of it. Although there is some authority for this view therefore, it seems safer to follow the more usually accepted one, which has the large balance of Catholic tradition in its favour, and to suppose that our Lady was already legally married. We know little of her previous history beyond certain traditions. Her parents are said to have been St. Joachim and St. Anne, and the former to have died during her infancy. St. John (xix. 25) apparently says that she had a sister; but there is no real reason to suppose that whoever is alluded to was nearer than first cousin, as it was a common usage among the Jews to call cousins "brethren" or "sisters": see on viii. 19. Our Lady was in all probability an only child. It is an ancient tradition (amplified in the Apocryphal Gospels) that she passed her early years in the Temple, according to a not uncommon custom with those consecrated to God (cf. ii. 37). At the time of her marriage to St. Joseph, it is believed that she was not more than thirteen or fourteen; but in those parts, persons of that age are much more grown up than with us. By this time St. Anne also was probably dead, for there is no mention of her in the Gospels.

28. *And the Angel being come in.* The time of the Annunciation is supposed to have been midnight on March 25th. Our Lady was quite probably at that very time praying for the advent of the Messiah; but nothing was further from her thoughts than that she was to be closely connected with it. Her vow of virginity (*v.* 34, note) shows that she was already sufficiently advanced in spirituality to value it above even the chance of having the Messiah descended from her.

Hail, full of grace. The word κεχαριτωμένη, which the Douay version, following the Vulgate, renders "full of grace," is quite inadequately expressed in the A.V. as "highly favoured"; and it is certainly remarkable that the early English Protestant versions—Wycliffe's, Tyndale's, Coverdale's, and Cranmer's Bibles—notwithstanding theological prejudice, adhere to "full of grace." The Greek word denotes a very special degree of grace to which our Lady had attained during the time of her preparation for the Divine Maternity.

the Lord is with thee, i.e., "God is with thee," words continuing the same sense as the opening phrase of the salutation.

Blessed art thou among women. This is again a further amplification of the former, and denotes that our Lady was raised distinctly above all the rest of womankind. Although the words are omitted here in the Vatican Codex, they occur in all the other chief MSS., and are almost certainly genuine.

Who having heard, was troubled at his saying, and thought 29
with herself what manner of salutation this should be.
And the Angel said to her: Fear not, Mary, for thou hast 30
found grace with God. Behold thou shalt conceive in thy 31
womb, and shalt bring forth a son; and thou shalt call his
name Jesus. He shall be great, and shall be called the 32
Son of the most High, and the Lord God shall give unto
him the throne of David his Father: and he shall reign
in the house of Jacob for ever, and of his kingdom there 33
shall be no end. And Mary said to the Angel: How 34
shall this be done, because I know not man? And the 35
Angel answering, said to her: The Holy Ghost shall
come upon thee, and the power of the most High shall

29. *Who having heard.* Though agreeing with the Vulgate, this is nevertheless a slight mistranslation. The word is ἰδοῦσα, = having *seen* him.

30. *Fear not, Mary*, &c. The salutation being over, the message of the Angel begins here and occupies four verses. It is couched throughout in Scriptural language (cf. Dan. vii. 14, 27; Mich. iv. 7; Ps. cxxxi. 11, and elsewhere). Our Lady, who had so long meditated on the Scriptures, could not fail to understand its meaning and the fact that it referred to the Messiah.

31. *Thou shalt call his name Jesus.* The holy name means Saviour. It was a very common name among the Jews, being identical with Josue or Joshua. Our custom of differentiating it is due to reverence, in order that the same name may not be used in another connection.

32. *He shall be called the Son of the Most High.* According to universal Scriptural usage, this means "He shall *be* the Son of the Most High" (cf. *v.* 76; also see Isa. ix. 6). This and what follows form the explanation of the words "He shall be great."

the Lord God shall give unto him the throne of David, his father. David, as the ruler of the people of God, was a type of Christ, and it was this throne that our Lord was to inherit, by becoming the Head of the Catholic Church.

33. *And of his kingdom there shall be no end.* This again is an allusion to Christ's Headship of the Church Triumphant in heaven; and of this there will be no end.

34. *How shall this be done, because I know not man?* Our Lady's question shows that she had made a vow of perpetual virginity. In any other hypothesis it would be meaningless. The mere fact of having hitherto "known not man" would have presented no difficulty, unless she had determined that this state of things was to be permanent.

35. *The Holy Ghost shall come upon thee.* To an ordinary Jew, the expression "the Holy Ghost" would not have contained any definite

overshadow thee. And therefore also the Holy which shall
36 be born of thee shall be called the Son of God. And
behold thy cousin Elizabeth, she also hath conceived a son
in her old age; and this is the sixth month with her that is
37 called barren; because no word shall be impossible with
38 God. And Mary said: Behold the handmaid of the Lord,
be it done to me according to thy word. And the Angel
departed from her.

The Visitation. The Magnificat.

(VERS. 39-56.)

39 And Mary rising up in those days, went into the hill
40 country with haste into a city of Juda. And she entered

meaning, for the doctrine of the Trinity was unknown to them. To our
Lady, that doctrine may have been specially revealed, and these words
would have been to her intelligible enough.

shall be called the Son of God. In like manner here, the term "Son
of God" would have been recognized generally as denoting "the
Messiah," but without any special reference to the Trinity. To our
Lady it had a far nobler and deeper meaning.

36. *Thy cousin Elizabeth.* See on v. 5. The word συγγενίς does
not mean anything more definite than "kinswoman." The exact relationship between our Lady and St. Elizabeth is not known.

37. *Because no word shall be impossible with God.* This means that
the conception of St. John was an actual miracle, and the Angel pointed
to that as proof that another can be worked at God's good pleasure.

38. *Behold the handmaid of the Lord, be it done to me according to
thy word.* The Blessed Virgin gave her consent in these words, which
are now said daily throughout the Catholic world in the Angelus. The
fulfilment of them is given by St. John (i. 14), "And the word was
made flesh and dwelt amongst us," for the Incarnation took place
immediately on her consent. These words accordingly also form part
of the Angelus.

39. *Into the hill country.* The province of Judea was almost the
same as the ancient kingdom of Juda. It included the original territories of Juda, Benjamin, Dan and Simeon, and was about 100 miles in
length and 60 in breadth. It was nearly all hilly in character; but the
name hill-country was commonly applied to a certain portion of it due
south of Jerusalem and extending to Hebron and beyond.

with haste. The double motive prompted the Blessed Virgin, (1)
to congratulate her cousin on being about to have a son, which she had
learnt from the Angel; and (2) to tell her of the great things which were
about to be accomplished in herself.

into the house of Zachary, and saluted Elizabeth. And it 41
came to pass, that when Elizabeth heard the salutation of
Mary, the infant leaped in her womb. And Elizabeth was
filled with the Holy Ghost. And she cried out with a loud 42
voice, and said: Blessed art thou among women, and
blessed is the fruit of thy womb. And whence is this to 43
me, that the mother of my Lord should come to me? For 44
behold as soon as the voice of thy salutation sounded in
my ears, the infant in my womb leaped for joy. And blessed 45
art thou that hast believed, because those things shall
be accomplished that were spoken to thee by the Lord.
And Mary said: My soul doth magnify the Lord: and my 46/47

into a city of Juda. See on *v.* 23. The suggested reading here of *Juttah* for Juda is, to say the least, improbable. Many have supposed that St. Joseph accompanied our Lady to Jerusalem. If the commonly received date be correct, the Pasch was at hand, for which both Joseph and Mary went yearly to Jerusalem (ii. 41). It is surmised that St. Joseph may have taken our Lady to Jerusalem in that way and then returned alone after leaving her at the house of St. Elizabeth.

41. *The infant leaped in her womb.* According to common belief, at the moment that the infant leaped in St. Elizabeth's womb, he was sanctified from original sin. Thus was the first special outpouring of the grace of the Incarnation worked through our Lady; and it was the fulfilment of the prophecy made by the Angel: see on *v.* 15.

42. *Blessed art thou among women and blessed is the fruit of thy womb.* The special inspiration of the Holy Ghost is noticeable in St. Elizabeth taking up the very words of the Angel, so that we now join the two salutations together to make a single one in the "Hail Mary."

43. *The mother of my Lord.* This expression clearly shows knowledge which St. Elizabeth could only have acquired by special inspiration.

45. *Blessed art thou that hast believed.* The allusion here to Zachary's want of belief is evident. Cf. our Lord's words to St. Thomas, John xx. 29.

46. *My soul doth magnify the Lord,* &c. We have here the first of the three Canticles recited daily in the Church's office, all of which occur in the first two chapters of St. Luke. The "Magnificat" is the only recorded saying of the Blessed Virgin of any length. It is Jewish in form, but Christian in sentiment. Considerable resemblance may be observed between it and the Canticle of Anna (1 Kings ii. 1-10), which may easily have been in our Lady's mind, and of course the Scriptural form of speech would have come very naturally to her, considering her continual meditation on holy writ. The whole Canticle may be divided into three parts. The first part, from *v.* 46 to the middle of *v.*

48 spirit hath rejoiced in God my Saviour. Because he hath regarded the humility of his handmaid ; for behold from
49 henceforth all generations shall call me blessed. Because he that is mighty hath done great things to me : and holy
50 is his name. And his mercy is from generation unto
51 generations, to them that fear him. He hath shewed might in his arm : he hath scattered the proud in the
52 conceit of their heart. He hath put down the mighty from

48, is an outburst of the feelings with which our Lady had been penetrated from the time of the Annunciation, of acknowledgment of God's favours and full attribution of everything to Him. In the second part, which ends with *v.* 53, she joins all mankind in her exaltation, the predominant idea being the greatness of God's works compared with the smallness of the instruments He uses. Cf. Matt. xi. 25 ; 1 Cor. i. 27-29 ; Apoc. iii. 17-18. The third and concluding part is a declaration of the fulfilment of prophecy.

48. *For he hath regarded the humility of his handmaid.* The Jewish idea of greatness and favour with God was always bound up with riches, temporal prosperity, and temporal greatness. See the first and last chapters of the Book of Job, where the idea is specially prominent. Also see Ps. cxxvii. ; Deut. v. 15; and elsewhere *passim.* The connection between temporal misery and spiritual blessedness, the reward of humility and lowliness, the blessings of poverty are all distinctively Christian. At this time they had not been preached, but they were part of the special revelation by which our Lady was being prepared. The word ταπείνωσιν does not mean humility in our sense, but rather "lowliness." Nothing was further from our Lady's mind than mentioning her own virtues.

for behold from henceforth all generations shall call me blessed. Here our Lady begins the second part of her canticle, associating all mankind with her rejoicing, because of the great work God is doing in her. Thus she is *causa nostrae lætitiæ.*

50. *His mercy is from generation to generations, to them that fear him.* The virtue of "fear of the Lord," one of the seven gifts of the Holy Ghost, is always quoted in the Old Testament as distinctive of a servant of God. Cf. Wisdom vii. 15 ; Job i. 1, 8, 9, ii. 3, and elsewhere. Such fear should be not a servile but a filial fear. This whole verse is taken from Ps. cii. 17.

51. *He hath scattered the proud in the conceit of their heart.* The Douay rendering here is particularly good. The sentiment itself is characteristically Christian and foreign to Jewish ideas.

52. *He hath put down the mighty from their seat.* This verse is an amplification of the preceding. The tense used is the aorist, and must be taken as *gnomic*, or representing God's customary acts, which our Lady understood and others did not.

their seat, and hath exalted the humble. He hath filled 53 the hungry with good things: and the rich he hath sent empty away. He hath received Israel his servant, being 54 mindful of his mercy. As he spoke to our fathers, to 55 Abraham and to his seed for ever. And Mary abode with 56 her about three months: and she returned to her own house.

The Birth of St. John.   The Benedictus.

(VERS. 57-80.)

Now Elizabeth's full time of being delivered was come, 57 and she brought forth a son. And her neighbours and 58

53. *He hath filled the hungry with good things.* This may be understood both spiritually and temporally. Those who hunger in this world, that is the poor, receive a rich share of God's graces, as well as temporal alleviation in due season. But those who "hunger and thirst after justice" will "have their fill" in a special way (Matt. v. 6).

and the rich he hath sent empty away. This can also be interpreted similarly to the first part of the verse.

54. *He hath received Israel.* The word ἀντελάβετο means rather more than received; *helped* or *assisted* would be better. By Israel is of course meant the Jewish race. The sense is a declaration of the fulfilment of the promise made to Abraham.

55. *As he spoke to our fathers.* This is in parenthesis, alluding to the continual remembrance of Almighty God, as shown in His revelations to the Patriarchs and Prophets.

to Abraham and to his seed for ever. These words should therefore be joined on to verse 54, and the sense is "being mindful of His mercy to Abraham and to his seed for ever." St. Paul refers to this concluding idea. See Gal. iii. 16, "To Abraham were the promises made, and to his seed . . . which is Christ." See also Mich. vii. 20.

56. *And she returned to her own house.* The Gospel does not say whether the Blessed Virgin returned to Nazareth before or after the birth of St. John. It would seem more natural that, after staying so long, she should wait to take part in the rejoicing described in verse 58; and though at first sight the order in which the events are mentioned in the Gospel seems to imply otherwise, a closer acquaintance with St. Luke's usual method of writing makes us think this not decisive. There are several instances where he finishes off the subject about which he is writing before proceeding to what happened at an earlier date. See Introduction.

58. *And they congratulated with her.* With the birth of her child, St. Elizabeth's time of seclusion came to an end, and her kinsfolk and acquaintance came to her to congratulate her.

kinsfolks heard that the Lord had shewed his great mercy
59 towards her, and they congratulated with her. And it
came to pass, that on the eighth day they came to circumcise the child, and they called him by his father's name
60 Zachary. And his mother answering, said : Not so, but he
61 shall be called John. And they said to her : There is none
62 of thy kindred that is called by this name. And they made
63 signs to his father, how he would have him called. And
demanding a writing-table, he wrote, saying: John is his
64 name. And they all wondered. And immediately his
mouth was opened, and his tongue *loosed*, and he spoke
65 blessing God. And fear came upon all their neighbours ;
and all these things were noised abroad over all the hill

59. *On the eighth day they came to circumcise the child.* The ceremony of circumcision had to be performed on the eighth day after birth
(Gen. xvii. 12 ; Lev. xii. 3 ; Luke ii. 21). It was usually performed
by the father, but in this case Zachary was unable to pronounce the
words, and it would have been done by another. The occasion was a
solemn one. Several witnesses had to be present, and the name was
given to the infant as at our christening.

they called him by his father's name Zachary. The verb is in the
imperfect, and the sense is that they were already giving him that
name.

60. *Not so, but he shall be called John.* St. Elizabeth had evidently
been told by her husband by means of signs all the details of his vision,
and knew that the child's name was to be John. These verses (59-61)
imply that Zachary was deaf as well as dumb, for he was not aware of
the dispute till people "made signs to him": see on *v.* 22.

63. *Demanding a writing-table.* A "writing-table" or tablet
would have been a small piece of wood on which wax was smeared or
sand strewn, so that words could be written with a metal *stilus*.
Zachary had no doubt been using one frequently during the nine months
of his dumbness. Such tablets were common in Rome, and no doubt
well known in Judea, as a regular means for writing short notes :
though for longer writings paper was used.

64. *And immediately his mouth was opened.* At the fulfilment of
the prophecy of the Angel, the "sign" came to an end, and Zachary
recovered his speech. The first use he made of it was to praise God.
Probably this praise was the Benedictus itself, though for obvious
reasons, and according to his usual custom, St. Luke finishes his narrative first, and then goes back to give the words of the Benedictus.

65. *And fear came upon all their neighbours.* This "fear" was due
to a consciousness of the nearness of the other world, as displayed by
these wonderful events.

country of Judea: and all they that had heard them laid 66
them up in their heart, saying: What an one, think ye,
shall this child be? For the hand of the Lord was with
him. And Zachary his father was filled with the Holy 67
Ghost: and he prophesied, saying: Blessed be the Lord 68
God of Israel: because he hath visited and wrought the
redemption of his people: and hath raised up an horn of 69
salvation to us, in the house of David his servant. As he 70
spoke by the mouth of his holy prophets, who are from the
beginning. Salvation from our enemies, and from the 71
hand of all that hate us. To perform mercy to our fathers; 72
and to remember his holy testament. The oath which he 73
swore to Abraham our father, that he would grant to us,
that being delivered from the hand of our enemies, we 74

67. *And he prophesied.* For the Scriptural meaning of prophecy, see *infra*, on *v.* 76.

68. *Blessed be the Lord God of Israel,* &c. The Benedictus is the second of the three Canticles given by St. Luke. It falls naturally into two divisions. The first (*vv.* 68-75) is the application of the prophesies of old to the Redeemer who had now come; the second (*vv.* 76-79) relates to the future work of Zachary's son, St. John Baptist.

69. *And hath raised up an horn of salvation to us.* The horn is frequently used in the Old Testament as a sign of power (cf. 1 Kings ii. 10; Ps. cxxxi. 17). An horn of salvation thus denotes a mighty deliverance.

in the house of David his servant. While the Jews bore the yoke of the Romans, they continually sighed for the time when the house of David was to be their deliverer. As of old in the family of David there was found power against their enemies, so now that of which they had been so long deprived was to be restored, but in a far higher sense.

70. *As he spoke by the mouth of his holy prophets.* This verse is parenthetic, alluding incidentally to the fulfilment of prophecy. Cf. *v.* 55.

71. *Salvation from our enemies.* This verse, therefore, joins on in sense to *v.* 69. "He hath raised up an horn of salvation to us, in the house of David his servant, salvation from our enemies, and from the hand of all that hate us"—i.e., from the Gentiles and Pagans.

72. *To perform mercy to our fathers,* i.e., "in answer to the prayers of our fathers."

73. *The oath which he swore to Abraham our father.* See Gen. xxii. 16-18, and xxvi. 3.

74. *That being delivered,* &c. The specially Christian character of the following words should be noticed. The object of deliverance from our enemies is not to be temporal or political greatness, but that "we

75 may serve him without fear, in holiness and justice before
76 him, all our days. And thou, child, shalt be called the
prophet of the highest : for thou shalt go before the face of
77 the Lord to prepare his ways. To give knowledge of salvation to his people, unto the remission of their sins.
78 Through the bowels of the mercy of our God, in which the
79 Orient, from on high, hath visited us. To enlighten them
that sit in darkness, and in the shadow of death: to direct
80 our feet into the way of peace. And the child grew, and
was strengthened in spirit : and was in the deserts until the
day of his manifestation to Israel.

may serve [God] without fear, in holiness and justice before him, all our days."

76. *And thou, child, shalt be called the prophet of the highest.* Here Zachary turns to his son and addresses him. "Thou shalt be called," i.e., shall *be*: see on *v.* 32. St. John was the last of the prophets. The others had shown what was to appear at a distance ; he was to point it out at the moment of its fulfilment. For the function of a prophet does not necessarily refer to the foretelling of future events ; but in a broader sense it may be applied to all preaching of higher spiritual truth, and making known by inspiration what is secret. Thus St. John prophesied when he said, "Behold the Lamb of God" (John i. 29). Cf. John iv. 18, 19, where our Lord says, "Thou *hast had* five husbands," and the Samaritan woman answers, "I see thou art a prophet."

thou shalt go before the face of the Lord to prepare his ways. This is a quotation from the prophet Malachias (iii. 1), and was afterwards applied to St. John by our Lord Himself (vii. 27 ; Matt. xi. 10).

77. *Unto the remission of their sins.* This was to be the special theme of St. John's preaching. The salvation of the people was to come not by deliverance from the yoke of the Romans, or the restoration of the kingdom of Israel, but by penance leading to forgiveness of sin.

78. *The Orient*, i.e., the Dawn. See Zach. iii. 8 and vi. 12. It here refers to the coming of the Sun of Justice ; the "true light that enlighteneth every man that cometh into this world" (John i. 9), of which the Baptist was to give testimony.

79. *To enlighten them that sit in darkness and in the shadow of death.* Cf. Isa. ix. 2, "The people that walked in darkness have seen a great light ; to them that dwelt in the region of the shadow of death, light is risen."

80. *And the child grew,* &c. This one verse gives us all the information we possess of the youth of St. John. How soon he left his father's house to lead the life of a hermit in the desert we are not told ; but it would seem that it was early, while he was yet young, and the numerous pictures which Christian art has produced showing St. John and our Lord together as children have little likelihood of foundation in fact. The "desert" or "wilderness" alluded to was the wild country lying between the "hill country" and the Dead Sea and not far from his home. The word "desert" was used of any wild region, though often not such as we should now designate by the name. Cf. ix. 10, " He went aside into a desert place," with John vi. 10, " Now there was much grass in the place." See also Mark vi. 39. The hilly region, however, was almost wholly barren and was infested by wild beasts and robbers, so that St. Luke must have had in his mind a life of solitariness and asceticism. This is confirmed from the other synoptists, who describe his "garments of camel's hair, with a leathern girdle about his loins," and his food as "locusts and wild honey." See Matt. iii. 4 ; and Mark i. 6.

until the day of his manifestation to Israel. When the time of St. John's " manifestation," or public preaching, came, he probably began near the same spot.

CHAPTER II.

Birth of our Lord.

(VERS. 1–7.)

AND it came to pass that in those days there went out a decree from Cæsar Augustus; that the whole ₂ world should be enrolled. This enrolling was first made

1. *A decree from Cæsar Augustus that the whole world should be enrolled.* This reference to an enrolment or census of "the whole world"—that is, of the whole Roman Empire—has given rise to much discussion. There is no account extant of an enrolment of the Jews at this time, and it has been argued that as Judea had not yet become actually a Roman province, it would not have had any part in a census decreed by Augustus. It is certain, however, that Judea was looked upon as a tributary kingdom or dependency, and Herod, who owed his kingship to the direct appointment of Rome, would have co-operated even if he had not received direct orders from the Emperor, as is more than possible. There is a record of the steps taken by Augustus in B.C. 7 to compile a full enumeration of his subjects. The people of Rome had from very early times been numbered by the Censors regularly every five years. Augustus resolved to take a special and complete census of the whole Roman world, and he appointed twenty-five Commissioners to take this enrolment in the different countries of the empire. A quarter of a century was expended on the work, and the resulting statistics were inscribed by Augustus with his own hand in a Register of the Empire, of which fragments are still extant, called the "Ancyra Marble." Josephus makes no direct mention of this enrolment extending to the Jews, but he is probably alluding to it when he says that they were called on to take the oath of fidelity to the Emperor, and that six thousand Pharisees refused to do so, and were accordingly punished by Herod. Such an administration of the oath of allegiance would naturally form part of the Imperial census, and we know of no other occasion to which it could refer.

2. *This enrolling,* &c. On the wording of this verse, a well-known difficulty arises. Cyrinus, or in the more common Roman form,

by Cyrinus the governor of Syria. And all went to be

Quirinus, is known to us as the Provincial Governor of Syria who was in office in A.D. 6, when Archelaus was deposed and Judea reduced to the position of an ordinary Roman province. Moreover, he *did* then carry out a census. But it seems to be quite clear that that census was not the one referred to here. Our Lord must have been born at latest before the death of Herod, which is fixed with little doubt in the year 750 of Rome, that is, B.C. 4, according to our present reckoning. Hence, of course, it follows that the early calculations on which the Christian era were based, were at fault; indeed, the exact date of our Lord's birth can hardly be said to be fixed with certainty even yet. But there is no reason to doubt that there were *two* consecutive censuses, at an interval of about ten years. In fact, the census of A.D. 6 may be distinguished from that of B.C. 4 by two things—(1) that it was accompanied in Judea by the levying of a tax, of which we hear nothing in B.C. 4 (for the word *taxed* used in the A.V. is clearly a mistranslation, which has been duly rectified in the R.V.); (2) that it led not merely to a protest of a certain number of Pharisees against the oath, but to an open Galilean revolt under Judas the Gaulonite (Acts v. 37). It appears, then, that St. Luke knew of both censuses, and refers here to the *first*, and in the Acts to the *second*. The one was no doubt as a matter of Roman policy, and used to prepare the way for the other; for we know that the complete enslavement of the Jewish people was effected by gradual measures. Further, it is known that the officers who took such a census as that of B.C. 4 were not necessarily the ordinary provincial governors. They were often extraordinary Imperial commissioners or "legates" for the district. It seems therefore that Quirinus was both legate of Syria (and probably military governor of that part of the East) in B.C. 4 and also the regular provincial governor in A.D. 6. If this explanation be correct, the idea conveyed by the text would be: "This was the first of the two enrolments made under the supervision of Quirinus, Governor of Syria." This would not, however, be an accurate translation word for word; the exact meaning of the Greek is: "This [Imperial] census was then for the first time made [in Judea] and it was under the supervision of Quirinus, Governor [then and afterwards] of Syria." The double census was memorable to all Jews as the epoch of their subjection by two stages to the Pagan empire, and the name of Quirinus was doubtless familiar to St. Luke, who was born in Syria about that time.

3. *All went to be enrolled, every one into his own city.* It is to be observed that in the method of the enrolment, the Jewish custom was followed of numbering all the people in their families or tribes: cf. Numb. i. 2-4. This was apparently a part of the politic arrangements for disguising the approach of the Roman authority. We know from Josephus that the name of Herod, as the Jewish king, was joined with the name of the Emperor in the oath of allegiance. Herod had evidently arranged this with his friends and masters at the Roman court, to smooth the way; and he had doubtless also got their assent to

4 enrolled, every one into his own city. And Joseph also went up from Galilee out of the city of Nazareth into Judea, to the city of David, which is called Bethlehem:
5 because he was of the house and family of David, to be enrolled with Mary his espoused wife, who was with
6 child. And it came to pass, that when they were there, her days were accomplished, that she should be delivered.
7 And she brought forth her first-born son, and wrapped him up in swaddling clothes, and laid him in a manger: because there was no room for them in the inn.

the taking of the census in the old national form. This made no difference in this *preliminary* enrolment, since a tax was not at once to be levied. On the second enrolment we hear of no similar grouping of families, and it was no doubt taken locally for taxing purposes in the ordinary Roman form. By then, also, Judea and Galilee were differently constituted, Judea being under a regular Roman provincial governor or Procurator: see on iii. 1. At this time, however, both formed part of Herod's kingdom.

4. *To the city of David which is called Bethlehem.* The name Bethlehem means "House of Bread." Being the city of David, it was the centre for all those who claimed royal descent. It was at that time but a small town, about six miles from Jerusalem, situated on a long hill, overlooking the plain famous in the stories of Jesse and of Ruth. At the summit of the hill now stands the Church of the Nativity: see on *v.* 7.

5. *To be enrolled with Mary his espoused wife.* The presence of our Lady at the enrolment was probably not absolutely necessary, but her time was at hand, and she naturally accompanied her husband. She was most probably aware, from her knowledge of the Scriptures, that the Messiah was to be born at Bethlehem, and she would thus have recognized the working of Divine providence in the events which led to the journey.

7. *Her first-born son.* Our Lord was of course her only son. In modern language, the phrase might indicate that there were other children: but in the case of the Jews it would imply no such meaning. The first-born sons had certain privileges, and there were also certain duties connected with them, as for example their presentation in the Temple and their redemption: see on *v.* 22. These were quite independent of whether there were other children or not; which of course would at the time be undecided. Hence the name "first-born" had a sort of technical meaning, and nothing would be implied by its use as to whether or not there were other children.

because there was no room for them in the inn. The inn or *khan* of a village such as Bethlehem is described as little more than an enclosed space surrounded by open recesses, with a paved floor or *leewan* raised a little above the level of the ground. There would be

Adoration of the Shepherds.

(VERS. 8–20.)

And there were in the same country shepherds watching, 8 and keeping the night-watches over their flock. And 9 behold an angel of the Lord stood by them, and the brightness of God shone round about them, and they feared with a great fear. And the angel said to them: 10 Fear not; for behold I bring you good tidings of great joy, that shall be to all the people. For this day is born to 11 you a Saviour, who is Christ the Lord, in the city of

no furniture, and the traveller would bring his own carpet and provide for himself as he pleased, and leave his animals in the courtyard. Those who arrived late might themselves have to occupy a corner of the yard, in company with mules, camels, and horses. Often there were caves in the vicinity, which would be used to accommodate such animals as could not fit into the yard. Such seems to have been the case in this instance. The cave where the Nativity is believed to have taken place, now surmounted by a church which dates from the reign of Constantine, appears to have been at some short distance from the khan itself, so that the earlier mysteries of our Lord's life took place in peace and seclusion. The tradition as to the place, which St. Jerome fully believed, was evidently accepted by the local Christians at the time when St. Helena sought out the Holy Places. It dates therefore from the fourth century at least, and there is no reason to think it spurious.

As to the day and hour of the birth of Christ, the Gospels are silent: but the universal tradition is that He was born in the middle of winter. The 25th of December may have been the exact date, or it may have been chosen to represent mid-winter, i.e., the time of the winter solstice, which was a great pre-Christian festival.

8. *There were in the same country shepherds.* The episode of the shepherds is again cast in the form of a Hebrew poem, with its characteristic doubling of the phrases, e.g., watching and keeping the night-watches. The words of the message may or may not be meant to be reported literally; but as before, the account is probably given on the authority of our Lady herself. The shepherds were with their sheep in the very place where David had received his call. The reference therefore to the city of David would appeal to them at once. It has sometimes been asserted that the fact of the shepherds being occupied with their sheep at night, shows that the Nativity must have taken place in the spring: but the best authorities tell us that in many parts of Palestine, to this day, shepherds are out with their sheep all night in the depth of winter.

11. *A Saviour, who is Christ the Lord.* Three titles are given to our Lord by the Angel. They are meant to indicate and sum up the

12 David. And this shall be a sign unto you. You shall find the infant wrapped in swaddling clothes, and laid in a
13 manger. And suddenly there was with the angel a multitude of the heavenly army, praising God, and saying:
14 Glory to God in the highest: and on earth peace to men
15 of good will. And it came to pass, after the angels departed from them into heaven, the shepherds said one to another, Let us go over to Bethlehem, and let us see this word that is come to pass, which the Lord hath
16 shewed to us. And they came with haste: and they found Mary and Joseph, and the infant lying in the
17 manger. And seeing, they understood of the word that

"good tidings," or Gospel, which was now first announced to the Jews, namely, that the Messiah had come. The word "a Saviour" would not have indicated to a devout Jew exactly what we understand by it. It would mean the Saviour who was to redeem Israel (cf. *infra*, xxiv. 21) from its degradation and bring in the Messianic kingdom, in which the kingdom of David was to be restored in greater glory. But the message says that this Saviour is to be (1) Christ, and (2) the Lord. To a Jew who knew the Prophets, as even these shepherds may well have known them, "Christ," that is "the Anointed One of God," was a natural title of this Messiah, as the "King of the Jews" and the "Holy One"—for the rite of anointing symbolized to them, as to us after them, a setting apart for holy uses. But the title which we translate as "the Lord" would be startling. The shepherds spoke of course the vernacular form of Hebrew which is styled Aramaic, and the word seems to represent, as it did already in the Septuagint, the name of God—that is, "the ineffable name." Its use here would convey to our Lady a declaration that the Saviour now born was in truth a Divine Person; but of course the shepherds would not understand anything so definite.

in the city of David. This was well known to be Bethlehem, and the shepherds understood it as such: see v. 15.

14. *On earth peace to men of good will.* There is some slight difference of reading here. According to the Vatican MS. the meaning is rather "peace, good will towards men," which meaning is adhered to in the A.V. The Revised Version approximates more to our translation, which agrees with the other chief MSS.

16. *They came with haste.* We are not told how they were guided to the place where the Holy Infant was; probably the angels told them more than is recorded.

17. *They understood of the word.* Both the A.V. and R.V. translate ἐγνώρισαν transitively, "made known." This seems to accord better with the sense and the context, as well as being more probably the actual meaning of the Greek word.

had been spoken to them concerning this child. And all ¹⁸ that heard wondered: and at those things that were told them by the shepherds. But Mary kept all these words, ¹⁹ pondering *them* in her heart. And the shepherds returned, ²⁰ glorifying and praising God, for all the things they had heard, and seen, as it was told unto them.

Early Ceremonies of our Lord's Life—Circumcision, Presentation in the Temple, Purification of the Blessed Virgin Mary.

(Vers. 21–39.)

And after eight days were accomplished that the child ²¹ should be circumcised; his name was called Jesus, which was called by the angel, before he was conceived in the womb. And after the days of her purification ²² according to the law of Moses were accomplished, they carried him to Jerusalem, to present him to the Lord.

18. *And at those things.* The word "and" is probably an interpolation. It does not occur in the early copies of the Vulgate, and the verse reads much more intelligibly without it.

19. *But Mary kept all these words,* &c. The antithesis here is instructive. The shepherds spoke to every one about what had taken place and all wondered: but to our Lady they were no source of wonder, for she had long been instructed in all these mysteries; and she spoke of them to no one, but kept pondering over them in her heart (cf. *v.* 50).

21. *His name was called Jesus.* Both St. Joseph and our Lady had learnt from an angel that He was to be called Jesus (Matt. i. **21**; Luke i. **31**). The account of the circumcision of our Lord may be compared with that of St. John i. 59, *seq.* It was in that case an occasion of rejoicing, and St. Elizabeth's friends and neighbours were present. In our Lord's case, there was no such congratulation, for He was born a stranger, in a village far from our Lady's home and acquaintance.

22. *The days of her purification.* All the Greek MSS. read αὐτῶν, "of *their* purification," and it is almost certainly the correct reading. St. Luke thus wrote as though both Mother and Child had to be purified; but this method of speaking was not used by the Jews themselves.

they carried him to Jerusalem. The first journey of the Holy Family after the birth of our Lord was to Jerusalem, for the double purpose of the Purification of our Lady and the Presentation of our Lord in the Temple as a first-born son, and His redemption. The

23 As it is written in the law of the Lord, *Every male open-*
24 *ing the womb shall be called holy to the Lord*. And to
offer a sacrifice according as it is written in the law of the
25 Lord, a pair of turtle doves, or two young pigeons. And
behold there was a man in Jerusalem named Simeon, and
this man was just and devout, waiting for the consolation

former rite took place after every childbirth; the latter only after that of a first-born son.

The law of Purification is given in the twelfth chapter of Leviticus. Every mother after childbirth was required to live in seclusion for a certain period—forty days if the child were a male, eighty days if a female—during which time she could not join in public worship, or mix with her neighbours, being legally "unclean." When the time was expired, she would offer the proper sacrifice, as described in Lev. xii. 6. At the same time, being a first-born son, our Lord had to be presented for the service of the Temple, and redeemed, or bought back, as prescribed by the law.

23. *Every male opening the womb*, &c. The law of the sanctification of the male first-born and their dedication to the service of God, was first given after the Israelites had escaped from Egypt: see Exod. xiii. 2. Later on this was changed, and all those of the tribe of Levi were consecrated to God instead (Numb. iii. 12, 13); but the firstborn of the other tribes were still regarded as marked for the Temple service, and had therefore to be redeemed by the legal payment of five shekels for each (or about fifteen shillings of our money) to form a Temple fund (*ibid.*, 39-51 and xviii. 15, 16). The shekel was a silver coin of the Temple, no longer current in ordinary life. It was partly to enable people to obtain this Temple money that the stalls of the money changers were placed in the outer court, for the payments commanded by the law could not be paid in the Roman coinage.

24. *A pair of turtle doves or two young pigeons*. The proper sacrifice was a yearling lamb for a holocaust or burnt offering, and a young pigeon or turtle dove for a sin offering (Lev. xii. 6). Those who were poor were allowed to substitute two turtle doves or two young pigeons (*ibid.*, xii. 8), and our Lady, with perfect humility, availed herself of the dispensation. With this offering they entered the Temple, that is the Court of the Women, at the further gate of which the priest would have received the offerings for sacrifice.

25. *A man in Jerusalem named Simeon*. Nothing further is known about Simeon beyond what is contained in these few verses. There was a famous Simeon alive at that time, the son of Hillel and the father of the celebrated Gamaliel, the instructor of St. Paul. Some have identified him with the one here mentioned; but there are considerable difficulties, one being that Simeon, son of Hillel, was alive many years after this, while the "Nunc Dimittis" is generally understood to point to its being near the end of the life of the Simeon here mentioned.

of Israel: and the Holy Ghost was in him. And he had 26
received an answer from the Holy Ghost, that he should
not see death before he had seen the Christ of the Lord.
And he came by the Spirit into the temple. And when 27
his parents brought in the child Jesus, to do for him
according to the custom of the law, he also took him 28
into his arms, and blessed God, and said: Now thou dost 29
dismiss thy servant, O Lord, according to thy word in
peace, because my eyes have seen thy salvation, which 30
thou hast prepared before the face of all peoples; a light 31
to the revelation of the Gentiles, and the glory of thy 32
people Israel. And his father and mother were wonder- 33
ing at those things, which were spoken concerning him.
And Simeon blessed them, and said to Mary his mother: 34
Behold this *child* is set for the fall, and for the resurrection of many in Israel, and for a sign which shall be

26. *He had received an answer*, i.e., to his constant prayer for the advent of the Messiah.

the Christ of the Lord. i.e., the Anointed of God. See note on *v.* 11. This is not, however, the same title as "Christ the Lord," there used by the Angel, but equivalent to the first part of it only.

28. *He also.* That is, he as well as the Holy Family and the priest.

29-32. The "Nunc Dimittis" is the last of the three canticles given by St. Luke. The spirit of it is one of perfect repose on the fulfilment of the one desire of Simeon's life; and hence it is recited daily at Compline.

30. *Thy salvation.* i.e., the Saviour; the abstract for concrete.

32. *A light to the revelation of the Gentiles.* This part of the prophecy of Simeon that our Lord was to be a light to the Gentiles is specially remarkable, as such an idea was then and for long afterwards far from the ordinary Jewish mind. But it is noticeable how the Prophets continually transcend this narrow conception: see Isa. xi. 9, 10, xix. 18-25; and in the last chapters almost *passim*. The very term light of the Gentiles occurs in xlix. 6: "It is a small thing that thou should'st be my servant to raise up the tribes of Jacob and to convert the dregs of Israel. Behold I have given thee to be the light of the Gentiles, that thou mayest be my salvation even to the farthest part of the earth."

and the glory of thy people Israel. Our Lord was specially the glory of the Jews, as belonging to their nation, having a Jewish mother, and as being the centre of all the Jewish prophets; in fact the very object for which the nation was established by God.

34. *For the fall and for the resurrection of many.* Cf. Isa. viii. 14. The expression is similar to that of the setting of a stone in a steep

35 contradicted. And thy own soul a sword shall pierce,
36 that out of many hearts thoughts may be revealed. And there was one Anna, a prophetess, the daughter of Phanuel, of the tribe of Aser; she was far advanced in years, and had lived with her husband seven years from
37 her virginity. And she was a widow until fourscore and four years; who departed not from the temple, by fastings
38 and prayers serving night and day. Now she at the same hour coming in, confessed to the Lord; and spoke of

valley track, over which some may stumble, and to which others may cling as to a rock of safety. All are given grace sufficient for salvation; but the greater the grace, the greater the guilt if it is rejected. See John ix. 41, xv. 24; Luke x. 13, 14, xx. 17, 18.

35. *Thy own soul a sword shall pierce.* This is the first of our Lady's seven Dolours or Sorrows. She must have been specially illuminated to understand the bitter meaning of this prophecy; otherwise it would be difficult for this to be comparable to the other six dolours. These were the Flight into Egypt, the Three days' loss, the Meeting of our Lord with the Cross, the death of our Lord, the reception of His dead body, and His burial.

that out of many hearts thoughts may be revealed. The sense of this phrase is not very clear. It probably refers back to the previous verse, and the "revelation of thoughts" is an allusion to the judgment on those who have made our Lord the source of their fall or resurrection respectively. The thoughts are their thoughts about Christ, and their reception of the Faith offered to them. The Jews were professedly ready to welcome the Messiah of the prophecies, and to accept the signs of His coming. Those whose inner "thoughts" were not sincere, but were self-seeking, or jealous, or rebellious, would be "revealed," especially in the final struggle and the condemnation and death of Christ. Those whose thoughts were sincere, like Nicodemus and Lazarus, would prove their sincerity by the same test.

36. *There was one Anna.* Nothing is known of Anna but what we find here, namely, that she was a prophetess, the daughter of Phanuel, of the tribe of Aser; that she had been seven years married before the death of her husband, and was now eighty-four years old. Moreover, she lived in the Temple, fasting and praying: see on i. 27. We may suppose that she had some connection with our Lady's life unknown to us.

It may be noted that our Lord at Bethlehem was revealed to, and worshipped by the shepherds, representing the poor, the humble and the docile; and by the Magi representing the Gentiles. Now, at His first entry into the Temple, He received the homage of that important class of devout Jews, whose chief occupation was to watch and pray for the coming of the Messiah.

him to all that looked for the redemption of Israel. And ₃₉ after they had performed all things according to the law of the Lord, they returned into Galilee, to their city Nazareth.

39. *After they had performed all things according to the law of the Lord.* To understand the precise meaning of the word "after," we must bear in mind that the next two verses, to which the phrase refers, cover a period of nearly twelve years; and the next dozen verses thirty years. It is therefore not at all necessary, or indeed possible, to suppose that the word *after* means *immediately* after in the sense that they set out for their ultimate home at Nazareth within a few days or weeks, or that they did not travel or sojourn elsewhere in the interval. The words involve no more than that they went back to Nazareth some time later, and had their home there for the rest of the life of St. Joseph, and the whole of the preparatory life of our Lord. It seems much the most probable that the visit of the Magi and the flight into Egypt (which are only mentioned by St. Matthew) took place between the Purification and this return to Nazareth. The feast of the Epiphany (January 6th) is not necessarily a commemoration of the traditional date; but if it were, it could not mean that the visit of the Magi happened twelve days after the Nativity, since the Holy Family were, as we see, in Jerusalem on the fortieth day after our Lord's birth; that is, if our date for Christmas be taken as correct, on February 2nd. We should have to suppose that tradition had placed the Epiphany a year and twelve days after, which is not impossible and has been thought by some to harmonize well with Matt. ii. 16.

On the other hand, this expression of St. Luke, "After they had performed," &c., does seem to preclude the idea of a seven years' exile in Egypt, such as is often quoted in books of devotion. About this we can be guided to some extent by secular history. We know that Herod died in the month of April of the year 4 B.C. If our Lord was born in that year, the Flight into Egypt must have taken place very soon after the Purification, probably early in February; and the sojourn of the Holy Family there need not have lasted more than a few months, where they would have found Archelaus reigning. His reign did not begin at once, for his succession was opposed and he went to Rome and got it confirmed: see on xix. 12. The language of St. Matthew would lead us to suppose that the natural thing would have been for the Holy Family to have returned to Bethlehem; and it was only because of their fear of Archelaus that they went to Nazareth. Probably St. Joseph when he went up to Bethlehem for the census had the intention of remaining there and practising his trade, so that the child might be brought up in the City of David. If we suppose the two years of St. Matthew (ii. 16) to be a measure of the time which had elapsed since the star was seen, and also that the star coincided with the Annunciation or the Nativity, we should have to put our Lord's birth earlier, say B.C. 5 or 6; and there would then have been a stay of many months in

The Hidden Life of Our Lord.

(VERS. 40–52.)

40 And the child grew, and waxed strong, full of wisdom: 41 and the grace of God was in him. And his parents went every year to Jerusalem at the solemn day of the pasch.

Bethlehem before the Magi came. St. Luke's language is not absolutely inconsistent even with this view.

40. *And the child grew*, &c. These few words are all that we are told of the sacred childhood. We can only supplement by what we know of the life and customs of those days, and what we should expect antecedently to have happened in the case of our Lord; and by a few of what may be called chance allusions in the Gospels, in describing His preaching at Nazareth later on. Thus we learn from St. Matthew (xiii. 55) that St. Joseph was a carpenter. Moreover we know that the law compelled every man to have some trade, and in view of the Oriental conservatism by which trade became almost a caste, we should naturally expect what we gather from St. Mark (vi. 3), that our Lord also was one. Thus He would have been brought up as a poor man, without even going through the form of learning, beyond what our Lady and St. Joseph, as His legal parents, were bound to teach Him (Deut. vi. 7). The work of a carpenter at a village like Nazareth would be of a very rude and rough description. It would consist chiefly of making implements of agriculture, yokes for oxen, ploughs, or the like, and perhaps rough household furniture. Every Sabbath, and at some other times, our Lord would have attended the synagogue, where He would have heard the Law and the Prophets (see on iv. 15); but a manual employment such as His was considered incompatible with anything like scholarship or study (Eccles. xxxviii. 25 *seq.*), so that when He preached the people asked in surprise, "How came this man by all these things? ... Is not this the carpenter?" (Mark vi. 2, 3), and "How doth this man know letters, having never learned?" (John vii. 15). It is well known that the Pharisees, and the other rulers among the Jews at that time, had come to despise the poorer classes, on the ground that they "knew not the law" (John vii. 49); that is, that they had had no opportunity for the minute study of it on which the Scribes and Doctors prided themselves. Equally they despised women and refused to teach them. Nevertheless it is certain that our Lady knew the Law and the Prophets intimately. It is possible that she might have acquired such a knowledge as one of the Temple maidens. It is also probable that there were in places like Nazareth synagogue schools, where some teaching was given to those boys who were sufficiently diligent and intelligent to profit by it. Many stories of this and of other incidents in our Lord's hidden life are given in the apocryphal Gospels; but most of them are evidently legendary.

41. *His parents went every year to Jerusalem.* There were three great Feasts, at which all were commanded to go to Jerusalem; these were the Pasch, Pentecost, and the feast of Tabernacles: see Exod. xxiii. 15-17, and Deut. xvi. 1-16. The Pasch was regulated, like our Easter, by the spring full moon, and was supposed to mark the beginning of the harvest. It was the 15th day of the Jewish month Nisan, which began always with a new moon, and was the first month of their year. The feast of Pentecost (Lev. xxiii. 15-22) was celebrated after seven full weeks (Deut. xvi. 9), and marked the end of the corn harvest, which in Palestine is now generally completed in or about our month of May. The feast of Tabernacles (Lev. xxiii. 34-6) was usually in October, the day being fixed by the autumn full moon, as the Pasch was by the spring moon, and it marked the completion of the fruit and wine harvest. The three events commemorated were respectively the escape from Egypt, the giving of the Law on Mount Sinai, and the wandering o the Israelites in the desert. At each of them the festivities were kept up for seven days; and at the feast of Tabernacles there was an eighth day added, known as the "great day" (John vii. 37).

Besides the three great feasts, there were two other minor ones, of later introduction. One of these, known as Purim, was instituted by Mardochai, to commemorate the overthrow of Aman. It was confirmed by Esther, and took place in the spring. It is thought by some that this is the feast alluded to in St. John v. 1. The other feast was instituted by Judas Machabæus to commemorate the dedication of the new altar of burnt offerings, after the profanation of the Temple by Antiochus, B.C. 168. It is referred to in St. John x. 22; and fell in December.

One more important commemoration must be referred to, though it was not a feast, namely, the Day of Atonement. It was in some respects the most solemn day of the whole year: see Lev. xxiii. 27-33. Every Jew was bound to fast on that day under pain of death, and on that day only the High Priest entered the Holy of Holies, with many ceremonies: see Heb. ix. 7. After this the curious ceremony took place of driving out into the wilderness the scape goat, which was supposed to bear with it the sins of the people, that were now expiated. The Day of Atonement was the tenth day of the seventh month (Tisri) of the Jewish year; and as theirs were lunar months and the year began with the new moon before the vernal equinox, it would occur some time about October, and five days before the feast of Tabernacles.

Though the law prescribed three visits to the Temple yearly, it seems clear that by the time of our Lord it had become usual to regard one as more particularly obligatory, namely, that for the feast of the Pasch. We know that the Jews "of the dispersion," when they made the pilgrimage to Jerusalem, arrived in time for the Pasch, and commonly stayed over Pentecost, which accounts for the facts noted in Acts ii. 5-11. Our Lady was exempt from the obligation, which only concerned men. The position of women generally among the Jews was one of inferiority. They were not even allowed to worship in the synagogue, except behind a lattice. Nevertheless it was quite customary

4

42 And when he was twelve years old, they going up into
43 Jerusalem according to the custom of the feast, and
having fulfilled the days, when they returned, the child
Jesus remained in Jerusalem; and his parents knew it
44 not. And thinking that he was in the company, they
came a day's journey, and sought him among their kins-
45 folks and acquaintance. And not finding him, they
46 returned into Jerusalem, seeking him. And it came to
pass, that after three days they found him in the temple
sitting in the midst of the doctors, hearing them and

for many of them to go up to the feasts, and our Lady, in doing so, would only have appeared to be acting as other religious women.

42. *When he was twelve years old.* The age of twelve formed an epoch in the life of every Jewish boy, who then, indeed, ceased to be a boy and became a man. He was bound by the law at that time to begin to learn a trade. It must be remembered that in southern countries boys grow to manhood at a much younger age than with us. At the age of twelve, then, he would be presented in the synagogue and given with a "phylactery," or frontlet for the head, on which were inscribed the Commandments, and which he would subsequently always wear on the Sabbath. This ceremony in our Lord's case had taken place soon after His twelfth birthday, several months before the Paschal festival. But this Pasch was the occasion of His first visit to Jerusalem after He was legally grown up, and it was indeed the first time He went in actual obedience to the law, which did not bind before that age.

44. *They came a day's journey.* There was always a large number of pilgrims going to and from Jerusalem at the seasons of feasts, forming different large companies or caravans, because the roads were not safe. The easiest route to and from Galilee would lie across Samaria (cf. John iv. 4; Luke ix. 51-3). The feast itself lasted seven days, and the journey in each direction would take three or four days. The total number of pilgrims is said to have been more than two millions; the caravan to Galilee must have numbered many thousands. The fact of a boy not being missed till evening would be in no way wonderful in the case of any one else; in our Lord's case it is specially instructive as showing that He mixed freely with His "kinsfolk and acquaintance," like any other Jewish boy.

45. *They returned into Jerusalem seeking him.* The three days' loss is the third of our Lady's Seven Dolours, and was in one sense the most bitter of all, for it was the only one in which she was separated from her Son.

46. *After three days,* i.e., on the third day. The first day was occupied by the journey towards Galilee; the second in the return to Jerusalem and inquiries among the various caravans; the following

asking them questions. And all that heard him were 47
astonished at his wisdom and his answers. And seeing
him, they wondered. And his mother said to him: Son,
why hast thou done so to us? behold thy father and I 48
have sought thee sorrowing. And he said to them: How 49
is it that you sought me? did you not know that I must
be about my father's business? And they understood not 50
the word, that he spoke unto them. And he went down 51
with them, and came to Nazareth: and was subject to
them. And his mother kept all these words in her heart.
And Jesus advanced in wisdom and age, and grace with 52
God and men.

day they found Him, in one of the halls of the Temple, near the
Israelites' porches. The doctors or teachers of the Law used to
assemble groups to hear them. They would sit on mats in a circle
round them and would be free to ask or answer questions: see on
x. 25.

47. *All that heard him were astonished.* This was apparently the
first time that our Lord had shown His wisdom in any public way.
The word ἐξίσταντο denotes great wonder or amazement.

48. *Seeing him they wondered.* The word this time is ἐξεπλάγησαν.
His parents had shown no wonder at the events of the Nativity, in
which they were already well instructed; but they did wonder at finding
our Lord employed in listening to the doctors in the Temple while they
sought Him sorrowing.

49. *Did you not know that I must be about my father's business?*
The sense of the last phrase (ἐν τοῖς τοῦ πατρός μου) is not very
certain. Our version agrees with the A.V., and the sense intended is
that God's work must take precedence of everything, even where it
causes pain to our earthly parents. But a possible rendering is, "Did
you not know that I must be in my father's house?" This is perhaps
more forcible and is a more direct answer to the words, "thy father
and I have sought thee." Why should they seek Him if He was in
His father's house? In either case we have in the first recorded words
of our Lord a declaration of His Divine sonship. In His last recorded
words, given also by St. Luke (xxiii. 46), He likewise calls God His
Father.

50. *They understood not the word.* Our Lord often spoke words
which Mary could not understand at the time and which she was
always pondering over (*vv.* 19 and 51). As she gradually grew
in grace, she would have understood His words continually better and
better, and would be always seeing fresh and deeper meanings in
them.

52. *Jesus advanced in wisdom, and age and grace.* i.e., as we might
say that the sun gets warmer as the summer comes on; for it does not

get intrinsically warmer, but only warmer so far as its effect on us is concerned. Our Lord's Divine knowledge was infinite; and His human knowledge was in itself perfect from the first. Even if we admit that besides His "infused knowledge," He obtained *acquired knowledge* as we do, such acquired knowledge could not really add to the sum total of what He already knew. "Advanced" means, therefore, not that His knowledge intrinsically increased, but that it gradually declared itself more and more to those among whom He lived. The case was obviously different as regards His bodily strength and development (v. 40). As He learnt to walk, for example, though He had no need to learn the art, nevertheless the exercise of it gradually made His limbs actually stronger, as in the case of other children. "Grace" in the text means, of course, not "grace" in our theological sense, but "favour"; and the reference to advancement in "grace with God and men" is (as with wisdom) to be understood of the outward and visible unfolding of beauties of character, and conveys no suggestion that His character was less perfect at first.

At the end of this chapter we must place the death of St. Joseph. From the absolute silence about him during the time of our Lord's ministry, we must take it as certain that he was dead. There are two distinct traditions about the time of his death; but the one which places it at the end of our Lord's hidden life seems the more probable. If we are to assume that he was in middle life at the time of the espousal, it would follow that he must have reached the age of seventy or over. This is not certain, however. In the earliest representations of him he often appears as quite young, in which case he need not have been much over fifty at the time of his death. Everything points to the probability that he died in the home at Nazareth, and it seems that our Lady did not live there continuously afterwards. When our Lord went to the teaching and baptism of John and to the retreat of the forty days, He was absent for months and He returned to Cana, where it appears that our Lady was staying with relatives or friends. Afterwards she went with Him to Capharnaum (John ii. 12), where they probably used St. Peter's house as a home for a considerable period of time: see on iv. 31.

CHAPTER III.

Preaching of St. John Baptist.

(VERS. 1–20.)

NOW in the fifteenth year of the reign of Tiberius Cæsar, Pontius Pilate being governor of Judea, and Herod being tetrarch of Galilee, and Philip his brother tetrarch of Iturea and the country of Trachonitis, and

1. *Now in the fifteenth year of the reign of Tiberius Cæsar.* The fifteenth year of the reign of Tiberius was A.U.C. 781–2, that is A.D. 28–9. As, however, Herod the Great had been then dead for almost thirty-two years and our Lord, though certainly born before his death, is said (*v.* 23) to have been at His baptism about thirty years old, we are at once confronted with a difficulty. Some have thought that the age *about* thirty is meant expressly not to be determinate within a year or two, and that our Lord was in reality thirty-two at the time of His baptism. A more common solution, however, is to suppose that the years of Tiberius are reckoned from the date of his associating himself with Augustus in the government of the empire two years earlier. In that case we can adhere to the ordinarily received view that our Lord's baptism took place in A.D. 27, and the previous year, when St. John began his preaching, may have been a sabbatical year: see on *v.* 7.

Pontius Pilate being governor of Judea, &c. The particulars which St. Luke next gives fix the time of the beginning of Gospel history, not only by the imperial date, but also by the concurrence of various authorities in Palestine, for the time during which all these rulers could be named together covers only a few years; and we thus get some means of checking the chronology adopted. They also contain an exact account of the political condition of these countries which were to be the scene of our Lord's preaching. Considerable changes had taken place during the thirty years of our Lord's hidden life. On the death of Herod the Great his kingdom was divided. Half of it, comprising Judea and Idumea, with Samaria, was granted by

Rome, though not without some struggle with the leading Jews, to his son Herod Archelaus: see on xix. 12. The other half was again divided, forming two "tetrarchies" (or fourth parts) which were treated as vassal states. One of these, which included Galilee and the territory east of the Jordan and the Dead Sea known as Perea, was given by Rome to another son by the same wife, Herod Antipas. He was therefor officially styled *Tetrarch*, a name afterwards extended to any tributary prince; but he was a vain man and was frequently called by the title of *king* (Mark vi. 14 and elsewhere), though the Roman suzerains had given him no right to use that title. The last division of the Herodian kingdom comprised Iturea and Trachonitis (i.e., the territory north and east of the Sea of Galilee), and this went to Philip, son of Herod by his wife Cleopatra, who inherited from his father a taste for building cities (such as Cæsarea Philippi, Bethsaida Julias, &c.). There was another Philip, a son of Herod by a third wife, called Mariamne, best known as the husband of Herodias whom Antipas afterwards married. Herodias was herself a grand-daughter of Herod the Great, and consequently the niece of both her husbands, Philip and Antipas. The following table will make these relationships more clear. Only those mentioned in the Gospels and Acts are included in it. It will be seen, and the full table would show still more clearly, that marriages of very near kin were scandalously common in this family.

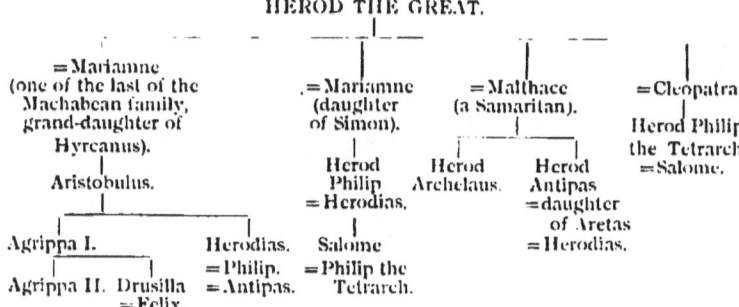

HEROD THE GREAT.

All of Herod's sons, except perhaps Philip, seem to have been cruel, cowardly, and time-serving. The Herodian party owed their position to the Emperor, and had powerful Jewish friends at the Roman court, and their chief aim was to keep up a good understanding between the Herods and Cæsar, by endeavouring to suppress as far as possible the Jewish national aspirations and habits. They were thus always at variance with the Pharisees, whose great aim was the preservation and observance of every religious external. In Judea the antagonism soon led up to a rebellion against Archelaus, provoked by his conspicuous misgovernment and cruelty (cf. Matt. ii. 22, and *infra.* on xix. 12). Augustus, who had never recognized him as more than an *Ethnarch* or

Lysanias tetrarch of Abilina, under the high-priests Annas 2 and Caiphas: the word of the Lord was made unto John

national ruler, deposed him altogether in A.D. 6; and with his deposition vanished the last vestige of Jewish independence. The country was made an appendage to Syria and a special "Procurator" or governor appointed, who lived usually not at Jerusalem, but at the Roman seaport of Cæsarea, though he came to Jerusalem with a cohort to keep order at the times of the chief festivals. Three of these Procurators ruled in rapid succession during the lifetime of Augustus; and after his death two others followed, the first Valerius Gratus, the second Pontius Pilate, who was appointed in the fourteenth year of Tiberius and held office for ten years. He was a harsh without being a strong ruler, and was apparently in fear that intrigues like those tried against Archelaus might oust him from his office, in which, like all Roman governors, he was seeking to make large gains. It is curious to note that Tacitus (Ann. xv. 45) also fixes the crucifixion of "Christus" by the words "Tiberio imperante per procuratorem Pontium Pilatum."

Lysanius tetrarch of Abilina. There is some difficulty about identifying this Lysanius. Two princes are known of that name, one some sixty years too early, the other—his grandson—about twenty years too late. We may conjecture that the one alluded to was the son of the former and the father of the latter. The date of the beginning and end of his reign are unknown. As we are not told when, if at all, our Lord was in his country, it is not very clear why his name is included in St. Luke's list, unless it be because Abilina was at one time afterwards under Herod Agrippa.

2. *Under the high priests Annas and Caiphas.* Annas was named High Priest by the Romans soon after the deposition of Archelaus, against whom he had used his great influence. Valerius Gratus, however, who succeeded as procurator after the accession of Tiberius, presently assumed the right to depose Annas after six years of office in favour of one Ishmael, son of Phabi, whom he again deposed soon afterwards to restore the office to Eleazar, one of the sons of Annas; and him in turn he also deposed to make room for one Simon, son of Camithos. These changes were probably all cases of mere political corruption, and eventually the family of Annas succeeded in defeating or outbidding their rivals, and they were restored in the person of Caiphas, who had married Annas's daughter. He seems to have been appointed by Valerius about A.D. 25, and to have held office, doubtless as a sort of substitute for his father-in-law, for several years, including the time of our Lord's ministry. The High Priesthood had already become a matter of court intrigue under the Herodian family, and the Romans in these rapid and arbitrary depositions, treated it as a mere dependence on the civil governor. The stricter Jews, however, appear to have treated these latter changes by heathen compulsion as illegal, and by them Annas was considered to be the real High Priest. This view was probably countenanced by Annas himself, and even after the

3 the son of Zachary, in the desert. And he came into all the country about the Jordan, preaching the baptism of

time of Caiphas, he was able to secure his position by obtaining the nominal appointment for two more of his sons, Jonathan and Theophilus, in succession. Annas was a man of strong character and vast wealth and influence. He was very unscrupulous, and his family (of whom, besides himself, seven in all were nominal high priests) was famous and hated for its tyrannous use of the chances of extortion afforded by the Temple traffic, so that the booths overthrown by our Lord were called "the shops of the sons of Annas." Thus when the High Priesthood is referred to in the Gospels and Acts, Annas is thought of as ruling jointly with Caiphas (cf. John xviii. 13-24, and Acts iv. 6). This is no doubt the reason of the mention of both names here.

3. *And he came into all the country about the Jordan.* Apparently St. John baptized at different stops on the river, between the Lake of Galilee and the Dead Sea. The Baptist's testimony to our Lord (and therefore probably His baptism also) is referred by St. John (i. 28) to a place which, in our version, agreeing with the Vulgate, is "Bethania beyond the Jordan"; but in the A.V., "Bethabara beyond Jordan." Neither name can be clearly fixed, but the place is believed to be near the ford a little north of the Dead Sea where one of the great caravan routes from the south and east crosses the river towards Jericho.

preaching the baptism of penance. The word translated here as *penance* (μετανοια lit. =change of mind and heart), in the A.V. is *repentance*. So in St. Matthew's account of St. John's preaching, "*Do penance*" (μετανοειτε) is replaced by *repent*. On the other hand in Mark i. 15, the Rheims version translates the same word in a similar context by *repent*. In each case the Rheims translators have followed the Vulgate. Moreover, elsewhere, while in the majority of cases (e.g. Luke x. 13, xiii. 3) the word is rendered by us *do penance:* in a considerable number of passages it is rendered *repent* (e.g. Luke xvii. 4), so that it has been asserted (as by Dr. Lingard) that in the Vulgate *pænitere* and *pænitentiam agere* are used indiscriminately. Neither translation gives the sense of the Greek quite completely. Probably, however, in using the word *penance*, the Rheims translators had in their mind its theological or technical sense. The *virtue* of penance includes repentance for past sin and something more besides, such as a purpose of amendment and change of life for the future. And the fact that penitential works are not excluded from the meaning of the Greek term in the New Testament may be seen by the use of the same word by St. Matthew (xii. 41) in giving our Lord's allusion to the conversion of the Ninivites, which we know to have been accompanied with fasting and the like (Jonas iii). It should be observed in this and other cases where the meaning of quasi-technical words in the New Testament Greek is in question, that the Greek is itself a translation of an unrecorded Aramaic word, for the precise sense of which the tra-

penance for the remission of sins ; as it was written in the 4
book of the sayings of Isaias the prophet : *A voice of one
crying in the wilderness : Prepare ye the way of the Lord,
make straight his paths. Every valley shall be filled ; and* 5
*every mountain and hill shall be brought low ; and the
crooked shall be made straight, and the rough ways, plain ;
and all flesh shall see the salvation of God.* He said there- 6
fore to the multitudes that went forth to be baptized by 7
him : Ye offspring of vipers, who hath shewed you to flee

dition handed down by the apostles may well be a safer guide than conjectures of Greek lexicography, useful as these may be. As a matter of fact, we know well that "works of mortification" very similar to what we should call "doing penance" had a distinct place at this time in the Jewish religious life : and St. Paul also gives (2 Cor. vii. 11) an explanation of the qualities which should go with true repentance, among which he clearly includes works of penance and mortification. It is also to be observed that the Baptist was himself an ascetic, and one of the chief things they noted in him was his acts of mortification : it is natural, therefore, to suppose that he did not leave " penance " out of account in preaching to his converts.

4. *As it was written in the book of the sayings of Isaias the prophet.* See Isa. xl. 3-5, which should be read with its full context. It is the commencement of the great Messianic message of "comfort" to Jerusalem, the "glad tidings" which this and the following chapters of the prophetic book conveyed. "The salvation of God" means (cf. ii. 30) the Messiah or Saviour of Israel and of the world. The quotation is made, as is commonly the case in the New Testament, from the Septuagint version, which differs slightly from any Hebrew text now known, but is in fact more ancient than any of these.

5. *Every valley shall be filled,* &c. The primary meaning of this relates to the preparation of the country for the passage of a king or great man. A derived meaning may apply it to the exaltation of the humble and the humiliation of the proud. In truth, however, St. John was not about to insist on any unusual humiliations or austerities, but only on each class of his hearers forsaking those sins to which they were specially liable.

6. *All flesh shall see the salvation of God.* The other evangelists break off the quotation before these words. They are characteristic of one of the features of St. Luke's Gospel, in which the universality of the redemption is so prominent. See Introduction.

7. *He said therefore to the multitudes that went forth to be baptized by him.* St. Luke alludes to "multitudes" going out to listen to St. John and to be baptized, and this is borne out by the three other evangelists. St. John the Evangelist evidently means to describe that a band of regular disciples lived with him, and that crowds came and went. Few things are more remarkable in all history than the unanimity with

8 from the wrath to come? Bring forth therefore fruits worthy of penance, and do not begin to say, We have Abraham for our father. For I say unto you, that God is

which all classes flocked out to hear him. He worked no miracles (John x. 41) and did nothing out of the ordinary; yet at the sound of his voice "all Jerusalem and Judea" (Matt. iii. 5; Mark i. 5) went out to listen to him and to be baptized. Our Lord Himself tells us the reasons which attracted them to St. John, namely, his constancy and his ascetic life: see vii. 24-28. The people must have been strongly conscious of their own sinfulness and helplessness, and the need they had of a redeemer, and were moved (as we see from v. 15, cf. John i. 20, &c.) by the vivid expectation that the Messiah was at hand. Some have thought (as has been said on v. 1, and cf. note on vi. i.) that this was a "sabbatical year." Every seventh year was kept as a year of rest (Lev. xxv. 2-4), when the lands were allowed to remain fallow, and during such a year, therefore, no agricultural work was done. If this is so, it would further account for the large numbers who went out to hear St. John. Those who went out confessed their sins (Mark i. 5), an expression always taken to mean not merely an acknowledgment of sin in general, but a confession made by each of some of his own individual sins, e.g., by the publicans of their extortions. All were "baptized" by St. John in the waters of the Jordan. This baptism had, of course, no sacramental efficacy; but it was more than a mere ceremony, and denoted a great and unusual outpouring of God's grace, to prepare men's minds for the coming of our Lord. It was performed, as we should say, "by immersion," that is, the penitent went into the water himself. Hence, a position near one of the fords where the Jordan was crossed was convenient, as in other parts of the valley the banks are steep and the river deep and swift. The rite of symbolical baptism was not known to the Mosaic Law, and it was a personal inspiration to St. John (John i. 33). Parallels existed as in the case of the "Proselytes of Righteousness," who were not circumcised, but "baptized" before witnesses and with a "profession of faith." This usage seems to have existed at this time, for there were disputes about it in details between the famous "schools" of Hillel and Shammai.

Ye offspring of vipers. This expression was aimed chiefly at the Pharisees and Sadducees (Matt. iii. 7). The Pharisees were a sect or school among the Jews, who aimed at being most national, both in politics and religion. Their religion had however become intensely and even absurdly formal. While they maintained the necessity of outward exactness in a host of little details, many of which were not in the written law at all, but had grown up traditionally, in many essential matters they were extremely lax. Our Lord came into continual conflict with them: see especially xi. 39-54, and Matt. xxiii. St. Paul was a Pharisee (Acts xxiii. 6), as was his illustrious teacher Gamaliel, and they were fairly numerous at the time of our Lord; and their dis-

able of these stones to raise up children to Abraham. For 9
now the axe is laid to the root of the trees. Every tree
therefore that bringeth not forth good fruit, shall be cut
down, and cast into the fire. And the people asked him, 10
saying: What then shall we do? And he answering, said 11
to them: He that hath two coats, let him give to him that
hath none; and he that hath meat, let him do in like
manner. And the publicans also came to be baptized, 12

tinctive nationalism made them always the popular party. Out of them
arose the "Zealots," whose excesses led to the final revolt and destruction of Jerusalem. There is no mention of them in the Old Testament because they grew to be a distinct body or class after the times of the Machabees. The Sadducees were to be found entirely among the upper classes, and were not liked by the people. Their religion was largely sceptical, and they did not believe in a future life after death: see on xx. 27. Much of the political power was in their hands. Annas and his family were Sadducees, as were the majority of the Sanhedrin. They had no scruple in making terms with the Romans, with whom the Pharisees were always ready to quarrel over questions of legality, such as, e.g., the oath of allegiance or the bringing of the Roman standards into the Temple. By comparing this chapter with vii. 30, we gather that though the Pharisees went out to hear St. John, not many of them submitted to his baptism.

9. *Every tree therefore*, &c. Cf. xiii. 7: "Cut it down therefore: why cumbereth it the ground?" Our Lord was comparing the Jewish nation to a fig tree which brought forth no fruit. St. John's comparison was similar to it. His carrying on the idea of "the wrath to come," is the judgment which should fall on Israel if they rejected the coming "kingdom."

10. *And the people asked him, saying what then shall we do?* St. Luke is the only evangelist who gives St. John's admonitions to these different sections of the multitude—(1) The common people, (2) The publicans, (3) The soldiers. His advice to each class was simple and practical, and wholly out of sympathy with Pharisaic ideas.

11. *He that hath two coats, let him give to him that hath none.* There were two kinds of garments worn by Jewish men, an inner and an outer: see on xxiii. 34. The word here denotes the outer garment. The meaning is simply that they were to give what they could spare to the poor.

12. *And the publicans also came to be baptized.* The publicans, or tax gatherers, were hated by the people, as they were agents of the new Roman government, and the taxes having only begun after A.D. 6, and being denounced by the Pharisees as contrary to the Mosaic Law, were not yet accepted quietly by any strict Jews. But the system which was in force throughout the Empire of "farming" the taxes, led to the publicans being very cruel and extortionate and oppressive to the

13 and said to him: Master, what shall we do? But he said to them: Do nothing more than that which is appointed 14 you. And the soldiers also asked him, saying: And what shall we do? And he said to them: Do violence to no man, neither calumniate any man: and be content with your pay. 15 And as the people was of opinion, and all were thinking in their hearts of John, that perhaps he might be the Christ:

poor. There were two classes of publicans—(1) Those who were directly responsible to Rome, and were usually themselves Romans of good position; and (2) Men hired by these to do the actual collecting. The latter are those always referred to in the Gospels, and their correct title would be not *publicani*, but *portitores*. They were of course Jews, and usually belonged to the lowest classes, as no one else could be found to undertake the work. They were looked upon as the scum of the population. The term "publican" is naturally and frequently bracketed with the term "sinner": see xv. 1, and elsewhere *passim*. In the conversion of Zaccheus, the chief publican of Jericho (xix. 2-9), we have an echo and possibly an after result of this preaching of St. John. Zaccheus's "*penance*" takes this form: "The half of my goods I give to the poor, and if I have wronged any man of anything (i.e., by extortion as a publican) I restore him fourfold": see on xix. 8.

13. *Do nothing more than that which is appointed you.* Here St. John's advice to them is practically to give up extortion. It is dead against the Pharisaic view that their whole calling and all payment of Roman taxes was unlawful. St. John implies, as Christ did in his answer about the "Coin of the Tribute" (xx. 25), that the *de facto* government is to be obeyed, and that they as its officers may do and ought to do their official duty, so long as they "do no more."

14. *And the soldiers also asked him.* The text seems to imply that these soldiers were on garrison duty; so that their most obvious temptations were (as with the publicans) to *exceed* their duty. Any Jews who served Rome would of course fall equally under the ban of the anti-Roman Pharisees. They would in their patrols be tempted to use violence for private anger or vengeance: and they would have many occasions of "calumniating"—the technical Latin term for making false accusations—either for spite or for extortion. No doubt both things were common. St. John said to them (as to the publicans), "do your duty and no more." "Be content with your pay" is not merely—perhaps not at all—a counsel against mutiny: it means, "do not seek to supplement it by corrupt means."

15. *All were thinking in their hearts of John that perhaps he might be the Christ.* It is said that the feeling of expectation and the hope that the Messiah was soon to come was more strongly felt among the people at this time than ever previously. It was therefore natural that many, seeing the power of St. John's preaching, should have taken him for the Messiah.

John answered, saying unto all: I indeed baptize you with water; but there shall come one mightier than I, the latchet of whose shoes I am not worthy to loose; he shall baptize you with the Holy Ghost and with fire. Whose fan is in his hand, and he will purge his floor; and will gather the wheat into his barn, but the chaff he will burn with unquenchable fire. And many other things exhorting did he preach to the people. But Herod the tetrarch, when he was reproved by him for Herodias his brother's wife, and

16. *There shall come one mightier than I.* Besides preparing the way for our Lord, St. John's office was to bear testimony of Him when He came: see John i. 29–34.

the latchet of whose shoes I am not worthy to loose. The sandals or shoes used in those days were little more than a flat sole attached to the foot by a latchet or thong. Apparently the shoe latchet was proverbially used to express something very small (Gen. xiv. 23). The duty of fastening or unfastening the sandals of a great man fell to the lowest of his slaves. St. John therefore expressed his own extreme littleness compared with our Lord.

He shall baptize you with the Holy Ghost and with fire. The word "fire" is used commonly as the symbol of the Holy Ghost's office in the world, representing the warmth of zeal, the light of illumination, and also—as what follows here will indicate—cleansing power. So at Pentecost the Holy Ghost came under the appearance of tongues of fire (Acts ii. 3–4).

17. *Whose fan is in his hand.* The metaphor here is taken from the process of threshing. A "fan" was a shovel with which the wheat was thrown up to the wind to separate it from the chaff. With the reference to unquenchable fire, cf. Matt. xxv. 41. The Jews of that day believed in a place of fire called Gehenna, into which the perfectly wicked went for ever, and the less wicked for a limited time: see on xii. 5.

19. *But Herod the tetrarch,* &c. The period of St. John's preaching is uncertain. Some consider that it lasted less than a year; others allow two years. His work was really over when he gave testimony (John i.) to our Lord's Messianic office. Some of his disciples thereupon followed our Lord, but that was before the beginning of His regular ministry. The Baptist's preaching and his separate following of disciples continued for a time as a distinct movement. There even arose a certain rivalry between them and the disciples of our Lord (John iii. 25), but at that point St. John's preaching was brought to an abrupt termination by Herod Antipas, who was weak and superstitious. He feared St. John (Mark vi. 20), and partly believed in him; and he also feared the people who looked up to him as a prophet (Matt. xiv. 3–5). St. John rebuked him for his marriage with his brother's wife, Herodias,

20 for all the evils which Herod had done, he added this also above all, and shut up John in prison.

Baptism of our Lord.

(VERS. 21-22.)

21 Now it came to pass, when all the people was baptized, that Jesus also being baptized and praying, heaven was 22 opened: And the Holy Ghost descended in a bodily shape as a dove upon him: and a voice came from heaven: Thou art my beloved Son, in thee I am well pleased.

which was at the same time adulterous, since his first wife was still alive, and also incestuous, as Herodias was his niece (see the genealogical table of the Herods given above). To silence him, therefore, he put him in prison.

20. *And shut up St. John in prison.* The prison selected was the fortress-palace of Machaerus, which had been built by Herod the Great, in the south of Perea, among the wild mountains east of the Dead Sea.

21. *Now it came to pass.* This verse and the following are, of course, chronologically anterior to what has gone before. This is a notable instance of St. Luke's method of pursuing one idea to the end, and then returning to describe collateral events. See Introduction.

Jesus also being baptized. Our Lord came to be baptized without any outward difference from others. He came as a sinner, that is bearing the sins of the world (John i. 29).

and praying. This detail is peculiar to St. Luke, though the baptism itself is mentioned by all four evangelists.

22. *The Holy Ghost descended in a bodily shape as a dove upon him.* This manifestation was meant primarily for St. John, as the sign by which he had been told that he was to know our Lord (John i. 33). It revealed the three Persons of the Blessed Trinity—the Father, whose voice was heard; the Son, present in the Sacred Manhood; and the Holy Ghost in the form of a dove. We must not forget, however, that to St. John the doctrine of the Trinity could be only known by a personal inspiration, if at all. And whatever word he used for what is here called by St. Luke the "Holy Ghost," it denoted to him rather the general work of the Spirit of God than a distinct Divine person.

and a voice came from heaven. There is no mention of the "voice" being heard by the people who were around. Possibly they heard something without distinguishing the words, as occurred on a similar occasion (John xii. 29). Even to St. John it would be difficult, unless he had a special Divine light, to appreciate the full meaning of the

The Genealogy.

(VERS. 23-38.)

23 And Jesus himself was beginning about the age of thirty years: being (as it was supposed) the son of Joseph, 24 who was of Heli, who was of Mathat, who was of Levi, who was of Melchi, who was of Janne, who was of 25 Joseph, who was of Mathathias, who was of Amos, who was of Nahum, who was of Hesli, who was of Nagge, 26 who was of Mahath, who was of Mathathias, who was of 27 Semei, who was of Joseph, who was of Juda, who was of Joanna, who was of Reza, who was of Zorobabel, who 28 was of Salathiel, who was of Neri, who was of Melchi, who was of Addi, who was of Cosan, who was of Helmadan, 29 who was of Her, who was of Jesus, who was of Eliezer, who was of Jorim, who was of Mathat, who was 30 of Levi, who was of Simeon, who was of Judas, who was of 31 Joseph, who was of Jona, who was of Eliakim, who was of Melea, who was of Menna, who was of Mathatha, who 32 was of Nathan, who was of David, who was of Jesse, who was of Obed, who was of Booz, who was of Salmon, 33 who was of Naasson, who was of Aminadab, who was of Aram, who was of Esron, who was of Phares, who was 34 of Judas, who was of Jacob, who was of Isaac, who was of 35 Abraham, who was of Thare, who was of Nachor, who was of Sarug, who was of Ragau, who was of Phaleg,

revelation; but he evidently understood it to some extent, and spoke of it to his disciples. So, also, St. John the Evangelist, who was a disciple of the Baptist, states the "testimony" of the latter (John i. 32-34; cf. also i. 14 and iii. 26) as if he alone had seen the heavenly sign. And the word "he" in Matt. iii. 16 and Mark i. 10 probably means the Baptist also.

Thou art my beloved Son. These words gave rise to certain early heresies, called "Adoptionist," in which it was supposed that our Lord's Divine character dated only from this time, and that His Lordship was accordingly an "Adoption." Certain early Syrian MSS. of the Gospel were corrupted to accord with this view, but it is quite clear that the true text is wholly inconsistent with it.

23-38. The genealogy here has given rise to much discussion in consequence of the apparently complete discrepancy between it and the

36 who was of Heber, who was of Sale, who was of Cainan, who was of Arphaxad, who was of Sem, who was of 37 Noe, who was of Lamech, who was of Mathusale, who was of Henoch, who was of Jared, who was of Malaleel, 38 who was of Cainan, who was of Henos, who was of Seth, who was of Adam, who was of God.

similar one in St. Matthew (i. 1–16). St. Matthew, writing for Jews, does not trace the genealogy back beyond Abraham, while St. Luke takes it back to Adam; and the two lists are written in reverse order, one tracing from son to father, and the other from father to son. These differences are, however, of no importance: the difficulty arises in the list of names which belong to the part common to the two. They agree between Abraham and David, in which period they represent, of course, the common record of the chiefs of the Jewish people; but between David and St. Joseph the lines seem totally distinct, except that they meet each other about the middle, in Salathiel and Zorobabel, after which they diverge again. St. Luke traces the descent from David through Nathan, the younger son; St. Matthew through Solomon, in the kingly line. In the former there are forty generations, in the latter twenty-six. The name of Salathiel is twenty-first from David in St. Luke, fifteenth in St. Matthew; and between Zorobabel and St. Joseph there are seventeen names in St. Luke and nine in St. Matthew. The former gives St. Joseph's father as Heli, the latter as Jacob.

The total destruction of genealogical records during the siege of Jerusalem renders it impossible now to obtain any documentary evidence to throw light on the question, beyond the two lists themselves, and hence we are left to conjecture in order to find an explanation. It is, however, quite certain that the Jews had many such lists and kept them, especially in the kingly and priestly lines, with great care. Hence it was possible in the Herodian census for every one to find his own tribe and family with certainty. It is quite obvious that the evidence of two lists in such a case as this cannot be a mere question of contradictory testimony or mistake; for the two are so different, and date from so nearly the same time, that they are obviously meant as different *schemes* of genealogy, following different but consistent plans of tracing the accepted Davidic descent of the Messiah. To the readers of the Gospels in the Apostolic period the two systems must have been consistent, and must have been both regarded as true—otherwise one would have of necessity been marked as spurious, and of this there is no trace anywhere. Several explanations have been suggested, but there is one which has found wide acceptance in principle, though with some reservation as to details. It dates back so early as the third century, and Julius Africanus, a Syrian writer, says that he learnt it from those who claimed to belong to the family of our Lord, among whom it was traditional. The explanation depends on the well-known law of " levirate " marriages among the Jews, which is stated in Deuteronomy (xxv. 5, cf. *infra* xx. 28) as follows :—

"When brethren dwell together and one of them dieth without children, the wife of the deceased shall not marry to another, but his brother shall take her and raise up seed for his brother."

It is said that Heli and Jacob, who are given by St. Luke and St. Matthew respectively as the father of St. Joseph, were half-brothers ; that their mother, Esther, was married successively to two men, called Mathan and Melchi ; and that the former was the father of Jacob, the latter of Heli. It is further said that Heli died childless, and, as directed by the law, Jacob married his widow, and had for a son Joseph, whose legal father therefore was Heli, but his real father Jacob. As Mathan and Melchi were not related, their genealogies might differ throughout ; but both were, in fact, descended from David. The fact of there being fewer generations in one line than in the other need not present any difficulty ; but the disparity is increased by St. Matthew omitting some names in his list, as we learn by comparison with the Old Testament. His object in these omissions seems to be in order to obtain a symmetrical arrangement, with three periods which included fourteen names each : see Matt. i. 17.

If we accept the principle of this tradition, three remarks may be made as to details :—

(1) In St. Luke Melchi is not given as father, but as great grandfather of Heli. It has been sometimes thought that the names have got misplaced ; but it is at least as easy to suppose that in the course of nearly three centuries, some confusion arose in the family tradition.

(2) It is more likely antecedently that St. Matthew would give the legal descent and St. Luke the natural one. We should therefore prefer to suppose that it was Jacob who died childless and that Heli was St. Joseph's actual father.

(3) It is by no means certain that the Salathiel and Zorobabel of St. Luke are identical with those named by St. Matthew. If their identity is assumed, a further supposition must be made to account for the presence of both in each list. It is, of course, quite easy to suppose that both Abiud and Reza were sons of Zorobabel ; the difficulty comes with respect to the father of Salathiel, whom St. Matthew calls Jeconias and St. Luke calls Neri. Now we know that Jeconias was to die childless, as a judgment on him, according to the prophecy of Jeremias (xxii. 30). It would seem natural, therefore, to suppose that he would adopt a son, so as to perpetuate the royal line, and that he would choose Salathiel, son of Neri, as he was known to be descended from David. If this very probable supposition be made, there is no further difficulty. St. Matthew's list was intended to show our Lord's royal descent, and he would accordingly trace it in the kingly line ; while St. Luke would rather aim at showing our Lord as the Son of Man, and therefore give his natural descent. This, indeed, gives us an additional reason for supposing that Heli, and not Jacob, was the true father of St. Joseph ; for St. Matthew's list would, in that case, be legal throughout, and St. Luke's would be natural throughout.

The genealogy would thus appear as in the following table :—

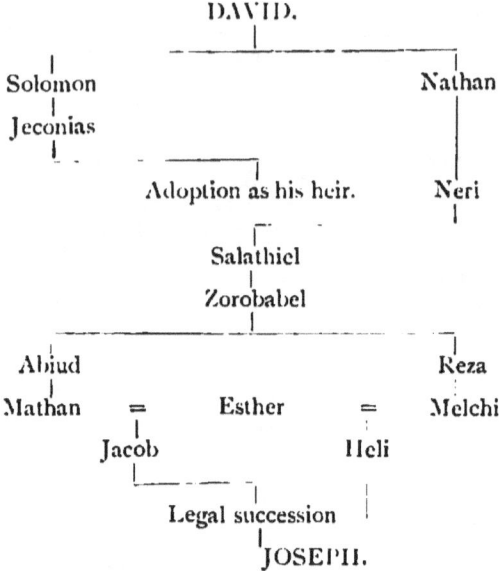

Another system, not very different in the result, assumes that St. Luke, with his usual tendency to record matters relating closely to our Lady, is giving her genealogy, Heli being, it is said, an alternative for the name of Joachim. Joseph, by the espousal, became his heir, and could therefore be said to be " of Heli." Others again see in the Greek text, in the absence of the article before St. Joseph's name only, a possible rendering which would make the sense "as it was supposed the son of Joseph, but in truth descended from Heli, who was of Mathat," &c. This supposition would lead to the same genealogy, and bearing in mind that our Lady and St. Joseph were probably cousins, it would be something as follows :—

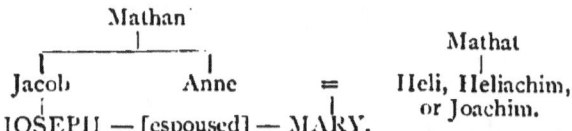

Thus it will be observed that, in consequence of the cousinship of Joseph and Mary, both tables would so give the *natural* chain of descent by which our Lord was connected through His Mother with the Davidic line (*ex semine David*).

CHAPTER IV.

The Fasting and Temptation.

(VERS. 1–13.)

AND Jesus being full of the Holy Ghost, returned from the Jordan, and was led by the Spirit into the desert, for the space of forty days; and was tempted by the devil. ² And he ate nothing in those days; and when they were

1. *And Jesus being full of the Holy Ghost.* The expressions "full of the Holy Ghost" and "was led by the Spirit" (cf. Mark i. 12, "The spirit *drove* him into the desert") must refer to the special sign of the descent of the "Spirit" at our Lord's Baptism. Our Lord was not, of course, ever out of His Divine communication with God the Father and the Holy Ghost; but these expressions show that on this occasion the guidance was of a very special nature.

into the desert. See on i. 80. St. Mark says (i. 13) that He was "with beasts," thus denoting that He spent the time away from all human beings. The place is traditionally believed to be a certain mountain west of Jericho, north of the famous road from that town to Jerusalem, and still known as "Mount Quarantine," i.e. the Mount of the Forty Days. See on xviii. 35.

2. *For the space of forty days.* A fast of forty days had precedents in the cases of Moses and Elias, the typical representatives of the Law and Prophets.

and was tempted by the devil. The two accounts of our Lord's temptations, given respectively by St. Matthew and St. Luke, differ only in their order, the second and third in St. Matthew being respectively third and second in St. Luke. Although as a rule we take St. Luke's arrangement of events as chronological, there seems some reason from internal evidence to suppose that in this instance St. Matthew and not St. Luke has adhered to the true order. For, (1) he connects the temptations with a note of time, "*then* the devil," &c. "*Again* the devil," &c. And (2) he gives the words at the end "Begone, Satan," which are omitted by St. Luke, and which appear to be a final rebuke to the tempter. Our Lord must

3 ended he was hungry. And the devil said to him: If thou be the Son of God, say to this stone that it be made bread. 4 And Jesus answered him: It is written: that *man liveth*

have spoken of these temptations Himself, for it is part of the common knowledge of the apostles, like all other things common to the synoptists. It is certainly not meant to be any *internal* struggle, but a direct attack on Him of an external spirit of evil. The word used (διάβολος) means in New Testament Greek also "a false accuser" or "adversary" (1 Tim. iii. 11; where we translate the word "slanderers." Cf. also John vi. 71). When used personally, it is the equivalent of Satan, which is a Hebrew word of the same signification (so used in the rebuke to St. Peter, Matt. xvi. 23). The Jews had held from the first the belief in the existence of spiritual intelligence other than men, some of whom were the ministers or messengers (ἄγγελοι = angels) of God, others His revolted servants, eager to do evil or to reduce mankind, as at the Fall. Of the latter, one commonly named *par excellence* Satan, or "*the* adversary," was the chief; and the gods of the heathen nations and cities, such as Moloch, Beelzebub, &c., were regarded as his subjects; hence the offer in *v.* 6.

The devil seems to have been allowed for the time being a certain preternatural control over the sacred body of our Lord: such at least is the more commonly received opinion, although the theory that the scenes referred to passed in some form of supernatural representation is not impossible. The account is in any case a mystery. It is supposed by many that the devil was not certainly aware of our Lord's Divinity, or He would not have engaged in a task that was necessarily fruitless; but that he suspected it, and so we seem to see in all these temptations a secondary purpose, of trying to extract a declaration that our Lord was God or that He was not. As to our Lord Himself, the temptations had this important difference from ours, that His human will was so united with His Divine will that there could be no inward hesitation or inclination to disobey. Externally, so far as the outward strain upon His human nature was concerned, His temptations were similar to ours. See Heb. iv. 15.

3. *If thou be the Son of God, say to this stone that it be made bread.* The subject of this, the first temptation, is again connected with the miraculous sign at our Lord's baptism. The devil recognized that He was endued with extraordinary powers and wished Him to use them selfishly to satisfy His bodily cravings. It was not, however, God's will that He should work a miracle for this end; He had been on earth thirty years and had never done so (John ii. 11). The office of miracles is not to suit the convenience of the worker; but to be "a sign" of a Divine mission and message to the onlookers.

4. *Man liveth not by bread alone.* See Deut. viii. 3. The text refers to the manna with which God fed the Israelites in a special way, as a continual sign of their dependence on Him.

not by bread alone, but by every word of God. And the 5
devil led him into a high mountain, and shewed him all
the kingdoms of the world in a moment of time. And he 6
said to him: To thee will I give all this power, and the
glory of them; for to me they are delivered, and to whom
I will, I give them. If thou therefore wilt adore before 7
me, all shall be thine. And Jesus answering said to him: 8
It is written: *Thou shalt adore the Lord thy God, and him
only shalt thou serve.* And he brought him to Jerusalem, 9
and set him on a pinnacle of the temple; and he said to
him: If thou be the Son of God, cast thyself from hence.
For it is written, that *he hath given his angels charge over* 10
thee, that they keep thee: and that *in their hands they shall* 11
bear thee up, lest perhaps thou dash thy foot against a stone.

5. *And the devil led him into a high mountain.* If the mountain here mentioned was that where our Lord had fasted, "all the kingdoms of the world" must be taken as simply meaning a large expanse of country which might be considered typical thereof. The words "in a moment of time," however, which are peculiar to St. Luke, suggest that Satan was allowed to represent them to our Lord in some preternatural way. The phrase "the kingdoms of the world" would probably indicate not only the Roman Empire, which then extended from the English Channel to Armenia, but also the Parthian Empire in the East, and the further kingdoms, such as the Chinese and Indian territories, which in fact have not even yet been brought to any great extent under the dominion of Christ.

6. *To thee will I give all this power.* Cf. John xii. 31 and xiv. 30, where Satan is called by our Lord "the prince of this world."

7. *If thou therefore wilt adore before me.* The temptation was to unlawful ambition. The adoration of the devil was the price to be paid. Devil-worship is by no means an unknown crime.

8. *Thou shalt adore the Lord thy God.* See Deut. vi. 13 and x. 20.

9. *If thou be the Son of God, cast thyself from hence.* The third suggestion of the devil was to what we call (by a proverbial reference to this very text) "tempting Providence," i.e., presuming unlawfully on God's providence over us by exposing ourselves to unnecessary risks in the expectation that he will work a miracle, or alter the appointed course of nature, to save us from our own act.

10. *He hath given his angels charge over thee.* The quotation is from Ps. xc. 11, but it is not quite complete, the words "in all thy ways" being omitted at the end of this verse. The distortion of meaning suggested is easily seen: for "in all thy ways" means in the appointed course of nature. It is this verse which has given occasion to the proverb that the devil can quote Scripture to his purpose; and is a warning against the glib misuse of isolated texts.

¹² And Jesus answering said to him: It is said, *Thou shall* ¹³ *not tempt the Lord thy God.* And all the temptation being ended, the devil departed from him for a time.

Preaching in Galilee. Rejection at Nazareth.
(VERS. 14-30.)

¹⁴ And Jesus returned in the power of the Spirit into Galilee, and the fame of him went out through the whole

12. *Thou shalt not tempt the Lord thy God.* Our Lord's answer is again from Deuteronomy (vi. 16). The meaning is not, as might at first sight appear, a declaration of our Lord's Divinity, or a rebuke to Satan for tempting Him. The words "the Lord thy God" do not refer to Christ directly, but to the God of the Jews (cf. Exod. xx. 2), and the text is a general admonition against tempting Providence in the sense just explained.

14. *And Jesus returned in the power of the Spirit into Galilee.* We enter with this verse on the public ministry of our Lord. By consulting St. John, we learn that our Lord began His preaching not in Galilee, but in Judea, and that the reason He retired into Galilee was the incipient opposition of the Pharisees, which showed itself very early. We can follow the sequence of events between our Lord's baptism and His final retirement to Galilee with some exactness. First we have the call of the first five disciples—SS. Peter, Andrew, John, Philip, and Nathanael (or Bartholomew) on the banks of the Jordan (John i. 35-51). Next we have our Lord's first return to Galilee, when He worked His first miracle at the marriage feast at Cana. Then St. John adds (ii. 12) that He went down to Capharnaum, with His mother and His brethren —i.e., cousins—and His disciples; but they remained there "not many days," as the Pasch or Passover was at hand, and Jesus went up to Jerusalem. This was the first Pasch of His ministry, during which He cleansed the Temple and also worked many miracles (iv. 45). Then after the festival, He began His regular ministry in Judea (iii. 22). At first He allowed His disciples to follow the not unusual custom of baptizing (see on iii. 7), though He did not Himself baptize (iv. 2). St. John was still preaching and baptizing at Ennon, on the Jordan, near Salim, in the north of Samaria, and not far from the confines of Galilee. And there seems to have been already signs of jealousy between the disciples of our Lord and St. John respectively (John iii. 23, *seq.* cf. on Luke vii. 19), but it was not till the opposition of the Pharisees appeared (John iv. 1) that He finally retired into Galilee, and just at this time St. John's preaching came to an end by his being put in prison (Matt. iv. 12). On this journey to Galilee took place the incidents connected with the woman of Samaria (John iv.). When they reached Galilee, St. John puts side by side the fact that the Galileans received Him and that He "Himself gave

country. And he taught in their synagogues, and was 15 magnified by all. And he came to Nazareth where he was 16 brought up: and he went into the synagogue according to his custom on the sabbath-day; and he rose up to read,

testimony that a prophet hath no honour in his own country." The expression "his own country" is used in several places in the Gospels to denote Nazareth, and it is very probable that St. John is here alluding to the rejection of our Lord at Nazareth chronicled by St. Luke in this chapter.

15. *He taught in their synagogues.* The word "synagogue" is a Greek term, meaning an "assembly." The Jewish synagogues were of comparatively recent introduction, dating only from after the return from captivity. By our Lord's time they existed in every town and village (Acts xv. 21) and served both as places of worship and also as law courts: see on xii. 11 and xxi. 12. They were usually plain, square buildings, bearing no outward religious sign, except such symbols as the pot of Manna or the seven-branched candlestick, and stood whenever possible on the highest ground of the town. They were also so arranged that those who worshipped in them had their faces turned towards Jerusalem. The men sat on one side, and the women, wearing veils and screened off by a lattice, on the other. There was at least one Rabbi, and usually more. These men were in charge of the synagogue, but their functions were in no sense priestly. There was a kind of committee with a president or "Ruler of the Synagogue," whose position as the civil chief of the Jewish community was well recognized by the Romans in the scattered colonies of Jews abroad (cf. viii. 41; xiii. 14; also Acts xviii. 8, 17). Besides on the Sabbath, there were meetings for prayer on the second and fifth days of the week, as well as on the feasts and fasts; but they were often so scarcely attended that it was necessary to hire "men of leisure" to make up the minimum legal congregation of ten. On the Sabbath it was otherwise, and the synagogues were often filled. At the end facing Jerusalem was an ark, containing the Book of the Law—a scroll written in Hebrew and protected by a decorated cover—and after prayers had been said, lessons were read out of the Scriptures. The books of Moses, which formed "the law" or Thora, were so arranged that they could be read through once in a year, and to these were added portions of the Prophets. After the lessons, a short explanation or exhortation followed. This was commonly delivered by a Rabbi; but any one was allowed to undertake it, and whenever a person of distinction was present, he would be invited to "preach." Our Lord used these occasions freely, as they formed the most favourable opportunities for His preaching. His followers accordingly embodied the service of the synagogue in the Christian liturgy, and the earlier part of the Mass is a development of it.

16. *He came to Nazareth.* For remarks on Nazareth and the Galileans generally, see on i. 26.

He went into the synagogue according to his custom. "According to

17 and the book of Isaias the prophet was delivered unto him. And as he unfolded the book, he found the place 18 where it was written: *The spirit of the Lord is upon me, wherefore he hath anointed me, to preach the gospel to the poor he hath sent me, to heal the contrite of* 19 *heart: to preach deliverance to the captives, and sight to the blind, to set at liberty them that are bruised, to preach the acceptable year of the Lord, and the day of* 20 *reward.* And when he had folded the book, he restored it to the minister, and sat down. And the eyes of all in 21 the synagogue were fixed on him. And he began to say to them: This day is fulfilled this scripture in your ears. 22 And all gave testimony to him: and they wondered at the

his custom" may mean His custom of teaching in synagogues during His ministry, stated in the previous verse. But it may mean His custom at Nazareth during the time when He was being "brought up." In this way the synagogue at Nazareth stood on a different footing in His regard from all others. In it He had worshipped week after week for thirty years. He had heard the Law and Prophets explained time without number by Rabbis and others. He would have been known by sight to the majority at least of the worshippers; but they had known Him simply as "the carpenter" (Mark vi. 3), or "the son of the carpenter" (Matt. xiii. 55), and nothing more. Doubtless He had never preached there before. Now His fame had spread, and the report of the great works He had already done at Capharnaum had reached His own village. Naturally therefore He was asked to preach.

18. *The spirit of the Lord is upon me,* &c. The text here is from Isa. lxi. 1, quoted according to St. Luke's custom from the Septuagint version. It refers to the mission of Christ. Whether our Lord chose it, or whether it came as the second lesson in the common order, we are not informed.

20. *When he had folded the book, he restored it to the minister.* The roll was held open with one roller in each hand till the lesson was done. It was afterwards rolled up and handed to the "minister," then, as now, an inferior functionary, who put it back in the "ark." He was, in fact, a kind of sexton.

21. *This day is fulfilled this scripture in your ears.* The first part of our Lord's discourse is here summarized. It was thus to the effect that He was the Messiah alluded to by Isaias. The message ought to have been pleasing to His hearers if they had not been biased by a small-minded envy of Him whom they had known as a child, and as a workman in their own streets.

22. *And all gave testimony to him,* i.e., to the truth of the reports concerning His preaching.

words of grace that proceeded from his mouth, and they
said: Is not this the son of Joseph? And he said to them: 23
Doubtless you will say to me this similitude: Physician,
heal thyself: as great things as we have heard done in
Capharnaum, do also here in thy own country. And he 24
said: Amen I say to you, that no prophet is accepted in
his own country. In truth I say to you, there were many 25
widows in the days of Elias in Israel, when heaven was
shut up three years and six months, when there was a great
famine throughout all the earth. And to none of them 26
was Elias sent, but to Sarepta of Sidon, to a widow woman.
And there were many lepers in Israel in the time of Eliseus 27
the prophet; and none of them was cleansed but Naaman

they wondered at the words of grace that proceeded from his mouth.
The first feelings were thus not precisely of admiration, but of wonder
how one whom they had known so well had become possessed of
these powers of eloquence.

23. *Physician, heal thyself.* This was no doubt a proverb current
among them, and in this case is similar to the reproach made to Him
during the Crucifixion: "He saved others, himself he cannot save"
(Matt. xxvii. 42).

*as great things as we have heard done in Capharnaum, do also here
in thy own country.* It appears from the line which our Lord's discourse now took, that the chief effect on that unworthy audience had
been to make them long to see miracles and wonders, and to extol
Him publicly as one of their own citizens. The "great things" at Capharnaum may have been the healing of the ruler's son (John iv.
46-53); or there may have been other unrecorded ones, even at this
early date.

24. *No prophet is accepted in his own country.* Our Lord's words
which follow are definitely words of rebuke. Their knowledge of
Scripture would confirm the fact. The prophets had been rejected by
the Jews (cf. vi. 23 and xi. 47 *seq.*).

25. *There were many widows in the days of Elias in Israel.* Our
Lord proceeded to point out that as the mission of the prophets was
not exclusively to the Jews, so His mission was not exclusively to His
own townspeople, or even to the Jews alone, as He had already
virtually asserted by preaching to the Samaritans (John iv.).

26. *To none of them was Elias sent,* i.e., to none of the widows of
Israel.

but to Sarepta of Sidon, to a widow woman. See 3 Kings xvii. 9.
Sarepta was a coast town of Phœnicia, between Tyre and Sidon. Of
Sidon probably means in the land about Sidon.

27. *None of them was cleansed but Naaman the Syrian.* See

²⁸ the Syrian. And all they in the synagogue, hearing these
²⁹ things, were filled with anger. And they rose up and
thrust him out of the city: and they brought him to the
brow of the hill, whereon their city was built, that they
³⁰ might cast him down headlong. But he passing through
the midst of them, went his way.

3 Kings xvii. 9. Both the widow of Sarepta and Naaman the Syrian were thus Gentiles. If, then, both Elias and Eliseus had special missions to the Gentiles rather than to their own nation, there ought to be no surprise in our Lord having a mission beyond the confines of His own town.

28. *All they in the synagogue were filled with anger.* The tone of our Lord's discourse had from the first been a disappointment to His hearers. They had hoped for a declaration of worldly greatness, of the restoration of their kingdom, and the like. Instead of this, He spoke of His mission to the poor, the outcast, the lepers, and, lastly, even to the hated and despised Gentiles. The further He proceeded the greater their disappointment, which quickly changed to positive anger, ending in an attempt to kill Him.

30. *But he, passing through the midst of them, went his way.* We are not told definitely whether this was a miraculous deliverance. Many have thought that it was not, but that the calm majesty of His presence prevented the people from actually laying hands upon Him (cf. John vii. 44, which seems a somewhat similar incident). And it is not necessary to suppose that any actual personal violence was used even in turning Him out of the synagogue; the tradition is, in fact, that no such treatment was allowed in the providence of God till the time of His passion.

It has often been discussed whether this was our Lord's only visit to Nazareth during His ministry, which resolves itself into the question whether it is or is not identical with the visit described by St. Matthew (xiii. 54-58) and St. Mark (vi. 1-6), which are evidently identical with each other. Like most questions of harmony, this cannot be certainly decided; but the following seem two strong reasons for thinking that the visits were *not* identical:

(1) St. Luke seems to place his account at the outset of our Lord's public life and as an explanation of why He began to reside at Capharnaum instead of Nazareth: while it is clear that the visit described by St. Matthew and St. Mark was *not* near the beginning of the ministry.

(2) The language of *v.* 23 suggests almost irresistibly that as yet our Lord had worked *no* miracles at Nazareth, but only at Capharnaum; and He certainly had no opportunity after that of working any during this visit; while both St. Matthew and St. Mark allude to a few as having been done by Him.

The Sabbath at Capharnaum.

(VERS. 31-44.)

And he went down into Capharnaum, a city of Galilee; 31 and there he taught them on the sabbath-days. And they 32 were astonished at his doctrine: for his speech was with power. And in the synagogue there was a man who had 33 an unclean devil, and he cried out with a loud voice,

31. *And he went down into Capharnaum.* For the next few months our Lord's head-quarters were at Capharnaum, which was consequently known as "His own city" (Matt. ix. 1). Its exact site is still a matter of dispute, but it was certainly near the north end of the lake. The ruins of what seems to be its famous synagogue and other signs point to the spot now called "*Tell-Hûm.*" It was the busiest town on the lake, and many of the best known incidents of our Lord's public life took place there. His home at this time may have been—and later on certainly was—in Peter's house, close to the synagogue; and the traditional site of this was marked by a Constantinian Basilica in the days when St. Helena identified and honoured the holy places.

32. *His speech was with power.* Cf. Matt. vii. 29: "He was teaching them as one having power and not as the Scribes and Pharisees." The scribes taught as mere interpreters of the law. Our Lord spoke as the lawgiver. "It was said to them of old . . . but *I say unto you* . . ." As to the burning effect of our Lord's teaching in its human eloquence on ordinary hearers, see xxiv. 32; and also John vii. 46.

33. *There was a man who had an unclean devil.* It is well known that in the history of the Church many cases have occurred of what is commonly called "possession by devils," which means that evil spirits are allowed for a time to have such power over a man that he is not responsible for his actions, which are not in fact his own at all, but those of the evil spirit who "possesses" him. It is said that in modern times, some cases of supposed lunacy have been in reality cases of demoniac possession, and have been cured by exorcism. There is no doubt that it would be often difficult to distinguish even now between the two classes of case. In later Jewish and early Christian centuries there was so great a horror and dread of evil spirits, and so little exact knowledge of the symptoms of mental diseases, since scientifically studied, that there was a tendency to call many things demoniac which we should call epileptic, or hysterical, or insane. The contemporary Jewish superstitions on the subject, as revealed in the Talmud, were gross and childish, and utterly unlike the simple teaching of the New Testament. The evangelists, however, as a rule leave no doubt that actual "possession" is intended in the cases they name. The phrase used

34 saying: Let us alone, what have we to do with thee, Jesus of Nazareth? art thou come to destroy us? I
35 know thee who thou art, the Holy One of God. And Jesus rebuked him, saying: Hold thy peace, and go out of him. And when the devil had thrown him into the
36 midst, he went out of him, and hurt him not at all. And there came fear upon all, and they talked among themselves, saying: What word is this, for with authority and power he commandeth the unclean spirits, and they go
37 out? And the fame of him was published into every
38 place of the country. And Jesus rising up out of the synagogue, went into Simon's house. And Simon's wife's mother was taken with a great fever, and they besought
39 him for her. And standing over her, he commanded the

is either δαιμόνιον ἔχειν (=to have an ["unclean" or "evil"] spirit) or δαιμονίζεσθαι. The similar Hebrew phrase is said to be common in Rabbinic books, and is no doubt the phrase meant by the Apostolic Greek. In the case before us St. Luke amplifies it by the epithet "unclean"; but the meaning is exactly the same.

34. *I know thee who thou art, the holy one of God.* The confident recognition of our Lord as "the Holy one of God" is a clear sign of actual possession. It is probable that the devils did not recognize His actual Divinity; but they would have clearly seen that He was a great Prophet. See *supra, v.* 3.

35. *When the devil had thrown him into the midst.* St. Mark says, "tearing him and crying out with a loud voice." Hence St. Luke's addition, "and hurt him not at all," is the more remarkable.

38. *Went into Simon's house.* This is the first mention of St. Peter in this Gospel, and nothing is said as to his antecedents till the following chapter, when he appears as a fisherman on the Lake of Genesareth. From St. John we learn that he was already a disciple of our Lord, and had with his brother been a disciple of the Baptist; but he had not as yet "left all things" to be permanently attached to Christ's following. We know also from St. Mark (i. 29) that James and John were also with our Lord when he entered Simon's house.

Simon's wife's mother was taken with a great fever. This is the only mention we have of Simon's wife. It is not certain whether she was still alive or not; but it is clear that through the rest of his life St. Peter followed our Lord and led a celibate life. The fact of St. Andrew and St. Peter's mother-in-law living in the same house with St. Peter himself suggests perhaps that his wife may have been dead; but, on the other hand, the words of our Lord (xviii. 29) addressed to him point rather to his having voluntarily left her.

39. *Rising she ministered to him.* She no doubt became after-

fever, and it left her. And immediately rising, she ministered to them. And when the sun was down, all they that had any sick with divers diseases, brought them to him. But he laying his hands on every one of them, healed them. And devils went out from many, crying out and saying: Thou art the Son of God. And rebuking them, he suffered them not to speak; for they knew that he was Christ. And when it was day, going out he went into a desert place: and the multitudes sought him, and came unto him: and they stayed him that he should not depart from them. To whom he said: To other cities also I must preach the kingdom of God: for therefore am I sent. And he was preaching in the synagogues of Galilee.

wards one of the regular ministering women, who showed their gratitude for having been cured in this way. See viii. 2.

40. *When the sun was down.* The law prohibited carrying the sick through the streets on the Sabbath, but the legal Sabbath ended at sunset, and accordingly then they brought their sick to be healed. This kind of scene no doubt went on on most Sabbath days during our Lord's ministry, and this one is given as a specimen of the rest. This particular Sabbath was evidently traditionally well known, for both St. Matthew (viii. 16) and St. Mark (i. 32) give an account of it.

41. *And devils went out of many.* It is important to notice that St. Luke distinguishes the two classes of miracles—the healing of the sick and the exorcism of demoniacs.

42. *When it was day, going out, he went into a desert place.* Apparently the healing of the sick on this Sabbath—and presumably therefore often on other Sabbaths—went on into the night, and it was not till sunrise that our Lord could retire to a "desert place," away from the city, to pray (Mark i. 35).

43. *To other cities also I must preach.* This is a warning to the people of Capharnaum, that although our Lord gave them a great deal of time and many Sabbath days (*v.* 31), He had other cities to preach to as well, and they could not expect to monopolize His ministry.

44. *And he was preaching in the synagogues of Galilee.* In some of the most authentic MSS.—including the two oldest, the Vatican Codex and the Sinaitic—the reading here is "the synagogues of Judea." It might be possible to construct a harmony afresh, and so that this passage coincided in time with the short Judean ministry mentioned by St. John (iii. 22); but it would not be altogether easy, and would especially clash with Mark i. 39. Moreover, in the verse immediately preceding and that immediately following, the scene is in

Galilee; so that if this verse was meant to allude to a Judean ministry, the whole would become very fragmentary. Nevertheless, the ordinary rule when there is a discrepancy is to accept the harder rather than the easier reading, as it is more probable that a copyist would substitute an easier for a harder than *vice versâ*. If we abide by the rule in this case, there is still a way out of our difficulty, and that is to suppose that the name Judea is here used in a broad sense, to denote all the country of the Jews, including therefore Galilee. As St. Luke wrote mainly for Gentiles, such a supposition is not unlikely; and indeed in several places in his Gospel he seems to be using it in that sense: see i. 5, vii. 17, xxiii. 5. See also Acts ii. 9, x. 37, xi. 1 and 29, xxvi. 20.

CHAPTER V.

Miraculous Draught of Fishes.

(VERS. 1–11.)

AND it came to pass that when the multitudes pressed upon him to hear the word of God, he stood by the lake of Genesareth, and saw two ships standing by the lake: but the fishermen were gone out of them and were

1. *He stood by the lake of Genesareth.* St. Luke is the only evangelist who uses this name. The word Genesareth means "the Garden of the Prince," and was the name of a fertile plain between Capharnaum and Tiberias. St. Matthew and St. Mark use the name "Sea of Galilee." St. John, writing many years later, calls it the "Sea of Tiberias," identifying it however (vi. 1) with the "Sea of Galilee." By that time Tiberias had become a flourishing town. It was founded by Herod Antipas during our Lord's lifetime and named after the Roman Emperor; and from its abstention from the Jewish revolt, was spared by Titus and made the capital of the province. When St. John wrote therefore it was the great town of the district. The word ($\lambda i \mu \nu \eta$) which we translate "lake" is used only by St. Luke, except in the Apocalypse ("the lake of fire," Apoc. xix. 20). It means properly a "marshy lake," and is appropriate here because the shores are marshy in various parts. The word sea ($\theta \acute{a} \lambda a \sigma \sigma a$) was originally used by the Greeks for the Mediterranean, and later for any great sheet of water. The Sea of Galilee is about fourteen miles long by nine broad and its level is some 600 feet below the Mediterranean. It was the centre of the most populous district of Galilee, and the fishing formed a source of considerable revenue to the inhabitants of its shores. The fish were cured and sold as a relish, large quantities being sent to Jerusalem and to the ports for export.

2. *And saw two ships standing by the lake.* Opinions are divided as to whether this incident is or is not identical with that of Matt. iv. 18 and Mark i. 16; but looking at the general surrounding circum-

3 washing their nets. And going up into one of the ships that was Simon's, he desired him to draw back a little from the land. And sitting he taught the multitudes out
4 of the ship. Now when he had ceased to speak, he said to Simon: Launch out into the deep, and let down your

stances, and the place occupied by each in the three Gospels respectively, there seems strong reason to think that it is. St. Peter and St. Andrew as well as St. John, and others, were *first* called by our Lord on the banks of the Jordan, at the outset of His ministry (John i. 37–42); but it is evident that this was not regarded as a permanent call to "leave all things and follow him," but only as one to pass on from being disciples of St. John to be disciples of the Teacher of whom St. John had given testimony. So in due time the sons of Jona and of Zebedee returned to their trade as fishermen at their native village of Bethsaida (= house of Fishery). After our Lord had finally called them from their boats, we do not find any trace of their leaving Him again, and in due time they were constituted Apostles (chapter vi.). Now in all these synoptic Gospels, the only call described is that on the shores of the lake, where they had been fishing, and in each case this call is given near the beginning of the Galilean ministry. The same four apostles are mentioned and the same promise is given that they should be fishers of men. The discrepancy sometimes alleged between St. Luke's account and those of the other two, is reconcilable in various ways. We may suppose, for example, that our Lord first came up while they were still fishing, and afterwards, when Simon and Andrew were washing their nets, He used their boat to preach from; and that after the sermon and the draught of fishes, He called first Peter and Andrew, and then James and John, who were mending their nets in their father's boat.

and were washing their nets. The word $\H{\epsilon}\kappa\tau\nu a$ seems to stand for any kind of net. Ἀμφίβληστρον is used by St. Matthew (iv. 18) and St. Mark (i. 16), and means a draw-net. A third word, σαγήνη, meaning a hauling net, occurs in St. Matthew (xiii. 47) in a different context.

3. *And going up into one of the ships that was Simon's.* The choice of the ship of Peter as the place from which His voice was to be heard has always been taken as a symbol of the teaching office of the Church: therefore from the times of the Catacombs, the ship of Peter has been always used as a figure of the Church itself. So also in some of the early Catacomb frescoes the picture of a man fishing is a symbol of the apostolic office, according to our Lord's words in *v.* 6.

4. *Launch out into the deep and let down your nets for a draught.* The idea of letting down the nets in broad daylight after having been unsuccessful all night must have appeared very hopeless; and it shows how St. Peter had already learnt to trust our Lord that he should have obeyed.

nets for a draught. And Simon answering, said to him: 5
Master, we have laboured all the night, and have taken
nothing; but at thy word I will let down the net. And 6
when they had done this, they enclosed a very great multitude of fishes, and their net broke. And they beckoned 7
to their partners that were in the other ship, that they
should come and help them. And they came, and filled
both the ships, so that they were almost sinking. Which 8
when Simon Peter saw, he fell down at Jesus's knees, saying: Depart from me, for I am a sinful man, O Lord.
For he was wholly astonished, and all that were with him, 9
at the draught of the fishes which they had taken. And 10
so were also James and John the sons of Zebedee, who
were Simon's partners. And Jesus saith to Simon: Fear
not; from henceforth thou shalt catch men. And having 11
brought their ships to land, leaving all things they followed
him.

5. *Master.* The word ἐπιστάτα (=teacher) is apparently used by St. Luke here and elsewhere as the nearest Greek equivalent to the Jewish Rabbi, which latter word the other evangelists retain.

6. *They enclosed a very great multitude of fishes.* The draught of fishes was evidently miraculous and likewise had a mystic meaning: cf. Matt. xiii. 47. Our Lord applied the parable when He said "from henceforth thou shalt catch men."

their net broke. This should be rather "was breaking" or bursting. The tense is the imperfect.

8. *Depart from me, for I am a sinful man, O Lord.* The mixture of impetuousness and humility in St. Peter's words exactly fits in with what we know of his character. By "depart from me" he meant from the neighbourhood of one unworthy and unclean.

10. *And so were also James and John, the sons of Zebedee.* This is the first mention by St. Luke of these two, though we know from other sources that they had been with our Lord at the time of at least one of the incidents of the previous chapter: see on iv. 38.

11. *Having brought their ships to land, leaving all things and followed him.* St. Mark adds of James and John that they left their father Zebedee in the ship, "with his hired men." Seeing that the two families—sons of Jona and Zebedee respectively—were in partnership, and had "hired men," they were probably not very poor; and the words "leaving all things" indicate as much. It may be noticed that St. Luke does not mention St. Andrew by name at all, but his presence is implied in *v.* 2.

The Cleansing of a Leper.

(VERS. 12–16.)

12 And it came to pass, when he was in a certain city, behold a man full of leprosy, who seeing Jesus, and falling on his face, besought him, saying: Lord, if thou wilt, thou

12. *When he was in a certain city.* The "certain city" alluded to is unknown. It was not Capharnaum, however, as appears both from the language here and from Mark ii. 1.

a man full of leprosy. The disease of leprosy was not uncommon in Palestine. Various regulations were laid down in the law to secure the complete isolation of the victims, which were partly of a religious nature, but partly sanitary, for the disease was highly contagious. A leper was condemned to isolation from all those not similarly afflicted. Thus it is enacted in the Law (Lev. xiii. 44-46): "Whosoever shall be defiled with the leprosy and is separated by the judgment of the priest shall have his clothes hanging loose, his mouth covered with a cloth, and he shall cry out that he is defiled and unclean. All the time that he is a leper and unclean he shall dwell alone, without the camp." Nevertheless the lepers were not always banished from the towns; they sometimes lived in isolated rooms or outhouses in the neighbourhood of their families. They were allowed even to attend the synagogues, provided that they occupied a special position, separated by a rail from the rest of the worshippers. The extreme loathsomeness of the disease was at the same time a guarantee that the laws of isolation would be observed. The disease is still a common one in many countries, and the horrors of the leper island in the Pacific were brought vividly before all English people in connection with Father Damien's death a few years ago.

True leprosy was considered incurable. There was, however, a form of white leprosy, which worked its own cure. This form was far less repulsive than the ordinary form, and did not lead to danger of death. The limbs did not corrupt inwardly, but externally, so far as the skin was concerned, it much resembled the ordinary form. A sufferer from this form of the disease would be classed with the others for the time being, and declared unclean. Eventually, however, the scales would fall off his body, and he would go to the priest to be certified as cleansed. In return, he was bound to offer three sacrifices, one for atonement, one as a sin offering, and the third as a burnt offering (Lev. xiv. 1–32).

For the ordinary leper, however, there was no hope. Yet he might linger on for ten or even twenty years in this living death, while the corruption gradually spread over his whole body, and his limbs one by one decayed. The disease has commonly been taken as a type of sin, which spreads gradually and brings corruption over the soul, so that it is loathsome to the eyes of God as a leper is to the eyes of men.

canst make me clean. And stretching forth *his* hand he touched him, saying: I will. Be thou cleansed. And immediately the leprosy departed from him. And he charged him that he should tell no man, but, Go, shew thyself to the priest, and offer for thy cleansing according as Moses commanded, for a testimony to them. But the fame of him went abroad the more, and great multitudes came together to hear, and to be healed *by him* of their infirmities. And he retired into the desert and prayed.

And a soul is cleansed from sin as the body from leprosy, only by the special work of our Lord.

In the case before us, St. Luke, himself a physician, uses the expression "full of leprosy," to show that the disease was far advanced, and that this was one of the worst cases. This parallel between leprosy and sin was familiar to the Jews, and it is probably because of it that prominence is given by all the synoptists to this particular one among the innumerable miracles of healing.

13. *He touched him, saying: I will. Be thou cleansed.* Even the external touch of our Lord was a great act of charity, for the law prohibited any contact whatever with a leper, under pain of sharing the "uncleanness." But such prohibition was not generally needed to keep people away. One of the hardest parts of the lepers' lot was the disgust with which every one turned away from them. Immediately, however, followed the much greater mercy of his cleansing.

14. *And he charged him that he should tell no man.* This command was frequently given by our Lord towards the beginning of His ministry. There was a great tendency to an outburst of popular enthusiasm, and their inclination would have been to proclaim Him king (John vi. 15), or something similar, so that a constant restraining influence was necessary. Under different circumstances, later on, He gave opposite directions: see on viii. 39.

offer for thy cleansing according as Moses commanded. See Lev. xiv.

15. *But the fame of him went abroad the more.* The only instances known of before when a true leper had been cleansed, were by Moses and Eliseus respectively, and this miracle of our Lord, so early in His ministry, would have at once stamped Him in the eyes of the people as one of the greatest of the Prophets. See 4 Kings v. 7, where Joram, being asked to cure Naaman, cries out: "Am I God, to be able to kill and give life, that this man hath sent me to heal a man of his leprosy?" The natural effect of our Lord working a miracle of this sort was that numbers came to see Him. St. Mark says (i. 45) there were so many that for some days He could not enter into the cities, but stayed without in the "desert places," apparently to avoid the chance of a rising among the excitable Galileans.

16. *And he retired into the desert and prayed.* This verse is of great importance as showing that, however busy and active was His life, our

Healing of a Paralytic.

(VERS. 17-26.)

17 And it came to pass on a certain day, as he sat teaching, that there were also Pharisees and doctors of the law sitting by, that were come out of every town of Galilee and Judea and Jerusalem; and the power of the Lord was to heal
18 them. And behold men brought in a bed a man who had the palsy: and they sought means to bring him in, and to
19 lay him before him. And when they could not find by what way they might bring him in, because of the multitude, they went up upon the roof, and let him down through the tiles with his bed into the midst before Jesus.

Lord always found opportunity to retire and pray from time to time, for our example. It is placed here probably as a sequel to the cure of the leper and with some antithesis between what the people did and what our Lord did. *They* talked about it far and wide (see Mark i. 45); but *He* retired and prayed. Some have thought that His prayer was meant as a preparation for the first encounter with the Pharisees, which now follows; but this is unlikely. The words with which *v.* 17 opens indicate clearly the beginning of a new subject.

17. *There were also Pharisees and doctors of the law.* See note on the Pharisees, on iii. 7. This is the first time they are mentioned as part of our Lord's audience, and they had come from all parts— "from every town of Galilee and Judea and Jerusalem"—and with them had come the "doctors of the law," whom St. Luke usually calls simply "lawyers." They were, in fact, identical with the Scribes: see on x. 25. There was as yet no open hostility on their part, though from the first they were jealous and suspicious of Christ's influence; and those from Jerusalem had probably come as spies, in consequence of our Lord's strong action in the first cleansing of the Temple, which had happened before this time (John ii. 15).

and the power of the Lord was to heal them. These words suggest distinctly that at that time the Scribes and Pharisees were intended to share in the blessings of our Lord's ministry, and some of them may have done so.

18. *And behold men brought in a bed a man who had the palsy.* St. Mark describes this more in detail, and says (ii. 3, 4) that the paralytic was carried on a small couch or litter by four men, and that the crowd was so great that they could not even get near the door. The scene was in a house at Capharnaum, very probably St. Peter's.

19. *They went up upon the roof.* Our Lord may have been in an upper room, but, more probably, the house had only one storey, as is often the case in the East. Like most houses in those parts, it would

Whose faith when he saw, he said: Man, thy sins are forgiven thee. And the scribes and Pharisees began to think, saying: Who is this who speaketh blasphemies? Who can forgive sins, but God alone? And when Jesus knew their thoughts, answering he said to them: What is it you think in your hearts? Which is easier to say, Thy sins are forgiven thee: or to say, Arise and walk? But that you may know that the son of man hath power on earth to forgive sins (he saith to the sick of the palsy) I say to thee, Arise, take up thy bed, and go into thy house. And immediately rising up before them, he took up the bed on which he lay; and went away to his own house, glorifying

have been oblong in shape, with a flat roof, so that it was easy to go on to it. There was often an outside staircase leading from the courtyard to the roof, so that a person escaping in haste from the housetop (Matt. xxiv. 17) would not go into the house.

and let him down through the tiles. These would have been their stone slabs, often used to this day.

20. *Man, thy sins are forgiven thee.* The Jews would have probably looked on this man's paralysis as the punishment of his sins; but there is no reason to suppose that our Lord was here referring to it as such. He probably only wished to give a general lesson on the importance of the wants of the soul above those of the body. The healing of the Pharisees alluded to above (*v.* 17) would have been of the soul, not of the body.

21. *Who is this who speaketh blasphemies?* The Pharisees and Scribes were here beginning their captiousness; but as yet they did not speak openly, and our Lord had to read their thoughts to be aware of it.

23. *Which is easier to say?* Of course both are equally easy, but the one can be put to a visible test, while the other cannot. Therefore our Lord established the truthfulness of one by proving that of the other.

24. *The son of man.* This title, which occurs here for the first time in this Gospel, was frequently used by our Lord of Himself, but never by others of Him; nor did any one ever address Him by it. It is generally used with some very pronounced meaning, as it is here. For it indicates His human origin only, and hence His use of it in this context is evidence that He claimed to be authorized as Man to forgive sins, and He established His claim by a miracle. The name was used in the Old Testament as a prophetic title of the Messiah, and, probably, refers to Dan. vii. 13, when, in his apocalyptic vision, he saw "one like the son of man [come] with the clouds of heaven." Cf. Matt. xxiv. 30, 44, &c.

25. *He took up the bed on which he lay.* To carry a bed or couch,

God. And all were astonished: and they glorified God. And they were filled with fear, saying: We have seen wonderful things to-day.

The Call of Levi and the Supper at his House.

(VERS. 27-39.)

27 And after these things he went forth, and saw a publican named Levi, sitting at the receipt of custom, and he said 28 to him: Follow me. And leaving all things, he rose up 29 and followed him. And Levi made him a great feast in his own house; and there was a great company of publi-

such as that on which the paralytic had lain, was not in itself wonderful. Such a bed was, in fact, little more than a mat and light quilted mattress, without any solid framework, so that he had been carried in it by the four corners, and it was carried by him by being simply rolled up and put on his shoulders. Even carrying it like this, however, when contrasted with the man's previous helpless state, gives a vivid idea of the completeness, as well as the suddenness of his cure.

27. *And saw a publican named Levi.* That Levi and St. Matthew are identical is certain, for in his own Gospel St. Matthew relates this whole incident and gives his name as Matthew. No doubt it was consideration for his feelings which induced St. Luke and St. Mark to forbear identifying in so many words the Apostle and the Publican; and it must have been his own humility which prompted St. Matthew to take the opposite course. It is commonly supposed that he took the name Matthew after his conversion, such a change being not uncommon among the Jews, as a mark of a change of state: cf. Abram to Abraham, Jacob to Israel, and Simon to Cephas or Peter. On the office of publican, see iii. 12. There is no reason to suppose that, before his conversion, St. Matthew was less cruel or extortionate than his fellow publicans. As this call happened in Capharnaum, that was where he followed his calling. It was a mercantile centre, and must have been an important place for taxes; the customs referred to had to do not only with the traffic on the lake, but also to the traffic which halted here on " the way of the sea from beyond the Jordan" (Matt. iv. 15) —that is, the great road from Damascus to Jerusalem, which passed either through or near the town.

29. *And Levi made him a great feast.* It must not be assumed that the feast was on the day of the calling. St. Luke naturally couples the events together, as is his custom, so as to finish off one subject before going on to another. In this case, it being St. Matthew's own feast, and his own conversion, we naturally turn to his Gospel for guidance. He describes both events, though through humility, he omits all mention of

cans, and of others, that were at table with him. But the 30 Pharisees and scribes murmured, saying to his disciples: Why do you eat and drink with publicans and sinners? And Jesus answering, said to them: They that are whole, 31 need not the physician: but they that are sick. I came 32 not to call the just, but sinners to penance. And they said 33 to him: Why do the disciples of John fast often and make prayers, and the disciples of the Pharisees in like manner; but thine eat and drink? To whom he said: Can 34 you make the children of the bridegroom fast, whilst the

his own name in connection with the feast. He separates the two by an interval, and we may reasonably conclude that they were separated. He puts the supper immediately before the raising of the daughter of Jairus, which St. Luke describes considerably later (ch. viii.). This raises certain fresh difficulties which will be there discussed; but whether or no St. Matthew places it in its exact chronological place, the mere fact that he separates it from his call which led up to it justifies us in assuming that the two were really separated, as they would almost necessarily have been, for a supper such as that must take time in order to get it ready and to invite the guests, &c.

30. *But the Pharisees and scribes murmured.* It would appear that they had not yet become accustomed to find fault with our Lord Himself. They naturally spoke first to those who were with Him and were His disciples; but the remarks may have been made in the hall when the banquet was going on and in our Lord's presence.

31. *They that are whole need not the physician: but they that are sick.* Our Lord answered for His disciples, with a clear enunciation of His feeling towards sinners as contrasted with that of the Pharisees. One of the most striking features of His ministry is the confidence with which sinners of all kinds constantly came to Him. See vii. 38, xv. 1, &c. The Pharisees, on the contrary, despised them, as is exemplified in the parable of the Pharisee and the Publican (xviii. 9-14).

33. *Why do the disciples of John fast often?* St. Mark implies (ii. 18) that some of the disciples of St. John joined with the Pharisees in asking this question, a fact which confirms the suggestion already made that this group of learned men, though curious and critical, were yet to some extent seekers after truth. But it must be remembered, on the other hand, that some of the disciples of the Baptist were already jealous of our Lord's teaching and success, while their own master was lying in prison.

34. *Can you make the children of the bridegroom fast?* Our Lord's meaning is this. There are times when mortification of this kind is unnecessary and out of season. Such a time would be that when He was in the midst of His disciples, as the bridegroom in the midst of the groomsmen, his chosen friends, assembled to rejoice with him in his

35 bridegroom is with them? But the days will come; when the bridegroom shall be taken away from them, then shall 36 they fast in those days. And he spoke also a similitude to them: That no man putteth a piece from a new garment upon an old garment: otherwise he both rendeth the new, and the piece taken from the new agreeth not with 37 the old. And no man putteth new wine into old bottles: otherwise the new wine will break the bottles, and it will 38 be spilled and the bottles will be lost. But new wine must 39 be put into new bottles; and both are preserved. And no man drinking old, hath presently a mind to new: for he saith, The old is better.

marriage feast. It was a time of joy and sensible sweetness, when the truths of faith were present before them, which made fasting for the time out of place. But such a season was by its nature only transient. It must pass away, and quickly, and then there would be no lack of fasting and mortification among His followers, i.e., when He should be taken away from them. The same idea is followed out by the Church when she dispenses with fasting and abstinence in festal seasons, such as Paschal time, Christmastide, &c.

36. *No man putteth a piece from a new garment upon an old garment.* The meaning of this "similitude" is not at first sight clear. The explanation usually given is something as follows. The new garment is meant to signify the New Law which our Lord came to promulgate; and it was to be accepted as a whole. If part of it were to be engrafted on a background of old customs and old observances, the two would disagree as new cloth would if patched on an old garment. The spirit of the new dispensation which He came to reveal must needs be embodied in new forms and new observances, and not merely grafted on the Mosaic law and Pharisaic tradition.

37. *No man putteth new wine into old bottles.* The bottles then and still in use in the East were commonly made of a single goat skin, from which the flesh and bones had been drawn out without cutting it. The neck of the animal became therefore the neck of the bottle. The idea of this similitude is the same as the last. It is only necessary to bear in mind that old bottles would often be cracked, and if fermentation ensued they would eventually burst.

38. *New wine must be put into new bottles.* Rather, new (νέον) wine must be put into *fresh* (καινούς) bottles. It is not so much the age of the bottle which is of importance, as the fact of its not having been used before.

39. *No man drinking old hath presently a mind to new.* This was an early hint which our Lord doubtless developed further than in these few words, of the teaching which scandalized the Jews, namely, that He

came to "fulfil," and in a way to replace their great possession—"the Law." That "old wine" it would be difficult for them, even with all good will, to forsake. Perhaps some one suggested this at the Feast. At any rate our Lord admitted it, and only indicated that although they may not "presently" (εὐθέως), and all at once relish this new wine of life, the time will come when they will learn that it is infinitely better than the old.

CHAPTER VI.

The Disciples in the Cornfields on the Sabbath.

(VERS. 1-5.)

AND it came to pass on the second first sabbath, that as he went through the cornfields his disciples plucked the ears, and did eat, rubbing them in their hands.

1. *And it came to pass.* This and the following episode are examples of incidents which occur in all three synoptic Gospels with practical identity, though not altogether in identical words: see Matt. xii. 1-8; Mark ii. 23-28. The variations are worth noting. St. Matthew alone adds *vv.* 5-7; St. Mark alone gives the striking saying in his *v.* 27; but St. Luke alone notes the technical point in which the breach of the law was chiefly supposed to consist, namely, that they "rubbed [the grains of corn] in their hands": see on *v.* 2.

on the second first sabbath. The specification of which Sabbath it was is also peculiar to St. Luke. The expression "second first" has been much discussed. The word used ($δευτερόπρωτος$) has no established sense in Greek, and is no doubt a translation of some Aramaic technical term which has been wholly lost. Some have taken it to mean the Sabbath after the second day of the Pasch; others the first Sabbath of the second year of a Sabbatical cycle: see on iii. 7; others again have taken it as the first Sabbath of the second month of the Jewish year, which would bring it to about three weeks after the feast of the Pasch, which was the fifteenth of the first month. The matter is, however, of little importance. The time of year would in each of these theories be about the same, i.e., the months of April or May, which is, in fact, the time of ripe corn in Palestine; for the wheat harvest was supposed to begin immediately after the Pasch, when the "first sheaf" was solemnly offered: see on ii. 41. The Pasch in question would be the second one of our Lord's ministry. Whether this Pasch is referred to in the fifth chapter of St. John, or whether, as many think, the reference there is to the Feast of Purim, in either case it would appear that the miracle recorded in connection with it was the occasion of the first outcry about our Lord breaking the Sabbath, which

And some of the Pharisees said to them: Why do you 2
that which is not lawful on the sabbath-days? And Jesus 3
answering them, said: Have you not read so much as
this, what David did, when himself was hungry and they
that were with him: how he went into the house of God, 4
and took and ate the bread of proposition, and gave to
them that were with him, which is not lawful to eat, but
only for the priests? And he said to them: The son of 5
man is Lord also of the sabbath.

became afterwards the continual source of their fault-finding. The two instances in this chapter are no doubt chosen as typical of many others which were the development of the one recorded by St. John. Since all the synoptists record the same two, it would appear that they had become traditional in the Apostolic Church as typical instances.

2. *Why do you that which is not lawful on the sabbath-days?* The fault found by the Pharisees is an example of their legal and ceremonial subtlety. The written law prohibited all kinds of work, and a mass of oral tradition had arisen, specifying what was lawful and what was not. Among the things which were forbidden by tradition was reaping and threshing corn. According to the fault-finders, "plucking the ears of corn" might be considered as falling under the former category, but "rubbing them with their fingers" was taken to be clearly a case of the latter. At the present time there are strict Jews in England who will not light a fire or even light gas on the Sabbath.

3. *Have you not read so much as this, what David did?* &c. The first part of our Lord's answer was the enunciation of a general principle equivalent to our proverb "Necessity has no laws." The instance quoted is described in 1 Kings xxi. David was flying from the face of Saul, and having no food for himself and his followers, he went to Achimelech, the High Priest, and prevailed on him to give him "the loaves of proposition," which were "hallowed bread." The law prescribed that it should be replaced week by week, and that the old bread should be eaten by priests: see Exod. xxix. 32, and Lev. xxiv. 9. The fact that the incident is recorded in the Scriptures should have been enough to establish in the minds of the Pharisees that it was praiseworthy, and our Lord's words are a reproach to them for not knowing or understanding what they prided themselves especially on knowing and understanding. The argument, then, is that, even if plucking ears of corn were a violation of the Sabbath, it would have been justifiable in the case of the disciples on account of their need, in the same way that it was in the case of David, who broke even the written law under circumstances of necessity.

5. *The son of man is Lord also of the sabbath.* This second part of our Lord's answer would have been even more distasteful to the Pharisees. In claiming to be Lord of the Sabbath, He was asserting His position as at least superior to Moses, who first promulgated the

Cure of the man with a withered hand.

(VERS. 6-11.)

6 And it came to pass also on another sabbath, that he entered into the synagogue, and taught. And there was a 7 man, whose right hand was withered. And the scribes and Pharisees watched if he would heal on the sabbath; that 8 they might find an accusation against him. But he knew their thoughts; and said to the man who had the withered hand: Arise, and stand forth in the midst. And rising he 9 stood forth. Then Jesus said to them: I ask you, if it be lawful on the sabbath-days to do good or to do evil; to

law of the Sabbath, and as in some sort head of the human race. Such a claim was not likely to be acknowledged by His hearers; yet it may have been necessary and fitting to enunciate clearly a power which was afterwards to be used very fully, when on the founding of the Church the laws of the Sabbath were finally abrogated in favour of those of the Christian Sunday.

In the other synoptical Gospels, further answers of our Lord are given: see Matt. xii. 5, 6, 7, and Mark ii. 27, which in effect amplify His claim to be "Lord of the Sabbath."

6. *And it came to pass also on another sabbath.* There is nothing to inform us precisely how soon after the journey through the cornfields we are to place the miracle on the man with a withered hand. All three of the synoptists, however, give the two incidents side by side, so that it would seem that they were both regarded as important landmarks in the development of the opposition of the Jewish rulers, and they may have occurred about the same period of the ministry.

7. *And the scribes and Pharisees watched if he would heal on the sabbath.* This is the first instance mentioned by St. Luke of the Pharisees deliberately watching our Lord for the sake of finding some accusation against Him, and marks a distinctly further stage in their opposition. If they could prove to the people that He "broke the law," they thought they could destroy His credit with them; for almost all those Jews who really cared for religion in that generation were fanatically devoted to "the Law"—as they were taught it by the "Doctors."

9. *I ask you if it be lawful,* &c. The Greek word ($\dot{\epsilon}\pi\epsilon\rho\omega\tau\tilde{\omega}$) implies that our Lord is putting a question consequent on something already said; and we can find the explanation by comparing St. Matthew's account. He tells us (xii. 10) that the Pharisees first asked Him, "Is it lawful to heal on the Sabbath days?" that they might accuse Him. Our Lord's words in St. Luke were no doubt in answer, and may be paraphrased as asking them a further question: Which is the greater violation of the Sabbath, to heal a sick man and save his life,

save life, or to destroy? And looking round about on 10 them all, he said to the man: Stretch forth thy hand. And he stretched it forth; and his hand was restored. And they were filled with madness; and they talked one 11 with another, what they might do to Jesus.

Choosing of the Twelve Apostles.

(VERS. 12-16.)

And it came to pass in those days, that he went out into 12 a mountain to pray, and he passed the whole night in the prayer of God. And when day was come, he called unto 13 him his disciples; and he chose twelve of them (whom also

or to do evil as they were doing by their plots to entrap Him and eventually destroy His life?

10. *And looking round about on them all.* The Pharisees appear to have understood His meaning, and were accordingly reduced to silence (Mark iii. 4), and our Lord, "looking on them with anger, and being grieved at the blindness of their hearts" (Mark iii. 5), worked the miracle before them all.

11. *They talked one with another what they might do to Jesus.* St. Matthew distinctly states (xii. 14) that they determined to put Him to death. As, however, He was in Galilee, nothing could be done without the concurrence of Herod, and this may have been the reason why they consulted with another party (Mark iii. 6) whom they usually held in abhorrence, namely the "Herodians"—the corrupt courtiers of the house of Herod, who were, like Herod himself, hardly real Jews at all.

12. *And it came to pass in those days.* Between the last episode and this, St. Mark tells us (iii. 7-12) that our Lord withdrew to the sea (of Galilee) "and that a multitude from all parts, even from about Tyre and Sidon, were attracted by his miracles and his teaching, as he preached from the boat by the shore."

he passed the whole night in the prayer of God. The choosing of the apostles forms the most decisive step of our Lord's whole ministry, marking His final determination, in consequence of the continued opposition of the Jewish rulers, to sever Himself from them finally, and train a band of His followers to found the Church independently of them. Before so decisive a step, as an example to us, He spent the whole night in prayer. The mountain is said to have been Kurn Hattin, behind Capharnaum.

13. *He chose twelve of them, whom also he named Apostles.* The word Apostle means originally "*messenger.*" The Apostolic office as instituted by our Lord is described by St. Mark (iii. 14). They were (1) to be with Him; (2) to go forth and preach; and (3) to exercise

14 he named Apostles): Simon whom he surnamed Peter,
and Andrew his brother, James and John, Philip and
15 Bartholomew, Matthew and Thomas, James *the son* of
16 Alpheus, and Simon who is called Zelotes, and Jude *the
brother* of James, and Judas Iscariot who was the traitor.

works of charity. After our Lord had left the world, a further office devolved on them, viz., witnessing to the Resurrection, as the basis of the Christian Faith (Acts i. 22). It was evidently our Lord's intention that the twelve should be the only ones to hold the Apostolic office strictly so-called. On the defection of Judas, however, another was appointed in his place, no doubt by our Lord's direction; and later on, for special reasons, St. Paul and St. Barnabas were raised to the Apostolic dignity, which involved a share in our Lord's command to preach the gospel to the whole world (Matt. xxviii. 19; Mark xvi. 15), or as we should now express it, "faculties" in every country. But no attempt was ever made to fill the places of the other apostles as they died, except only that of St. Peter. At the present day, therefore, the Pope, as his direct successor, alone has Apostolic power and jurisdiction.

14-16. There are four enumerations of the twelve apostles in the New Testament, three being in the synoptical Gospels, and the fourth in the Acts of the Apostles. The general harmony of the four lists is evident to the eye; the merely apparent discrepancies only concern the two names before the last, and can be easily explained. The four lists are as follows:—

St. Matthew x.	St. Mark iii.	St. Luke vi.	Acts i.
SIMON, WHO IS CALLED PETER	SIMON, TO WHOM HE GAVE THE NAME PETER	SIMON, SURNAMED PETER	PETER
Andrew	James	Andrew	John
James	John	James	James
John	Andrew	John	Andrew
Philip	Philip	Philip	Philip
Bartholomew	Bartholomew	Bartholomew	Thomas
Thomas	Matthew	Matthew	Bartholomew
Matthew	Thomas	Thomas	Matthew
James, son of Alpheus	James, son of Alpheus	James, son of Alpheus	James of Alpheus
Thaddeus	Thaddeus	Simon Zelotes	Simon Zelotes
Simon the Cananean	Simon the Cananean	Jude, brother of James	Jude, brother of James
Judas Iscariot	Judas Iscariot	Judas Iscariot	

It will be noticed that the order varies, but some points of agreement may be noticed in all four. Thus each list begins with St. Peter and ends with Judas Iscariot, except the fourth one, in which the name of Judas does not appear, as at the time described he was dead. Then if we divide each list into three groups of four, we shall find the same four names in each group, and three of the first four—though not in each list the *first* three—are Peter, James, and John, who were always closest to our Lord, and with Him on all occasions of special importance (e.g., the raising of Jairus's daughter, ix. 51; the transfiguration, ix. 28; the agony in the garden, Matt. xxvi. 37, Mark xiv. 33. See also Mark xiii. 3, when all the four of this group are close to our Lord). Again, in two out of the three Gospel lists, the names are given in pairs; and as we know that our Lord sent them out to preach two by two, the idea is suggested that they are enumerated in the order of the couples who preached together. If we follow the lists in St. Matthew and St. Luke, though they are not quite in the same order, we get the same couples with the exception of the last two. In the last St. Matthew gives Simon as the companion of Judas Iscariot, while St. Luke gives Jude; and the last couple but one is, of course, correspondingly altered. It seems probable, to judge from the other couples, that St. Jude would not have been separated from his brother, and we may note that the last four in St. Luke are not coupled quite like the others. It is perhaps permissible to conjecture that St. Luke put all the last four together, and in an inverted order advisedly, so as to avoid any unpleasant feeling which might have survived in the mind of Simon, from the recollection of having preached with Judas Iscariot. If this were so, then we should be justified in taking St. Matthew's list as it stands. On the other hand, it is also possible that it was St. Jude who did actually preach with Judas Iscariot, and that St. Matthew inverted the order and placed him next to his brother; and in that case St. Luke's order would be exactly correct.

That St. Peter should come first as Prince of the Apostles and the rock on which the Church was to be founded, would be naturally expected. Throughout the Gospels he always speaks as chief of the Apostolic College, and our Lord's special commissions were given to him by name (Matt. xvi. 18; John xxi. 15-17; and elsewhere). Of St. Andrew we know little except that he was the brother of St. Peter, and probably the elder of the two. They were sons of Jonas, who lived at Bethsaida of Galilee, a little fishing village close to Capharnaum: see on ix. 10.

The next couple were also brothers and also of Bethsaida. Their father's name was Zebedee, their mother's Salome. They were called Boanerges, or Sons of Thunder. The elder of the two is known as St. James the Greater, to distinguish him from the other apostle of the same name. He was the first to suffer martyrdom, being killed by Herod Agrippa in Jerusalem about nine years after our Lord's Ascension (Acts xii. 2). His relics are said to be at the celebrated shrine of Compostella in Spain. St. John, his brother, was the youngest of all the apostles, the "beloved disciple," and the one "whom Jesus loved" (John xiii. 23, xxi. 20). He eventually outlived the others by many years, and he alone of all the apostles ended his life without martyrdom; for though he was at one time condemned to death by being put into a cauldron of boiling oil, a miracle was worked in his favour, and after being banished for many years in the island of Patmos—a very small island in the Ægean Sea, off the south-west coast of Asia Minor—he eventually died in extreme old age, close on 100 A.D., as Bishop of Ephesus.

Philip and Bartholomew come next. The former of these came from Bethsaida (John xii. 21), the latter from Cana of Galilee (John xxi. 2), where our Lord had worked His first miracle. It seems certain that St. Bartholomew is identical with Nathaniel, whose first call is described by St. John; for—(1) St. John speaks twice of Nathaniel and never of Bartholomew; (2) the other evangelists speak of Bartholomew and never of Nathaniel; (3) both Nathaniel and Bartholomew are always coupled with Philip. The name Bartholomew signifies son of Tolmai, and would have borne the same relation to Nathaniel as Barjona to Simon.

Matthew and Thomas come next. The former we have already come across as the publican Levi: see v. 27. St. Thomas is known chiefly by his natural despondency of character (John xi. 16, xx. 25) and his slowness to believe in the Resurrection. St. Matthew must have been a Galilean; for he was living at Capharnaum when he was first called to follow our Lord. St. Thomas was probably also from Galilee. His surname, Didymus (John xi. 16, xxi. 2), means a twin, but we have no record of his brother.

We now come to the last group. The most important of these four is St. James the Less, who is probably the same James that was afterwards Bishop of Jerusalem, and as such took an important part in the history of the early Church (e.g., Acts xii. 17, xv. 13-21, xxi. 18; Gal. i. 19). He and his brother Jude were known as the *brethren* of the Lord, being in reality His cousins, through their mother Mary, wife of Cleophas or Alpheus, who is believed to have been the cousin or sister of our Lady : see on viii. 19. They both came from Nazareth (Mark vi. 3). St. Jude is clearly identical with Thaddeus of St. Matthew and St. Mark : it is simply a case of a double name like Levi and Matthew. The surname Lebbæus is given in all the best MSS. of St. Matthew (x. 3), but is omitted in the Vulgate and therefore also in the Douay version. It was probably a place name. Next we have Simon Zelotes, or the Zealot. The Zealots were a famous sect, who, without any prudence or thought of consequences, rebelled on every possible occasion against Roman impositions and Roman government. It is instructive to note that our Lord's band of apostles was able to unite side by side one of these Zealots and a man like St. Matthew who had been an actual collector of the hated taxes.

The last on the list is Judas, surnamed Iscariot, or man of Kerioth, a little town in Judea ; and he was the only one of the twelve who came from Judea. Needless to say, at the moment our Lord chose him, He knew He would one day say of him, "It were better for that man if he had never been born" (Matt. xxvi. 24). Such, however, is God's ordinary providence. Many there are whom He daily brings into existence to whom one day the same words will be applicable. He does not refuse the benefit of creation to those who He sees will misuse it ; nor did He withhold the apostolic vocation from Judas because He knew he would be unfaithful.

Sermon on the Plain.

(VERS. 17-49.)

And coming down with them, he stood in a plain place, 17 and the company of his disciples, and a very great multitude of people from all Judea and Jerusalem, and the sea-coast both of Tyre and Sidon, who were come to hear 18 him, and to be healed of their diseases. And they that were troubled with unclean spirits, were cured. And all 19 the multitude sought to touch him, for virtue went out from him, and healed all.

17. *He stood in a plain place.* From the fact recorded here, the sermon which follows has become known as the "Sermon on the Plain." Only one other long consecutive sermon of our Lord addressed to the people is recorded in the Gospels, which is that known as the "Sermon on the Mount" (Matt. v., vi., vii.). The two sermons resemble each other in many ways. Whether or not they were the same sermon, two opposite opinions have been held by commentators. Those who believe them to be identical rely on the general similarity of ideas throughout, especially in the opening and closing verses; and they take "a plain place" to mean a plateau such as is often found some way up a mountain. Those who hold the opposite opinion point to various differences in the two sermons, as, for example, to the fact that there are in St. Matthew eight beatitudes and no corresponding woes; and in St. Luke only four beatitudes, but also four corresponding woes. A more important difference perhaps is the omission of much which concerns the relation of Christ's teaching to that of the Old Law—the lessons of almsdeeds and prayers, including the promulgation of the Pater Noster, or Lord's Prayer. This is explained in the former view by supposing that St. Luke, writing for Gentiles, recorded only what suited his purpose. If this be correct, it would follow that he had summarized freely, and that we are at a considerable distance from the *ipsissima verba* of our Lord. But it is not at all certain that the Sermon on the Mount was a single sermon of our Lord's at all. Some have maintained that it is a collection of His sayings put together by St. Matthew, to explain the relation between the new dispensation and the old. Certainly a good deal of what occurs in the Sermon on the Mount is to be found elsewhere in St. Luke's Gospel in a very different context; but it is of course possible that our Lord may have repeated some of His sayings more than once.

The crowd described by St. Luke as listening to our Lord were from all Judea and Jerusalem, and the sea coast of Tyre and Sidon. That described by St. Matthew was from Galilee, Judea and Jerusalem, Perea, and Decapolis. Possibly neither enumeration is meant to be

7

(a) BEATITUDES AND WOES (vers. 20-26).

20 And he, lifting up his eyes on his disciples, said: Blessed complete. St. Mark does not give any sermon; but the crowd which he notes (iii. 8) as following our Lord about this time is from Galilee, Judea and Jerusalem, Idumæa, beyond Jordan [Perea] and the parts about Tyre and Sidon, which covers both the lists of St. Matthew and St. Luke.

It is usually stated that there are four beatitudes in the Sermon on the Plain, corresponding with the four woes. If we take them as four, however, we must consider those in the Sermon on the Mount to be nine, for the last of the four in St. Luke corresponds not with the eighth in St. Matthew, but with the development of the subject which follows the eighth. In truth there is not much resemblance in the order of ideas between the two sets of beatitudes, except at the end. If we wish to make them correspond, we have to invert the order in St. Luke, and give his second one a special meaning. The following synopsis of the two sets puts it in a clear light:—

ST. MATTHEW. *Sermon on the Mount.*	ST. LUKE. *Sermon on the Plain.*
1. Blessed are the poor in spirit, for theirs is the kingdom of heaven.	1. Blessed are ye poor, for yours is the kingdom of God.
2. Blessed are the meek, for they shall possess the land.	
3. Blessed are they that mourn, for they shall be comforted.	3. Blessed are ye that weep, for you shall laugh.
4. Blessed are they that hunger and thirst after justice, for they shall have their fill.	2. Blessed are you that hunger now, for you shall be filled.
5. Blessed are the merciful, for they shall obtain mercy.	
6. Blessed are the clean of heart, for they shall see God.	
7. Blessed are the peacemakers, for they shall be called the children of God.	
8. Blessed are they that suffer persecution for justice sake, for theirs is the kingdom of heaven.	
Blessed are ye when men shall revile you and persecute you and speak all that is evil against you, untruly for my sake: be glad and rejoice, for your reward is very great in heaven.	Blessed shall you be when men shall hate you, and when they shall separate you, and shall reproach you, and cast out your name as evil, for the son of man's sake. Be glad in that day and rejoice, for your reward is great in heaven.

20. *Blessed are ye poor.* St. Matthew gives the poor in spirit. Of course spirituality is necessary to sanctify poverty; but actual poverty

are ye poor: for yours is the kingdom of God. Blessed 21
are ye that hunger now: for you shall be filled. Blessed
are ye that weep now: for you shall laugh. Blessed shall 22
you be when men shall hate you, and when they shall
separate you, and shall reproach you, and cast out your
name as evil, for the son of man's sake. Be glad in that 23
day and rejoice; for behold, your reward is great in heaven.
For according to these things did their fathers to the
prophets. But wo to you that are rich: for you have your 24
consolation. Wo to you that are filled: for you shall 25
hunger. Wo to you that now laugh: for you shall
mourn and weep. Wo to you when men shall bless you: 26
For according to these things did their fathers to the false
prophets.

facilitates the acquisition of poverty of spirit. A poor man is used to giving up his own will, and his feeling of helplessness at the hands of others ought to lead him to a feeling of dependence on God. It is of course possible for a rich man to become as a poor one and to acquire detachment, but as a state, riches render salvation more difficult : see on xviii. 24, 25. In the religious language of the Jews—as in the Psalms —"the poor" commonly meant all humble and trustful servants of God and this is no doubt what St. Matthew had in his mind.

21. *Blessed are ye that hunger now.* If this sermon be identified with the Sermon on the Mount, those that hunger now must be the same as those that hunger after justice; i.e., that hunger spiritually. Apart from St. Matthew's Gospel, we should have taken it as a development of the preceding beatitude and apply it to bodily hunger ; but the reward of "having their fill" will of course be spiritual in any case.

22. *According to these things did their fathers to the prophets.* It is a sign of a true prophet, as it is a sign of the true religion, to be persecuted unjustly.

they shall separate you and reproach you. The separating, or cutting them off from their company, means casting them out of the synagogues (see John ix. 34, 35), and is the same as the "persecution" of St. Matthew.

23. *Be glad in that day and rejoice.* Cf. Acts v. 41, "[The Apostles indeed went from the presence of the council, rejoicing that they were accounted worthy to suffer reproach for the name of Jesus."

24. *But wo to you.* This expression is rather one of grief and pity than of reproach. Those who are now filled are in truth unfortunate, for "they have had their reward."

26. *For according to these things did their fathers to the false prophets.* There is little record of the false prophets. It was the

(*b*) THE LAW OF CHARITY TO OUR NEIGHBOUR (vers. 27-38).

27 But I say to you that hear: Love your enemies, do good
28 to them that hate you. Bless them that curse you, and
29 pray for them that calumniate you. And to him that striketh thee on the *one* cheek, offer also the other. And him that taketh away from thee thy cloak, forbid not to
30 take thy coat also. Give to every one that asketh thee, and of him that taketh away thy goods, ask them not again.

duty of the Scribes and Priests to decide on the credentials of those who claimed to be prophets, and to tell the people whether to attend to their teaching or not: see on xx. 4.

27. *But I say to you that hear.* Cf. Matt. v. 44, where the emphasis on the "I" is to mark the contrast with the Jewish doctors of the law, whose teaching St. Luke may well have omitted to notice, as being of no great moment to Gentile readers. On the other hand, St. Luke draws out an antithesis between the disciples to whom the first part of the Sermon was primarily addressed, and the application to all those "that hear," which now follows. These are not told to rejoice in persecution, which is a degree of excellence at which few could aim; but they *are* told to exercise universal charity, which was a virtue imperfectly understood or practised among the Jews. Four degrees of evil are given, in increasing proportion, to be met with four degrees of good. Thus, their being our enemies, hating us, cursing us, and calumniating us, is to be met on our side by loving them, doing good to them, blessing them, and praying for them.

29. *And to him that striketh thee on one cheek, offer also the other.* The virtue of patience is closely connected with the instructions of the preceding verses. The instances our Lord gives involve the highest exercise of the virtue, and denote a spirit at which all should aim. A literal compliance with them, however, is rarely obligatory, and usually not even desirable. To "offer the other cheek," might be simply placing an additional occasion of sin before our neighbour: to refrain from retaliation where it is not necessary for self defence, is usually possible and obligatory on all. St. Matthew (v. 40) makes it plain that the "taking of the cloak and coat—i.e., the outer and inner garment—was meant as a case of legal oppression, by sueing for a debt and trying to take that which the law did not allow to be taken.

30. *Give to every one that asketh of thee.* Cf. Deut. xv. 7-9: "If one of thy brethren that dwelleth within the gates of thy city in the land which the Lord thy God wilt give thee, come to poverty: thou shalt not harden thy heart, nor close thy hand, but shalt open it to the poor man." It need hardly be added that this is no precept of *indiscriminate* almsgiving, which in these days of charitable organizations is not usually either wise or charitable. But all are bound to give alms. The proposition that only the rich, and often not even they, are

And as you would that men should do to you, do you also to them in like manner. And if you love them that love you, what thanks are to you? for sinners also love those that love them. And if you do good to them who do good to you, what thanks are to you? for sinners also do this. And if ye lend to them of whom ye hope to receive, what thanks are to you? for sinners also lend to sinners, for to receive as much. But love ye your enemies; do good, and lend, hoping for nothing thereby: and your reward shall be great, and you shall be the sons of the Highest; for he is kind to the unthankful, and to the evil. Be ye therefore merciful as your Father also is merciful. Judge not, and you shall not be judged. Condemn not, and you shall not

bound under sin to give to the poor, has been condemned by the Church.

31. *And as you would that men should do to you, do you also to them in like manner.* This seems a summing-up of what has gone before. If we are guided in our dealings with others by what we should wish to be done if we were in their places, we shall not be far from perfect charity.

32. *Sinners also love those that love them.* By the word "sinners," our Lord means to designate those whose motive is not connected with their sense of duty. In effect such men will always be sinners, for they have no motive to give them strength to resist the downward tendency of their nature.

33. *What thanks are to you?* Cf. xiv. 12–14. The motive of self-interest or vain glory often takes the merit out of works ostensibly charitable.

34. *If ye lend to them of whom ye hope to receive.* This takes up the second part of Matt. v. 42.

35. *Hoping for nothing thereby.* The meaning of the Greek verb ἀπελπίζειν is disputed. Some agreeing with the early Syriac version, translate it "disappointing no men": but the Vulgate is clear, and there is no reason to question St. Jerome's rendering.

your reward shall be great and you shall be the sons of the Highest. Two motives are put before us: (1) a great reward in heaven, and (2) we shall be "sons of the Highest," and shall as sons grow in our likeness to Him. Cf. Matt. v. 9: "Blessed are the peace-makers, for they shall be called [i.e., shall *be*] the children of God."

36. *Be ye therefore merciful.* This verse is a deduction from the last. If we are children of God, we must imitate Him, and our mercy should be modelled on His. It may be noted that, if the two sermons are identical, the whole of Matt. vi. is passed over at this point.

37. *Judge not and you shall not be judged.* Cf. the Lord's Prayer, xi. 4, and Matt. vi. 12; also see Matt. xviii. 21–35. Our own

38 be condemned. Forgive, and you shall be forgiven. Give, and it shall be given to you: good measure and pressed down and shaken together and running over shall they give into your bosom. For with the same measure that you shall mete withal, it shall be measured to you again.

(c) SELF KNOWLEDGE (vers. 39-45).

39 And he spoke also to them a similitude: Can the blind
40 lead the blind? do they not both fall into the ditch? The disciple is not above his master: but every one shall be
41 perfect, if he be as his master. And why seest thou the mote in thy brother's eye, but the beam that is in thy own
42 eye thou considerest not? Or how canst thou say to thy brother: Brother, let me pull the mote out of thy eye, when thou thyself seest not the beam in thy own eye? Hypocrite, cast first the beam out of thy own eye; and then shalt thou see clearly to take out the mote from thy
43 brother's eye. For there is no good tree that bringeth forth evil fruit: nor an evil tree that bringeth forth good

charity of judgment is to be the measure of God's judgment of us, as our own forgiveness is to be the measure of what we may expect from Him.

38. *Into your bosom*—i.e., the loose folds of their ample garments, above the girdle, which often served as a pocket to carry such things as gifts of corn for which no vessel was at the moment obtainable.

39. *Can the blind lead the blind?* This comparison is used elsewhere by our Lord (Matt. xv. 14), and applied directly to the Pharisees and Scribes. Probably here also He had them chiefly in view. See Matt. xxiii. 16 : " Wo to you, blind guides."

41. *Why seest thou the mote in thy brother's eye?* A "mote" was a little chip or dry twig of wood. The antithesis between a mote and a beam was a Jewish proverb, representing what was small and great respectively. It is used here to point out the readiness of men to overlook huge faults in themselves, while they pick out faults almost invisible in others. The " eye " (as in Matt. vi. 22) is a figure of moral consciousness in general.

43. *For there is no good tree that bringeth forth evil fruit.* The connection between this and what has gone before seems to be that as the nature of the fruit depends on the tree, so the good we shall do to others will depend on our first cleansing ourselves, and casting out the "beams" from our eyes ; and on the fact that as the disciple is not better than his master, those who would teach goodness to others must, unless they will be blind guides, be good themselves.

fruit. For every tree is known by its fruit. For men do not gather figs from thorns; nor from a bramble bush do they gather the grape. A good man out of the good treasure of his heart bringeth forth that which is good: and an evil man out of the evil treasure bringeth forth that which is evil. For out of the abundance of the heart the mouth speaketh.

(d) PERORATION (vers. 46-49).

And why call you me Lord, Lord: and do not the things which I say? Every one that cometh to me, and heareth my words, and doth them, I will shew you to whom he is like. He is like to a man building a house, who digged deep, and laid the foundation upon a rock. And when a flood came, the stream beat vehemently upon that house, and it could not shake it; for it was founded on a rock. But he that heareth, and doth not; is like to a man building his house upon the earth without a foundation: against which the stream beat vehemently, and immediately it fell, and the ruin of that house was great.

44. *For every tree is known by its fruit.* Our Lord in His similes almost universally appealed to what was characteristic of the place where He happened to be, and what would thus be familiar to His hearers. The case here is no exception. Gardens and orchards abounded in the neighbourhood, and while the interior would contain vines and fig trees, the whole would be surrounded with a thorny hedge of "prickly pear," interspersed with many "bramble bushes," or thorny shrubs.

45. *Out of the abundance of the heart the mouth speaketh.* The conversation of our unguarded moments is the best index of the worth of our lives. This is still the same line of thought. Out of our character we shall speak; so only the good can preach goodness usefully.

48. *He is like to a man building a house*, &c. The similitude with which our Lord concludes implies that those who hear His words and become disciples will have to undergo great trials and persecutions, against which, as He said earlier in the discourse (vv. 22-23), they will become proof by their lives being founded on His, as a house may be founded on a rock.

CHAPTER VII.

Cure of the Centurion's Servant.

(VERS. 1–10.)

2 AND when he had finished all his words in the hearing of the people, he entered into Capharnaum. And the servant of a certain centurion, who was dear to him,

1. *He entered into Capharnaum.* Capharnaum was still our Lord's home at this period, and for some time afterwards. The miracle on the centurion's servant is recounted by St. Luke as our Lord returned to Capharnaum after the Sermon on the Plain, and by St. Matthew almost immediately after the Sermon on the Mount—a circumstance relied on by those who assert the identity of the two sermons; but on the other hand, the miracle which intervenes in St. Matthew seems to be identical with that given by St. Luke (v. 12), much earlier and before the call of the apostles.

2. *The servant of a certain centurion.* A *centurion* was originally a commander of one hundred soldiers. Every Roman legion was divided into ten *cohorts*, each cohort into three *maniples*, and each maniple into two *centuries*. Thus a legion was supposed to number six thousand men; but in point of fact it usually numbered considerably fewer, so that there were less than one hundred men in a so-called century. A centurion had superior officers over him, and likewise inferior officers under him. It will thus be seen that a cohort to some extent corresponds with our *regiment* or *battalion:* the century to our *company*, and the centurion to our *captain*, who is usually in command of from sixty to one hundred men. The Roman troops of Judea had their head-quarters at the great seaport of Cæsarea, where the Procurator also lived. It is said that five cohorts were stationed there, and only one at Jerusalem; but at the time of the feasts, reinforcements were sent up to preserve order: see on iii. 1. In Galilee there would be fewer Roman soldiers, for it was under Herod's rule; but there were *some*, for the Imperial officers never allowed the vassal princes any chance of feeling independent. A small garrison is known to have

being sick, was ready to die. And when he had heard of 3 Jesus, he sent unto him the ancients of the Jews, desiring him to come and heal his servant. And when they came 4 to Jesus, they besought him earnestly, saying to him, He is worthy that thou shouldest do this for him. For he 5 loveth our nation : and he hath built us a synagogue. And 6 Jesus went with them. And when he was now not far from the house, the centurion sent his friends to him, saying : Lord, trouble not thyself. For I am not worthy that thou shouldest enter under my roof. For which cause neither 7 did I think myself worthy to come to thee ; but say the word, and my servant shall be healed. For I also am a 8 man subject to authority, having under me soldiers : and I say to one, Go, and he goeth ; and to another, Come, and he cometh ; and to my servant, Do this, and he doth it.

been kept at Capharnaum, as a trade and customs' centre ; and the beautiful marble synagogue there was built for the Jews by this Roman, who had no doubt been stationed there for years and had become a "proselyte," as not a few Romans in all parts of the world were at that time.

3. *He sent unto him the ancients of the Jews.* The Jews naturally detested the Roman soldiers, and the Pharisees declared the emblems they carried to be idolatrous, because they contained a figure of the Emperor, to which absurd honours were paid. Hence the fact of this centurion being so highly esteemed by the "ancients," or chief men of the synagogue, would be hardly possible if he were not a proselyte.

5. *He hath built us a synagogue.* If Tell Hum is really the site of ancient Capharnaum and the ruins of a marble building are those of this very synagogue, they show that the centurion did his good work with great liberality ; for it was evidently once a magnificent building.

6. *Lord, trouble not thyself.* In St. Matthew's account of the same miracle, the centurion himself is made to utter the words here used by his friends. Either of two explanations is possible. (1) St. Matthew may have been speaking in general language, in which case he might regard a message sent by the centurion as equivalent to words used by him ; or (2) otherwise we must suppose that he met our Lord outside his house, and then himself repeated what he had already instructed others to say.

I am not worthy that thou shouldest enter under my roof. The words of this humble protestation are said daily in the Mass applied to the priest and faithful as they are about to receive our Lord in Holy Communion.

8. *For I also*, &c. The meaning of this verse is that if he, a centurion, subject to authority and accustomed to obey, could nevertheless command those under him, how much more would Christ, the Lord of

9 Which Jesus hearing, marvelled: and turning about to the multitude that followed him, he said: Amen I say to you, I have not found so great faith not even in Israel. And 10 they who were sent being returned to the house, found the servant whole who had been sick.

Raising of the Widow's Son.

(VERS. 11-17.)

11 And it came to pass afterwards, that he went into a city that is called Naim; and there went with him his disciples, 12 and a great multitude. And when he came nigh to the

heaven and earth, be able to command the forces of nature, and heal his servant without necessarily coming to him. It implies, therefore, a very strong confession of our Lord's Divine power—which few people understood so clearly at this early stage of the ministry.

9. *I have not found so great faith, not even in Israel.* The faith of the centurion was a lesson even to the Jews; and accordingly our Lord worked the desired miracle.

11. *A city that is called Naim.* This is one of the very few places connected with Gospel history of which the exact site is known. The word signifies "Beautiful," and its situation fully bears out the title. It was about twenty-five miles from Capharnaum, on one of the main roads from Damascus and the Lake to Jerusalem and Egypt. Our Lord arrived there the next day, according to one reading, or soon afterwards, according to ours. The difference depends only on the gender of the article. If it is ἐν τῇ ἑξῆς, we understand ἡμέρᾳ; if it is ἐν τῷ ἑξῆς, we understand χρόνῳ.

12. *A dead man was carried out.* The Jews always disposed of their dead by burial. The funerals were accompanied with much ceremony. The body was prepared by a kind of partial embalming in spices, and was bound up with linen bands. Cf. John xix. 40. Then it was carried on a plain bier or litter, or sometimes an open coffin, to the place of burial, which was, when possible, a vault, catacomb, or rock tomb. Such are the tombs of the kings now shown near Jerusalem, and there is a series of very similar rock tombs still to be seen in the hills near Thabor, not far from Naim. The tombs were always outside the city, and no habitation could be made over them, for all who passed over or touched them became legally unclean; hence the custom of "whitening." The procession to the tomb was a mournful sight. In front of the bier walked flute players, drawing plaintive notes from their pipes, while the hired mourners sang with much demonstration of grief. In the present case, being the funeral of the only son of a widow, well known in the small town, an unusually large number of people were following.

gate of the city, behold a dead man was carried out, the only son of his mother; and she was a widow: and a great multitude of the city was with her. Whom when the Lord 13 had seen, being moved with mercy towards her, he said to her: Weep not. And he came near and touched the bier. 14 And they that carried it, stood still. And he said: Young man, I say to thee, arise. And he that was dead, sat up, 15 and began to speak. And he gave him to his mother. And there came a fear on them all: and they glorified 16 God, saying: A great prophet is risen up among us: and God hath visited his people. And this rumour of him 17 went forth throughout all Judea, and throughout all the country round about.

13. *He said to her: Weep not.* The present miracle belongs to the class of unsolicited favours bestowed by our Lord. Probably nothing was further from the widow's mind than asking His help, and the idea of her son being raised to life again would never have occurred to her.

14. *They that carried it stood still.* Our Lord evidently spoke with authority, for the bearers of the body stopped instinctively, and waited to see what was to happen.

15. *He that was dead sat up.* There are only three recorded instances of our Lord raising the dead, two of which occur in St. Luke, the second being the daughter of Jairus (viii. 54, 55). We may assume that he, as a physician, must have inquired into the evidence, and satisfied himself that these astounding miracles were authentic. It is quite possible that the young man of Naim and the daughter of Jairus might have been alive when he wrote, for neither would have been more than fifty years old. The name is not mentioned in either case; perhaps for reasons similar to those supposed in the case of the family of Lazarus: see on x. 38. In two of the three cases recorded it was an only child. The words of our Lord to the disciples of St. John (*v.* 22) seem to indicate that there were other cases than those recorded, and that these are related, as in the case of the lepers, the palsied, the blind, &c., merely as examples of a class.

16. *A great prophet is risen up*, i.e., one who can do at a word the greatest thing which Elias (3 Kings xvii. 22) and Eliseus (4 Kings iv. 34) had done.

17. *This rumour of him went forth.* On a trade road, and by the city gate, there were many whose business would take them at once into Judea; and such an event would be spread by rumour from khan to khan all along the route.

throughout all Judea. The term Judea here seems to mean all the country of the Jews—including Galilee and Perea: for the rumour is said in the next verse to have reached St. John, who was then in Perea: see on iv. 44.

Deputation from St. John Baptist. Christ's Witness to Him.

(VERS. 18-35.)

¹⁸ And John's disciples told him of all these things. And ¹⁹ John called to him two of his disciples, and sent them to Jesus, saying : Art thou he that art to come ; or look we ²⁰ for another ? And when the men were come unto him, they said : John the Baptist hath sent us to thee, saying : Art thou he that art to come ; or look we for another ? ²¹ And in that same hour, he cured many of their diseases, and hurts, and evil spirits : and to many that were blind

18. *And John's disciples told him.* The evangelist seems to connect the rumour of the miracle at Naim with St. John's message. If this is so, some interval of time must have elapsed for the report to reach him. He was in prison, as he had been for months past, at Machærus (see on iii. 20), but his disciples were allowed some intercourse with him, and he was not altogether cut off from the outside world though he was probably not allowed by his gaolers to preach or teach any more.

19. *Art thou he that art to come?* The message of St. John does not imply any wavering of *his own* faith. For if this had really been a mark of doubt, and a message sent by one seeking for a sign to prevent his final unbelief, it is impossible to suppose that our Lord would have taken this very occasion to deliver a long eulogy on the merits of St. John, mentioning especially his constancy (*v.* 24). The true explanation is easily suggested. St. John's whole mission had been to preach the coming of our Lord. His character had been throughout one of self-effacement (iii. 16, 17, and John i. 20 *seq.*). Nevertheless, among his disciples a worldly spirit had shown itself, and there had already been signs of jealousy between them and our Lord's disciples (see John iii. 26 ; Matt. ix. 14). We know that some of St. John's disciples did not even at the last accept our Lord's Gospel, and that even after Pentecost there were those who had "only John's baptism." Now he most probably knew that his death was not far distant, and looking forward to it, seeing his own disciples left as sheep without a shepherd, would naturally be eager that they would turn from him to our Lord. But at that time such was not their inclination. He therefore sent two of them to Him ; with perfect trust that He would remove all doubts from their minds, and would meet the difficulty which John found himself unable to overcome, whether by reason of their obstinacy or of his own lack of freedom to instruct them properly.

he gave sight. And answering, he said to them: Go and 22 relate to John what you have heard and seen : The blind see, the lame walk, the lepers are made clean, the deaf hear, the dead rise again, to the poor the gospel is preached. And blessed is he whosoever shall not be scandalized in 23 me. And when the messengers of John were departed, 24 he began to speak to the multitudes concerning John. What went you out into the desert to see? a reed shaken with the wind? But what went you out to see? a man 25 clothed in soft garments? Behold they that are in costly apparel and live delicately, are in the houses of kings. But what went you out to see? a prophet? Yea, I say to 26 you, and more than a prophet. This is he of whom it is 27 written : *Behold I send my angel before thy face, who shall*

22. *The blind see, the lame walk.* (See Isa. xxxv. 4 and 5, and lxi. 1.) Our Lord no doubt was referring to both these texts, the latter of which He had made the subject of His discourse at Nazareth (iv. 18, 19). The answer may be taken in a threefold sense. First, He pointed to these miracles as His credentials and as evidences of His mission. Secondly, He pointed out works of mercy which were distinctive marks of a true religion (cf. James i. 27). Thirdly, each of these corporal works had an allegorical reference to the spiritual works of the Church. The faithful receive light and strength, so that the blind see and the lame walk. They are cleansed from the leprosy of sin. Those whose souls were dead rise again ; and the poor in spirit have a special insight into the Divine wisdom. These things He may of course have expounded further either to them or to the twelve, as with the parables.

23. *Whosoever shall not be scandalized in me.* For the meaning of " scandalize," see on xvii. 1. The concluding words may have been addressed to the disciples of St. John or to the Pharisees and other bystanders who were listening with a hostile spirit. These two classes had actually come together and formed a deputation not very long before to address our Lord (Mark ii. 18).

24. *What went you out into the desert to see?* Our Lord ended with a final testimony of St. John, who had begun by testifying to Him. He gives two reasons why all the people went out to hear him. The first was his fixity and firmness of purpose, the second his ascetic life : see on iii. 1. We may suppose that at the end of *v.* 24, and again at the end of *v.* 25, there is probably a break, and that our Lord in fact went on to enforce and amplify the point of each of His questions to the crowd.

26. *A prophet?* There is some question as to this word in the text, for it is absent in the Sinaitic and others of the best MSS. It is also absent in St. Matthew's account. Some think that its insertion here is

28 *prepare the way before thee.* For I say to you: Amongst those that are born of women, there is not a greater prophet than John the Baptist. But he that is the lesser 29 in the kingdom of God, is greater than he. And all the people hearing, and the publicans, justified God, being 30 baptized with John's baptism. But the Pharisees and the lawyers despised the counsel of God against themselves, 31 being not baptized by him. And the Lord said: Whereunto then shall I liken the men of this generation? and to 32 what are they like? They are like to children sitting in the

a gloss; but it is equally probable that its omission was due to an erroneous fancy that St. Luke must have used exactly the same words as the other Gospel.

more than a prophet. St. John was more than a prophet, for he had himself been prophesied of, and he was an eye-witness of the fulfilment of the prophecies of old. On the meaning of the word prophet, see on i. 76.

28. *He that is the lesser in the kingdom of God.* The meaning of this is somewhat obscure. Perhaps our Lord was drawing a distinction between the person and office of the Precursor. No greater preacher or prophet of the Old Dispensation had existed, but the least in the new kingdom, or under the New Law, had a more exalted office than even St. John. Some, however, think that the "kingdom of God" here refers to heaven, and that the meaning is that the least in heaven is greater than the greatest on earth. The parallel text in St. Matthew (xi. 11) does not altogether solve the difficulty, but perhaps throws some light on it, for he adds immediately the well known words, "And from the days of John the Baptist until now, the kingdom of heaven suffereth violence and the violent bear it away," meaning perhaps that since our Lord's ministry had begun, this new kingdom with its higher spiritual glory and privilege was open to the humblest, if they chose to overcome the obstacles in themselves and their surroundings, and procure by conquest their right to enter in and bear the prize. See also Luke xvi. 16.

29. *And all the people hearing.* The words which follow are probably still our Lord's, and hence refer to a past time. Those who listened to St. John and received his Baptism, even the outcast publicans, corresponded with the designs of God. The others, who should have known God's "counsel," by pride turned the purposes of Providence to their own condemnation.

31. *And the Lord said.* These words are absent in all the best MSS., and they obscure, what is probably the fact, that the whole is part of the same discourse. They were probably inserted by some copyist, under the impression that *vv.* 29 and 30 were an interpolation by the evangelist, and not our Lord's words at all.

32. *We have piped to you and you have not danced.* The meaning

market-place, and speaking one to another, and saying: We have piped to you, and you have not danced: we have mourned, and you have not wept. For John the Baptist 33 came neither eating bread nor drinking wine; and you say: He hath a devil. The son of man is come eating 34 and drinking; and you say: Behold a man that is a glutton and a drinker of wine, a friend of publicans and sinners. And wisdom is justified by all her children. 35

Supper at the Pharisee's house. Anointing of Christ's Feet.

(VERS. 36-50.)

And one of the Pharisees desired him to eat with him. 36 And he went into the house of the Pharisee, and sat down

of this is clear, though the details of the allusion are not known with certainty. It has been thought to refer to games played by children who alternately acted weddings and funerals; and "this generation" is likened to those perverse ones who would not join in either. When you play them music they don't want to dance; if you humour them and offer them a sad theme, they turn round and object to that as readily.

33. *You say: he hath a devil.* Cf. Luke i. 15; Mark i. 6. Like these ill-tempered and perverse children, nothing would please the Pharisees, neither the wonderful abstinence of St. John, nor the outwardly more social life of our Lord. Yet both the one and the other were the outcome of true wisdom, according to different circumstances, and "children of wisdom" will look on it in this light; that is, they will take neither amiss, but will see how in each "wisdom" is "justified." Probably the word σοφία here is used with a reference to the use of it in the Septuagint, where it often indicates (in the later books) the "Divine Wisdom" in a sense which almost anticipates the λόγος of St. John.

36. *And he went into the house of the Pharisee.* There is no indication in what town the Pharisee's supper took place. The last town mentioned is Naim, and some have thought, without any reason, that it took place there. If "the sinner" mentioned was, as Catholics generally believe, the same person as Mary Magdalen, it is more probable that the supper was at Magdala, which was a flourishing town not far distant, on the western shore of the lake of Genesareth, where she is understood to have lived in the days of her sinfulness. Whether she was married there, or whether, as some suppose, she chanced to have there some property in her own right—for the family was wealthy —we can only conjecture. If she were merely absent from her home as

37 to meat. And behold a woman that was in the city, a sinner, when she knew that he sat at meat in the Pharisee's 38 house, brought an alabaster box of ointment: and standing behind at his feet, she began to wash his feet with tears, and wiped them with the hairs of her head, and kissed his 39 feet, and anointed them with the ointment. And the Pharisee, who had invited him, seeing it, spoke within himself, saying: This man, if he were a prophet, would know surely who and what manner of woman this is that toucheth him, 40 that she is a sinner. And Jesus answering, said to him: Simon, I have somewhat to say to thee. But he said:

a sinner and an outcast, she would hardly have had a *name* indicating this town.

37. *A woman that was in the city, a sinner.* On the reasons for identifying this sinner with Mary Magdalen, see on viii. 2. St. Luke might naturally refrain from identifying them in so many words, through a feeling of consideration for one so holy as Mary Magdalen became, just as he never identifies Matthew and Levi. On the question of her identity with Mary of Bethany, see on x. 39. If they were identical, St. Luke would have had additional reasons for reticence about the sinner, for there were reasons for his not speaking much about the family of Bethany: see on x. 38. It will be remembered that there is a story that she was converted by catching, as she passed the door, a *look* of the Lord's face; as with Peter in the courtyard.

38. *Standing behind at his feet.* In a large house the dining-hall looked on the courtyard and would be open for spectators, and any one was free to enter: see on xiv. 1. The guests used to *recline* at table, so that the best position for anointing our Lord's feet would be behind Him. The ointment had no doubt been bought by the sinner for her own use, and her idea of pouring it out like water on our Lord's feet was probably meant as an abandonment of her life of pleasure, and a sign of her complete repentance. It must have been valuable, for it was carried in an alabaster box, but there is nothing to show that it was of the very costly sort that was used, probably by Mary Magdalen again, at the anointing before our Lord's Passion. All unguents were much used in the East, and the fashion found its way from thence to Imperial Rome—Cf. Horace, *passim*.

39. *That she is a sinner.* The Pharisaical idea of a sinner was as some one unclean and to be avoided. The Christian idea is the very opposite of this. Mary Magdalen must have already known something of our Lord's spirit for her to be bold enough to approach Him; but He was doubtless commonly spoken of everywhere, as He said (*v.* 34), both by friend and foe, as "the friend of sinners."

40. *Simon.* The name Simon was very common among the Jews. There are seven named in the Gospels, two of whom were apostles.

Master, say *it*. A certain creditor had two debtors, the one 41
owed him five hundred pence, and the other fifty, and 42
whereas they had not wherewith to pay, he forgave them
both. Which therefore of the two loveth him most?
Simon answering said: I suppose that he to whom he for- 43
gave most. And he said to him: Thou hast judged rightly.
And turning to the woman, he said unto Simon: Dost 44
thou see this woman? I entered into thy house, thou
gavest me no water for my feet; but she with tears hath
washed my feet, and with her hairs hath wiped them.
Thou gavest me no kiss; but she, since she came in, hath 45
not ceased to kiss my feet. My head with oil thou didst 46
not anoint; but she with ointment hath anointed my feet.
Wherefore I say to thee: Many sins are forgiven her, 47
because she hath loved much. But to whom less is
forgiven, he loveth less. And he said to her: Thy sins 48

There is, therefore, no necessity to identify this Simon with Simon the Leper (Matt. xxvi. 6; Mark xiv. 3). It is certainly a remarkable coincidence that the two anointings were both at the house of a man named Simon, though the time, place, and surroundings are different. It has been ingeniously supposed that this Simon was the same, and even that he was Mary's father, who had cast her off in her sin and whose house she would not have dared to enter again but that Jesus was there. It will be obvious that this theory would give, if it were true, a double force to the dramatic story of our Lord's words from this to the end of the chapter; but of course it is only the merest conjecture.

44. *Thou gavest me no water for my feet.* It is evident that Simon had not treated our Lord very considerately—probably because he did not recognize Him as a Rabbi, and wished to show his friends that he did not. To give water for the feet and a kiss of welcome would have been only ordinary courtesy. To anoint our Lord's head would have been a mark of greater honour, though by no means unusual. For any notable Rabbi Simon would have done all these things and more: cf. Ps. xxii. 5, &c.

45. *Since she came in.* Many ancient MSS. read, "Since I came in," and this has been followed in the A.V. The difference depends on the question whether we think of her as coming in with our Lord or after He had sat down. The latter seems more likely.

47. *Many sins are forgiven her.* The forgiveness is the consequence of the love and *vice versâ*. The two go hand in hand. The more we detach ourselves from our sins and give ourselves whole-heartedly to God, the more we shall grow in the love of God and *vice versâ*.

48. *Thy sins are forgiven thee.* Our Lord pronounces a formal absolution, apparently for the purpose of giving the penitent the assur-

are forgiven thee. And they that sat at meat with him began to say within themselves: Who is this that forgiveth sins also? And he said to the woman: Thy faith hath made thee safe, go in peace.

ance she was waiting for, and doubtless as a type of sacramental absolution.

49. *Who is this that forgiveth sins also?* Cf. v. 21.

50. *Thy faith hath made thee safe.* It was the faith of the "sinner" that had been the guiding principle of her turning to Jesus as her Saviour, and hence it was that which led her to conversion. That "faith" was not only her confidence in His attributes of mercy and forgiveness, without which she would not have ventured to approach Him, but also, as we may infer from His final words, an acceptance of Him as the Messiah, by reason of all she had heard and seen of His works, and His preaching in Galilee. It may well be that it was precisely *because* she knew how He preached the Kingdom of God to the poor and the outcast, that she, whom the harsh justice of the Pharisees had only hardened, was led to believe that His "good tidings" were the Word of God

CHAPTER VIII.

Missionary Journeys with the Twelve. The Ministering Women.

(VERS. 1-3.)

AND it came to pass afterwards, that he travelled through the cities and towns, preaching and evangelizing the kingdom of God; and the twelve with him. And certain women who had been healed of evil spirits and infirmities; Mary who is called Magdalen, out

> **1.** *And it came to pass afterwards.* The words ($\dot{\epsilon}\nu\ \tau\tilde{\varphi}\ \kappa\alpha\theta\epsilon\xi\tilde{\eta}\varsigma$) which we render "afterwards" denote a new phase or period of our Lord's ministry. Capharnaum was no longer the centre from which He went to preach to villages near at hand. He now made a wide circuit in Galilee, "through the cities and towns."
> *And the twelve with Him.* He ($\alpha\dot{\upsilon}\tau\dot{o}\varsigma$) is contrasted with οἱ δώδεκα and γυναῖκές τινες—Himself, and the twelve, and certain women. The twelve, whose training was now His chief care, were henceforward always with Him. They formed a little community and had goods in common, for we know that Judas carried the common purse (John xii. 6).
> **2.** *And certain women who had been healed.* The picture is completed by St. Luke with the mention of the ministering women. Their motive in following was gratitude for the cures wrought on them; but their presence was a necessity now that a community had been formed by the apostles. Women were accustomed to minister to the Rabbis, whose rapacity in this respect was rebuked by our Lord (xx. 47: Matt. xxiii. 14; Mark xii. 40). In allowing them to join in the missionary journey, our Lord broke through the narrow circle which Eastern custom had drawn round women, and emancipated them in the noblest sense.
> *Mary who is called Magdalen.* The name Magdalen must be from the town Magdala, on the shore of the lake. From this time forward Mary Magdalen appears as the most prominent of the holy women, and (except in John xix. 25) she is always placed first when others are

3 of whom seven devils were gone forth, and Joanna the wife of Chusa, Herod's steward, and Susanna, and many others who ministered unto him of their substance.

Parable of the Sower.

(VERS. 4–8.)

4 And when a very great multitude was gathered together and hastened out of the cities unto him, he spoke by a

mentioned. The only particular given as to antecedents is that " seven devils " had gone forth from her: cf. Mark xvi. 9. The expression " seven devils " occurs in connection with only one other incident in the Gospels (see on xi. 26), and then evidently denotes a sinful state of life, or a guilty surrender to the possession of devils. Cf. xxii. 3 and John xiii. 27, where a somewhat similar expression is used of Judas when he finally yielded to the temptations of Satan. It seems natural, even apart from the authority of tradition, to connect the sudden appearance of Magdalen from whom seven devils had been cast, with the sinner whose conversion has just been recorded, and whom we should naturally expect to find as a follower of our Lord. The identity of the two has been commonly accepted since the time of St. Gregory, at least in the Western Church. On the identity of either with Mary of Bethany, there has been more difference of opinion: see on x. 39. Here it may just be remarked that on the supposition of their being identical, we should find an easy explanation of these women " ministering unto Him of their substance," for the family of Martha and Mary were rich.

3. *Joanna, the wife of Chusa, Herod's steward.* The name of Joanna occurs again in connection with the Resurrection (xxiv. 10). Some have identified Chusa, Herod's steward, with the "ruler" ($\beta a\sigma i\lambda\iota\kappa\dot{o}\varsigma$ = *lit.* king's officer): cf. John iv. 46. St. Luke seems to have known something of Herod's court, possibly from Manahen, Herod's foster brother, whom he mentions in the Acts (xiii. 1) as a convert to Christianity. See ix. 7–9.

and Susanna. Of Susanna we know nothing further. According to all tradition, our Lady would have been with these holy women, though she is mentioned by name only once or twice.

and many others. Cf. Matt. xxvii. 55; Mark xv. 41.

4. *He spoke by a similitude.* This similitude is the first of the regular series of parables of our Lord, and is given as such by all three synoptists. See Matt. xiii. 3; Mark iv. 3. There was nothing new in itself in our Lord making use of a similitude, or parable, to teach the people; already He had often done so incidentally: see v. 36–39, vi. 47–49, vii. 31–35, 41–43. It was a usual way of teaching in the East, and used commonly by the Rabbis. It has been said that the Western mind thinks in abstraction, but the Eastern in imagery.

similitude. The sower went out to sow his seed. And as 5
he sowed some fell by the way side, and it was trodden
down, and the fowls of the air devoured it. And other 6
some fell upon a rock; and as soon as it was sprung up,

Our Lord had often used this method before, but now He began to teach *exclusively* in parables (Mark iv. 33), and hence the parables became, in many cases, longer and more complete. His reasons are recorded by St. Matthew (xiii. 13-15). The enmity of the Pharisees and of the chief men among the Jews was making itself felt, and a considerable proportion of His hearers were not listening for instruction, but as spies and emissaries sent to ensnare Him. The new form of teaching gave them little chance of anything definite to take hold of, while it enabled those who wished for instruction to obtain it. The subjects chosen by our Lord were always such as His hearers would be familiar with. Thus, for example, teaching in Galilee, He gave the parable of the Sower and Seed, the Cockle, the Mustard Seed, &c.; in Judea, a pastoral country, the Lost Sheep; at other times, instances from every day life, such as the Lost Groat, the Debtor and Creditor, the Leaven, &c. Some, e.g., the Good Samaritan and the Prodigal Son, are supposed to have been true stories, well known to many of our Lord's hearers, and specially chosen by Him to convey certain moral lessons. It is important to bear in mind that whether they were histories or not, the parables were each meant to convey certain truths, and those only. We must not look for special teaching in every detail. It would, for example, be quite as idle to take the parable of the Sower as showing the number of the elect to form a comparatively small class of men, as it would be to deduce from the parable of the Lost Sheep that ninety nine per cent. of the human race never went astray; and that the one per cent. who did so were brought back again. Each is meant to convey its own lesson: the one to point out the different effect of God's Word according to the dispositions with which it is received; the other to show God's will for the conversion of every sinner. So also with the Prodigal Son. One side of God's dealing with sinners is shown, namely, His readiness to forgive; but the picture of God seeking the obdurate sinner is not brought prominently forward: see on chap. xv.

5. *The sower went out to sow*, &c. St. Luke does not tell us where the parable was delivered; but from St. Matthew and St. Mark we learn that it was by the edge of the lake, and—as once recorded by St. Luke (v. 1)—our Lord preached from a boat, while the multitude stood on the shore. The subject of the parable was familiar to those who lived in the neighbourhood of Lake Genesareth, where the land was rich and usually well cultivated. Across the fields were beaten tracks, where seed would be trodden down by the passers by, and would fail to take root; while the birds would be ready to eat any which was left exposed.

6. *And other some fell upon a rock.* Rocky or stony places were

7 it withered away, because it had no moisture. And other some fell among thorns, and the thorns growing up with
8 it, choked it. And other some fell upon good ground; and being sprung up yielded fruit a hundred fold. Saying these things, he cried out: He that hath ears to hear, let him hear.

Explanation and Discourse to the Twelve.
(Vers. 9–18.)

9 And his disciples asked him what this parable might
10 be. To whom he said: To you it is given to know the mystery of the kingdom of God: but to the rest in parables, that seeing they may not see, and hearing
11 may not understand. Now the parable is this: The seed
12 is the word of God. And they by the way side are they

common enough. St. Matthew and St. Mark mention want of soil in such places as the cause of the seed withering; St. Luke notes want of moisture, which, however, is implied in the expression that the seed was scorched by the sun, which the other synoptists use.

7. *And other some fell among thorns.* The thorns would be weeds, not unlike our thistles, which grew to a considerable size—and it is furthermore characteristic of many noxious weeds that they grow very rapidly.

8. *Yielded fruit a hundredfold.* The other two evangelists add, some sixty fold and some thirty. St. Mark adds a few descriptive details of the growth of the fruit.

10. *To you it is given to know the mystery of the kingdom of God.* To understand our Lord's answer we must turn to St. Matthew (xiii. 10 *seq.*), where we find that the apostles first asked why our Lord had begun to teach only in parables. The first part of His answer refers to that question. The fact that many of the people, though they saw and heard, did not understand, was, of course, not God's wish, but the effect of their want of disposition. And although those in bad dispositions hear without understanding at the moment, they may remember the parable afterwards, and when they come to good dispositions its teaching will be clear and helpful. Our Lord said to all (*v.* 8): "He that hath ears to hear, let him hear."

11. *The seed is the word of God.* In its primary sense our Lord Himself is the sower. In a secondary sense we may take it to denote any one who preaches the Word of God, and, indeed, any means (e.g., books or example) whereby His truth is made known.

12. *They by the way side are they that hear.* The first class of

that hear; then the devil cometh, and taketh the word
out of their heart, lest believing they should be saved.
Now they upon the rock, *are they* who when they hear, 13
receive the word with joy: and these have no roots: for
they believe for awhile, and in time of temptation they fall
away. And that which fell among thorns, are they who 14
have heard, and going their way, are choked with the
cares and riches and pleasures of this life, and yield no
fruit. But that on the good ground, are they who in a 15
good and very good heart, hearing the word, keep it, and
bring forth fruit in patience. Now no man lighting a 16
candle covereth it with a vessel, or putteth it under a bed;
but setteth it upon a candlestick, that they who come in
may see the light. For there is not anything secret, that 17
shall not be made manifest; nor hidden, that shall not be

hearers who fail to profit by the Word are those who are callous and indifferent.

the devil cometh. See on iv. 2. The direct statement of our Lord Himself is a proof of the existence of a personal devil, and one who is always on the alert to take grace away from those who receive it.

13. *They upon the rock.* The second class is one with which we are very familiar, in whom excitement and enthusiasm for the moment is the important factor. Thus Herod heard John gladly (Mark vi. 20), but it was only the gladness of the moment. Such people have nothing to fall back upon in time of temptation or trial, when the first impulsive enthusiasm has passed away.

15. *And bring forth fruit in patience.* This expression should be noticed. That our chief work is to continue in patience is brought prominently forward throughout the epistles of St. Paul and elsewhere in the New Testament: cf. Rom. v. 3, 4, viii. 25; 2 Cor. vi. 4; Heb. xii. 1; Apoc. xiii. 10, &c., &c.

16. *No man lighting a candle covereth it with a vessel.* The next three verses include a parable addressed specially to the apostles. They are the light of the world, a light which is not to be hidden, but to shine before men. The other two synoptists describe our Lord as saying that the candle is not to be placed "under a bushel." A bushel was a dry measure, equivalent to about a peck with us. St. Luke speaks instead of the vessel which contains it, as more intelligible to his readers who were for the most part unfamiliar with Jewish measures and times. See Matt. v. 15; Mark iv. 21.

17. *There is not anything secret that shall not be made manifest.* The sense of this follows easily on the preceding verse, and leads up to the following. All truths, however secret at present between our Lord and His apostles, were to be shortly published over the

18 known and come abroad. Take heed therefore how you hear. For whosoever hath, to him shall be given; and whosoever hath not, that also which he thinketh he hath, shall be taken away from him.

The Mother and Brethren of our Lord.

(VERS. 19-21.)

19 And his mother and brethren came unto him; and 20 they could not come at him for the crowd. And it was told him: Thy mother and thy brethren stand without

face of the earth. Hence the responsibility on their shoulders to listen to His words. If they are faithful in this, many graces will be given them for their future ministry. That this is the true sense is clear from the context. The more obvious meaning, if *v.* 17 stood alone, would be a reference to the discovery of secret crimes at the day of judgment: cf. *infra.* xii. 2, where such is evidently the meaning. In the case before us, however, this would not accord with the context before and after.

19. *And his mother and brethren came unto him.* This incident is given by the other two synoptists *before* the parable of the sower. If it occurred afterwards it must have been between the announcement of the parable and its explanation, as the multitudes were still surrounding our Lord.

The word "brethren," according to scriptural usage, may be taken to mean any near relative; but the question as to who the brethren of our Lord actually were, that is, what was their relationship to Him, cannot be considered yet certainly decided. Their names are given by St. Mark (vi. 3) as James, Joseph (? Joses), Judas, and Simon. St. Matthew tells us that among those present at the crucifixion was Mary, mother of James, and Joseph; and as St. John mentions in the same context, His mother's sister, Mary of Cleophas (more properly Clopas: see on xxiv. 18), it is natural to identify Mary of Cleophas as sister of our Lady, and mother of James and Joseph. Then St. Luke calls the apostles James (the less) and Jude the sons of Alpheus, and the names Alpheus and Cleophas come from the same Hebrew original; and as St. James is called by St. Paul (Gal. i. 19) "the brother of the Lord," this seems at first to bind together and establish the whole theory. According to this view, accepted by St. Jerome, St. Augustine, and the Latin fathers generally, Mary of Alpheus or Cleophas, was our Lady's sister, and some of the "brethren" (but not necessarily all of them) were her children. The chief difficulty in the way of accepting this is the fact that it implies two sisters having both the same name, Mary, which is most unlikely. A second reason of a different kind, but not to be altogether set aside, is that it certainly would appear *a priori* more fitting and

desiring to see thee. Who answering said to them: My ²¹ mother and my brethren, are they who hear the word of God, and do it.

The Storm on the Lake.

(VERS. 22-25.)

And it came to pass on a certain day, that he went into ²² a little ship with his disciples, and he said to them: Let us go over to the other side of the lake. And they launched

more likely that our Lady should have been an only child. To meet these two objections it has been supposed that the two Marys were not sisters but cousins. This would make the "brethren" second cousins of our Lord, which theory may perhaps be provisionally accepted; though second cousin is certainly a distant relationship to be denoted by the word ἀδελφοί. The supposition of the "brethren" being sons of St. Joseph by a former marriage, though supported by some of the Greek fathers, has little else to recommend it; and that of "his mother's sister" and "Mary of Cleophas" (John xix. 25) being two distinct persons, would necessitate a complete reconsideration of many points which have been long regarded as settled.

21. *My mother and my brethren are they who hear the word of God and do it.* It has often been assumed by non-Catholic writers that this answer was in some sense a rebuke, as though our Lord's mother and brethren had come at an unseasonable time. There is no evidence whatever of this. None of the evangelists who narrate the incident either say or imply that our Lord did not immediately go to them; and the fact that He utilised the occasion to give His hearers a spiritual lesson, is exactly in keeping with what we know as to His customary way of acting throughout the ministry. His meaning would be to point to His love for His mother and brethren; and to explain that His love for others would be of the same kind, in proportion only to the degree of their love of God. If He had meant anything else, and if the interruption had been really unseasonable, surely on the most extreme Protestant view of the position of the Blessed Virgin, our Lord would hardly have rebuked her publicly before all the people.

22. It appears from St. Mark (iv. 35) that the next incident related happened in the evening of the day on which our Lord spoke the parable of the Sower; and from St. Matthew (viii. 18) that crowds surrounded Him on the shore. Possibly the explanation of the parable belongs to a later time, when our Lord was alone with His disciples, perhaps during the first part of the time when they were in the boat, and the crowd on the shore would be those who had listened to the parable. This would in that case be another illustration of St. Luke's

23 forth. And when they were sailing, he slept; and there came down a storm of wind upon the lake, and they were 24 filled, and were in danger. And they came and awakened him, saying: Master, we perish. But he arising rebuked the wind and the rage of the water; and it ceased, and there 25 was a calm. And he said to them: Where is your faith? Who being afraid, wondered, saying one to another: Who is this (think you) that he commandeth both the winds and the sea, and they obey him?

The Demoniac in the Country of the Gerasens.

(VERS. 26-39.)

26 And they sailed to the country of the Gerasens which

habit of finishing off one subject before going on to another; and in this instance, St. Matthew and St. Mark do likewise, so as not to separate the parable from its explanation.

23. *There came down a storm of wind upon the lake.* Sudden storms are characteristic of all lakes or inland seas, and the lake of Genesareth is specially noted to this day for the suddenness and violence of its storms. It was quite possible that the boat might have capsized. Our Lord was sleeping—St. Mark adds the detail that He was on a pillow in the hinder part of the ship—and the alarm of the apostles was perfectly natural.

24. *Master, we perish.* In the original Greek, the word Master (ἐπιστάτα) is repeated twice, showing the apostles' agony of mind. *But he arising rebuked the wind and the rage of the water.* Our Lord's power over winds and waves depended on His Divinity. Had the faith of the apostles been more perfect, they would have realized better that the Providence of God is not suspended by sleep. The whole incident is typical of the troubles and dangers of life which are continually coming on us. It often needs great faith not to be discouraged, nor to think that God has deserted us. It refers in a special manner to the troubles and dangers which the Church, of which the barque of Peter is the type, has to face. We know, however, that Christ will not desert her, nor cease to watch over her. "Ecce non dormitabit neque dormiet qui custodit Israel" (Ps. cxx. 4).

25. *Where is your faith?* St. Luke as usual spares the twelve and relates the rebuke in milder terms than St. Mark or St. Matthew.

26. *And they sailed to the country of the Gerasens.* The readings here vary between Gadarenes, Gerasens, and Gergesenes. The A.V. reads Gergesenes here and in the corresponding passage of St. Matthew; but Gadarenes in that of St. Mark. The Douay version,

is over against Galilee. And when he was come forth to 27
the land, there met him a certain man who had a devil now
a very long time, and he wore no clothes, neither did he
abide in a house, but in the sepulchres. And when he saw 28
Jesus, he fell down before him; and crying out with a
loud voice, he said: What have I to do with thee, Jesus,
Son of the most high God? I beseech thee do not torment me. For he commanded the unclean spirit to go out 29
of the man. For many times it seized him, and he was
bound with chains, and kept in fetters; and breaking the
bonds he was driven by the devil into the deserts. And 30
Jesus asked him, saying: What is thy name? But he
said: Legion; because many devils were entered into him.

following the Vulgate, adopts the reading Gerasens in all three. Gerasa was a large and flourishing town, some fifty miles from the lake and near the confines of Arabia. Being a large town it may possibly have given its name to the surrounding district. Gadara was at the south end of the lake, but much nearer to it. Gergesa has been identified with Kerzha, which is nearly opposite where Capharnaum probably was; so that it appears the most probable reading of the three. The population of the country on the other side of the lake was chiefly pagan. The ten cities which originated the name of Decapolis, were almost entirely Greek. The people were full of earthly ambition, and had no special longing for a Messiah or any craving after heavenly truths.

27. *There met him a certain man who had a devil.* St. Matthew mentions (viii. 28) two demoniacs. It is probable enough that that one was much more violent than the other and better known. The description points to a case of extreme savageness. Such a person would be expelled from the towns and would live in caves or tombs of outlying districts. The text says that he wore no clothes. This is not, of course, to be taken literally: the word used ($\iota\mu\acute{a}\tau\iota o\nu$) denotes the outer garment; an inner garment ($\chi\iota\tau\acute{\omega}\nu$) of some sort he no doubt had: see on iii. 11.

28. *I beseech thee, do not torment me.* It is possible that the devils were seeking, by their cries, to obtain from our Lord a declaration of His Divinity. In any case, the presence of one who was great and holy would be to them a " torment."

30. *And Jesus asked him, saying: What is thy name?* It is noticeable how at the approach of our Lord the demoniac is at once tamed. He who had so often broken bands and fetters now talked and answered quietly. Our Lord's object seems to be to point out the personality of the devils as distinct from that of the sufferer.

But he said: Legion. The introduction of a Latin word ($\Lambda\epsilon\gamma\iota\omega\nu$) is remarkable; but since the Roman occupation the apostles may have become familiar with such terms, and even if they did not know that a

31 And they besought him that he would not command them
32 to go into the abyss. And there was there a herd of many swine feeding on the mountain; and they besought him that he would suffer them to enter into them. And he
33 suffered them. The devils therefore went out of the man, and entered into the swine; and the herd ran violently
34 down a steep place into the lake, and was stifled. Which when they that fed them saw done, they fled, and told it in
35 the city and in the villages. And they went out to see what was done; and they came to Jesus, and found the man, out of whom the devils were departed, sitting at his feet, clothed, and in his right mind, and they were afraid.
36 And they also that had seen told them how he had been
37 healed from the legion. And all the multitude of the country of the Gerasens besought him to depart from them; for they were taken with great fear. And he going up into
38 the ship returned back again. Now the man, out of whom the devils were departed, besought him that he might be
39 with him. But Jesus sent him away, saying: Return to thy

legion contained six thousand men, they would at least know that a large number was meant.

because many devils were entered into him. This is a remark of the evangelist. It has been hazarded that they numbered two thousand, the number of the swine.

31. *Into the abyss,* i.e. the prison of lost spirits. See Rom. x. 7; Apoc. ix. 1–11, xi. 7, xvii. 8, xx. 1, 3.

32. *And he suffered them.* The entrance of the devils into the swine has no parallel in the Gospels. It has been conjectured that they belonged to Jews; if so, there was an open violation of the Law, and their destruction would have had the appearance of a judgment from God. There is little force, therefore, in the consideration sometimes urged, that the destruction of property would scandalize the bystanders.

37. *All the multitude of the country of the Gerasens besought him to depart from them.* The country was semi-pagan, and the people had no disposition for repentance, and they besought our Lord to depart. We may contrast this with the very opposite conduct of the Samaritans under somewhat similar circumstances (John iv. 40).

39. *Tell how great things God hath done to thee.* The instruction to the demoniac to publish his cure to every one is notable as being the only time that our Lord bade one whom He had cured to publish the fact. At other times He enjoined secrecy. The reason is easy to see. In this case there was no prospect of a popular outburst of enthusiasm

house, and tell how great things God hath done to thee: And he went through the whole city, publishing how great things Jesus had done to him.

Healing of the Woman with an Issue of Blood. Raising of the Daughter of Jairus.

(VERS. 40-56.)

And it came to pass, that when Jesus was returned, the 40 multitude received him: for they were all waiting for him. And behold there came a man whose name was Jairus, 41 and he was a ruler of the synagogue: and he fell down at the feet of Jesus, beseeching him that he would come into his house. For he had an only daughter almost twelve 42 years old, and she was dying. And it happened, as he went, that he was thronged by the multitudes. And there 43

in His favour, and there were no Pharisees to take offence. On the other hand, the proclaiming of the miracle might lead others to faith in Christ, and the man himself to a more perfect realization of the greatness of the favour he had received.

40. *For they were all waiting for him.* Those on shore would have recognized the sail on the lake as that of our Lord's boat, for the others had been driven back overnight by the storm: so they all assembled to meet Him. The exact chronology of events which follow is uncertain. St. Matthew states that they happened on the day on which he gave his feast, and this incident St. Luke puts some time earlier. See v. 29. It has already been pointed out, however, that the feast could not easily have been on the very day of St. Matthew's call, for it would have taken some time to get ready. Both St. Luke and St. Mark give the miracle on the daughter of Jairus immediately after our Lord's return from the other side of the lake. It is possible that St. Matthew's banquet intervened between His return and going to the house of Jairus; otherwise we must suppose that St. Matthew does not mean by "as he was speaking these things" (ix. 18) more than a general note of time, like the expression "In illo tempore" used at the beginning of the Gospel in the Mass.

41. *He was a ruler of the synagogue.* The office of Ruler of the Synagogue was, of course, in no sense sacerdotal: see on iv. 15.

42. *And she was dying.* St. Matthew describes Jairus as saying that his daughter was "even now dead." Perhaps he is summarizing what he said at first with what he said after the messengers arrived (v. 49).

43. *A certain woman having an issue of blood.* An issue of blood was looked on as a special scourge from heaven and, as in all such

was a certain woman having an issue of blood twelve years, who had bestowed all her substance on physicians,
44 and could not be healed by any: She came behind him, and touched the hem of his garment; and immediately
45 the issue of her blood stopped. And Jesus said: Who is it that touched me? And all denying, Peter and they that were with him said: Master, the multitudes throng and
46 press thee, and dost thou say, Who touched me? And Jesus said: Somebody hath touched me; for I know that
47 virtue is gone out from me. And the woman seeing that she was not hid, came trembling, and fell down before his feet: and declared before all the people for what cause she had touched him, and how she was immediately healed.
48 But he said to her: Daughter, thy faith hath made thee
49 whole; go thy way in peace. As he was yet speaking, there cometh one to the ruler of the synagogue, saying to
50 him: Thy daughter is dead; trouble him not. And Jesus hearing this word, answered the father of the maid: Fear

cases, a retribution for past sin. The woman was therefore in a pitiable state. St. Luke says that the physicians' remedies had been unavailing. St. Mark, not himself a physician, adds that they had caused her much pain, and made her worse instead of better.

46. *Somebody hath touched me.* Our Lord, of course, knew exactly what was happening, but preferred to accommodate His words to His hearers. The touch of the woman would have brought with it ceremonial uncleanness; hence His words would have had a special meaning in her ears.

47. *And the woman seeing she was not hid, came trembling.* The woman therefore confessed with some fear and "trembling"; but added in justification of her conduct how she had been immediately healed. Cf. Mark v. 33.

48. *Daughter, thy faith hath made thee whole.* These words were, no doubt, designed by our Lord to point out that this was the determining cause; for to attribute the cure to mere external contact would be akin to the spirit of externalism which pervaded the Pharisees and many others of the Jews.

49. *Thy daughter is dead: trouble him not.* It is noticeable how the people assumed that, as soon as death had occurred, there was no more hope of a miraculous cure. Martha and Mary assumed the same thing before the raising of their brother Lazarus. See John xi. 21, *seq.*

50. *Fear not; believe only and she shall be safe.* Our Lord may well have had in mind, in addressing these words to Jairus, the striking miracle which had just been worked, and which He had just declared

not; believe only, and she shall be safe. And when he 51
was come to the house, he suffered not any man to go in
with him, but Peter, and James, and John, and the father
and mother of the maiden. And all wept and mourned 52
for her. But he said: Weep not; the maid is not dead,
but sleepeth. And they laughed him to scorn, knowing 53
that she was dead. But he taking her by the hand, cried 54
out, saying: Maid, arise. And her spirit returned, and 55
she rose immediately. And he bid them give her to eat.
And her parents were astonished, whom he charged to tell 56
no man what was done.

to be a reward of faith. It was, as it were, a promise that if he showed a like faith he would receive a similar favour.

51. *He suffered not any man to go in with him, but Peter, and James, and John.* We have here for the first time the three favourite apostles together with our Lord. These three and the father and mother were the only privileged witnesses of the miracle.

52. *All wept and mourned for her.* Those who wept would have been hired mourners, who began their wail immediately after death. See 2 Paral. xxxv. 25. St. Matthew describes them (ix. 23) as "the minstrels and the multitude making a rout." The presence of these "minstrels," or hired mourners, is very important, as certifying to the reality and certainty of the maiden's death.

the maid is not dead, but sleepeth. Cf. John xi. 11. Our Lord's meaning was, of course, not that death had not taken place, but that it was to be only like a sleep, inasmuch as the maiden was to wake from it.

54. *Maid arise.* St. Mark gives the actual words used by our Lord, *Talitha cumi*: St. Luke gives the Greek equivalent.

55. *Her spirit returned,* that is, she lived again; her body and soul were once more united. This is a phrase commonly used in the Old Testament, but only here in the New Testament.

56. *Whom he charged to tell no man.* See on *v*. 39. It was, of course, impossible to keep such a miracle secret. The injunction of our Lord was against the natural tendency there would have been to publish it abroad immediately and to make the house of Jairus a centre for people to assemble and see the maiden, which would have led to a display of popular enthusiasm. Such was not the object of the working of the miracle, and it would have been clearly bad in every way for the ruler. He was therefore to tell no man; that is, to let the rumour take its course and himself to return thanks to God.

CHAPTER IX.

Mission of the Apostles.

(Vers. 1-6.)

THEN calling together the twelve apostles, he gave them power and authority over all devils, and to ² cure diseases. And he sent them to preach the Kingdom ³ of God, and to heal the sick. And he said to them: Take nothing for your journey, neither staff, nor scrip, nor bread,

    1. *Then calling together the twelve apostles.* We have here an important development in the training of the apostles—they are now sent forth by themselves to minister to those who were unable to come to our Lord, and to prepare others for His arrival. From St. Matthew we learn (x. 5) that their first mission was to the Jews only. They were given power to cast out devils and to heal the sick. We know also (Mark vi. 7) that they went out in couples: see note on vi. 14; also cf. *infra* x. 1.

    3. *Take nothing for your journey.* The instructions quoted by St. Luke are much less full than those given by St. Matthew. The purport is the same. Some of the details applied by St. Matthew to this occasion agree with those given by St. Luke in connection with the mission of the seventy-two. The occasions are so similar that there is no difficulty in supposing that these particular instructions were given twice, and some actually occur twice in St. Luke.

    The picture given is our Lord's description of what an apostle should be. They were to go forward without preparations and without thought of the morrow; to take neither staff, nor scrip, nor bread, nor money. St. Mark (vi. 8) gives the words "save a staff only." It may be that some had staves, and that our Lord's meaning is that those who have not any are not to procure them; or it may be, as many think, that the forbidden "staff" was a different kind, used as a weapon. A "scrip" was a small bag thrown over the shoulders and used to carry a few necessaries. They were not to occupy their minds over these things,

nor money, neither have two coats. And whatsoever house 4
you shall enter into, abide there, and depart not from thence.
And whosoever will not receive you, when ye go out of that 5
city, shake off even the dust of your feet for a testimony
against them. And going out they went about through the 6
towns, preaching the gospel and healing everywhere.

Death of St. John the Baptist.

(VERS. 7-9.)

Now Herod the tetrarch heard of all things that were 7
done by him; and he was in a doubt because it was said
by some, that John was risen from the dead: but by other 8
some, that Elias hath appeared; and by others, that one

but to give themselves to the work of their ministry and trust to Providence. This, it must be remembered, was not so extraordinary a command as it may seem to us, for hospitality to such travelling teachers was customary. The word for money in St. Mark (χαλκόν) meant a very small brass coin, but St. Luke, as often, softens it to a less violent and more literary expression.

4. *Whatsoever house you shall enter into, abide there.* Strangers in an Oriental village would receive many invitations; the acceptance of such would distract the apostles from their work. Restlessness and the spirit that is ever desiring change is one of the most frequent obstacles in the way of apostolic work in every age; and one specially noticeable in modern life.

5. *Shake off even the dust of your feet.* It was customary for Pharisees entering Judea from a Gentile land, to shake off the dust of their shoes, in token of their want of fellowship with the heathen nations. The same symbol was to be used by the apostles to those who would not listen to them: cf. Matt. xviii. 17, "If he will not hear the church, let him be to thee as the heathen and publican."

7. *Now Herod the tetrarch heard of all things that were done by him.* St. Luke here again shows some knowledge of what occurred at the court of Herod: see on viii. 3. The words "by him" are omitted in all the best MSS. except the Alexandrian, and the passage reads more easily without them. The sense in either case is that the mission of the twelve in different directions spread the fame of our Lord's work so that it reached the ears of Herod.

8. *By some that John was risen from the dead.* The rumours as usual took various shapes, but Herod's guilty conscience made him sensitive to all of them. Though he was a Sadducee and the rumours involved a belief in the resurrection of the dead, this did not prevent them filling his mind with alarm.

9 of the old prophets was risen again. And Herod said: John I have beheaded; but who is this of whom I hear such things? And he sought to see him.

Feeding of the Five Thousand.

(Vers. 10-17.)

10 And the apostles, when they were returned, told him all they had done: and taking them he went aside into a
11 desert place apart, which belongeth to Bethsaida. Which when the people knew they followed him, and he received them, and spoke to them of the kingdom of God, and

9. *John I have beheaded.* Herod speaks as though the beheading of St. John was recent. St. Luke gives no account of it, though he gives two references to his imprisonment (iii. 20, vii. 19), and now he alludes to his beheading as if it was well known. For details of it see Matt. xiv. 3-12 or Mark vi. 17-29. If this had recently occurred it is not wonderful that Herod's mind was still disturbed about it, for we know that he had partly believed in John as a prophet. There would have been a mixture of curiosity and fear in his feeling towards our Lord. He did not succeed in gratifying his desire to see Him till the day of the Crucifixion, when we are again told he had long desired to see Him, simply in order to witness some wonder (Luke xxiii. 8).

10. *Taking them he went aside into a desert place.* We are not told how long the apostles were on their mission; it may have been weeks or even months. On their return our Lord took them to "a desert place" to rest.

which belongeth to Bethsaida. It is now known that there was a second Bethsaida besides the fishing suburb of Capharnaum, and its discovery removes an old difficulty about the desert place. This second Bethsaida, or Bethsaida Julias, was at the north end of the lake and on the *east* of the inlet of the Jordan, and its ruins still exist, though they have only lately been identified. The country around Bethsaida Julias is on the north-east shoulder of the lake up to the slopes of the mountains of Gaulon. It would be exactly what is usually described in the Gospel as desert: see on i. 80.

11. *Which when the people knew, they followed him.* From the other Gospels we learn that the multitude saw our Lord's ships, in which were the apostles, sailing up the lake, and they followed on foot; and, the distance being considerable, many of them found themselves far from their homes. Though our Lord had taken the apostles thither for the sake of rest, when all the people flocked out He could not but receive them, and He rewarded their trust in Him by a most striking miracle.

There are only two incidents in our Lord's public life recorded by all

healed them who had need of healing. Now the day began to decline. And the twelve came and said to him: Send away the multitude, that going into the towns and villages round about, they may lodge and get victuals: for we are here in a desert place. But he said to them: Give you them to eat. And they said: We have no more than five loaves and two fishes: unless perhaps we should go and buy food for all this multitude. Now there were about five thousand men. And he said to his disciples: Make them sit down by fifties in a company. And they did so. And made them all sit down. And taking the five loaves and the two fishes, he looked up to heaven, and

four evangelists. The procession of palms is one; the feeding of the five thousand is the other. The special importance of the latter lies in its having been the occasion of the sermon on the Eucharist (John vi.), of which the miracle was the type. The early Christians were so accustomed to identify the two as type and prototype, that when wanting a figure of the Blessed Sacrament, they used commonly to draw, not the Last Supper, but the Multiplication of the Loaves, as may be seen to this day in the Catacombs. In fact, the words adopted by the Church in that part of the canon immediately preceding the Consecration are taken from the account of this miracle. The fact that St. John, contrary to his rule, records it and enlarges on its Eucharistic meaning is one of the indications that his Gospel, written long after, was intended to bring out this and other important Catholic doctrines into relief. Besides the spiritual significance, the miracle itself is a remarkable illustration of our Lord's marvellous compassion and ready tenderness for all human suffering. It took place shortly before the feast of the Pasch (John vi. 4), which, according to our computation, was the third during the ministry and one year before the Passion.

13. *We have no more than five loaves and two fishes.* From St. John we learn that our Lord first asked Philip what was to be done, and that Andrew called attention to the boy with the loaves and fishes.

14. *Make them sit down by fifties in a company.* When the companies of fifty were arranged, it became easy to count the number that were there. It appears that there were about one hundred companies. St. Matthew says that this does not include women and children, who would, according to custom, sit apart. It seems probable, from the circumstances under which the crowd came together, that the women and children would not have been numerous.

16. *He broke and distributed to his disciples.* The word for distributed is ἐδίδου and should be simply "gave," as in the A.V. Being in the imperfect, after a succession of words in the aorist, it represents a continued action; and possibly indicates that the multiplication took place in our Lord's hands.

blessed them: and he broke and distributed to his disciples,
17 to set before the multitude. And they did all eat, and were filled. And there were taken up of fragments that remained to them, twelve baskets.

Confession of St. Peter.

(VERS. 18-27.)

18 And it came to pass; as he was alone praying, his disciples also were with him: and he asked them, saying:
19 Whom do the people say that I am? But they answered, and said: John the Baptist; but some say Elias; and others say that one of the former prophets is risen again.

17. *Of fragments that remained to them, twelve baskets.* These "baskets" (κόφινοι) were wallets carried by Jews when on a journey, in which to take their food, so as to avoid having to buy from Gentiles. The twelve baskets would have impressed the miracle vividly on the minds of the apostles and have served for their own use for several days. Apparently each apostle dispensed to the crowd, and each therefore had to collect, and saw what was over. Hence the number of baskets.

Another very similar miracle was performed by our Lord at another time (Matt. xv. 32-38: Mark viii. 1-9). The fact that both are recorded, in two cases by the same evangelist, is very instructive. Had St. Matthew recorded one and St. Luke the other, harmonists would undoubtedly have thought the occasions identical, and sought for explanations of the different number of loaves and fishes on the two occasions. As it is, we see an illustration of the fact that our Lord must have often repeated His actions and His miracles, and this illustration of it ought to help us in the principles of harmony, and to warn us against forcing into unreal agreement two narratives which may well relate to different though similar occasions.

18. *Whom do the people say that I am?* The confession of St. Peter must have been separated from the miracle just recorded very considerably, both in time and place. The multiplication of loaves was about the time of the Pasch; the confession of St. Peter probably in the late summer or early autumn. During the interval our Lord seems to have left Galilee (Matt. xv. 21) on a long missionary circuit, but we have no very definite account of His movements. St. Matthew (xvi. 13) and St. Mark (viii. 27) both tell us that the confession of St. Peter took place near Cæsarea Philippi. St. Luke says that it was made apart from the multitude, while our Lord was praying along with His disciples.

19. *But they answered,* &c. The three different rumours are repeated here from *v*. 8.

And he said to them: But whom do you say that I am? 20
Simon Peter answering, said: The Christ of God. But 21
he strictly charging them, commanded they should tell this
to no man, saying: The son of man must suffer many 22
things, and be rejected by the ancients and chief priests
and scribes, and be killed, and the third day rise again.

20. *Simon Peter answering, said: the Christ of God.* The confession made by St. Peter, in the name of the apostles, was in virtue of a direct inspiration of God (Matt. xvi. 17). It was no doubt the case that he did not practically apprehend in all its fulness the doctrine which he here professed, and which he believed theoretically. His subsequent history and that of the other apostles fully bears this out. It was not till after the Resurrection that they began to realize what at this time they speculatively believed. But the confession was the formal declaration of his faith and that of the other apostles, and the culmination of that stage of their training. It formed, therefore, a most important epoch in the ministry of our Lord, and was the occasion of His first formal announcement that He was about to found a church, and that St. Peter was to be its head: "Thou art Peter, and upon this rock I will build my church" (Matt. xvi. 18). This St. Matthew naturally dwells on, as one of the central points of his Gospel, the relation between the Old Law and the New. St. Luke, on the other hand, does not mention Christ's charge to St. Peter, and we must seek for another reason for the prominence which he gives to the whole incident. The reason appears in the following verses.

21. *But he strictly charging them.* The tendency of the apostles, as of all the people, was to assume that if our Lord were the Messiah, the time would shortly come for Him to declare Himself as such, and to establish the Messianic Kingdom with power and majesty. The two facts, that our Lord was the Messiah, and that He was to be put to death, must have appeared to any Jew of that day mutually contradictory. They had so far learnt the former only. In order that they should rightly understand it, it was necessary now to teach them the doctrine of the Cross, which our Lord began to do from that time. The one doctrine was the complement of the other, and it was for this reason that our Lord commanded them not to publish His Divinity till they had learnt that He was to be put to death.

22. *The son of man must suffer many things.* St. Matthew says (xvi. 21) more definitely: "*From that time* Jesus began to show to His disciples that He must go to Jerusalem, and suffer many things from the ancients and scribes and chief priests, and be put to death, and the third day to rise again." St. Luke puts the same in rather shorter language. The profession of faith made by St. Peter was a declaration that they ought to be now fitted to receive the doctrine of the Cross, learn to put aside their ideas of His future temporal greatness, and to learn that He was to suffer and be put to death without their taking scandal thereby. That their faith was still weak is clear from the way in which St. Peter

23 And he said to all: If any man will come after me, let him deny himself and take up his cross daily, and follow
24 me. For whosoever will save his life, shall lose it; for he
25 that shall lose his life for my sake, shall save it. For what is a man advantaged, if he gain the whole world, and
26 lose himself, and cast away himself? For he that shall be ashamed of me and of my words, of him the son of man shall be ashamed when he shall come in his majesty, and
27 that of his Father, and of the holy Angels. But I tell you of a truth: There are some standing here that shall not taste death till they see the kingdom of God.

received the first preaching of Christ's sufferings, and the rebuke which our Lord addressed to all the disciples: see Mark viii. 32, 33.

23. *And he said to all.* The character of our Lord's preaching to the people changed at the same time. The words which follow were addressed to the people, and not to the apostles only: this is indicated not merely by the words "to *all*," but also by Mark viii. 34. They form a development of His saying about Himself; He was to be crucified, and His disciples must also bear their share of the Cross; and they are part of the text practically common to the three synoptists. His hearers would not, indeed, at that time have understood the meaning of the reference to His crucifixion. Death on the cross was itself, however, familiar to them, and they would have seen that it was an invitation to penance. The full meaning—the lightening of all penance by union with the sufferings of Christ—neither the apostles nor the people would have understood till after the Resurrection.

24. *Whosoever will save his life shall lose it.* The meaning is, whoever shall make his temporal life his only aim shall lose his eternal life, and that all temporal losses for Christ's sake will purchase eternal rewards. The same solemn declaration is recorded on three other occasions: Matt. x. 39; Luke xvii. 33; John xii. 25; besides being given by all three synoptists on the present occasion.

26. *He that shall be ashamed of me*, &c.: cf. xii. 9.

27. *There are some standing here*, &c. These words have been taken by many as referring to the Transfiguration, the account of which follows, and their meaning would in that case be that some standing here—i.e., the three chosen apostles—should see in their lifetime what we shall all see after we have "tasted death," the glory of our Lord manifested. Others, however, refer the words "the Kingdom of God" rather to the founding and growth of the Church and her marvellous strength against all the powers of evil. Cf. Mark viii. 39, where the words "coming in power" are added, and seem to suggest some such meaning. Cf. Rom. i. 16, x. 18, &c. Others again refer the words to the fall of Jerusalem, which is often spoken of by our Lord in this sense, and the figure of His coming at the last day. In that case the words

The Transfiguration.

(VERS. 28-36.)

And it came to pass about eight days after these **28** words, that he took Peter and James and John, and went

would mean that some of those standing before Him would live to see the destruction of Jerusalem. Cf. *infra*, xxi. 32. The words are in any case again common, with slight variations, to the three synoptists, and *in all* they are followed (after a short interval) by the transfiguration itself: cf. Matt. xvi. 28 ; Mark viii. 39.

28. *About eight days after these words.* St. Matthew (xvii. 1) and St. Mark (ix. 1) both say "after six days." We must conclude that six full days had intervened, and that St. Luke followed the ordinary Roman usage of counting the day at the beginning, and that at the end.

And went up into a mountain to pray. The mountain of the transfiguration has from very early times been believed to be Thabor, which stands in the middle of Galilee, about eight miles east of Nazareth. The view from the top is one of the finest in all Palestine, and it was a Rabbinic saying that the temple should have been built there. In an early century after Christ, three tabernacles according to St. Peter's words, were erected on it to mark the site of the transfiguration, and another where our Lord is said to have given His injunction of secrecy till after the Resurrection. Of late years, some doubt has been thrown on the tradition, and the alternative of Mount Hermon has been put forward. It is argued that (1) Hermon was a much higher mountain than Thabor, and was in the neighbourhood of Cæsarea Philippi ; (2) that according to Josephus and others, at the summit of Thabor there was a Roman fort and a village; and (3) that when St. Mark (ix. 29) says that after the transfiguration "departing from thence, they passed through Galilee," he must be supposed to refer to a point outside the province, rather than to one in the very middle of it. These arguments admit of a ready answer. (1) Six days would be ample time for our Lord to pass from Cæsarea Philippi to Thabor. (2) Many authorities deny that the fort existed in our Lord's time, and it is very probable that an old disused hill fort at this spot was rebuilt and garrisoned by the Romans when the troubles became serious in Palestine some ten or twenty years after this time. Even if a fort did exist, however, there would have been little difficulty in finding a secluded spot on the mountain top. (3) St. Mark's words are not inapplicable, and the reference in his mind may well be to the fact that our Lord was now re-entering Galilee on a missionary circuit, though He had seemed at an earlier time to have abandoned it. It appears, in short, that the tradition identifying Thabor with the transfiguration is so old and venerable, while the assignment of Hermon to it is so recent, that it ought to require very strong and even unanswerable reasons to make us forsake the ancient belief in favour of the new ; and it seems that such reasons do not exist.

20 up into a mountain to pray. And whilst he prayed, the shape of his countenance was altered, and his raiment 30 became white and glittering. And behold two men were 31 talking with him. And they were Moses and Elias, appearing in majesty. And they spoke of his decease that he 32 should accomplish in Jerusalem. But Peter and they that were with him were heavy with sleep. And waking, they saw his glory, and the two men that stood with him. 33 And it came to pass that as they were departing from him, Peter saith to Jesus: Master, it is good for us to be here: and let us make three tabernacles, one for thee, and one

29. *And whilst he prayed.* This detail is peculiar to St. Luke.

the shape of his countenance was altered. This probably refers only to our Lord's glorified expression, which now, as after the Resurrection, would produce sufficient change to cause even hesitancy in recognition.

his raiment became white and glittering. St. Mark, writing under the direction of St. Peter, who himself witnessed it, adds (ix. 2) that the whiteness was such "that no fuller on earth can make white." It is to be noted that we have two further references to this miracle by eye-witnesses: John i. 14 and 2 Peter i. 17.

30. *And they were Moses and Elias.* To every Jew, Moses and Elias represented the law and the prophets respectively. Our Lord had come on earth for the fulfilment of the law (Matt. v. 17, and John v. 46), and also in fulfilment of prophecy (Luke xxiv. 27).

31. *And they spoke of his decease.* This detail also is peculiar to St. Luke. The word is ἔξοδος, meaning only "departure" out of the world, and might be applied either to His crucifixion or His ascension; but the apostles would have only gathered vaguely what was to happen. The subject of His death was really closely bound up with the manifestation of His glory like the doctrine of the Cross with that of His Divinity, as has just been said. The glory for a short space revealed at the transfiguration was only to be reached through death at Jerusalem: cf. xxiv. 26.

32. *But Peter and they that were with him were heavy with sleep.* Our Lord had gone up in the evening, the night being His favourite time for long prayer; and hence the sleep of the three apostles was natural.

33. *Let us make three tabernacles,* that is, "tents" such as the people dwelt in during the feast of Tabernacles. The Hebrew word which is always rendered as "tents" in the Old Testament meant (at least in later times) huts or booths covered with boughs of trees. St. Peter said this as though to call back Moses and Elias, who were departing. He probably had some vision in his mind of our Lord establishing His kingdom, and preaching in glory from the summit of the mountain, and all the people coming up to hear Him.

for Moses, and one for Elias: not knowing what he said. And as he spoke these things there came a cloud, and overshadowed them: and they were afraid, when they entered into the cloud. And a voice came out of the cloud, saying: This is my beloved Son, hear him. And whilst the voice was uttered, Jesus was found alone. And they held their peace, and told no man in those days any of these things which they had seen.

The Demoniac Boy.

(VERS. 37–50.)

And it came to pass the day following, when they came down from the mountain, there met him a great multitude. And behold a man among the crowd cried out, saying: Master, I beseech thee, look upon my son, because he is my only one. And lo, a spirit seizeth him, and he suddenly crieth out, and he throweth him down and teareth him so that he foameth, and bruising him he hardly departeth from him. And I desired thy disciples to cast

34. *There came a cloud and overshadowed them.* Cf. Matt. xvii. 5: "a bright cloud," or "cloud of brightness." It seems to mean a glory so intense that nothing could be seen in it, which enveloped our Lord, Moses, and Elias, and gradually spread so that the two apostles entered into it.
35. *This is my beloved son, hear him.* This is the second great manifestation of our Lord by a voice from heaven recorded by St. Luke. The other was at His baptism: see iii. 22.
36. *And they held their peace.* The apostles said nothing about what they had seen, in deference to our Lord's express command (Mark ix. 8) till after the Resurrection. The reason of that command would be the same as that of the similar one above: see v. 21.
37. *The day following.* Our Lord had gone up the mountain overnight: see on v. 32.
there met him a great multitude. St. Mark gives the scene of our Lord's descent from the mountain with great vividness. He says that the disciples were surrounded by a great multitude, and the Scribes were questioning them; and that when they saw Him, they were astonished and ran towards Him and saluted Him. He asked them the subject of their dispute, in answer to which the father of the demoniac boy told his story.
40. *I desired thy disciples to cast him out, and they could not.* The reason of the failure of the disciples was given by our Lord. See

him out, and they could not. And Jesus answering said: O faithless and perverse generation, how long shall I be with you and suffer you? Bring hither thy son. And as he was coming to him, the devil threw him down and tore him. And Jesus rebuked the unclean spirit, and cured the boy, and restored him to his father. And all were astonished at the mighty power of God: but while all wondered at all the things he did, he said to his disciples: Lay you up in your hearts these words, for it shall come to pass that the son of man shall be delivered into the hands of men. But they understood not this word, and it was hid from them, so that they perceived it not. And they were afraid to ask him concerning this word. And there entered a thought into them, which of them should be greater. But Jesus seeing the thoughts of their heart, took a child and set him

Matt. xvii. 20, "This kind is not cast out but by prayer and fasting." They had not yet been trained by ascetic practices and suffering to a degree of spiritual power sufficiently high to enable them to cope with certain of those strange and exceptional manifestations of the spirits of evil.

41. *O faithless and perverse generation.* These words were addressed to all, but they had a special reference to the want of faith of the apostles (Matt. xvii. 19), who had failed to perform the exorcism required. But no doubt the want of faith of the people and the boy's parents was a concurrent cause of the failure. Our Lord frequently attributed His miracles to the faith of the sufferer: e.g., viii. 48.

44. *The son of man shall be delivered into the hands of men.* Again, after this display of our Lord's power, the enthusiastic hopes of His followers would have risen, and ideas of the Messianic Kingdom would have come before them. See below, on *v.* 46. Our Lord therefore put before them once more the subject of His approaching passion, as He seems to have done on many such occasions during the period which followed.

45. *They understood not this word*—i.e., they did not fully understand it. It seemed to give them forebodings that were distasteful to their worldly hopes, and they did not venture to question Him further.

46. *Which of them should be greater.* This may be read as a commentary on the preceding verse. They did not venture to ask our Lord about the prophecy of failure, for their ideas still ran on His establishing an earthly kingdom, and they were discussing which of them should have the higher place therein. It must be observed, however, that there is some difficulty in working out exactly the order of

by him, and said to them: Whosoever shall receive this 48
child in my name, receiveth me: and whosoever shall
receive me, receiveth him that sent me. For he that
is the lesser among you all, he is the greater. And 49
John answering, said: Master, we saw a certain man
casting out devils in thy name, and we forbade him,
because he followeth not with us. And Jesus said to 50
him: Forbid *him* not: for he that is not against you, is
for you.

time, and it seems probable by reference to the parallel passage in St.
Matthew (xviii. 1) and St. Mark (ix. 34), that other events came in
between this prophecy of the Passion and the group of events covered
by *vv.* 46-50.

48. *Whosoever shall receive this child in my name receiveth me.*
There is something in the open straightforwardness of a child, as well
as its innocence, that was peculiarly in harmony with our Lord's
teaching: cf. Matt. xviii. 1-6 and 1 Cor. xiv. 20. The sense, however,
of the phrase is not clear as it stands, for it seems to have no reference
to the apostles' questionings. St. Luke's account follows closely here
with St. Mark (ix. 36, 37), but the key of both is given by St. Matthew,
who describes it more in full (xviii. 2-6). From his Gospel we learn
that, after setting the child " in the midst " (as a pattern and object
lesson of simplicity and lowliness), our Lord added, "Amen I say to you,
unless you be converted *and become as little children*, you shall not
enter into the kingdom of heaven. Whosoever therefore shall humble
himself *as this little child*, he is the greater in the kingdom of heaven.
And he that shall receive one such little child in my name receiveth me ;
but he that shall scandalize one of these little ones that believe in me," &c.
The fact is that our Lord thought it best not to answer their questioning
directly. Peter in a sense was already " the greatest," and had often
been so marked. Peter, James, and John were also in a sense greater
than the rest, and had just been so honoured at the transfiguration.
But they were unfit (as the petition of James and John [Mark x. 34-45 ;
Matt. xx. 20-28] soon showed) to be trusted with any outside recognition of rank until they had got the earthly glories of the Messianic
Kingdom out of their minds. Therefore our Lord's answer simply is
that in His new kingdom, he that is lowliest and most childlike is really
the greatest.

49. *We forbade him, because he followeth not with us.* It should be
noted that the ground of the opposition of the apostles to this man was
not that he did not follow our Lord, but that he was not one of themselves. The incident is linked with the last. St. John means " surely
we as apostles have exclusive rights and may assert them."

50. *Forbid him not: for he that is not against you is for you.* Our
Lord in His answer did not deny the privilege alluded to. He merely
said, " Do not forbid those who are in My name warring against evil."

Preparation for Judean Ministry. Journey through Samaria.

(VERS. 51–56.)

51 And it came to pass when the days of his assumption were accomplishing, that he steadfastly set his face to go

If there was need to interfere with them, He could do it Himself, without any of the mischief which self-assertion on their part might cause, especially to themselves.

51. *He steadfastly set his face to go to Jerusalem.* With this verse we enter on a new section of our Lord's ministry, a great part of which is recorded by St. Luke alone; and it occupies some nine chapters of his Gospel. It is not necessary to suppose that the section describes throughout a single consecutive journey, or that all the events are here grouped together in one exact order of time. The section is clearly meant to record and illustrate the last stage of His missionary work, before His final journey to Jerusalem, which begins at xviii. 31. During the time covered by these nine chapters, St. Luke describes our Lord " setting his face " towards Jerusalem, as the time of His death drew near. A direct journey would have taken only a few days. What the narrative suggests is a larger missionary journey or journeys: see on xiii. 22. From St. John we learn that our Lord was twice in Jerusalem during the last year of His life before He came there for the Pasch to suffer; viz., at the Feast of Tabernacles in October (John vii. 2) and at the Dedication Feast in the winter (*ibid.*, x. 22). Many commentators have identified the journey described by St. Luke with the former of these, but there are grave objections to this supposition. St. John describes it (vii. 10) as a private and hurried journey, while St. Luke says that He sent messengers before His face into every city and place where He was to come, and the like. St. Luke's language, " When the days of his assumption were accomplishing," seem also to imply rather a later date than October. If this be so, we must rather connect the journey with the Feast of Dedication at which our Lord was present (John x. 22 *seq.*). It is, however, quite possible, as Tischendorf and other critics suppose, that St. Luke groups, as one great missionary period, a mass of events and teachings belonging to the whole time between the close of the Galilean ministry, i.e., the transfiguration, and the final return to Jerusalem to die. That whole period is overshadowed by the idea of His approaching death, and lasted, on any view, only a few months. This period probably covers the " preaching through all Judea," alluded to by St. Peter (Acts x. 37). It differed from the preaching in Galilee in the following particulars :—

(1) It was much shorter in duration—only a few weeks or, at most, months. Our Lord had originally left Judea on account of the opposition of the Pharisees (see on iv. 14), and for a long time He retired before His enemies. Now the time had come for Him to face their

to Jerusalem. And he sent messengers before his face: 52
and going they entered into a city of the Samaritans, to

opposition. It was clear that His preaching in Judea would emphasize
the differences between Him and them, and would soon bring matters
to a crisis there: hence He had to make the most of the time that
remained. Therefore, while there was more vigorous opposition on
the part of the Pharisees, there was also greater activity among those
helping Him. Instead of sending out twelve, He sent out seventy-two:
see x. 1.

(2) The training of the apostles was further advanced, and hence the
character of our Lord's preaching to them was somewhat different. It
involved frequent reference to His coming passion and death. See, for
example, ix. 44, xii. 50, xiii. 32, xvii. 25, xviii. 31. This difference also showed itself when He was preaching to the people.

(3) The final rupture with the Pharisees being at hand, our Lord
spoke much more plainly about them than before: cf. xi. 39–54,
xii. 1, &c.

(4) The illustrations from which the parables were taken were
those specially suited to a Judean audience: see remarks on the
Good Samaritan, the Lost Sheep, the Pharisee and Publican, the
Pounds, &c.

52. *And he sent messengers before his face.* The messengers mentioned were very probably of the seventy-two, whose choice is described
in the following chapter. They were probably chosen before our Lord
left Galilee, and were to go "before his face into every city and place
whither he himself was to come": see on x. 1.

into a city of the Samaritans. This is the first mention by St. Luke
of the Samaritans. They hold a curious position in relation to the
Jews. Their country was situated between Judea and Galilee, and as a
result, numbers of Galileans frequently passed across by the great trade
roads on their way to and from the Pasch and other festivals at
Jerusalem. The only other way was on the east side of the Jordan,
which was considerably longer. One result of the frequency with
which the Galileans crossed the territory of the Samaritans, was a continual friction between the two peoples. St. John says categorically
(iv. 9) that they held no intercourse with one another, and notes both
the surprise of the Samaritan woman and that of our Lord's disciples at
His speaking with her. By origin the Samaritans were a mixed people,
many immigrants having been sent from Persia and Medea to colonize
the land, in the time of the captivity of the Jews. A few Israelites only
had been left; but they intermarried, and were able to teach the new
race something of the Jewish faith. The result was, that their religion
became eventually a sort of mixture of Judaism and Paganism. With
the Jews they looked forward to a Messiah or Deliverer, and they had
learnt to worship Jehovah; but they also at first worshipped their own
gods, and though by the time of our Lord they had become in some
sort monotheists, they had cut themselves off from the sympathy of the

53 prepare for him. And they received him not, because his
54 face was of one going to Jerusalem. And when his
disciples James and John had seen this, they said: Lord,
wilt thou that we command fire to come down from heaven
55 and consume them? And turning, he rebuked them,
56 saying: You know not of what spirit you are. The son of
man came not to destroy souls, but to save. And they
went into another town.

Jews by establishing a sanctuary on Mount Garizim, which at one time even rivalled Jerusalem. When the Jews themselves rebuilt Jerusalem and strove to restore the Law in absolute purity, they came into sharp conflict with this hybrid people, and despised and anathematized them accordingly; and this antagonism continued to the end. Indeed, a separate Samaritan community still exists at Shechem.

53. *And they received him not.* It must be remembered that our Lord was going about surrounded by a numerous following, and His approach would have caused almost as much commotion as the general caravans which crossed Samaria at the times of the festivals. He was now commonly believed to be the Messiah, and the Samaritans would have resented any claim to that title on the part of one, who was going, not to Garizim, but to Jerusalem.

54. *Wilt thou that we command fire to come down from heaven?* The A.V., following the *less* critical text, adds, "as Elias did," referring to 4 Kings i. 10. The words are no doubt an early gloss, and are rejected by Tischendorff and most other authorities. It is perhaps worthy of remark that one of those who wished to call down fire from heaven on the Samaritans became afterwards one of their first evangelizers: see Acts viii. 14. The over-zeal indicated here and in v. 49 was the result of that impetuous character which led our Lord to call them "Boanerges" (Mark iii. 17).

55. *You know not of what spirit you are.* These words, as well as the conclusion of our Lord's remark in the next verse, are omitted by several of the best MSS.; but they are almost certainly genuine, for they were known to the early Fathers, and there is no conceivable reason why they should have been interpolated. The contrast between the spirit of the world and of Jesus Christ is in harmony with what has gone before in the preceding verses, and the rebuke also harmonizes with the context. Our Lord was labouring to wean the apostles from their very imperfect idea of His "kingdom."

56. *The son of man came not to destroy souls but to save.* The use of the title, "Son of Man," is here apparently expressive of one of the great motives of our Lord to seek and save sinners—the fact that He had a Human Nature like them, and that is a motive which would have specially appealed to those who, through daily intercourse with Him, knew Him intimately as the "Son of Man."

Three Applicants for the Apostolate.

(VERS. 57–62.)

And it came to pass as they walked in the way, that a 57 certain man said to him: I will follow thee whithersoever thou goest. Jesus said to him: The foxes have holes, and 58 the birds of the air nests; but the son of man hath not where to lay his head. But he said to another: Follow 59 me. And he said: Lord, suffer me first to go, and to bury my father. And Jesus said to him: Let the dead 60 bury their dead; but go thou, and preach the kingdom of

57. *A certain man said to him, I will follow thee withersoever thou goest.* The three incidents which conclude this chapter are connected in subject-matter with the beginning of the following one. Our Lord was about to choose seventy-two disciples to preach, and was therefore collecting candidates. Whether the applications were or were not exactly at this time, we cannot say. St. Matthew, who is the only evangelist who alludes to them, puts two of the applications together, but in quite a different context.

58. *The son of man hath not where to lay his head.* Our Lord's answer seems to be similar to that to the sons of Zebedee, "You know not what you ask" (Mark x. 38). The applicant here was a scribe (Matt. viii. 19), and probably a man of some position and means. Probably, like the rich young man at a later date (xviii. 23), he had not realized the complete self-sacrifice required for the Apostolate. The title, "Son of Man," as before, emphasizes our Lord's human side, and it indicates that, though a Man and a Typical Man, He had chosen a life of less comfort than the beasts. The words here form a remarkable commentary on our Lord's absolute homelessness in the latter part of His ministry, when Capharnaum had ceased to be "His own city": see on viii. 1.

59. *Suffer me first to go and to bury my father.* This is usually taken to mean living with his father till his death. It may, however, be taken literally as having reference to the law by which a "Nazarite," or one consecrated to God, became legally unclean by contact with a dead body: see on i. 15. St. Matthew gives (viii. 21, 22) the incident, calling the person addressed, "another of his disciples."

60. *Let the dead bury their dead.* The sense of this is very obscure. Some have explained it as "let the spiritually dead bury those who are physically dead." This is not, however, a very satisfactory interpretation. Perhaps it was meant paradoxically. It is possible to imagine a general in the midst of a battle, addressing similar words to a soldier who wished to stop fighting for a time to bury the dead. He would point to the urgency of the work of fighting the enemy, which could not be delayed, and the fact that however fitting and proper

61 God. And another said: I will follow thee, Lord, but let me first take my leave of them that are at my house.
62 Jesus said to him: No man putting his hand to the plough, and looking back, is fit for the kingdom of God.

burial rites may be, they are as nothing compared to the urgency of a life and death struggle. He might say, "let the dead take care of themselves; but those who are alive must go on fighting." Something like this is indicated by the fact that St. Luke supplies the words, "but go thou and preach the kingdom of God," which St. Matthew had not thought it necessary to put down, as the bare paradox sufficiently suggested to his mind the whole lesson.

61. *Let me first take my leave of them that are at my house.* This leavetaking meant delay and hesitation, and the request was indicative of a class of mind that would be easily distracted from work, and our Lord's refusal is connected with the fact that the crisis is now at last, and there is not a moment to lose, for He is going up to the final conflict.

62. *Putting his hand to the plough and looking back.* The light ploughs of the East require continual attention, otherwise they easily overturn. A ploughman who is distracted and looking about him will therefore do little real work. Hence it is a very suitable simile to the life of a distracted apostle. The courage to cut oneself off from home and relatives is one of the most elementary, as well as important, qualities for any priesthood. Cf. xiv. 26 *seq.*

CHAPTER X.

Mission of the Seventy-two Disciples.

(VERS. 1–16.)

AND after these things the Lord appointed also other seventy-two: and he sent them two and two before his face into every city and place whither he himself was

1. *After these things.* These words leave the exact time undetermined. The section ends with words of warning against the chief towns on the Lake of Galilee—Capharnaum, Bethsaida, Corozain—and our Lord quotes not only Sodom, but also Tyre and Sidon, in judgment against them. The natural inference is that He was at that time still in Galilee, and that a number of His hearers came from "the coasts of Tyre and Sidon," where he had recently preached (Matt. xv. 21; Mark vii. 24). *Vv.* 13–15 have a parallel in Matt. xi. 21–24; but they are probably here in their right place, and are most naturally understood as a final farewell to Galilee, where the greater part of our Lord's ministry had lain. If we take it in this way, we may, perhaps, suppose that the seventy-two were appointed at the beginning of our Lord's journey southwards, and that, having alluded (ix. 52) to one episode in the earlier part of their ministry, St. Luke now gives the words of their commission, and of our Lord's last condemnation of Galilee. It is also quite possible that the account of the return of the seventy-two is likewise displaced so as to put it with the sending: see on *v.* 17.

the Lord. ὁ Κύριος is a term which implies Christ's Divinity, the Greek word being that which was commonly used in the Septuagint to render the Hebrew word for God; as in the remarkable quotations in which Christ uses it to indicate His own claim to be Divine: "How then doth David in spirit (i.e., being inspired) call him 'Lord,' saying 'The Lord said to my Lord'?" &c. The different uses of the word must be distinguished. (1) Κύριε, = Lord, is a form of address, and not necessarily more than a compliment to any one of rank: e.g., Matt. xiii. 27; xxv. 24, &c., and so "not every one that saith Lord,

Lord," is necessarily confessing His Divinity. In this use it is often a servant's name for his lord and master, and is equivalent to the Latin Dominus, or the master of a slave, as in Matt. xiii. 27 ; but it is not necessarily even that, as the use of it by the five virgins (Matt. xxv. 11) may show. As an address, the word Κύριε is, of course, very often used to Christ, and in such cases we can only judge from the context whether it is meant as a recognition of a Divine nature or not. In very many cases it would be stretching it too far to suppose this. (2) Κύριος, simply used in the sense of "dominus," is equivalent to the master or lord of any person or thing which is regarded as his property. In this sense it is common enough, e.g., Luke xx. 15, "The Lord of the vineyard." Cf. Matt. xxi. 40 ; Mark xii. 9. See also x. 2, "The Lord of the harvest"; Matt. vi. 24, "No man can serve two masters." Here, of course, again, we must judge by the context whether there is any hint at a Divine reference. (3) ὁ Κύριος, the direct sense of the Septuagint as equivalent to the one Lord and God of the Jews, is also often found in the New Testament apart from quotations, as for example, "The angel (or messenger) of the Lord" (Matt. i. 20), "The temple of the Lord" (Luke i. 9), "In the name of the Lord" (Luke xiii. 35), &c., &c. There is seldom much difficulty in recognizing this use. (4) ὁ Κύριος, in the Christian sense, as we say "our Lord," meaning that their "master" Christ was in fact God, and one with the Κύριος of the Septuagint. This occurs frequently in the Epistles of St. Paul ; but it does not follow that it was exclusively Pauline, for it occurs in non-Pauline Epistles, and was evidently in common Christian use from early times. St. Luke uses it frequently, but in the other synoptic Gospels it occurs only in Mark xvi. 19 in direct narrative, though occasionally (as in Matt. xxi. 3, xxviii. 6) it is recorded as used by our Lord or some one else.

appointed also other seventy-two. The mission of the seventy-two is peculiar to this Gospel. They were probably all, or nearly all, from Galilee, and were, no doubt, chosen from among those who had been regular followers of our Lord for some time past. There is a slight variation of reading as to their number, some of the best MSS. giving seventy and others of equal rank giving seventy-two. The number is supposed to have been chosen after that of the Sanhedrin, and about their number also there is a difference of opinion between seventy and seventy-two. Considering the importance and deep mystical significance attached to numbers in Rabbinical and also early Christian times, the discrepancy is curious ; but it may perhaps be explained by the fact that both numbers would be accounted mystical. In reality the question is of little importance. Whichever the number, it was very large compared with that of the apostles, who had been up to then the only missionaries. From St. Luke's language, it seems clear that the twelve were not included among the seventy-two, and that they journeyed with our Lord. There is no reason to suppose that the seventy-two had a *permanent* ministry : indeed, this seems to be one mark of difference between the very similar account of the sending of these and of the twelve. Hence the seventy-two are not referred to

to come. And he said to them: The harvest indeed is 2
great, but the labourers are few. Pray ye therefore the
Lord of the harvest, that he send labourers into his
harvest. Go: Behold I send you as lambs among wolves. 3
Carry neither purse, nor scrip, nor shoes; and salute no 4
man by the way. Into whatsoever house you enter, first 5
say: Peace be to this house: and if the son of peace be 6
there, your peace shall rest upon him: but if not, it shall
return to you. And in the same house remain, eating and 7
drinking such things as they have. For the labourer is
worthy of his hire. Remove not from house to house.

in the Acts; and perhaps the same reason may account for their omission by St. Matthew and St. Mark.

2. *The harvest indeed is great, but the labourers are few.* The words used here are given by St. Matthew as an introduction to his account of the mission of the twelve. Several other phrases also which St. Luke gives among the instructions to the seventy-two are given by St. Matthew as instructions to the twelve. Cf. Matt. x. 10 *seq.* It has already been pointed out that the occasions are so similar that nothing is more probable than that many of the instructions given were identical, and it is obvious that neither evangelist gives in full all that our Lord said.

3. *Behold I send you as lambs among wolves.* Cf. Matt. x. 16, where our Lord sends the apostles as sheep among wolves. The distinction between lambs and sheep may possibly have been meant by our Lord in the same way as it was certainly meant in His words to St. Peter after the Resurrection, "Feed my lambs, feed my sheep" (John xxi. 15-17).

4. *Carry neither purse, nor scrip, nor shoes.* Cf. ix. 3. The injunctions here set before the seventy-two have been made the foundation of the rules of some of the religious orders, such as the preaching friars of St. Dominic, and those followers of the poverty of Christ, the brethren of St. Francis, who have carried them out, even literally, at a time when much in the Church was marked with feudal power and splendour.

5. *Peace be to this house.* These words are still used by the ministers of Christ, when they enter the house of a sick man to minister to him.

6. *The son of peace,* i.e., a peaceful man. This is a Hebrew figure of speech. There are several instances of it in this very Gospel: "Children of wisdom" (vii. 35), "Children of this world, children of light" (xvi. 8), and elsewhere. Cf. the name of St. Barnabas, "the son of consolation" (Acts iv. 36).

7. *The labourer is worthy of his hire.* This appears to have been a proverb among the Jews. It expresses a principle on which is based

8 And into what city soever you enter, and they receive you,
9 eat such things as are set before you: and heal the sick that are therein, and say to them: The kingdom of God
10 is come nigh unto you. But into whatsoever city you enter, and they receive you not, going forth into the streets
11 thereof, say: Even the very dust of your city that cleaveth to us we wipe off against you. Yet know this that the
12 kingdom of God is at hand. I say to you, it shall be more tolerable at that day for Sodom, than for that city.
13 Wo to thee, Corozain, wo to thee, Bethsaida. For if in

the duty of all the faithful to contribute to the support of their pastors. "The Lord ordained that they that preach the Gospel should live by the Gospel" (1 Cor. ix. 14). There is no one who is in so true a sense working for us, as he who gives his whole life to spiritual ministration to those committed to his charge. They therefore receive the offerings of the faithful, not by favour, but by right, as a workman receives his wages.

8. *Eat such things as are set before you.* The primary meaning is, doubtless, "Be content with any fare that comes"; and St. Francis of Sales used to look on this spirit as the perfection of mortification—to take simply what God sends us, without wishing for either better or worse; and it is a kind of mortification specially suited for these latter days of self-indulgence and the worship of "comfort." But some critics have compared this with the Pauline insistence against Jewish *scruples* of eating (1 Cor. x. 27, &c.), and understand it here as meaning that they were not to refuse, as the Jews did, to eat with Samaritans.

9. *And heal the sick that are therein.* Healing the sick was probably understood by the seventy-two to include the power of exorcism of those possessed, and apparently it *did* so include it. Cf. *v.* 17. To the ordinary Jewish mind there was no strict line of demarcation between disease and possession. They put down all such ills to the agency of evil spirits: see on iv. 33.

11. *Even the very dust of your city that cleaveth to us we wipe off against you.* See on ix. 5.

Yet know this that the kingdom of God is at hand—i.e., whether or not the people receive it, the time of grace is now and the time of justice will come shortly.

12. *More tolerable at that day for Sodom.* Sodom was a city on which the vengeance of God fell in a very marked manner. See Gen. xix. 24. Our Lord's meaning here is that even the inhabitants of Sodom were less guilty than they who rejected His ministration, inasmuch as they sinned against less light and grace. Cf. John xv. 24, "If I had not done among them the works that no other man hath done, they would not have sin."

13. *Wo to thee, Corozain.* St. Matthew puts these warnings to the cities of the lake in a different context, but, as has been said, they are

Tyre and Sidon had been wrought the mighty works that have been wrought in you, they would have done penance long ago, sitting in sackcloth and ashes. But it shall be more tolerable for Tyre and Sidon at the judgment, than for you. And thou, Capharnaum, which art exalted unto heaven: thou shalt be thrust down to hell. He that heareth you, heareth me: and he that despiseth you, despiseth me. And he that despiseth me, despiseth him that sent me.

Return of the Seventy-two.

(VERS. 17–24.)

And the seventy-two returned with joy, saying: Lord,

probably in their right place here. Corozain was an inland town some two or three miles from Capharnaum. It is very remarkable that, whereas our Lord here quotes it as one of the towns where most miracles had been wrought, there is not a single one mentioned in all the Gospels as having taken place there. This fact alone illustrates the very large number of sayings and doings of our Lord which are unrecorded.

wo to thee, Bethsaida. By Bethsaida must be meant the town of Andrew and Peter and James and John, rather than Bethsaida Julias: see on ix. 10.

they would have done penance long ago. See on iii. 3 and xvii. 3.

14. *It shall be more tolerable for Tyre and Sidon.* Both of these were heathen towns; yet their reception of our Lord will be a witness against the Jews themselves.

15. *Thou shalt be thrust down to hell.* "Ἕως ᾅδου. On Hades and Gehenna, see on xvi. 22 and xii. 5 respectively.

16. *He that heareth you, heareth me.* These words form the conclusion of our Lord's charge to the seventy-two, and are words of encouragement, as identifying them with Himself in their preaching. It should be observed that He does not speak to the seventy-two as to the twelve of the persecutions and even martyrdom which the latter were to face; these were after His death, and the mention of them is an indication that the preaching office of the twelve (Matt. x. 7) was permanent.

17. *And the seventy-two returned.* We are not told how long the mission of the seventy-two lasted. According to his usual custom, St. Luke follows out the story to its end; but it by no means follows that the mission may not have lasted several weeks or even months. The next few chapters (more than any other part of the Gospel) read like a selection of anecdotes rather than like a continuous history, and the

18 the devils also are subject to us in thy name. And he said to them: I saw Satan like lightning falling from heaven.
19 Behold, I have given you power to tread upon serpents and scorpions, and upon all the power of the enemy, and nothing
20 shall hurt you. But yet rejoice not in this that spirits are subject unto you: but rejoice in this, that your names
21 are written in heaven. In that same hour he rejoiced in the Holy Ghost, and said: I confess to thee, O Father, Lord of heaven and earth, because thou hast hidden these things from the wise and prudent, and hast revealed them to little ones. Yea, Father, for so it hath seemed good

several parentheses (xiii. 22; xvii. 11) seem meant to remind us at regular intervals that all belong to the period when our Lord was journeying "towards Jerusalem"—i.e., to His Passion.

18. *I saw Satan like lightning falling from heaven.* These words have been explained in different ways. Some think that they are a warning against spiritual pride which caused Satan's fall. The following two verses are quite in keeping with this meaning. Others, however, think that our Lord was alluding to the exorcisms of the seventy-two, in which "Satan" was cast out, and that it means—"I witnessed, as you did, and saw the evil spirit cast out at your word as swiftly as the lightning falls from heaven."

19. *Behold I have given you power to tread upon serpents and scorpions.* So also in Mark xvi. 18, and see Acts xxviii. 3-6 for an instance. Our Lord's phrase was no doubt meant to refer in part to the well known words of Ps. xc. 13; and He uses these common dangers of Eastern life as types of all "the power of the enemy"—which word is of course the exact equivalent of Satan.

20. *Your names are written in heaven.* The exact meaning of the phrase "to be written in heaven," or "in the Book of Life," is to be in favour with God, either by *present* sanctification, or by *efficacious* predestination. It does not necessarily imply here that each of the seventy-two went to heaven on his death.

21. *He rejoiced in the Holy Ghost.* The A.V. has "in spirit," following a Greek reading now abandoned by many of the modern critics in favour of that found in the Vulgate. We must remember that the phrase "the Holy Spirit," as referring distinctly to the Third Person of the Blessed Trinity, would not be clearly understood by the disciples until after our Lord's resurrection; but St. Luke's use of it here, in strict connection with the relation of the Father and the Son, was no doubt meant to convey to us the doctrine of the Holy Trinity, which to him, as a disciple of St. Paul, must have been a vivid reality. See 2 Cor. xiii. 13, &c. That the doctrine was expressly revealed by our Lord before His ascension appears clearly by the Baptismal Formula (Matt. xxviii. 19).

in thy sight. All things are delivered to me by my Father, and no one knoweth who the Son is but the Father ; and who the Father is but the Son, and to whom the Son will reveal *him*. And turning to his disciples, he said : Blessed are the eyes that see the things which you see. For I say to you that many prophets and kings have desired to see the things that you see, and have not seen them ; and to hear the things that you hear, and have not heard them.

Parable of the Good Samaritan.

(Vers. 25-37.)

And behold a certain lawyer stood up, tempting him ; and saying : Master, what must I do to possess eternal

I confess to thee, O Father. Cf. Matt. xi. 25. The words of our Lord here given are remarkable in that they resemble the long dogmatic discourses given by St. John which do not elsewhere find a parallel in synoptical Gospels. Our Lord must have often spoken in this way. Apparently, St. John's meditations on such discourses served to impress them deeply on his mind and they accordingly occupy a very prominent place in his Gospel. Of course our Lord's rejoicing was not because His words were hidden from any one, but because *although* many had failed to understand them, through their want of proper dispositions, *the little ones* of this world (whom He especially loved for their absence of pride) received them to their profit.

22. *And who the Father is but the Son.* Cf. John xvii. 25 ; also viii. 19.

23. *Blessed are the eyes that see the things which you see.* Hence He congratulates His disciples on hearing and seeing as they did, and of their opportunities of knowing both Him and His Father. See John xiv. 9 : "He who seeth me, seeth the Father also." Looking back on all that was greatest in Hebrew history, it appeared how kings and prophets had passed away long before they could behold the revelation such as was now given to these peasants of Galilee. Therefore they exceeded even kings and prophets in privilege and dignity. Cf. John viii. 56 : "Abraham your father rejoiced that he might see my day : he saw it and was glad."

25. *A certain lawyer stood up.* The titles "lawyer," "doctor of the law," "scribe," seem to be used indiscriminately by St. Luke for the whole class of those who made it their business in life to study and comment upon the Law and the Prophets. This class was supposed to have had its origin in the so-called "Great Synagogue" founded by Nehemias (B.C. 430), which is the name given to a succession of Jewish teachers, numbering in all one hundred and twenty. It came to an end

26 life? But he said to him: What is written in the law?
27 how readest thou? He answering, said: *Thou shall love the Lord thy God with thy whole heart, and with thy whole soul, and with all thy strength, and with all thy mind,*
28 *and thy neighbour as thyself.* And he said to him: Thou
29 hast answered right: this do, and thou shalt live. But he willing to justify himself, said to Jesus: And who is my

about B.C. 300 and its work devolved on a new body of men who were sometimes called Scribes, and also Teachers (i.e., doctors) of the law. It was their duty therefore to study the law, to apply it to the circumstances of the times, and then to instruct others. All their instructions were by word of mouth, and in the Temple courts they held a kind of class for boys and youths: and it was one of these that our Lord was attending when found after the three days' loss: see on ii. 46. The Scribes were looked on as great men of their day, and addressed by the title Rabbi, or even Rabboni. Outside Jerusalem, they exercised their functions in the synagogues. The more famous Rabbis were held in extraordinary honour. As a body they were at this time Pharisaical, and the Scribes and Pharisees are usually bracketed together in the Gospels; but there were some who belonged to the Sadducees. These Teachers were the people convened by Herod to answer the Magi, and they exercised great influence on the decisions of the Sanhedrin in judicial matters, even in our Lord's time; but since the destruction of Jerusalem, which deprived the priests of their power, the influence of the Scribes has been supreme.

26. *What is written in the law?* The lawyer or scribe here mentioned would have attracted great attention by his question, on account of the office he held. It appears from St. Luke's language that it was not sincerely meant; but it professed to be referring his teaching to the judgment of our Lord. Our Lord answered referring him to the Scriptures, in which he was supposed to be well versed.

27. *Thou shalt love the Lord thy God,* &c. The words given here and in the following verse, may be regarded as a summary of various texts. See Deut. vi. 5: Lev. xix. 18, and elsewhere. Possibly the scribe gave them in full, and the summarizing may be the work of St. Luke. The former text was one of those inscribed on the phylacteries which the Jews wore (see on ii. 42), and they were repeated in their customary daily prayers.

29. *He willing to justify himself.* Having answered his own question, the scribe naturally appeared rather foolish, as if he had asked something with an obvious answer. That he should wish to "justify himself" before the bystanders was natural enough; so he tried to appear as if he had expected the answer and was leading up to a difficulty or a further questioning about it, and asked, "Who is my neighbour?"

neighbour? And Jesus answering, said: A certain man 30
went down from Jerusalem to Jericho, and fell among
robbers, who also stripped him, and having wounded him,
went away leaving him half dead. And it chanced that 31
a certain priest went down the same way; and seeing him,
passed by. In like manner also a Levite, when he was 32
near the place and saw him, passed by. But a certain 33
Samaritan being on his journey, came near him; and
seeing him, was moved with compassion. And going up 34
to him, bound up his wounds, pouring in oil and wine:
and setting him upon his own beast, brought him to an

30. *A certain man went down from Jerusalem to Jericho.* Many have thought that the parable which follows—the "Good Samaritan"—was a true history, well known to the people. In any case our Lord apparently used a local illustration if, as we suppose, He was then between Jericho and Jerusalem. There is strong probability that this was so, especially as immediately afterwards we find Him at Bethany (v. 28) which was between the two cities. Possibly He may have been near the *khan* or inn where people were accustomed to break the journey, which is alluded to in the parable. The road was well known as a dangerous one, and was infested by brigands and robbers, and for this reason known as the "way of blood." For a description of Jericho, see on xviii. 35.

31. *A certain priest went down the same way.* The context shows that the victim was a Jew, and hence he had every right to look for sympathy from a priest. The latter would be very probably on his way to the priestly city of Jericho (see on i. 23) after offering sacrifice at Jerusalem.

32. *In like manner also a Levite.* It has been conjectured that possibly he was aware that the priest had passed, and thought he need not trouble to do what the priest had omitted.

33. *A certain Samaritan being on his journey, came near him.* See on ix. 52. The Jews not only held no intercourse with the Samaritans, but they despised and hated them, and looked on them even as emissaries of Satan. Cf. John viii. 48: "Thou art a Samaritan and hast a devil." Hence the charitable care of the Jew in distress was a literal obedience of our Lord's command to "do good to them that hate you" (vi. 27). The Jewish Doctors of the Law would certainly *not* consider any Samaritan as being included in the term "my neighbour" in the texts just quoted. Cf. Matt. v. 43.

34. *Pouring in oil and wine.* These were the common remedies of the day. Cf. Mark vi. 13, where the apostles are described as anointing the sick with oil—a practice which was sometimes of miraculous efficacy, and which gave rise to the ceremony afterwards raised by our Lord to the dignity of a Sacrament, viz., Extreme Unction.

35 inn, and took care of him. And the next day he took out two pence, and gave to the host, and said: Take care of him; and whatsoever thou shalt spend over and above, 36 I at my return will repay thee. Which of these three in thy opinion was neighbour to him that fell among the 37 robbers? But he said: He that shewed mercy to him. And Jesus said to him: Go, and do thou in like manner.

Supper at Bethany.

(VERS. 38–42.)

38 Now it came to pass as they went, that he entered into a certain town: and a certain woman named Martha

35. *He took out two pence.* For the value of a "penny" (denarius) see on vii. 41. It meant in practice an ordinary day's wage. We are probably intended to suppose that the Samaritan was a poor trader, travelling from Samaria by the usual road to Jericho and Jerusalem, and that therefore he would return by the same way in a very few days after doing his business, and probably with a little more money at his command. The whole idea is the helpful and unselfish charity of a poor man who did not for a moment hesitate to "love as himself" this alien, who would in ordinary life have scorned and repelled him. Incidentally we may note the great literary skill with which St. Luke has put the whole picture together. The complete incident is related in the short space of six verses; yet it abounds with graphic detail.

37. *Go, and do thou in like manner.* The primary lesson enforced by our Lord is plain enough. The lawyer was compelled to applaud the Samaritan for looking on a Jew as his "neighbour"; whom then have we any right to exclude? It is often supposed that our Lord meant also by this parable to suggest an allegory. The man who fell among thieves is thought to represent the human race, fallen among its spiritual enemies, and helpless by the wayside. The Priest and Levite passing by are taken to denote the inability of the Jewish Law and Sacrifices to raise him up again; and finally the good Samaritan is taken to be our Lord Himself, "despised and rejected," who has done what the Jewish Church could not; has tended our wounds and brought us to a place of safety.

38. *He entered into a certain town.* The "certain town" must be Bethany, the home of Martha and Mary (John xi. 1). All the synoptists exercise a certain reserve in their mention of members of this family. The reason of this is uncertain. Some have thought that the strong feeling of the Jewish rulers against Lazarus (John xii. 10) must have survived after our Lord's death and threatened their safety even when the synoptic Gospels were written, so as to make it more prudent

received him into her house. And she had a sister called 39 Mary, who sitting also at the Lord's feet, heard his word.

not to mention any of them too prominently. The reticence itself is quite evident. Thus on this occasion Bethany is described as "a certain town." So also, the name of Lazarus is not even mentioned in any of the three synoptical Gospels, though it was the raising of him to life that was the final cause of the determination to put our Lord to death. The anointing of Christ is told by St. Matthew and St. Mark, but the name of the woman is not given, and it is described as at the house of Simon the leper, whose relation to Martha and Mary is matter of conjecture, though he *may* have been their father. When St. John wrote his Gospel, however, the fall of Jerusalem had taken place, and all such considerations ceased to have any force. It is from him that we learn about Lazarus, and that Martha and Mary were his sisters, and that they lived at Bethany.

39. *A sister called Mary.* St. John also says (xi. 2) that Mary was she that anointed our Lord ; and in describing the second anointing, he mentions her by name (xii. 3). In the former text, from the tenses used in the Greek (aorist after the imperfect) it would seem that he could not have been referring to the second or subsequent anointing, but to the one which had already taken place. If this is so, it is decisive as to the identity of Mary of Bethany with the sinner of Luke vii. 37. But even apart from grammatical considerations, it seems certain that St. John must have been referring to the "sinner," and that the second anointing was by the same person as the first ; for if two different persons had done the same thing, it would cease to be a distinguishing mark of either. The probable identity of the "sinner" with Mary Magdalen has already been mentioned, and there are likewise independent positive reasons for identifying Mary of Bethany with Mary Magdalen : see on xxiv. 10. It is of course necessary to suppose that she had ceased for the time to follow our Lord from place to place, and was now living with her sister at Bethany ; but it is not probable that the holy women were always with our Lord's company. If the chronology which we have adopted be correct, the incident here described occurred immediately before the feast of Dedication and within a few weeks of the raising of Lazarus, at the time of which we also find Mary described as living with her sister (John xi). And if the identity of the three persons be admitted, we can form in our minds a picture in which the characteristics of each fit together in harmony. It seems fitting that she who had "many sins forgiven her" because she had "loved much" should "sit at the Lord's feet" and "hear his word" ; and should likewise at another time follow Him about, ministering to Him out of her substance ; and then that she should stand with our Lady beneath the Cross ; and finally be rewarded by being the first to see our Lord risen. The identity of the three is the basis of the office of St. Mary Magdalen in the Roman Breviary and Missal, and it has been the general tradition of the Western Church since the time of St.

40 But Martha was busy about much serving. Who stood and said: Lord, hast thou no care that my sister hath left me alone to serve? speak to her therefore, that she help me. 41 And the Lord, answering, said to her: Martha, Martha, thou art careful, and art troubled about many 42 things. But one thing is necessary. Mary hath chosen the best part, which shall not be taken away from her.

Gregory. Two exceptions of note may be mentioned, both having their origin in France. The first was in the sixteenth century, when Jacques Lefèvre, a learned Dominican writer and a humanist, wrote a book called *Maria Magdalena*, in which he attempted to prove that the sinner, Mary Magdalen, and Mary of Bethany were three distinct persons. The book has a special interest for us, as it was answered, at the request of the Archbishop of Paris, by Blessed John Fisher, Bishop of Rochester, in his work *de Unica Magdalena*. See Bridgett's Life, chap. vi. The movement did not come to much at that time, but it was renewed towards the end of the seventeenth century, apparently at Douay, though it was not connected at all with the English College there. For a time a separate feast was kept in France of St. Mary of Bethany: but this did not last very long and at the present day few Catholics are found, even in France, to doubt the identity of the three persons.

The whole question may be summed up thus:—

Was the "sinner" the same person as Mary Magdalen? See on vii. 37 and viii. 2.

Was the "sinner" the same person as Mary of Bethany? See above.

Was Mary of Bethany the same person as Mary Magdalen? See on xxiv. 10.

If the first two questions be answered in the affirmative, the answer to the third of course follows as an immediate deduction; but it seems well to refer to independent grounds for thinking the affirmative answer to the third at least quite probable. See the article, *St. Mary Magdalen in the Gospels*, in the *Dublin Review* for July, 1872.

40. *But Martha was busy about much serving.* These words suggest that the providing for the wants of our Lord and those with Him caused some little trouble, and Martha's expostulation about her sister who was not helping her was very natural.

42. *But one thing is necessary.* The meaning of our Lord's answer is not very easy to understand. Yet it would seem that the only object St. Luke could have had in mentioning the whole incident was to convey some lesson through these words. The meaning "one dish alone is necessary," though supported by considerable authority, and even suggested by an early variant reading found in some of the very best MSS., seems utterly unworthy of the context. The following paraphrase gives a more probable sense, and one commonly accepted: "Though the cares of life are numerous and absorbing, one thing only is necessary throughout, namely growth in the knowledge of God, which will ultimately lead to our salvation. Mary's choice to devote herself exclusively to contemplation is the higher choice and that which leads most directly to the highest good. Such choice shall not be taken away from her." This meaning has been adopted in the Church's liturgy and applied to our Lady of whom this Mary is taken as the type, and this incident forms the Gospel for the feast of Assumption, when the Church commemorates our Lady entering on the contemplation of her Son, which was the fulfilment of her vocation in this world. The same meaning has also been adopted in support of the fact of the excellence of the contemplative life as a state in itself higher than that of an active life, for those who are truly called to it, as we must suppose Mary eminently *was*.

CHAPTER XI.

The Lord's Prayer.

(VERS. 1-4.)

AND it came to pass, that as he was in a certain place praying, when he ceased, one of his disciples said to him: Lord, teach us to pray, as John also taught his dis-

1. *As he was in a certain place.* We may fairly assume that our Lord had by this time retired to the Jordan valley, so that some interval must have elapsed since the end of the last chapter. We know also from St. John (x. 40) that immediately after the feast of Dedication, our Lord went down from Jerusalem to Perea "into that place where John was baptizing first." This suggests that possibly the feast of Dedication took place immediately after the supper at Bethany, and that our Lord was on His way to it when He stayed at the house of Martha and Mary; and that the events which now follow came immediately or soon afterwards, i.e., about three months before our Lord's passion and death. This would have been several years, at least, since the Baptist first began to baptize; but many of the religious-minded people there would vividly remember him; and it appears from the words of the fourth Gospel, that apart from the twelve, there were few of our Lord's regular followers with Him in this retreat.

Lord teach us to pray. The above consideration furnishes an answer to what might otherwise appear a very considerable difficulty. It might have been urged that after its first promulgation (Matt. vi. 9-13), the "Lord's Prayer" would have passed into daily use among His immediate followers; and it would seem difficult to suppose that it had become unknown, or that the disciples could have made such a request as "Lord teach us to pray." But it is clear that at this time the "many that resorted to Him" were mostly new disciples from the neighbourhood, who would know little or nothing of the Sermon on the Mount. Most of these were familiar with St. John Baptist and his disciples; few had so much as seen our Lord.

as John also taught his disciples. Apparently, though this is the sole

ciples. And he said to them: When you pray, say: Father, 2 reference to it, St. John had also given a form of prayer which these devout people still used. It was not unusual for a Rabbi to teach his disciples a form of prayer.

2. *And he said to them*, &c. The form of the Lord's Prayer given here is considerably shorter than that given by St. Matthew. Whether our Lord Himself gave it in its abbreviated form, or whether St. Luke summarized it, is uncertain. Some MSS. have a longer form, with the three phrases—" Who art in heaven," " Thy will be done as in heaven so on earth," "but deliver us from evil "—inserted, thus making it practically identical with the form in St. Matthew. The A.V. adopts this form; but there seems little doubt that the Catholic text is the true one, and that these three phrases are due to copyists who were familiar with the prayer in its usual shape. The R.V. coincides nearly with ours, and the phrases are omitted. There is nothing improbable in the idea that St. Luke, who avoids repetitions when he can, may have shortened the form, by omitting the words which seem to be explanatory rather than essential. There is reason to believe that the full form became fixed in liturgical use at a very early date: and we know that it was always used in the Mass. For convenience of reference, we put here the two forms (St. Matthew's and St. Luke's) side by side, the three doubtful phrases in the latter being within brackets:—

ST. MATTHEW vi. 9-13.

Our Father who art in heaven, hallowed be thy name. Thy kingdom come. Thy will be done on earth as it is in heaven. Give us this day our supersubstantial bread. And forgive us our debts, as we also forgive our debtors. And lead us not into temptation, but deliver us from evil. Amen.

St. LUKE xi. 2-4.

[Our] Father [who art in heaven] hallowed be thy name. Thy kingdom come. [Thy will be done on earth as it is in heaven.] Give us this day our daily bread; and forgive us our sins, for we also forgive every one that is indebted to us. And lead us not into temptation [but deliver us from evil].

It will be seen that neither form coincides exactly with the English text in use amongst us, which is probably traditional from Catholic times. It is practically identical with that in the Book of Common Prayer, except for the omission of the doxology at the end. The only other difference is the substitution of *who* for *which* in the first clause. This denotes a comparatively recent revision, and appears to be due to Bishop Challoner; for in the early editions of the *Garden of the Soul*, the prayer appears in the form now in use.

2. *Father.* This title as applied to God is distinctively Christian. Cf. Rom. viii. 15: " You have not received the spirit of bondage again in fear; but you have received the spirit of adoption of sons, whereby we cry Abba " (Father).

Thy kingdom come. The " kingdom " is used by our Lord in three

3 hallowed be thy name. Thy kingdom come. Give us this
4 day our daily bread. And forgive us our sins, for we also
forgive every one that is indebted to us. And lead us not
into temptation.

senses. (1) The kingdom of heaven (Luke xxii. 29, 30; see also xxiii. 42, and James ii. 5); (2) the kingdom of the Church (John xviii. 36, Matt. xiii. 38); and (3) the kingdom of Christ in each individual soul (Luke xvii. 21; see also Rom. xiv. 17). In some of these texts and many others, more than one of these meanings can be applied. In the Lord's Prayer, all three meanings seem to be intended. Thus we pray that Christ may come and reign in our souls; that His Church and the preaching of the Gospel may spread in the world; and that we may in the end come to reign with Him in the kingdom of heaven. The following petition, here omitted, is really a duplicate or explanation of the second sense just explained.

3. *Our daily bread.* The word ($\epsilon\pi\iota o\acute{\nu}\sigma\iota o\varsigma$) which we here translate "daily" is not found in Greek, except in this and the parallel text; and it is impossible to say what Hebrew or Aramaic word it may represent, for the prayer was no doubt given not in Greek but in the vernacular dialect. From its probable etymology it is said to equal either "sufficient" (so St. Cyril's commentary), or "necessary for the coming day" (so Lightfoot, &c.). This meaning practically coincides with the *quotidianum* of the Vulgate, and with the traditional meaning adopted by the Church. It also agrees with the chief English non-Catholic versions. In St. Matthew's Gospel, however, the *same* Greek word in the same context is rendered in the Douay Version "supersubstantial" (i.e., "spiritual"), also in accordance with the Vulgate, and hence also with Wycliffe's Bible, and this rendering has the support of some modern critics. But all the other English versions—including the R.V.—give "daily" in St. Matthew as well as in St. Luke. Many have thought that "supersubstantial" was simply a mistranslation, and that the original was mistaken for some such word as $\epsilon\pi o\acute{\nu}\sigma\iota o\varsigma$, which would be from $\epsilon\pi\acute{\iota}$ and $ο\grave{\upsilon}\sigma\acute{\iota}\alpha$ (= Being or Substance) and might have exactly the force of "supersubstantial." St. Jerome probably had some such derivation in his mind when he inserted this Latin word; but it is difficult to see why he should not have used the same rendering in St. Luke. And it is not a little remarkable that, notwithstanding St. Jerome's very great influence in such matters, the Church never accepted this word in her Liturgy, though with that exception, the version used in the Mass corresponds exactly, word for word, with the Vulgate. If the ordinary rendering ("daily") be adopted, the deeper application of the phrase to spiritual sustenance or to the Eucharist—such as has been common enough in the Church from the time of Origen onwards—is not excluded as a secondary application; and St. Jerome may have had some reason, now lost, for his evident belief that our Lord's word conveyed directly some such sense.

4. *For we also forgive every one that is indebted to us.* Again the forgiveness of our enemies, as a test or measure of the forgiveness which

On Perseverance in Prayer.

(VERS. 5-13.)

And he said to them : Which of you shall have a friend, 5
and shall go to him at midnight, and shall say to him :
Friend, lend me three loaves, because a friend of mine is 6
come off his journey to me, and I have not what to set

we are to expect from God, was specially Christian. Cf. Matt. v. 38-48 and Mark xi. 25, 26. The word "trespass" does not occur in any of the chief English versions except Tyndale's (A.D. 1534). Probably he took it from the form in common use, and it was the later translators who changed it; for though Wycliffe's version is earlier, being translated from the Latin, it stands on a different basis. St. Matthew has "debts" in *v.* 12, and "offences" (A.V. trespasses) in *v.* 14, as an explanation : "debt" is clearly Hebraism for "sin," and the Aramaic word would no doubt be equally well translated by either.

And lead us not into temptation. By this we can perhaps understand generally "lead us safely through our temptations," or "lead us not into such temptation as would prove fatal to us"; but the further prayer for actual delivery from temptations which would in the ordinary course come upon us seems a legitimate one, and probably at the same time intended by our Lord. The full meaning would thus be, "lead us away from temptation ; but if it be God's will that we should undergo certain particular temptations, then may we have the grace to overcome them."

5. *Which of you shall have a friend.* St. Luke next records a series of sayings as to the manner in which we ought to pray, two of which find a parallel in Matt. vii. 7-9. We cannot certainly say whether our Lord repeated this part of the Sermon on the Mount, or whether St. Luke inserted it here as a related subject, or whether we are to consider the text in St. Matthew as displaced in chronological order. But the question is quite immaterial.

Friend lend me three loaves. The first quality mentioned is perseverance. We are to act as if we wished to weary Almighty God with our importunity. Cf. the Parable of the Unjust Judge, xviii. 1-8. It is often necessary for our own good that the answer to our prayer should be delayed. If we rightly understand our position towards Almighty God, we shall continue asking with perseverance. The parable given here is meant to illustrate this. Our Lord employed, as He constantly did, the imagery of homely Jewish life, which would seize at once the attention of His hearers, and remain vivid for all time.

6. *A friend of mine is come off his journey.* As those familiar with southern climates are well aware, people used commonly to travel at night to avoid the heat, and would therefore arrive late.

7 before him. And he from within should answer and say: Trouble me not, the door is now shut, and my children 8 are with me in bed; I cannot rise and give thee. Yet if he shall continue knocking, I say to you, although he will not rise and give him, because he is his friend; yet because of his importunity he will rise, and give him as many as he 9 needeth. And I say to you, Ask, and it shall be given you: seek, and you shall find: knock, and it shall be opened to 10 you. For every one that asketh receiveth: and he that seeketh, findeth: and to him that knocketh, it shall be 11 opened. And which of you if he ask his father bread, will he give him a stone? or a fish, will he for a fish give him 12 a serpent? Or if he shall ask an egg, will he reach 13 him a scorpion? If you then being evil, know how to give good gifts to your children, how much more will your Father from heaven give the good Spirit to them that ask him?

7. *Trouble me not.* The answer is in every way discouraging. The friend has shut his house and retired to rest for the night, and shows no inclination to rise again. Cf. the reluctance to open again in the case of the Foolish Virgins (Matt. xxv. 11, 12).

the door is now shut. We do not know exactly how they secured their houses, but apparently it was a complicated matter; and in the daytime they were very open.

8. *Because of his importunity he will rise.* The argument is of course from the less to the greater. The man in the parable obtained what he wanted by his perseverance, although his friendship had proved insufficient to obtain it. How much more can we count on obtaining by continued prayer what God so wishes to bestow.

9. *Ask and it shall be given you.* The second quality of prayer is confidence, which is enforced by our Lord by these words so constantly quoted. Cf. Matt. vii. 7.

11. *If he ask his father bread, will he give him a stone?* Cf. Matt. vii. 9. The shape and colour of the loaves in common use resembled that of good sized stones; hence the devil's suggestion to our Lord (iv. 3), "say to this stone that it be made bread."

12. *If he shall ask an egg, will he reach him a scorpion?* It is said that a scorpion when curled up might resemble an egg, so that a proverb existed, "an egg for a scorpion."

13. *How much more will your Father from heaven.* The argument again is from the less to the greater. As we are evil by nature compared with Him, and yet we are commonly devoted to our children, how much more will our heavenly Father be devoted to us.

Christ among His Enemies.
(Vers. 14-36.)

And he was casting out a devil, and the same was dumb; 14 and when he had cast out the devil, the dumb spoke: and the multitudes were in admiration at it. But some of 15 them said: He casteth out devils by Beelzebub the prince

14. *And he was casting out a devil.* The incident here recorded is clearly separated altogether from the sayings just told. The miracle is probably the same as one of two recorded by St. Matthew (ix. 32 and xii. 22). In the latter place St. Matthew gives the same discussion as to the kingdom divided against itself, and the strong man armed, which comes also, without mention of the miracle, in Mark iii. 22. In Matt. xii. the man is said to be blind as well as dumb. The miracle in Matt. ix. is a dumb man simply, and is similar, both in its circumstances and in the comments to which it gave rise, though they are only mentioned shortly. The two cures in St. Matthew are probably distinct, as he would hardly record the same miracle twice. Both of them would seem at first sight to be recorded as if they took place in Galilee, and in the earlier part of the ministry; but there are indications which might warrant us in referring Matt. xii. to a later time, when Christ's death was near at hand. We may take it that these were two similar cases at different times, and that both provoked the taunt of the Pharisees, which was doubtless often repeated.

15. *Some of them.* In Matt. xii. 25 it is the Pharisees; in Mark iii. 22 it is "the scribes who were come down from Jerusalem."

He casteth out devils by Beelzebub. St. Luke summarizes their questions under two heads. First they asserted that His miracles were performed by the agency of "Beelzebub, the prince of devils." Beelzebub was the name of that form of Baal locally worshipped at Accaron, one of the cities of the Philistines (4 Kings i. 2, 3, 16), for consulting whom Elias predicted the death of Ochozias. The meaning of the word has been the subject of much discussion. In the Septuagint version of the passage just quoted it is rendered βααλ μυῖαν (= Lord of Flies), and Josephus (Antiq. ix. 2, 1) has the same interpretation. It has been supposed that it was Baal worshipped under the mystic form of a beetle, copied from the sacred Scarabæus, so commonly used in Egyptian worship. Many scholars say that Βεελζεβούλ, which is the invariable Greek reading in all the Gospels, means "Lord of the Dungheap," and is a contemptuous Jewish play on the name, not only because beetles are associated with filth, but also because in the Talmud "filth" is used for idolatry. Later Hebraists doubt this etymology, and think that Baal-Zebul (Zebhul) means in the Hebrew of the Rabbis "Lord of the House or Temple," and that there is a direct allusion to this meaning in Matt. x. 25: "If they have called the good-man of the house Beelzebub, how much more them of his household?" In this

16 of devils. And others tempting, asked of him a sign from 17 heaven. But he seeing their thoughts, said to them: Every kingdom divided against itself shall be brought to desola- 18 tion, and house upon house shall fall. And if Satan also be divided against himself, how shall his kingdom stand? because you say, that through Beelzebub I cast out devils. 19 Now if I cast out devils by Beelzebub: by whom do your children cast them out? Therefore they shall be your 20 judges. But if I by the finger of God cast out devils: 21 doubtless the kingdom of God is come upon you. When a strong man armed keepeth his court: those things are in 22 peace which he possesseth. But if a stronger than he come upon him and overcome him: he will take away all his armour wherein he trusted, and will distribute his

view, Baal-Zebul must have been the proper Philistine title of honour, and Beelzebub a parody of it, in reference, as explained, to his Scarab symbol. A recent scholar suggests that the New Testament name may be read for Baal-Zibbul (= Lord of Sacrificing to Idols). In that view Matt. x. 25 would have a further emphasis: "If the real 'Lord of the Temple' is called the 'Lord of Idolatry,'" &c. There would still, of course, be a contemptuous intention in the Hebrew parody of the Philistine name. This theory has the great advantage that it supplies a reason not supplied by the others, why the particular name should be linked with the title "Prince of Devils."

16. *Others tempting, asked of him a sign from heaven.* On this head of Christ's questioners, cf. the devil's temptations (iv. 3–13), which were all directed towards obtaining from our Lord a miraculous sign from heaven at his bidding.

17. *Every kingdom divided against itself.* This is the first answer to the former accusation. It is one from reason or common sense. If Satan were to fight against himself, it is obvious that it would lead to his own ruin.

19. *By whom do your children cast them out?* This second reply is an *argumentum ad hominem*. Exorcism was not uncommon among the Jews, and was freely practised, it appears often successfully, by the disciples of the Pharisees themselves. See Acts xix. 13. Our Lord then asked the Pharisees whether they would accuse their own disciples also of working by the power of Beelzebub.

20. *But if I by the finger of God.* Cf. Exod. viii. 19.

21. *When a strong man armed keepeth his court.* This parable is a development of the same line of thought as the first answer. The "strong man armed" is the devil, the "Prince of this world" (John xii. 31; xvi. 11), who had no one to oppose him till a stronger than he —that is Christ—came to take away his armour and distribute his spoils.

spoils. He that is not with me, is against me: and he 23
that gathereth not with me, scattereth. When the unclean 24
spirit is gone out of a man, he walketh through places
without water, seeking rest: and not finding, he saith: I
will return into my house whence I came out. And when 25
he is come, he findeth it swept and garnished. Then 26
he goeth and taketh with him seven other spirits more
wicked than himself, and entering in they dwell there.
And the last state of that man becomes worse than the
first. And it came to pass: as he spoke these things, a 27
certain woman from the crowd lifting up her voice said to
him: Blessed is the womb that bore thee, and the paps
that gave thee suck. But he said: Yea rather, blessed 28

23. *He that is not with me is against me.* Our Lord proceeds to insist in a kind of parable suggested by the subject, on the impossibility of standing still in the spiritual life. It would be of no use to have devils expelled, unless those from whom they had gone would become active servants of God.

24. *When the unclean spirit is gone out.* Thus a second parable is made a continuation of the first.

through places without water—i.e., the desert, where the evil spirits were supposed to dwell. But the unclean spirit will not rest there after being expelled. Sooner or later he will return and seek re-admittance, for our sins are prone to come back to us; and his success or otherwise will depend on how he finds his former dwelling.

25. *He findeth it swept and garnished.* This means that the soul is empty, with no good habits planted in place of the former bad ones, so that it is to him like a house "swept and garnished," and made ready for his return.

26. *Seven other spirits more wicked than himself.* The expression of possession by seven devils is used in only one other connection in the Gospels—that of Mary Magdalen: see on viii. 2. In both cases the context shows a life of sin to be denoted, that is an indwelling of evil spirits, for which the victim was culpable. The number "seven" is no doubt mystically used, and it is often taken to symbolize the seven deadly sins. These lists of sins were known even to the Jews in our Lord's day, and this list may possibly be so old.

27. *Blessed is the womb that bore thee.* We may infer from St. Matthew (xii. 46), that at this moment our Blessed Lady came up and could not get to Him at first because of the crowd. Her presence may have suggested the exclamation of the woman in this verse.

28. *Who hear the word of God and keep it.* Our Lord uses the occasion for insisting on the lesson that great as was the privilege of His Mother in bearing such a Son, yet that was not her greatest title to our reverence and homage. It was a greater privilege still to have the

are they who hear the word of God, and keep it. And the multitudes running together, he began to say: This generation is a wicked generation: it asketh a sign, and a sign shall not be given it, but the sign of Jonas the prophet. For as Jonas was a sign to the Ninivites, so shall the son of man also be to this generation. The queen of the south shall rise in the judgment with the men of this generation, and shall condemn them, because she came from the ends of the earth to hear the wisdom of Solomon; and behold more than Solomon here. The men of Ninive shall rise in the judgment with this generation, and shall condemn it, because they did penance at the preaching of

grace to avoid all sin, and this is one which we can all in our measure share with her: cf. on viii. 21.

29. *The sign of Jonas the prophet.* Our Lord next answered the other class of fault-finders, who were asking for a sign "from heaven," i.e., some sign coming down from the region of God and the angels over which the spirits were supposed not to have power: see on *v.* 16. He spoke a kind of parable which St. Matthew gives more in full (xii. 40). "As Jonas was in the whale's belly three days and three nights, so shall the Son of Man be in the heart of the earth three days and three nights." We of course have no difficulty in seeing here the allusion to His death and burial and resurrection the third day; but at the time this would not have been intelligible to the people. They would have only seen that the answer was meant as a rebuke to them. In truth, they had seen signs enough, and much more than enough, had they been in earnest, without wanting to see such a "sign from heaven" as they seem to have asked for. See John xi. 47, where the word ($\sigma\eta\mu\varepsilon\iota\alpha$) translated "miracle" is the same as that here rendered "sign." The spirit of their question is denoted by the word "tempting," used by the evangelist (*v.* 16).

31. *The queen of the south*—i.e., the Queen of Saba. See 3 Kings x. 1; and 2 Par. ix. 1. The ancient Sabæan kingdom was a part of Arabia, far to the south of Palestine.

32. *The men of Ninive.* See Jonas iii. 5. Ninive, the capital of the Assyrian empire, and one of the most famous of ancient cities, was situated on the upper Tigris, in Mesopotamia. The modern Mossoul is not far from its site. The history of Assyria is only known to us in fragments, and chiefly from its monuments, of which the most familiar is the great winged bull. The inscriptions recovered from time to time give us a certain further fragmentary knowledge. Jonas was a contemporary of Jeroboam II. King of Israel (Jonas i. 1 and 4 Kings xiv. 25). His visit to Ninive would not probably have occurred during the reign of either Asshur-dan III. (B.C. 773-755) or of Asshur-nisasi (B.C. 755-743) when, as the inscriptions tell us, the country was sadly

Jonas; and behold more than Jonas here. No man 33 lighteth a candle, and putteth it in a hidden place, nor under a bushel: but upon a candlestick, that they that come in may see the light. The light of thy body is thy eye. If 34 thy eye be single, thy whole body will be lightsome: but if it be evil, thy body also will be darksome. Take heed 35 therefore that the light which is in thee be not darkness. If then thy whole body be lightsome, having no part of 36 darkness; the whole shall be lightsome, and as a bright lamp shall enlighten thee.

Dinner with the Pharisee.

(VERS. 37-54.)

And as he was speaking, a certain Pharisee prayed him 37 that he would dine with him. And he going in, sat down

reduced by insurrections and pestilence, and the people would thus have been prepared by calamity to pay heed to the call to repentance. The Ninivites were of course heathens; hence the sternness of our Lord's words in holding up their penance at the preaching of Jonas in condemnation of the Jews.

33. *No man lighteth a candle.* Here again we come on a group of "sayings," which are not apparently connected with the previous story. The parallel passages are to be found in Matt. v. 15 and vi. 22. But whether that context or this is their chronological place we cannot say. Probably they were often repeated in the course of our Lord's many journeys and preachings.

under a bushel. St. Luke here uses the word "bushel," which before he seemed to avoid: see on viii. 16.

34. *If thy eye be single.* A further comparison is here used. The light was before them, and they had only to use their eyes to see it; if they did not do so, the fault was theirs. The application of the light was for inward illumination. A single eye stands for a firm intention, the soul being illuminated by God only. Hence the antithesis to *single* is *evil*.

35. *The light which is in thee be not darkness.* The light within us becomes darkness when our conscience itself loses its perception, which is one of the first results of a life of sin.

37. *A certain Pharisee prayed him that he would dine with him.* The account which follows marks the culmination of the opposition of the Pharisees to our Lord, which has been traced by St. Luke from its beginning. This scene may probably be supposed to happen on the Perean journey, and the context indicates a time near the end. For the words which our Lord addressed to the ruling class could not but

38 to eat. And the Pharisee began to say, thinking within
39 himself, why he was not washed before dinner. And the
Lord said to him: Now you Pharisees make clean the
outside of the cup and of the platter; but your inside is
40 full of rapine and iniquity. Ye fools, did not he that
made that which is without, make also that which is

have been considered a final rupture with them; from henceforth they were His open and undisguised enemies. It seems certain therefore that this occurred within a few weeks of His last return to Jerusalem for the Pasch. Our Lord would not have spoken so openly and in such strong language, unless He had been about to face them finally and accept the consequences. The discourse itself should be carefully compared with the great denunciation recorded in the twenty-third chapter of St. Matthew, which formed our Lord's last public discourse in the Temple. The chief difference on this occasion was only that our Lord's words were delivered less publicly, in the private house of one of the Pharisees, instead of in the Temple before all the people. The general purport of the two is the same, and a careful perusal of them gives a vivid picture of Pharisaism as actually existing, and its absolute opposition to the spirit of the Gospel.

38. *Why he was not washed before dinner.* The washing alluded to was part of the Oral Law, and though not usually observed by the common people, would be superstitiously expected from one who was a religious teacher. It was accompanied by various minute ceremonies and prayers. For example, one rule was that the hands must be held downwards in washing, lest some water rendered unclean by touching the hands might run upon the arms and thus render a fresh washing necessary.

39. *Now.* This is more emphatic than appears in any English version; and contrasts what was *then* the state of the Pharisees with what had previously been the case.

you Pharisees make clean the outside. The occasion for our Lord's denunciation was offered by the captiousness of His hosts. From the context it is evident that they had asked Him in no friendly spirit and that their object was under a pretext of pretended friendliness to find something to blame Him for. Our Lord therefore took up the ideas which were passing through their minds. He contrasted their outward ablutions with their inward laxity and wickedness. In truth, the ideas of thought and intention or charitable feeling of any sort which hold so important a place in the mind of a Christian, were quite foreign to their whole system.

40. *Did not he that made that which is without, make also that which is within?* Our Lord's answer to them is then that the soul is more important than the body: for both the one and the other were created by God, and He will look to cleanliness of heart more than to that of the body.

within? But yet that which remaineth, give alms; and 41
behold all things are clean unto you. But wo to you 42
Pharisees, because you tithe mint and rue and every herb,
and pass over judgment, and the charity of God. Now
these things you ought to have done, and not to leave the
other undone. Wo to you Pharisees, because you love 43
the uppermost seats in the synagogues, and salutations
in the market-place. Wo to you, because you are as 44
sepulchres that appear not, and men that walk over, are
not aware. And one of the lawyers answering, saith to 45
him: Master, in saying these things, thou reproachest us

41. *That which remaineth.* Τὰ ἐνόντα. The sense of these words is not clear. Some think they refer to giving alms of that which remains; others think they have some reference to the inner life of the Pharisees; others again that it means the contents of the cup and platter.

give alms. A little charity or alms deeds would do more to cleanse them than all their ceremonies. Our Lord is here, of course, not condemning the outward ceremonies of the Law prescribed by Moses, but only the absurd importance attached to them which obscured instead of assisting " the weightier things of the Law, judgment, and mercy, and faith " (Matt. xxiii. 23). This idea is developed in the next verse.

42. *You tithe mint and rue.* Mint and rue were two herbs, on all of which tithes were paid (Deut. xiv. 22). The absurdity of insisting on such minute matters and omitting real and grave obligations is evident. Nevertheless, our Lord does not condemn even the minutest of such observances. "These things (referring to the judgment and charity of God) you ought to have done and not to leave the other (i.e., observance of minute ceremonial) undone."

43. *The uppermost seats in the synagogues.* These consisted of a semicircular row, around the reader's desk, and facing the people. A similar arrangement may be seen in many foreign churches of the Protestant communion, where the "Pastors" and other leading members of the congregation sit behind the Communion Table, facing the people.

44. *You are as sepulchres that appear not.* As those who walk over a grave are unaware of the corruption inside—and were, in their usages, accounted to be defiled unawares—so they who had intercourse with the Pharisees knew nothing of the corruption of their hearts. If contact with a grave caused legal uncleanliness (Numb. xix. 16), what is to be said of the state of their own souls?

45. *One of the lawyers*, i.e., a Scribe: see on x. 25. So many of the Scribes were Pharisees that they would naturally suppose themselves to be included in our Lord's condemnation. They held such a position,

46 also. But he said: Wo to you lawyers also; because you load men with burdens which they cannot bear, and you yourselves touch not the packs with one of your fingers. 47 Wo to you who build the monuments of the prophets: 48 and your fathers killed them. Truly you bear witness that you consent to the doings of your fathers: for they 49 indeed killed them, and you build their sepulchres. For this cause also the wisdom of God said: I will send to them prophets and apostles, and some of them they will 50 kill and persecute. That the blood of all the prophets which was shed from the foundation of the world, may be 51 required of this generation. From the blood of Abel unto the blood of Zacharias, who was slain between the altar, and the temple. Yea I say to you, it shall be

however, that they could hardly believe that our Lord would venture to speak thus of them before others. Hence this question, which must be taken as one of expostulation.

46. *Wo to you lawyers also.* Our Lord did not shrink from the challenge, and at once used words equally strong, addressed to the Scribes directly.

you load men with burdens. The "burdens" referred to the ever-increasing restrictions of the "Oral Law." Cf. Acts xv. 10. The Scribes would commonly find pretexts to excuse themselves from many of these burdens.

48. *Truly you bear witness that you consent.* Those who built the monuments to the prophets did so professedly to honour them, and as if disapproving of the deeds of their persecutors. Our Lord uses a sort of spiritual illustration. They are really continuing the works of their fathers, just as the building of a monument follows naturally after death.

49. *I will send to them prophets,* &c. The words here are not meant for a quotation, and our Lord is describing the Providence of God, and using an ordinary method of talking in putting it in the form of a speech.

51. *From the blood of Abel unto the blood of Zacharias.* The murders of Abel and Zacharias were respectively the first and last in the historical books of the Old Testament. The death of Zacharias is described (2 Paral. xxiv. 19-22) as having taken place "in the porches of the Lord's house," that is, in the porches of the Priests, in front of the temple itself, and between it and the Altar of Holocausts. In the sermon recorded by St. Matthew, Zacharias is called (xxiii. 35) son of Barachias; but though there was a Zacharias son of Barachias, he could not have been the one alluded to, as in his day the temple was in ruins. Various explanations have been suggested; but the simplest seems to

required of this generation. Wo to you lawyers, for you 52 have taken away the key of knowledge: you yourselves have not entered in, and those that were entering in you have hindered. And as he was saying these things to 53 them, the Pharisees and the lawyers began vehemently to urge him, and to oppress his mouth about many things. Lying in wait for him, and seeking to catch something 54 from his mouth that they might accuse him.

be to attribute it originally to the error of the copyists, who confused the two persons.

52. *You have taken away the key of knowledge.* A key was the symbol for a Scribe, who was supposed to open the meaning of the Scriptures. They are here denounced for misinterpreting them, and withholding their consolation from the people.

53. *As he was saying these things*, i.e., as he finished saying these things. The Vatican codex, and many others, have "When he had gone forth from thence," which seems the better reading. The Pharisees thus appear to have surrounded our Lord as He went out, and to have pursued Him with angry questions.

54. *Seeking to catch something.* "Catch," i.e., in Greek θηρεῦσαι, as hunters try to snare and kill their prey.

CHAPTER XII.

On Pharisaism and the Pharisees.

(VERS. 1–12.)

AND when great multitudes stood about him, so that they trod upon one another, he began to say to his disciples: Beware ye of the leaven of the Pharisees, which is ² hypocrisy. For there is nothing covered, that shall not ³ be revealed: nor hidden, that shall not be known. For whatsoever things you have spoken in darkness, shall be published in the light: and that which you have spoken in the ear in the chambers, shall be preached on the house- ⁴ tops. And I say to you, my friends: Be not afraid of them who kill the body, and after that have no more that they

1. *And when great multitudes stood about him.* The opening of this chapter follows on the closing of the last without any break. We must take it therefore as simply a continuation of the same narrative. It appears that the words used in the Pharisee's house had been noised abroad, and it was known that there had been an angry attack on our Lord. Many of the people still believed in Him, and on coming out of the house, He was soon among friends. His words may be taken as a reply to what the Pharisees had said. He began at once with a two-fold warning to His followers, (1) to avoid the spirit of the Pharisees; (2) not to be afraid of them. The first point is given by a simile, comparing such spirit in its all-pervading nature with the effect of leaven on bread. See *infra*, xiii. 21.

2. *There is nothing covered that shall not be revealed.* The words here evidently refer to the day of judgment, when we shall see all things as they are and all hypocrisy will be made manifest. The same words have already been commented on (see on viii. 17), where the context shows the application of them to be different from that intended here.

4. *And I say to you, my friends.* The apostles are here called our Lord's friends in antithesis to the Pharisees, now openly His enemies.

can do. But I will shew you whom ye shall fear : fear ye 5
him, who after he hath killed, hath power to cast into hell.
Yea, I say to you, fear him. Are not five sparrows sold for 6
two farthings, and not one of them is forgotten before God?
Yea, the very hairs of your head are all numbered. Fear 7
not therefore : you are of more value than many sparrows.
And I say to you, whosoever shall confess me before men, 8
him shall the son of man also confess before the Angels of

Cf. also John xv. 13-15. The advice here therefore is that Christ's
friends have nothing to fear from those His enemies, who cannot work
against Divine Providence, and even when allowed to persecute the
body, cannot touch the soul.

5. *I will shew you whom ye shall fear.* "The fear of the Lord is
the beginning of wisdom" (Ps. cx. 10). "Fear God and keep his
commandments, for this is all man" (Eccles. xii. 13). This fear
should of course be not a *servile* but a *filial* fear. But it is to be a true
fear of judgment and hell : see on i. 50.

Fear ye him who after he hath killed, hath power to cast into hell.
The word (γέεννα) which we translate "*hell*" is a transcription from the
Hebrew Gehenna, meaning originally Valley of Hinnom, or of the Sons
of Hinnom, south of Jerusalem. Solomon had erected there "high
places" for sacrifices to the idol Moloch, and other idolatrous kings
revived these rites from time to time. To put an end to these abomina-
tions, Josias made the valley a receptacle for dead bodies (4 Kings xxiii.
10, 13, 14), so that it became ceremonially unclean. Later on the sewage
of the city was conducted into it. It has been said that the dead bodies and
carcases of animals were burnt there by continual fires ; but whether this
was so or not, it is hardly wonderful that the name of a place so full of
abomination in the eyes of the Jews should be adopted to designate
hell, the place of eternal torments, "where their worm dieth not and the
fire is not extinguished."

6. *Are not five sparrows sold for two farthings?* Cf. Matt. x. 29-30.
The word (ἀσσάριον) which we translate "*farthing*," was a bronze coin
equal in value to one-tenth of a "*denarion*," which it has been said was
equivalent to about eightpence of our money ; so that the *assarion* was
worth nearly a penny. Later on it was reduced in weight, and sixteen
went to the denarion, so that its value became less than a halfpenny.
The "*quadrans*" of St. Matthew and St. Mark, which we also translate by
the word "*farthing*," was only one-fourth part of the above. The
denarion represented the ordinary daily wage of a labourer. See Matt.
xx. 9.

8. *Whosoever shall confess me before men.* "Confessing Christ" may
be direct or indirect. The highest way of confessing Him is that of the
martyrs ; but every good act done in His name is indirectly a confession
of Christ. Thus the Church keeps the feasts of saints, who were not
apostles or martyrs, under the title of confessors.

9 God. But he that shall deny me before men, shall be
10 denied before the Angels of God. And whosoever speaketh a word against the son of man, it shall be forgiven him: but to him that shall blaspheme against the Holy Ghost it
11 shall not be forgiven. And when they shall bring you into the synagogues, and to magistrates and powers, be not solicitous how or what you shall answer, or what you shall
12 say. For the Holy Ghost shall teach you in the same hour what you must say.

On Covetousness.

(Vers. 13–21.)

13 And one of the multitude said to him: Master, speak to my brother that he divide the inheritance with me.

10. *To him that shall blaspheme against the Holy Ghost, it shall not be forgiven.* The sin of blasphemy against the Holy Ghost has sometimes been taken to mean despair, which is a final act and leads to certain damnation. But this meaning does not fit well with the context. Our Lord is giving His apostles motives for confidence in their ministry, and this is one of them, namely, the gravity of the sin of those who refuse the gifts of grace and thus blaspheme the Holy Ghost. It is perhaps possible to suppose that our Lord meant to emphasize the gravity of the sin, and the fact that it would ordinarily lead to final impenitence, without meaning to pronounce absolutely that it would not under any circumstances be forgiven.

11. *And when they shall bring you into the synagogues.* The officials of the synagogue had power to inflict minor punishments, such as excommunication, temporary or permanent, with or without scourging. See Matt. x. 17; John ix. 22 and xii. 42. Such officials were found in every town. "Magistrates" and "powers" were apparently general names for higher tribunals, Jewish or Roman.

12. *For the Holy Ghost shall teach you in the same hour what you must say.* See Acts vi. 8, 10; and 2. Tim. iv. 17.

13. *Master, speak to my brother that he divide the inheritance with me.* The lessons that follow in this and the next two chapters seem to be a selection illustrative of our Lord's teaching at this period, but without any exact reference to the chronological order in which they were delivered. Several of the phrases and sentences occur elsewhere in the Gospels, sometimes in quite a different context. There is, however, no reason to suppose that they are out of place here. Our Lord would have frequently repeated many of His sayings, and especially at this time when many of those listening were not His regular followers. The incident of this man's appeal to our Lord was made by

But he said to him: Man, who hath appointed me judge 14
or divider over you? And he said to them: Take heed 15
and beware of all covetousness: for a man's life doth not
consist in the abundance of things which he possesseth.
And he spoke a similitude to them, saying: The land of a 16
certain rich man brought forth plenty of fruits. And he 17
thought within himself, saying: What shall I do, because
I have no room where to bestow my fruits. And he said: 18
This will I do: I will pull down my barns, and will build
greater: and into them will I gather all things that are
grown to me, and my goods. And I will say to my soul: 19
Soul, thou hast much goods laid up for many years, take
thy rest, eat, drink, make good cheer. But God said to 20
him: Thou fool, this night do they require thy soul of thee;
and whose shall those things be which thou hast provided?
So is he that layeth up treasure for himself, and is not rich 21
towards God.

Him the occasion of suggesting various lessons on covetousness, and is evidently mentioned here for the sole purpose of introducing the subject.

16. *And he spoke a similitude to them.* The parable of the Rich Fool is given only by St. Luke. It resembles that of the Rich Man and Lazarus—also peculiar to St. Luke—in that the riches described were not acquired by any injustice. The man's sins were not positive but negative; what we commonly call sins of omission. The possession of riches brings with it obligations, and a man who uses them simply for his own comfort and luxury is guilty in the sight of God, and may be punished by a sudden judgment by which he loses them all.

17. *Where to bestow my fruits.* The frequent repetition of the word μοῦ—*my* fruits, *my* barns, *my* goods, &c.—is probably not accidental. It denotes the man being full of the idea of the possessions being his own.

18. *My barns.* The word ἀποθήκας has rather a wider meaning than "barns." It stands rather for storehouses of any sort.

19. *Eat, drink, make good cheer.* This is, of course, his idea of enjoying life. Like so many in the noonday of health and happiness, nothing is further from his mind than that one day he will have to give an account of his stewardship.

20. *This night do they require thy soul of thee.* The present tense is emphatic. They are already requiring the man's soul.

21. *So is he that layeth up treasure for himself.* This is a summing up of the above sins of the man in the parable. Being "rich before God" implies generosity in His service and, in this case, devoting at least a portion of his goods to the service of his fellow-men, by alms-

On the Providence of God.

(VERS. 22-32.)

22 And he said to his disciples: Therefore I say to you, be not solicitous for your life what you shall eat;
23 nor for your body, what you shall put on. The life is more than the meat, and the body is more than the
24 raiment. Consider the ravens, for they sow not, neither do they reap, neither have they storehouse nor barn, and God feedeth them. How much are you more valuable
25 than they? And which of you by taking thought can add
26 to his stature one cubit? If then ye be not able to do so much as the least thing, why are you solicitous for the
27 rest? Consider the lilies how they grow: they labour not, neither do they spin. But I say to you, not even Solomon in all his glory was clothed like one of these.
28 Now if God clothe in this manner the grass that is to-day in the field, and to-morrow is cast into the oven; how

deeds or charitable work for the poor, which will be accepted as if done for the just judge Himself (Matt. xxv. 40).

22. *Be not solicitous.* That is, "cast your care on [God], for He hath care of you" (1 Peter v. 7). Compare verses 22-31 with Matt. vi. 25-33. These lessons follow naturally in the parable which precedes them. There can be no two more opposite spirits than on the one hand the thirst for riches and the *apparent* security which they give, and on the other the abandonment of self to the providence of God here described, which gives the only *true* security in this world. It need hardly be pointed out that solicitude is one thing and prudent care another. The latter is indeed the condition without which we should have no right to look for God's special providence in our favour.

23. *The life is more than the meat:* that is, the gift of life which God gives us without our co-operation is the greatest gift; and He who gave the greater can and will in due season give the less—which is necessary for its preservation. And so also with the body and the clothes which are a necessity for it.

24. *Consider the ravens.* Lastly, our Lord puts forward the unceasing providence of God for irrational creatures as an incentive to us to trust more in His providence for us.

25. *Which of you by taking thought.* This begins a further line of argument. Our Lord contrasts the power of God with the helplessness of man, even over small things.

can add to his stature one cubit. The word ἡλικία is taken by some as a man's "age"; but our rendering—"stature"—is probably more correct. A Jewish cubit was about twenty-one inches.

much more you, O ye of little faith? And seek not you ²⁹ what you shall eat, or what you shall drink: and be not lifted up on high. For all these things do the nations ³⁰ of the world seek. But your Father knoweth that you have need of these things. But seek ye first the kingdom of ³¹ God and his justice, and all these things shall be added unto you. Fear not, little flock, for them their measure ³² of wheat in due season?

Counsels of Charity.

(Vers. 33–34.)

Sell what you possess and give alms. Make to your- ³³ selves bags which grow not old, a treasure in heaven which faileth not: where no thief approacheth, nor moth cor-

29. *Be not lifted up on high.* The word ($\mu\epsilon\tau\epsilon\omega\rho i\zeta\epsilon\sigma\theta\alpha\iota$) means, literally, to be suspended [in the air]. Our translation here is somewhat obscure. Possibly our Lord was referring to the pride and arrogance which are the natural sequence of trust in riches and over-anxiety. Being suspended may, however, indicate want of decision or certainty, according to our phrase "in suspense." This meaning is adopted by the A.V. "neither be ye of doubtful mind." The Geneva bible gives a third meaning, "neither let your minds wander in these speculations." The old Latin texts vary considerably: "nolite solliciti esse," "non abalienatis vos," &c.

30. *For all these things do the nations of the world seek.* Although in the choice minds of antiquity, there was here and there, as in Socrates, Seneca and others, a growing sense of the personal nearness of God, it was very dim and wavering. The eagerness with which the Persian rites of Mithra were welcomed by the heathen world, not long after the time of Christ, testifies to the longing there was for a consciousness of personal relation with the Infinite; but the Gentile nations as a whole had no clear notion of God's fatherly care; and it would be very disappointing if we, who have had experience of so much of it, should descend to their level.

32. *Fear not, little flock.* The "little flock" probably meant the apostles and our Lord's immediate followers, to whom these words were primarily addressed. This verse is an explanation of the previous one, of the meaning of the word "kingdom," and it seems to be the only part of this section which has no counterpart in the Sermon on the Mount.

33. *Sell what you possess.* Cf. Matt. xix. 21, "If thou will be perfect, go sell what thou hast and give to the poor, and thou shalt have treasure in heaven: and come, follow me." Here the counsel seems

34 rupteth. For where your treasure is, there will your heart be also.

On Watchfulness.

(Vers. 35-48.)

35 Let your loins be girt, and lamps burning in your hands.
36 And you yourselves like to men who wait for their lord, when he shall return from the wedding: that when he cometh and knocketh, they may open to him immediately.
37 Blessed are those servants, whom the Lord when he cometh, shall find watching. Amen I say to you, that he will gird himself, and make them sit down to meat, and
38 passing will minister unto them. And if he shall come in the second watch, or come in the third watch, and find
39 them so, blessed are those servants. But this know ye, that if the householder did know at what hour the thief would come, he would surely watch, and would not suffer
40 his house to be broken open. Be you then also ready: for at what hour you think not, the son of man will come.
41 And Peter said to him: Lord, dost thou speak this parable

more general; to be intended for all and not only for those called to be "perfect," i.e., to absolute evangelical poverty. Nevertheless, it has a very special meaning when applied to these.

34. *Where your treasure is, there will your heart be also.* Thus those who work for a reward in the new world gradually have their hearts weaned from the affairs of this world.

35. *Let your loins be girt.* This is the first necessary for beginning work for those who wear loose and flowing garments such as were in common use at that time.

36. *Who wait for their lord.* Those waiting for the return of their lord do so in the spirit of longing for his arrival. Such should be our feeling, longing for the day of God's manifestation to us. Cf. 2 Tim. iv. 6-8.

when he shall return from the wedding. Cf. the parable of the Ten Virgins, Matt. xxv. 1-13.

38. *In the second watch.* The Jews divided the night into three watches, the Romans into four. Our Lord would of course have followed the Jewish division.

39. *At what hour the thief would come.* Our Lord here promises to come like a thief in the night, that is, unexpectedly.

41. *Dost thou speak this parable to us.* The nature of the question here naturally suggests that St. Peter was acting as spokesman for the

to us, or likewise to all? And the Lord said: Who (thinkest thou) is the faithful and wise steward, whom his lord setteth over his family, to give them their measure of wheat in due season? Blessed is that servant, whom when his lord shall come he shall find so doing. Verily I say to you, he will set him over all that he possesseth. But if that servant shall say in his heart, My lord is long a coming; and shall begin to strike the men-servants and maid-servants, and to eat and to drink, and be drunk: the lord of that servant will come in the day that he hopeth not, and at the hour that he knoweth not, and shall separate him, and shall appoint him his portion with unbelievers. And that servant who knew the will of his lord, and prepared not *himself*, and did not according to his will, shall be beaten with many stripes. But he that knew not and did things worthy of stripes, shall be beaten with few stripes. And unto whomsoever much is given, of him much shall be required: and to whom they have committed much, of him they will demand the more.

others. In any case, his inclination to take the lead was recognized both by the others and by our Lord.

42. *The faithful and wise steward.* As on many other occasions, our Lord answered one question by another, setting before St. Peter the dignity and responsibility of the office of those who were to be stewards, i.e., pastors of the Church. Some have also seen here a direct allusion to St. Peter's primacy, as though he was *the* steward whose duty it was to be faithful and wise.

44. *Over all that he possesseth.* This is the final reward. Cf. xxii. 29.

46. *Shall separate him.* The Greek word is διχοτομήσει and seems to mean something much stronger than "separate." The A.V. gives "cut him in sunder."

47. *Shall be beaten with many stripes.* It is only just that one who knew, i.e., realized, the will of his Lord and still failed to do it, should suffer "many stripes."

48. *But he that knew not.* Ignorance of the law may be a complete excuse for doing what is materially sinful. This would be what is called by theologians "*invincible ignorance.*" Ignorance which is not invincible may be a palliation of guilt, though the ignorance itself is partially culpable. Thus one who has lived all his days in a heathen country may be invincibly ignorant of the existence of the Catholic Church. If he is ignorant all his life of what is necessary for salvation —the existence of one God who rewards the good and punishes the wicked —such ignorance cannot be invincible and must be to some extent

Other Counsels.

(VERS. 49-59.)

49 I am come to cast fire on the earth ; and what will I but
50 that it be kindled ? And I have a baptism, wherewith I
am to be baptized: and how am I straitened until it be
51 accomplished. Think ye that I am come to give peace
52 on earth? I tell you no, but separation. For there shall
be from henceforth five in one house divided ; three against
53 two, and two against three. The father *shall be divided*
against the son, and the son against his father, the mother
against the daughter, and the daughter against the mother,
the mother-in-law against her daughter-in-law, and the
54 daughter-in-law against her mother-in-law. And he said
also to the multitudes: When you see a cloud rising from
the west, presently you say : A shower is coming ; and so
55 it happeneth : and when *ye see* the south wind blow, you
56 say : There will be heat : and it cometh to pass. You
hypocrites, you know how to discern the face of the heaven

culpable. But the circumstances of his life form a palliation of his guilt, and his punishment in the next world will be very much less severe than that of an unfaithful Catholic. And there seem to be many people, even in this country, in great centres of population, who are in this respect hardly better off than they would be in a heathen country ; while others have similar excuse but in very varying degrees. In every case God will take all such circumstances into account in pronouncing His judgment.

50. *I have a baptism wherewith I am to be baptized.* Our Lord of course refers here to His passion and death, for which He continually longed. Cf. Mark x. 32.

51. *That I am come to give peace.* See on ii. 14. The peace which our Lord promised was an internal one, not incompatible with external trials, which His followers have always had to undergo.

52. *Three against two, two against three.* This is not our Lord's wish, but what in fact will be often the case and what we have so often seen—people suffering for conscience' sake from those in the same house.

54. *When you see a cloud rising from the west.* A cloud from the west, and therefore from towards the Mediterranean, was a clear sign of rain. Cf. 3 Kings xviii. 44, 45.

55. *When you see the south wind blow.* The south wind would blow direct from the desert and therefore bring heat.

56. *You hypocrites.* The word "hypocrite" was applied by our Lord

and of the earth : but how is it that you do not discern this time? And why even of yourselves do you not judge that which is just? And when thou goest with thy adversary to the prince, whilst thou art in the way endeavour to be delivered from him : lest perhaps he draw thee to the judge, and the judge deliver thee to the exacter, and the exacter cast thee into prison. I say to thee, thou shalt not go out thence, until thou pay the very last mite.

on many occasions to the Pharisees: see the great denunciation of Matt. xxiii. Originally the word meant merely one who answered : then it became applied to an actor ; and afterwards to any one who pretended what was not and thus deceived people. The Pharisees in their pride not only deceived others, but also themselves. Cf. Matt. xxiii. 13 *seq*.

57. *Even of yourselves*, i.e., without the necessity of its being pointed out to you in this very special manner.

58. *Whilst thou art in the way with him*. The words "in the way," or "in via," are commonly used in reference to our passage through this life. Hence while the primary meaning seems to be simply a general lesson of worldly prudence, and of coming to terms with those who have anything against us, a secondary application has been seen by some, applying it definitely to doing penance for our sins in this life.

the judge deliver thee to the exacter. At the judgment seat the devil will be truly our "adversary" (1 Peter v. 8), having noted down all that can be brought against us.

59. *Thou shalt not go out from thence till thou pay the very last mite.* This must denote punishment in judgment on our sins ; and some have even seen a definite allusion to the prison of purgatory, where we shall have to remain till we pay "the very last mite." The word λεπτόν denotes the very smallest coin, equal to about half a farthing : see on xxi. 2.

CHAPTER XIII.

Parable of the Fig Tree.

(Vers. 1-9.)

AND there were present at that very time some that told him of the Galileans, whose blood Pilate

1. *There were present.* Παρῆσαν = rather "there came." Cf. Matt. xxvi. 50, where the word used is the same.

at that very time. This denotes that the arrival of these people took place just as our Lord was talking of the signs of judgment, which seemed to apply to the case of the victims they described.

the Galileans whose blood Pilate had mixed with their sacrifices. The position of Pilate as procurator of Judea has been already explained: see on iii. 1. He was a tyrannical ruler, much hated by the people. His first act, on his appointment some two or three years before this time, had been to bring the silver eagles and other military effigies to Jerusalem, which the Jews violently resented, not only because they were signs of the Roman dominion, but also because they looked on them as idolatrous: see on vii. 3. The former procurators had refrained from doing what would be a cause of exasperation among the Jews, and Pilate soon found it necessary to retract the step he had taken, and to take them back to Cæsarea. There is no other record extant of the particular massacre of the Galileans mentioned here, but tumults and bloodshed, about and even in the temple, were by no means uncommon at the time of the feasts at Jerusalem. Cf. for example the sudden and dangerous riot about St. Paul in Acts xxi. Some have thought that these victims were followers of Judas of Galilee, who headed a revolt at the time of the census (Acts v. 37)—that is of the second census in A.D. 6, when the Jews were first made to pay tribute. We cannot suppose, however, from the language of the Acts, that the sect lasted on into Pilate's time. The words of St. Luke clearly indicate that the massacre took place recently, and at the temple during the act of sacrifice. The question of *when* it took place is not an easy one. It cannot well

had mingled with their sacrifices. And he answering ² said to them: Think you that these Galileans were sinners above all the men of Galilee, because they suffered such things? No, I say to you: but unless ³ you shall do penance, you shall all likewise perish. Or ⁴ those eighteen upon whom the tower fell in Siloe, and slew them: think you that they also were debtors above all the men that dwelt in Jerusalem? No, I say ⁵ to you: but except you do penance, you shall all like-

have been at one of the three great festivals, though these were the usual occasions when Pilate went up to Jerusalem, and also when the Galileans came there in large numbers. The last great feast was that of Tabernacles, and our Lord had been present during the latter part, including the last or "great" day, the eighth day, peculiar to that feast only. Had the incident occurred then, our Lord would have witnessed it, and it would have been needless to describe it. Hence it had apparently happened since. There must always have been Galileans coming to or staying at Jerusalem, and these men, whose numbers are not stated, but who need not have been more than ten or twenty, were probably zealots under a vow who insulted the Roman guards, and were slain in the temple court by soldiers coming down the stairs from Fort Antonia, much as is described by St. Luke himself in Acts xxi.

2. *Think you that these Galileans were sinners.* As we have already seen, the Jews commonly looked on temporal affliction or calamity as a judgment for sin. Cf. John ix. 2. "Rabbi, who hath sinned, this man or his parents, that he should be born blind?" The object of our Lord's words is to teach us that such is not at all necessarily the case, but that often calamities may, in the providence of God, be meant to serve for us as warnings to the survivors, and even to be special graces to bring them to penance.

3. *Unless you shall do penance, you shall all likewise perish.* Note the word likewise (ὡσαύτως), i.e., suddenly and unexpectedly. In this sense it is true of all men. But it was to be true of the Jewish nation in a special sense that the unrepentant part of them would perish ὡσαύτως, by tumult, and murder, and ruin, all at Jerusalem, and in the temple itself.

On the words "*penance*," "*do penance*," see on iii. 3, and also x. 13 and xvii. 3.

4. *Those eighteen upon whom the tower fell in Siloe.* There is no other record of the fall of a tower in Siloe any more than of the massacre of the Galileans. But it is known that about this time Pilate was building an aqueduct which would naturally come into the port of Siloe at the south-east angle of the city, and he had incurred the wrath of the Jews by spending on it some of the corban or temple money. They therefore looked on the whole as sacrilegious,

6 wise perish. He spoke also this parable: A certain man had a fig-tree planted in his vineyard, and he came 7 seeking fruit on it, and found none. And he said to the dresser of the vineyard: Behold for these three years I come seeking fruit on this fig-tree, and I find none. Cut it down therefore; why cumbereth it the 8 ground. But he answering said to him: Lord, let it alone this year also, until I dig about it, and dung it. 9 And if happily it bear fruit: but if not, then after that thou shalt cut it down.

and if this accident was connected, as it probably was, with the work, they would have regarded it as a direct judgment from God. It may in fact have been a water-tower built on bad foundations, and burying those who were working at it. An inscription on one of the water-channels connected with the work has lately been discovered.

6. *And he spoke to them a parable.* The sense of the parable which follows is a continuation of the ideas which have just preceded. Our Lord meant to say that it would be well for us to examine our own lives and see whether we are bringing forth the fruit of penance. Cf. iii. 8.

7. *Behold for three years I come.* Here the first meaning evidently applied to the Jewish people, and some have even seen an application of the three years' fruitlessness to the three years of our Lord's ministry. Others take it to be simply an allusion to the time a fig-tree would ordinarily take to come to maturity. If the fig-tree be taken as the Jewish people, it is noticeable that one of our Lord's miracles, the parabolic sentence on the fig-tree at Bethphage: "May no fruit grow on thee henceforward for ever," acquires a special meaning. In the wider sense the parable applies to every human soul.

Cut it down therefore. The sudden death of the Galileans in the temple, or of the workmen at Siloe, was in each case like the cutting down of the tree. God will not take this course till He has given ample opportunity for amendment; but if no amendment comes, sooner or later He will say: "Cut it down;" and to the careless life that is so cut off, the end will always seem sudden and unaccountable.

8. *Lord, let it alone this year also.* These words are evidently intended to denote a definite respite granted to the Jewish nation, whether we take it as meaning the remainder of Christ's ministry, or the forty years before the destruction of Jerusalem. So also it is often the case that a soul is having its last chance as a respite from punishment, without being aware that it is so.

9. *If happily it bear fruit.* The rest of the sentence is, of course, to be understood.

A Sabbath-day Miracle.

(VERS. 10–17.)

And he was teaching in their synagogue on their 10 sabbath. And behold there was a woman who had a spirit 11 of infirmity eighteen years: and she was bowed together, neither could she look upwards at all. Whom when Jesus 12 saw he called her unto him, and said to her: Woman, thou art delivered from thy infirmity. And he laid his 13 hands upon her, and immediately she was made straight, and glorified God. And the ruler of the synagogue, 14 (being angry that Jesus had healed on the sabbath,)

10. *And he was teaching in their synagogue on their sabbath.* We have here a specimen of the Sabbath-day disputes during the last period of the ministry, probably in Perea. It resembles generally those of an earlier date, but the language, both of our Lord and of His enemies, is stronger and more definite, as the conflict had become more acute. There is no absolute reason to suppose that this incident took place after the dispute described in chap. xi., though it may have done so. The words "on their sabbath" should read "on the sabbaths," and it thus appears that our Lord was still in the habit of taking part in the synagogue worship, at least occasionally, as before. Thus they had not as yet used their legal power of "excommunicating" Him. It would be very difficult for the temple chiefs ever to do so by any universal sentence, though it was done in particular cases commonly enough, as is indicated in John ix. 22, xii. 42, &c. In our Lord's case, as He passed from place to place, He was continually addressing new hearers, and though many, both of friends and enemies, followed Him about, it would have been difficult to enforce "excommunication" at any fresh village or town. The people did not ask for miracles on the Sabbath till after sun-down, when it was legally over (cf. iv. 40), and the ruler's remark in *v.* 14 implies that the more censorious thought they ought not even to give occasion for them by being there. Our Lord chose, however, when occasion offered, to effect cures and to use the opportunity for a doctrinal explanation of the new law of the Sabbath.

11. *A woman who had a spirit of infirmity.* It is not at all necessary to suppose that this was a case of actual demoniacal possession. St. Luke's expression, "a spirit of infirmity," may easily have been figurative, and our Lord's words (*v.* 12) do not imply any exorcism. The only thing definitely specified is a disease which caused the woman to be "bowed together" so that she could not look upwards at all.

14. *The ruler of the synagogue.* See on iv. 15.
being angry that Jesus had healed on the sabbath. We may note the much more definite way in which the ruler of the synagogue

answering said to the multitude: Six days there are wherein you ought to work. In them therefore come, and
15 be healed: and not on the sabbath-day. And the Lord answering him, said: Ye hypocrites, doth not every one of you on the sabbath-day loose his ox or his ass from the
16 manger, and lead them to water? And ought not this daughter of Abraham, whom Satan hath bound, lo, these eighteen years, be loosed from this bond on the sabbath-
17 day? And when he said these things, all his adversaries were ashamed: and all the people rejoiced for all the things that were gloriously done by him.

The Mustard-seed and the Leaven.
(VERS. 18–21.)

18 He said therefore: To what is the kingdom of God like,
19 and whereunto shall I resemble it? It is like to a grain

ventured to speak against healing on the Sabbath than the Pharisees had done at the beginning of the ministry. Originally indeed they had only found fault with a miracle which involved what they termed "work" on a Sabbath—such as carrying a bed. Cf. John v. 10. And they spoke then in a more tentative way. See Matt. xii. 10. Now, however, it had become a sort of watchword, a recognized occasion of accusing our Lord. There had no doubt been very many other Sabbath-day miracles, unrecorded in the Gospels, leading up gradually from one state of things to the other.

15. *Doth not every one of you on the sabbath-day loose his ox or his ass?* This is an *argumentum ad hominem*. Their own common-sense taught them that they could do such things on the Sabbath; to deny it would be hypocrisy. And a comparison seems further meant between loosing an ox or an ass, and loosing a child of Abraham, which follows.

16. *Whom Satan hath bound.* This expression again does not necessarily indicate diabolical possession. Such manner of speaking was common and well recognized in a figurative sense.

17. *And all the people rejoiced.* It appears from this verse that the general sympathy of the people was still with our Lord. They rejoiced in the miracle and in the discomfiture of the ruler. There are indeed many indications that Pharisaism, while appealing to the educated or half-educated classes, left the simple people of the country largely unaffected, and naturally so, for the Pharisaic teachers despised them, and looked on them as accursed in their ignorance.

19. *It is like to a grain of mustard-seed.* Cf. Matt. xiii. 31; Mark iv. 31. The mustard-seed is like God's kingdom because of (1) its

of mustard-seed, which a man took and cast into his garden, and it grew, and became a great tree, and the birds of the air lodged in the branches thereof. And again he 20 said: Whereunto shall I esteem the kingdom of God to be like? It is like to leaven, which a woman took and 21 hid in three measures of meal, till the whole was leavened.

On the Difficulty of Salvation.

(VERS. 22–30.)

And he went through the cities and towns teaching and 22 making his journey to Jerusalem. And a certain man 23 said to him: Lord, are they few that are saved? But he

great growth; and (2) its secret growth. The seed is very small, and the expression, "small as a mustard-seed" had passed into a proverb. Yet it grew into "a great tree"—not in the sense of a forest tree, of course, for He is comparing it to *other garden-herbs*, and the word in St. Matthew is "plant." It is said that a variety of the mustard plant grows in that region as much as ten feet, and some even say twenty feet high.

21. *It is like to leaven.* The peculiarity of leaven is its all-pervading effect from an apparently slight and secret cause. A measure ($\sigma\acute{a}\tau o\nu$) was one-third of an *ephah*, which was an ordinary baking. Hence the *three* measures mentioned.

22. *And he went through the cities and towns.* Many commentators see in this verse the beginning of a new missionary journey. It seems, however, hardly natural that St. Luke should mention the beginnings of several successive journeys without alluding to their ends. He has told us (ix. 51) that as the time of our Lord's death approached, His face was set towards Jerusalem, and we have already stated that it seems simpler to regard the whole section—ix. 51 to xviii. 30—as one protracted missionary record. It is true that we have to allow one short break, as our Lord was in Jerusalem for the feast of Dedication. But there is no reason to think that His visit was for more than a few days, and there is some indication that His disciples did not accompany Him, for at the supper at Bethany (x. 38) He must have been alone. If we take this view, the verse we are now discussing must be considered as a sort of parenthesis, which might be paraphrased in English thus: "We shall now proceed to describe other typical incidents and sayings of our Lord which occurred at this time, when He was going through the cities and towns making His journey to Jerusalem."

23. *Lord, are they few that are saved?* The question as to the number of the elect has always been one on which religious men have

24 said to them: Strive to enter by the narrow gate: for many, I say to you, shall seek to enter, and shall not be 25 able. But when the master of the house shall be gone in, and shall shut to the door, you shall begin to stand without, and knock at the door, saying, Lord, open to us: and he answering shall say to you, I know you 26 not whence you are: then you shall begin to say: We have eaten and drunk in thy presence, and thou hast 27 taught in our streets. And he shall say to you: I know you not whence you are: depart from me, all ye workers 28 of iniquity. There shall be weeping and gnashing of teeth; when you shall see Abraham and Isaac and Jacob, and all the prophets in the kingdom of God, and you 29 yourselves thrust out. And there shall come from the east and the west and the north and the south; and shall 30 sit down in the kingdom of God. And behold, they are last that shall be first, and they are first that shall be last.

occupied themselves. In this case it seems to have been suggested by those sterner aspects of our Lord's teaching which He was insisting on at that period.

24. *Strive to enter by the narrow gate.* Cf. Matt. vii. 13. Our Lord always refused to answer in so many words as to the number who will be saved, and rather directed His hearers to the proper frame of mind to aim at. To save one's soul is like entering a narrow gate. In the case of an eastern traveller on a camel this demands great care, and may require that he shall first unload much of what he has brought with him from his journey. If it refer to another gate on which people press from all sides, and which at a certain time may be shut, then it requires skill and diligence to get in while the opportunity is still offered to us— that is, before we are cut off, like the fig tree.

26. *We have eaten and drunk in thy presence.* No external privilege, not even contact with our Lord Himself, will avail on that day. On the contrary, such may be the cause of greater judgment.

28. *Weeping and gnashing of teeth.* This is our Lord's regular expression to denote the state of the lost, and it appears to indicate anguish and rage. The vision of the patriarchs was the current Jewish picture of heaven—as in "Abraham's bosom" (xvi. 22) with which compare this verse; but He goes on to widen the idea by showing that the Gentiles shall also come, even where the "children of Abraham" are shut out.

29. *There shall come from the east and the west.* Cf. Isa. xlv. 6. This is so evidently a prophecy of the salvation of the Gentiles who came from afar, that the Pharisees must have recognized it as such.

30. *They that are first shall be last.* These well-known words are

The Pharisees and Herod.

(VERS. 31-35.)

The same day there came some of the Pharisees, saying 31 to him: Depart and get thee hence, for Herod hath a mind to kill thee. And he said to them: Go and tell 32 that fox, Behold I cast out devils, and do cures to-day and to-morrow, and the third day I am consummated.

a continuation of the same sense. They may mean either (1) the Pharisees who made themselves great in this world should find themselves least in the next; or (2) the Jews who received their call first in point of time shall find themselves last. The words "the first shall be last" are recorded as used by our Lord more than once, and were probably proverbial.

31. *Herod hath a mind to kill thee.* Our Lord was therefore still in Perea, which was part of the tetrarchy of Herod. If the incident took place just at the end of the ministry, as seems likely, He may have been expected to pass on His journey to Jerusalem, where He was going for the feast (xxiii. 7). The object of the Pharisees appears to have been to get our Lord to go back into Judea, where He would be more under the power of the Sanhedrin. Cf. John x. 39 and 40, "They sought therefore to take him; and he escaped out of their hands. And he went again beyond the Jordan." The plea about Herod was clearly hypocritical, but there must have been an element of truth in the rumour, for our Lord sent in answer a message to Herod, which He would not have done had the whole been a fabrication (see next note). Very possibly Herod feared our Lord, as he had feared St. John, as Josephus tells us, because of His influence with the people, which might at any time be turned against himself. He also probably feared Him because of his own guilty life, against which our Lord would have testified as St. John did. And he may still have half believed that John had come to life again in Him. But just as in the case of John himself, his feelings were mixed, for we know from xxiii. 8 that "for a long time he had desired," partly no doubt out of curiosity, to see our Lord.

32. *Go and tell that fox.* This is the only instance recorded of our Lord using a word of contempt. The name implied low cunning: and Herod, from all we know of him, must have been a very contemptible person. From the form of the message many suppose that these Pharisees had really been sent by Herod. A possible theory is that they were plotting to get our Lord out of Perea to Jerusalem, in the hope of seizing Him, or denouncing Him to Pilate as an "enemy of Cæsar"; and that they, by their temporary alliance with "the Herodians," had actually got Herod to use some threat, and then conveyed it to Jesus for their own ends. If so, the word "fox" is meant for them as well as for him.

to-day and to-morrow; and the third day I am consummated.

33 Nevertheless I must walk to-day and to-morrow, and the day following, because it cannot be that a prophet perish
34 out of Jerusalem. Jerusalem, Jerusalem, that killest the prophets, and stonest them that are sent to thee, how often would I have gathered thy children as the bird doth
35 her brood under her wings, and thou wouldst not? Behold your house shall be left to you desolate. And I say to you that you shall not see me till the time come, when you shall say: Blessed is he that cometh in the name of the Lord.

These words cannot refer to the last three "days" of the ministry: they probably mean simply a short time, or perhaps rather a definite and appointed time.

33. *I must walk*, i.e., "I must proceed on my way and go on with my work; and neither Herod nor the temple chiefs can stop me."

it cannot be that a prophet perish out of Jerusalem. The deduction seems to be that there is no reason for apprehension in Herod's threats; for Providence has arranged that the end shall come not in Perea, but, as has been the case with so many prophets, in Jerusalem.

34. *Jerusalem, Jerusalem*, &c. Cf. Matt. xxiii. 37. Probably these words of warning to Jerusalem were used by our Lord twice. The context on the second occasion shows that it cannot be there read as an isolated saying. We might suppose it to be such here, and introduced out of the order of time for similarity of subject: but this seems less probable than the simple explanation that as He had so often yearned over Jerusalem, He twice made use of this remarkable sentence.

how often would I have gathered thy children. The words "how often" are important, as they seem to refer to the frequent visits to Jerusalem recorded by St. John, but on which the synoptists are silent.

35. *You shall not see me till the time*, i.e., "you, the unbelieving people of Jerusalem, shall not see me after my death until," &c.

when you shall say: Blessed is he that cometh in the name of the Lord. These words cannot, as some have imagined, refer to the triumphal entry of our Lord into Jerusalem, on the day of Palms, if for no other reason, because the same prophecy was repeated by Him after that day. It seems most natural to take them as an abandonment to last to the end of time, when He shall come in judgment and they will be compelled to recognize Him as the Messiah. Some refer these words to the belief that the Jews are to be converted before the last day, and suppose therefore that they will fulfil this saying by receiving Him with acclamation on the judgment day (cf. Rom. xi. 25—27); but it seems better to suppose that the Jerusalem which is to receive Him with blessing is not the old Jerusalem, but the new; i.e., the city of the Apocalypse.

CHAPTER XIV.

Sabbath-day Meal with the Pharisees.

(VERS. 1–14.)

AND it came to pass when Jesus went into the house of one of the chief of the Pharisees on the sabbath-day to eat bread, that they watched him. And behold, there was 2 a certain man before him that had the dropsy. And Jesus 3

1. *One of the chief of the Pharisees.* The Pharisees had no grades of distinction among themselves, so that this phrase must have been used in a popular sense.
on the sabbath-day to eat bread. Sabbath-day dinners were quite usual among the Jews, though the cooking had to be done the day before (Exod. xvi. 23). Upon this point the law was observed with scrupulous care by devout Pharisees, who used to watch on Friday evenings until three stars could be seen in the sky, that they might be quite sure of the moment when, according to the tradition of the Rabbis, the Sabbath rest had begun. We have already commented on the Sabbath-day disputes of this period of the ministry: see on xiii. 10. We cannot say whether the incident of this chapter took place before or after that of chap. xi.; but it is clear that it was in a different place and concerned different people.

2. *There was a certain man before him that had the dropsy.* It has already been remarked that at an oriental house, during the progress of a repast, the banquet hall was accessible to outsiders, who were often present as spectators. Thus it was possible for the dropsical man to be there without being one of the guests. It would appear that he had been placed there by the Pharisees especially to see what our Lord would do; or at least they allowed him to stay with that purpose in view. From the nature of his disease, he would have been very conspicuous, and his unsightliness would render his presence otherwise unwelcome.

3. *And Jesus answering.* The above conclusion is strengthened by these words. There is no mention of any question being asked, so that our Lord's "answer" must have been an answer to the presence of the dropsical man and to the Pharisees' thoughts.

answering, spoke to the lawyers and Pharisees, saying: Is
4 it lawful to heal on the sabbath-day? But they held their
peace. But he taking him, healed him, and sent him
5 away. And answering them, he said: Which of you shall
have an ass or an ox fall into a pit; and will not imme-
6 diately draw him out on the sabbath-day? And they could
7 not answer him to these things. And he spoke a parable
also to them that were invited, marking how they chose the
8 first seats at the table, saying to them: When thou art
invited to a wedding, sit not down in the first place, lest
perhaps one more honourable than thou be invited by him;
9 and he that invited thee and him, come and say to thee,
Give this man place: and then thou begin with shame to

4. *But they held their peace.* The plan of the Pharisees thus reacted on themselves. The lawyers were bound to profess knowledge of the law, and our Lord in anticipating their thoughts put them in the same difficulty which they had meant for Him. Their silence indicated their frame of mind. They had no wish to have the question answered or even discussed: their only object was to get an excuse for finding fault.

5. *Which of you shall have an ass or an ox.* Nearly all the Greek MSS. read "a son or an ox," &c. See Deut. v. 14, where in explaining the laws of the Sabbath "thy son" is put first among rational creatures and "thy ox" first among irrational. To fall into an unprotected pit or well, would have been a not uncommon accident. Nevertheless, an intelligent being would be better able to protect himself or to extricate himself than an animal, and this consideration may perhaps have led to the substitution of reading. The above is, however, almost certainly the correct one, and if the meaning is "if his son, or even his ox shall fall into a pit," it becomes more forcible.

7. *He spoke a parable also.* Having answered what was in their minds, our Lord proceeded to speak some strong words to the Pharisees. As in chap. xi., we see that the hostility had now become so open that there was no longer any reason for our Lord to hold back.

8. *Sit not down in the first place.* The tables at a banquet were commonly arranged in triplets, forming three sides of a square. The middle seat at each table was the highest place.

9. *Then thou begin with shame to take the lowest place.* The motive put before the Pharisees is only that of worldly prudence. They would not gain their own ends by choosing a place from which they might be asked to remove; and if they had to move, they would find by that time nothing but the lowest places unoccupied; whereas if they selected the lowest place of all, they would be asked by the host on his arrival to move up higher. To a class so jealous of precedence and outward marks of esteem, in the synagogue and elsewhere, the lesson would come home with singular force.

take the lowest place. But when thou art invited, go, sit down in the lowest place : that when he who invited thee cometh, he may say to thee : Friend, go up higher. Then shalt thou have glory before them that sit at table with thee. Because every one that exalteth himself, shall be humbled : and he that humbleth himself, shall be exalted. And he said to him also that had invited him : When thou makest a dinner or a supper, call not thy friends, nor thy brethren, nor thy kinsmen, nor thy neighbours who are rich : lest perhaps they also invite thee again, and a recompense be made to thee. But when thou makest a feast, call the poor, the maimed, the lame, and the blind. And thou shalt be blessed, because they have not wherewith to make thee recompense : for recompense shall be made thee at the resurrection of the just.

The Heavenly Banquet.

(VERS. 15-24.)

When one of them that sat at table with him, had heard these things, he said to him : Blessed is he that shall eat

11. *Every one that exalteth himself shall be humbled.* Though the first motive was worldly prudence, our Lord went on to draw out of it a moral lesson that he that exalteth himself shall be humbled, and *vice versâ*, words which, though familiar enough to us, must have sounded strangely novel when first spoken.

12. *Call not thy friends.* There seems to be here a contrast intended between the Pharisees who were sitting inside the banquet hall, and the poor who were assembled outside. True hospitality and charity would show itself in giving to the latter rather than the former, and this would have its reward in the next world. Of course this is in no way meant as a prohibition to invite our friends, but only as pointing out that this sort of hospitality was not worthy of an everlasting reward as the other kind was.

14. *Recompense shall be made thee at the resurrection of the just,* i.e., the Heavenly Banquet. These words also would add both to the lesson and to the reproof, inasmuch as the resurrection was the doctrine which the Pharisees themselves ardently maintained against the Sadducees. Here they are taught at once its vital reality and its actual consequences.

15. *Blessed is he that shall eat bread in the kingdom of God.* The guest was here taking up the sense of what our Lord had said. To "eat bread" indicated a banquet, and it was commonly supposed that the Messianic age would be a time, amongst other things, of feasting.

16 bread in the kingdom of God. But he said to him: A
17 certain man made a great supper, and invited many. And
he sent his servant at the hour of supper to say to them
that were invited, that they should come, for now all things
18 are ready. And they began all at once to make excuse. The
first said to him, I have bought a farm, and I must needs
19 go out and see it; I pray thee, hold me excused. And
another said, I have bought five yoke of oxen, and I go to
20 try them: I pray thee, hold me excused. And another
said, I have married a wife, and therefore I cannot come.
21 And the servant returning told these things to his lord.
Then the master of the house being angry, said to his
servant: Go out quickly into the streets and lanes of the
city, and bring in hither the poor and the feeble and the

The man probably, however, was one of those who had heard our Lord speak of "the heavenly banquet," which was to be the fulfilment of what was promised in this world. So his chance remark led up to the parable.

16. *A certain man made a great supper.* Our Lord answered with a parable showing how little sought after is this heavenly banquet. A somewhat similar, but clearly not identical parable, is given by St. Matthew (xxii. 1-10). The purport of each is the same. They relate primarily to the call of the Jews and their unfaithfulness, and to the subsequent call of the Gentiles: but their meaning may be extended to include all unfaithfulness to any vocation. This is one of the many cases where we have an illustration of the fact that our Lord repeated parables of the same type more than once—probably often—to different hearers.

17. *He sent his servant at the hour of supper.* This was the ordinary custom, and did not imply any expected unwillingness to come on the part of the guests. The people had already, we are to understand, been invited for that day. Now the servants came with the customary reminder, "The supper is ready."

18. *They began all at once to make excuse.* The sense of this phrase in Greek is not very clear. ἀπὸ μιᾶς may mean "to make excuses of the one type." They do not indicate that they had agreed together; but merely that each preferred his own worldly affairs. None of the occupations pleaded in excuse were *unlawful*; now they were only preferred unduly to the Lord's call. They are sometimes classified as (1) avarice; (2) worldly care; and (3) sensuality. But the story does not seem to imply this. They are ordinary calls of life, and the "thorns" that choke the word of God.

21. *Into the streets and lanes of the city.* Some have seen a distinction between those mentioned here and those in *v.* 23, that whereas

blind and the lame. And the servant said: Lord, it is 22 done as thou hast commanded, and yet there is room. And the lord said to the servant: Go out into the high-23 ways and hedges ; and compel them to come in, that my house may be filled. But I say unto you, that none of 24 those men that were invited shall taste of my supper.

Conditions for following Christ.

(VERS. 25-35.)

And there went great multitudes with him ; and turning, 25 he said to them : If any man come to me, and hate not 26 his father, and mother, and wife, and children, and brethren, and sisters, yea and his own life also, he cannot be

the former were in the city, the latter were out of it, which they interpret to mean that this one class were those poor whom the Pharisees looked down on and despised, publicans or sinners, or the common ignorant people, who were still of the house of Israel ; while the other class outside the city are recognized as the Gentiles.

23. *Compel them to come in.* The deduction from the context is that these men responded to the call and duly filled many of the vacant places. But it needed hard work to "compel" the Gentiles who knew not God. Cf. 2 Tim. iv. 2.

24. *None of those men that were invited.* The punishment named was that none of those invited should taste the supper. The Pharisees could hardly fail to observe the meaning of this and its application to themselves. Our Lord clearly meant that the Gentiles would fill the places left vacant by their unworthiness.

25. *There went great multitudes with him.* There is no connection between this verse and what has gone before, and we may suppose St. Luke here passes to a different tract of time. The sayings of our Lord which follow certainly belong however to the last period of His ministry, during which the sterner aspects of His preaching were more particularly enforced. He had been proclaiming the doctrine of the Cross and of self conquest for some months past. Now He went a step further, and some part of what follows seems addressed especially to His more immediate and closer followers. At least, the conditions enumerated can be applied with special force to these.

26. *And hate not his father.* This is given as the first and most necessary condition. Cf. Matt. x. 37. "Hating one's father" has, of course, a comparative meaning. Cf. xvi. 13 : "He will hate the one and love the other," of the "two Masters." The love for one's parents must be less strong than that for God, so that we should be ready, if necessary, to leave them for His sake. More than this is however meant,

my disciple. And whosoever doth not carry his cross and come after me, cannot be my disciple. For which of you having a mind to build a tower, doth not first sit down and reckon the charges that are necessary, whether he have wherewithal to finish *it*. Lest after he hath laid the foundation, and is not able to finish it, all that see it begin to mock him, saying: This man began to build, and was not able to finish. Or what king about to go to make war against another king, doth not first sit down and think whether he be able with ten thousand to meet him that with twenty thousand cometh against him? Or else whilst the other is yet afar off, sending an embassy, he desireth conditions of peace. So likewise every one of you that doth not renounce all that he possesseth, cannot be my disciple. Salt is good. But if the salt shall lose its

As soon as intercourse with our parents or friends becomes an obstacle to our perfection, in that respect it becomes to us a danger, and therefore a thing to turn away from. It should be added that no feeling of personal aversion was intended, or would be even lawful; but only an aversion to such intercourse as might be detrimental to our higher interests, and such a feeling is compatible with the highest and truest love for our parents themselves. The whole has additional force when applied, on the one hand, to the apostles and first disciples: and on the other, to those who, like them, are called to a life of absolute detachment from the interests of this world. To such, these words have a special meaning, calling on them to forsake all sensible intercourse with those naturally dearest to them, with a view to corresponding with the sublime vocation of union with God to which they are called.

27. *Whosoever doth not carry his cross.* The full meaning of this expression would, of course, not have been intelligible at this time. See xviii. 34.

28. *Which of you having a mind to build a tower.* The second condition which our Lord touches on, is equivalent to simply calling attention to the advisability of counting the cost, before embarking on any serious business. This is only ordinary prudence. Again, there is a special meaning applicable to those called to the religious life, and the rule enforced by the Church as to the duration and character of the noviceship.

31. *What king about to go to make war.* This is a variant of the second, but reminds us that in addition to much work, there has to be positive fighting, in which it is necessary that we should be victorious.

34. *Salt is good.* Cf. Matt. v. 13, where our Lord's special followers are called "the salt of the earth." The meaning seems to be

savour, wherewith shall it be seasoned? It is neither 35 profitable for the land, nor for the dunghill, but shall be cast out. He that hath ears to hear, let him hear.

here that our Lord's disciples should be as salt, full of freshness and vigour. It must be remembered that salt is not, even now, the cheap and ready commodity in the East that it has in late years become with us. It was, and still is, very commonly taxed as something of a luxury. Hence, because of its price, it would often be kept until spoiled. There is therefore a force which the hearers would have readily understood when Christ said "Salt is good," &c.

35. *He that hath ears to hear, let him hear.* This seems to have been a formula used by our Lord more than once, to attract special attention to His words. See viii. 8.

CHAPTER XV.

Parable of the Lost Sheep.

(VERS. 1-7.)

NOW the publicans and sinners drew near unto him to hear him. And the Pharisees and the scribes murmured, saying: This man receiveth sinners, and

1. *The publicans and sinners drew near unto him.* The sense seems to be " were drawing near unto him," or " were accustomed to draw near unto him " ; and St. Luke puts this fact as an introduction to the three parables on sinners which he is about to give. There is no reason to suppose that these three parables were all delivered together. Like those which follow, on the use of riches and other subjects, they no doubt belong to this period of the ministry, and hence are for the most part peculiar to St. Luke ; but the grouping of them seems by subject rather than by time, and we may take the next two chapters as simply a collection of some of the chief parables delivered during the ministry in Judea and Perea. The three before us in this chapter relate to God's dealings with sinners. It would be impossible to bring this out satisfactorily in one parable, as the mercy of God is so far beyond anything of which we have practical experience in this life, so that no single illustration would serve the purpose. If, for example, in the parable of the Prodigal Son, we were told that his father followed him into the "far country" and was at his side all through his misdeeds, begging him to return and offering him a free pardon ; and that after his return and reinstatement, he went off again, and again his father followed him, and that the same happened time after time, it would carry little weight, as it would not be within the range of human possibility. The different qualities of our Lord's dealings have therefore to be shown in different parables, so that each one may be more or less in keeping with what might ordinarily happen. Thus we have here the Lost Sheep, the Lost Groat, and the Prodigal Son. The first two show a picture of God seeking out a sinner like a sheep who has wandered astray, or a piece of money lost. In the parable of the Prodigal Son, the free will

eateth with them. And he spoke to them this parable, 3
saying: What man of you that hath an hundred sheep: 4
and if he shall lose one of them, doth he not leave the
ninety-nine in the desert, and go after that which was lost
until he find it? And when he hath found it, lay it upon 5
his shoulders, rejoicing: and coming home call together 6
his friends and neighbours, saying to them: Rejoice with
me, because I have found my sheep that was lost. I say 7
to you, that even so there shall be joy in heaven upon one
sinner that doth penance, more than upon ninety-nine just
who need not penance.

of the sinner is made apparent, both in his yielding to temptation and his after repentance; and then God's forgiveness of the repentant sinner is placed before us. Each parable ends with a similar moral lesson—the rejoicing of the saints and angels, and of God Himself, at the conversion of the sinner.

2. *And the Pharisees and scribes murmured.* There seems to be a contrast intended here between the publicans and sinners, who as by instinct continually drew near to our Lord, and the Pharisees, to whom murmuring against Him had become almost a second nature. Possessed with the thought of ceremonial cleanliness and defilement, they were indignant because Christ, a teacher and a Rabbi, not only received sinners, but exposed Himself to actual uncleanness by eating with them.

3. *He spoke to them this parable.* The tense here is the aorist, denoting the transition from a habit and custom to a particular occasion.

4. *What man of you that hath a hundred sheep.* The surroundings of a pastoral country such as Judea would make the simile of this parable appeal very specially to the people. The care of a shepherd for his sheep in those countries is more typical than with us. He always goes in front of them as their leader and they follow of their own accord. He acts as their guide, directing them where to go, what dangers to avoid, and the like, always by his example, as he walks before them. And when any accident does befall any of them, or when, as in this parable, they go astray, he is at hand to help them or to go and seek the wandering ones.

5. *Lay it upon his shoulders rejoicing.* The picture of our Lord returning, with the sheep on His shoulders, has become familiar to us in Christian art, and has been so from the first, for it is perhaps the commonest of all the representations in the Catacombs. It is as if He were returning in triumph, as though the recovery of the lost sheep was *His* victory and *His* gain.

7. *There shall be joy in heaven.* The joy in heaven over every repentant sinner is commonly quoted as illustrating the Communion of Saints, and the continual interest which they take in our welfare. It is

Parable of the Lost Groat.

(VERS. 8-10.)

8 Or what woman having ten groats: if she lose one groat doth not light a candle and sweep the house and seek dili-
9 gently, until she find it? And when she hath found it, call together her friends and neighbours, saying: Rejoice with
10 me, because I have found the groat which I had lost. So I say to you, there shall be joy before the Angels of God upon one sinner doing penance.

Parable of the Prodigal Son.

(VERS. 11-32.)

11
12 And he said: A certain man had two sons; and the younger of them said to his father: Father, give me the portion of substance that falleth to me. And he divided

hardly necessary to point out that joy at the recovery of a sinner is a feeling of itself, and different in kind from the satisfaction which God takes in one who preserves his innocence. Our Lord would never have meant that the former was the preferable state; but that the repentance of a sinner produced a certain kind of joy which in the other case would not be called forth. Cf. *vv.* 31, 32.

8. *What woman having ten groats.* A "groat" or drachma was a Greek coin, corresponding to the Latin *denarius*, and worth about 10d. The women used to hang them round their necks as ornaments. Hence one would easily be missed, and would be more truly a loss to be recovered by searching than if the money was for spending. Comparing this parable with that of the lost sheep, the only difference seems to be that the sheep went astray through its thoughtlessness, while the groat was lost as the result of mere accident. It would, however, be over-straining the comparison to see any very special meaning in this. Our Lord was intending to insist on the joy at the repentance of a sinner as of the finding of something precious which was lost, and this is illustrated by both parables.

11. *A certain man had two sons.* In the third parable on the subject of sinners, our Lord puts forward more distinctly sin as the work of the sinner. The picture at the beginning shows us the happiness of the two sons at home with their father; then comes the younger one's desire for liberty, his request to his father, and the father's conduct in not refusing his consent, but allowing his son the use of his freedom, although he knew it might be to his ruin. In the same way God allows us the use of our free will, though He often knows that we shall use it amiss.

12. *The portion of substance that falleth to me.* The second son

unto them his substance. And not many days after, the 13
younger son gathering all together, went abroad into a far
country: and there wasted his substance living riotously.
And after he had spent all, there came a mighty famine in 14
that country, and he began to be in want. And he went, 15
and cleaved to one of the citizens of that country. And
he sent him into his farm to feed swine. And he would 16
fain have filled his belly with the husks the swine did eat:
and no man gave unto him. And returning to himself, he 17
said: How many hired servants in my father's house abound
with bread, and I here perish with hunger? I will arise, 18
and will go to my father, and say to him: Father, I have

would inherit one third, the eldest one two thirds of the father's estate (Deut. xxi. 17): but of course they had no right to ask for it in the lifetime of the father. Nevertheless, at the request of the younger he divided his property between them both, so that the elder also received his share.

13. *Went abroad into a far country.* The journey to a far country typifies the alienation from God produced in every soul by sin. When we lose the state of grace, He is no longer close to us as before, and we are like people in a far country.

14. *There came a mighty famine in that country.* The apparent misfortune of the famine was in reality a blessing for the prodigal, for the trouble it led him into became afterwards the occasion of his repentance.

15. *He sent him into his farm to feed swine.* The depth of degradation was reached in the eyes of the Jews when the unfortunate youth was sent to feed swine, which they regarded as unclean, and which were not allowed in their own land, but were kept with impunity in this "far country."

16. *With the husks the swine did eat.* The husks here alluded to were a coarse fruit which were the food of pigs, which only the poorest of the poor would eat, and only when in the extremity of want.

17. *And returning to himself.* This phrase implies that hitherto the prodigal had acted like a man out of his senses, and that it was only now that he began to see what he had done. And his first conclusion was that of course he could not hope for full restoration to his ancient position, but it might be possible to become as one of his father's servants.

18. *I have sinned against heaven and before thee.* It is to be noted that the prodigal recognizes not only the injustice he has done to his parent, but also his sin before God, which was in itself, of course, far more serious. In these days it often happens that while the rights of our neighbours are keenly realized, our duties towards God are overlooked in popular estimation.

19 sinned against heaven, and before thee: I am not now worthy to be called thy son: make me as one of thy hired
20 servants. And rising up he came to his father. And when he was yet a great way off, his father saw him, and was moved with compassion, and running to him, fell upon his
21 neck and kissed him. And the son said to him: Father, I have sinned against heaven, and before thee, I am not
22 now worthy to be called thy son. And the father said to his servants: Bring forth quickly the first robe, and put it on him, and put a ring on his hand, and shoes on his feet:
23 and bring hither the fatted calf, and kill it, and let us eat
24 and make merry: because this my son was dead, and is come to life again: was lost, and is found. And they
25 began to be merry. Now his elder son was in the field, and when he came and drew nigh to the house, he heard
26 music and dancing: and he called one of the servants, and
27 asked what these things meant. And he said to him: Thy brother is come, and thy father hath killed the fatted
28 calf, because he hath received him safe. And he was angry, and would not go in. His father therefore coming out
29 began to entreat him. And he answering, said to his

20. *When he was yet a great way off, his father saw him.* The conduct of the father went as far as would seem possible in an earthly father, and yet was very far short of the way in which our heavenly Father receives us when we are repentant. He "fell on his neck and kissed him," and did not allow him even to finish his confession and petition for pardon.

22. *Bring forth quickly the first robe.* The "first robe" is often taken figuratively as typifying baptismal innocence, now restored to him; the ring as the mark that he is once more the child of God; and the shoes the sign that he is to walk again in the paths of virtue.

25. *Now his elder son was in the field.* The annoyance of the elder brother and the father's answer forms really a second parable distinct from the former part, and destined to teach a separate lesson. The feeling of some sort of suspiciousness at God's love for sinners is not uncommon, as if it was an encroachment on what ought to be the lot of the just. It was quite in keeping with ordinary Pharisaism, and the Pharisees must have recognized these words as meant for themselves.

28. *His father therefore coming out began to entreat him.* The father's solicitude for the welfare of his elder son also may here be noted. He is no less anxious to bring him to a good frame of mind than he was in the case of the prodigal.

29. *For so many years do I serve thee.* The word $δουλεύω$ represents

father: Behold, for so many years do I serve thee, and I have never transgressed thy commandment, and yet thou hast never given me a kid to make merry with my friends: But as soon as this thy son is come, who hath devoured ³⁰ his substance with harlots, thou hast killed for him the fatted calf. But he said to him: Son, thou art always with ³¹ me, and all I have is thine. But it was fit that we should ³² make merry and be glad, for this thy brother was dead, and is come to life again; he was lost, and is found.

the service of a slave, and he omits the word "father" altogether, forming a contrast between his address and that of the prodigal. Thus it may happen that to have committed sin and repented may even be turned into a blessing, if we are able on that account to realize better the fatherliness of God's care for us.

30. *This thy son.* It would appear that the form used is not accidental. He does not care to call the prodigal his brother, so great is his contempt for him.

31. *Son, thou art always with me, and all I have is thine.* Our Lord's answer, which He put into the mouth of the father of the parable, is very instructive. He simply compares the two states, both the subject of joy, but joy of different kinds. Those who have not fallen into sin are so united to God that all He has is theirs. On the other hand, the repentance of a sinner is the subject of a joy, even of a triumph, in the work of grace in his soul, and the two feelings in no way interfere with each other. Cf. on *v.* 7.

If the usual secondary meaning of the parable be taken, the prodigal stands for the Gentiles who are ultimately reclaimed and brought into the Church, while the elder brother stands for the Jews, who trusted to themselves alone as just, and resented every good work done for the Gentiles. In truth, however, our Lord is here putting the case of the Jews and Pharisees with great mildness, for He assumes that they are and have always been just; whereas He might have pointed to their proper place alongside the prodigal in the far country.

CHAPTER XVI.

Parable of the Unjust Steward.

(VERS. 1-13.)

AND he said also to his disciples: There was a certain rich man who had a steward: and the same was
2 accused unto him, that he had wasted his goods. And he called him, and said to him: How is it that I hear this of thee? give an account of thy stewardship: for now

1. *There was a certain rich man.* There is more connection of subject between the parables of last chapter and those which follow here than might at first sight appear. The parable of the prodigal has brought into prominence the evils of the misuse of riches; those which follow here are on their proper use, though the word riches is to be understood in its broader sense, as applying to all possessions, physical and moral, which God has entrusted to us. The general sense of the parable of the steward is plain enough. We are stewards of what we possess in this world, and not owners. Some day we shall have to give up our stewardship and render an account of it. If we are wise, therefore, we shall imitate the forethought of the steward of the parable, by using all we have with a view to our eternal future. If, as is often supposed, the story was a true one and well known to the people, we should not be justified in looking for any further meaning in the details of the parable. In any case, it would be difficult to find any satisfactory interpretation of them, beyond that of leading up to the great lesson of *vv.* 8 and 9.

that he had wasted his goods. This means, of course, that from the master's point of view the goods had been wasted. The steward had used them for his own purposes.

2. *Render an account of thy stewardship.* Every steward has to keep accounts of his stewardship, so as to be able to render them at the appointed time. To ask for an account was therefore quite a matter of course; but it was accompanied with a notice that the time of his stewardship was at an end.

thou canst be steward no longer. And the steward said within himself: What shall I do, because my lord taketh away from me the stewardship? To dig I am not able; to beg I am ashamed. I know what I will do, that when I shall be removed from the stewardship, they may receive me into their houses. Therefore calling together every one of his lord's debtors, he said to the first: How much dost thou owe my lord? But he said: an hundred barrels of oil. And he said to him: Take thy bill and sit down quickly, and write fifty. Then he said to another: And how much dost thou owe? Who said: An hundred quarters of wheat. He said to him: Take thy bill and write eighty. And the lord commended the unjust steward, forasmuch as he had done wisely: for the children of this world are wiser in their generation than the children of light. And I say to you: Make unto you friends of the mammon of iniquity, that when you shall

3. *To dig I am not able.* οὐκ ἰσχύω=I am not strong enough.
to beg I am ashamed. The honourable position he had held unfitted the steward physically for earning his bread, and made him ashamed to live on alms.

5. *Every one of his lord's debtors.* It seems from the context that the debtors referred to were those who occupied the rich man's lands, and paid rent in the shape of a certain proportion of their crops.

6. *An hundred barrels of oil.* The "barrel" here named was a measure equivalent to about seven or eight of our gallons.

7. *An hundred quarters of wheat.* A "quarter" was equivalent to about the same as our own.
Take thy bill and write eighty. The fact of the first debtor having his bill reduced by half and the second only by a fifth, is one of those little details which is suggestive of the whole being a history. In real life we can easily imagine the steward venturing on a greater reduction with one man than with another.

8. *The lord commended the unjust steward.* The "lord," i.e., the rich man, praised the forethought and cleverness of the steward. The words which follow are our Lord's own, and not those of the lord in the parable.
in their generation, i.e., in their ordinary worldly dealings with men like themselves. The meaning is, therefore, that men of the world have more wisdom and forethought in their dealings with each other, than the children of light in those with God and the saints.

9. *Make unto you friends of the mammon of iniquity.* Here we have our Lord's application of the parable. "Mammon" is an Aramaic word, signifying riches, and it is introduced bodily by St.

10 fail they may receive you into everlasting dwellings. He that is faithful in that which is least, is faithful also in that which is greater: and he that is unjust in that which is
11 little, is unjust also in that which is greater. If then you have not been faithful in the unjust mammon; who will
12 trust you with that which is the true? And if you have not been faithful in that which is another's; who will give you
13 that which is your own? No servant can serve two masters, for either he will hate the one, and love the other: or he will hold to the one, and despise the other. You cannot serve God and mammon.

Luke, no doubt, from the difficulty of finding a Greek equivalent. It is here called "mammon of iniquity" because it is, in fact, the source of so much sin and wickedness. See 1 Tim. vi. 10. In its broader sense it stands for all worldly possessions and interest. See *v.* 13. We may use our possessions and our faculties to make friends in the next world or in this. We may make God Himself our friend; or we may make the saints whom we pray to and honour our intercessors; or the souls in purgatory, who by the help of our prayers enter heaven the sooner; or the poor of this world, whom we have aided by our charity, and whose prayers will help us to obtain our everlasting dwelling in heaven.

10. *He that is faithful in that which is least.* Our Lord now gives three contrasts, illustrative of that between things of this world and those of the next. The first is between the littleness of things of this world, and the greatness of the things of the next, and was frequently made by our Lord in much the same form. See Matt. xxv. 21, 23; Luke xix. 17, and elsewhere.

11. *If you have not been faithful in the unjust mammon.* The second contrast is between true riches and false ones. The "unjust mammon" is, of course, the same as the "mammon of iniquity" above—the Greek word being the same in both cases. It is our good use then of the mammon of iniquity which is to purchase to us our right to the true riches of heaven, which are without deceit and do not lead to misuse.

12. *In that which is another's.* Thirdly, what is another's is contrasted with what is our own. Our possessions in this world are not our own; we are only stewards of them, and sooner or later our stewardship comes to an end. Those in heaven are in the truest sense our own property. We cannot give them away, and no one can take them from us. Cf. Matt. vi. 19, 20; Luke xii. 33; John xvi. 22. The meaning is then that by faithfulness in the use of what is lent to us in this world, we are to gain the true riches which are to be our own in heaven.

13. *No servant can serve two masters.* The word for serve here is $\delta ουλεύειν$=to be a slave to. For "servant" the word is οἰκέτης. The

Warnings to the Pharisees.

(VERS. 14–18.)

Now the Pharisees who were covetous, heard all these things: and they derided him. And he said to them: You are they who justify yourselves before men, but God knoweth your hearts; for that which is high to men is an abomination before God. The law and the prophets were until John; from that time the kingdom of God is preached, and every one useth violence towards it. And it is easier for heaven and earth to pass, than one tittle of

strict meaning is therefore that no servant can be a slave to two masters. Cf. Matt. vi. 24.

You cannot serve God and mammon. This is a sort of summing up of what has gone before. No service is so exacting as that of the thirst for wealth and riches. St. Paul calls it an actual idolatry (Col. iii. 5). And in a broader sense, all those who serve worldliness in any form are "covetous."

14. *The Pharisees who were covetous heard all these things.* Hitherto our Lord had been addressing His disciples only. Hence the Pharisees who listened did so of their own accord; and heard things which evidently appealed to their conscience.

and they derided him. This word (ἐξεμυκτήριζον) occurs again in connection with our Lord's crucifixion (xxiii. 35), and is expressive of extreme contempt. This was the answer of the Pharisees to our Lord's words; but the effect was to turn these words on to themselves, and He now addressed them directly.

15. *Who justify yourselves before men.* The Pharisees were hypocrites, and deceived men by feigning themselves just; and they likewise deceived themselves to a great extent: see on xii. 56. Their pride would not allow them to suspect their own justice. Before God, however, who sees the heart, they were truly an abomination.

16. *The law and the prophets were until John.* "The law and the prophets" stands for the old dispensation; and here our Lord distinctly states, therefore, that with St. John's preaching was inaugurated a new era.

every one useth violence towards it. Cf. Matt. xi. 12. See also above note on vii. 24. The expression βιάζεται seems to denote the earnestness with which people seek after this new kingdom.

17. *The one tittle of the law to fall.* The sense of this seems to be similar to our Lord's insistence in the Sermon on the Mount that the new dispensation was not the destruction of the old, but its fulfilment. Cf. Matt. v. 17, 18.

18 the law to fall. Every one that putteth away his wife, and marrieth another, committeth adultery: and he that marrieth her that is put away from her husband, committeth adultery.

Dives and Lazarus.

(VERS. 19-31.)

19 There was a certain rich man, who was clothed in purple 20 and fine linen: and feasted sumptuously every day. And there was a certain beggar named Lazarus, who lay at his 21 gate, full of sores, desiring to be filled with the crumbs that fell from the rich man's table, and no one did give 22 him; moreover the dogs came and licked his sores. And it came to pass that the beggar died, and was carried by the Angels into Abraham's bosom. And the rich man

18. *Every one that putteth away his wife.* Again the connection with what has gone before is a little obscure. It may possibly be found in the history of St. John's fearless protest against Herod's adulterous and incestuous marriage. The Pharisees had failed to protest against it, while St. John had lost his liberty, and finally even his life, by denouncing it.

19. *A certain rich man, who was clothed in purple and fine linen.* The second parable on the use of riches puts before us a contrast, which forms one of the most characteristic touches of St. Luke's Gospel. The "purple and fine linen" with which the rich man was clothed represent respectively outer and inner garments of a costly description. The expression has become proverbial among us. The sumptuous daily feasting completes the picture of one who, while committing no positive sin of injustice, was nevertheless a victim to the vices of luxury and selfishness to which riches naturally expose us.

20. *A certain beggar named Lazarus.* The name Lazarus (=Helped of God) has also become proverbial, to represent a typical poor servant of God, like the name Magdalen for a penitent. This is the only proper name which occurs in any of our Lord's parables, and this added to the detail given (*v.* 27) that the rich man had five brothers, both suggest this to be a true history.

21. *Moreover the dogs came and licked his sores.* These words complete the contrast in the description of the poor man. He was full of sores, or ulcers, an outcast, outside the gate of the rich man's house, abandoned by every one, so that even the dogs—i.e., the wild dogs such as abounded in every town in the East—showed him more feeling than his fellow-men.

22. *And he was buried in hell.* This seems to be a slight misreading, for which the Vulgate is originally responsible. The A.V.

also died: and he was buried in hell. And lifting up his 23
eyes when he was in torments, he saw Abraham afar off,
and Lazarus in his bosom: and he cried, and said: Father 24
Abraham, have mercy on me, and send Lazarus that he
may dip the tip of his finger in water, to cool my tongue,
for I am tormented in this flame. And Abraham said to 25
him: Son, remember that thou didst receive good things
in thy lifetime, and likewise Lazarus evil things: but now
he is comforted, and thou art tormented. And besides all 26
this, between us and you there is fixed a great chaos: so
that they who would pass from hence to you, cannot, nor
from thence come hither. And he said: Then, father, I 27
beseech thee that thou wouldst send him to my father's
house, for I have five brethren, that he may testify unto 28
them, lest they also come into this place of torments. And 29

reads, "And was buried; and in hell he lifted up his eyes," &c., and
this agrees with all the Greek MSS. The word here translated "hell"
is not γέεννα, but ᾅδης. It is a well-known defect of our versions, that
the same word is used as a rendering for such different Greek equivalents. The word ᾅδης, or Hades, only means the other world, and it
included in the Jewish mind two places of an opposite kind, one of
which was the Bosom of Abraham and the other Gehenna. On the
latter, see on xii. 5. Nevertheless, the context here shows that the
rich man was in fact in hell, so that our translation conveys a not
incorrect idea of the original. The exact sense should be that the rich
man was buried, and from his place in the next world, he called out,
&c., thus showing that he was in hell.

25. *Thou didst receive good things in thy lifetime.* The answer of
Abraham is twofold: (1) the punishment is just, for the rich man had
received good things in this world and had trusted in his riches, which
now failed him. (2) The punishment is final and irrevocable.

27. *For I have five brethren.* It may be asked how, if the rich man
was in hell, he could show any charity to his relatives, and whether he
would not have rather wished to draw them there after himself. Some
have met this by supposing him to have been only in purgatory, and
have pointed to the language of Abraham, who called him "son," in confirmation of this theory. It is not likely, however, that our Lord could
have meant this; for the Jews had no definite idea of purgatory, and He
would not have used language which in its obvious sense would have
been misleading to them. It is easier to suppose that the meaning
intended to be conveyed was the rich man's own feeling of grievance, at
not having been warned more definitely of the fate that awaited him.
Abraham probably calls him "son" because he was a Jew, as appears
in the following verse.

29. *They have Moses and the prophets*—i.e., the Scriptures, read

Abraham said to him: They have Moses and the prophets;
30 let them hear them. But he said: No, father Abraham, but if one went to them from the dead, they will do pen-
31 ance. And he said to him: If they hear not Moses and the prophets, neither will they believe if one rise again from the dead.

weekly in the synagogues, and expounded by the Scribes. In other words, they had the ordinary and sufficient means of salvation.

30. *But if one went to them from the dead.* The petition of the rich man was for something beyond the ordinary means, for a special sign. Cf. xi. 16.

31. *Neither will they believe if one rise again from the dead.* The words of the final answer were prophetical, as we can now see plainly enough. The Jews who were incredulous before, were not converted by our Lord's own resurrection from the dead. Nevertheless, our Lord's resurrection *was* the appointed sign which should have convinced them. See xi. 29; John iii. 19; Acts i. 22, &c.

CHAPTER XVII.

Various Teachings of Our Lord.

(VERS. 1–10.)

AND he said to his disciples : It is impossible that scandals should not come : but wo to him through whom they come. It were better for him, that a millstone were hanged about his neck, and he cast into the sea, than

1. *And he said to his disciples.* The teachings of our Lord which follow are quite miscellaneous in character ; it seems as if St. Luke is gathering together various miscellaneous sayings of our Lord which have not found a place elsewhere. There does not seem any special connection between them all, and though they probably belong to this period of the ministry, there is nothing to show more precisely the circumstances under which they were delivered.
it is impossible that scandals should not come. A scandal means a stumbling block, and the word is used here for anything which may be a cause of sin to others. It is certain, as the world exists, that scandals will come ; nevertheless, in each individual instance, the author of the scandal is responsible for it. Of course there is such a thing as what we now call "Pharisaical Scandal," which is no real scandal at all, for the person is scandalized quite unreasonably. Such, for example, would be the scandal taken by the Pharisees at our Lord's miracles on the Sabbath, which led them to speak against Him. They were sufficiently instructed to know better, and the source of their sin was not our Lord, but themselves. In many cases, however, where people are less well instructed, charity may dictate the omission of what is otherwise lawful, for fear of scandal, even though such scandal be in itself unreasonable. Cf. 1 Cor. viii. 13 : "If meat scandalize my brother, I will never eat flesh, lest I should scandalize my brother."
2. *That a millstone were hanged about his neck.* The kind of millstone here referred to belonged, not to one of the small hand-mills worked by women (see *v.* 35), but to a large one such as an ass would work. It was therefore a very large stone. The expression of

3 that he should scandalize one of these little ones. Take heed to yourselves. If thy brother sin against thee, reprove
4 him: and if he do penance, forgive him. And if he sin against thee seven times in a day, and seven times in a day
5 be converted unto thee, saying, I repent: forgive him. And
6 the apostles said to the Lord: Increase our faith. And the Lord said: If you had faith like to a grain of mustard-seed, you might say to this mulberry-tree, Be thou rooted up, and be thou transplanted into the sea: and it would
7 obey you. But which of you having a servant plowing or feeding cattle, will say to him when he is come from the
8 field: Immediately go, sit down to meat: and will not *rather* say to him: Make ready my supper, and gird thyself, and serve me whilst I eat and drink, and afterwards
9 thou shalt eat and drink? Doth he thank that servant,

our Lord seems to have been a proverbial one. It is said in the Talmud that a married man with slender means "studies the law with a millstone round his neck." It thus typifies a man in great difficulties. The application intended here is obvious.

one of these little ones, i.e., one who is helpless as a little child. Our Lord expressed on many occasions His peculiar tenderness towards the qualities typified in little children. The helplessness, in many cases, of those who are scandalized, adds a special guilt to the sin of scandal.

3. *If he do penance.* The word (μετανοέω) translated in this verse as "do penance" is the same as that in the next, rendered "repent:" see on iii. 3.

4. *Seven times a day.* This phrase stands for generally a large number—larger than any likely to be reached in actual life.

6. *Faith like to a grain of mustard-seed*, i.e., the very smallest amount of faith, which will, however, grow till it affects our whole life. Cf. Matt. xiii. 32; Mark iv. 31. The power of faith has been shown in the extraordinary works and miracles performed by some of the Saints, works as great and as far above nature as the removal of a mulberry tree here described.

7. *Which of you having a servant plowing.* The words which follow are meant to impress the duties we owe to God as His servants. There is no absolute need to suppose them addressed to the apostles only, and the sort of Pharisaical self-importance against which they are directed suggests a larger audience.

9. *Does he thank that servant.* The implication is that he at least does not owe him gratitude as of right, for the servant has only done what was his duty and what his master has therefore a full title to expect.

for doing the things which he commanded him? I think 10
not. So you also, when you shall have done all these
things that are commanded you, say: We are unprofitable
servants; we have done that which we ought to do.

The Ten Lepers.
(Vers. 11-19.)

And it came to pass, as he was going to Jerusalem, he 11
passed through the midst of Samaria and Galilee. And as 12
he entered into a certain town, there met him ten men that
were lepers, who stood afar off; and lifted up their voice, 13
saying: Jesus, master, have mercy on us. Whom when 14
he saw, he said: Go, shew yourselves to the priests. And
it came to pass, as they went, they were made clean. And 15
one of them when he saw that he was made clean, went
back, with a loud voice glorifying God. And he fell on 16
his face before his feet, giving thanks: and this was a

10. *We are unprofitable servants.* The meaning is that God does not stand in need of man's service; and it need hardly be pointed out that there is no question here as to the rewards which He has promised for that service, if voluntarily undertaken. The tendency of the Pharisees was to extol themselves and their own importance, and to look on it even as a sort of favour to God that they should obey Him at all. It is against this spirit, which in its measure is common enough in all ages, that our Lord is here addressing Himself.

11. *He passed through Samaria and Galilee.* This verse seems to have the same parenthetical character as xiii. 22. It probably fixes the incident as some time back, when our Lord began His journey from Galilee through Samaria to Judea.

12. *Ten men that were lepers.* See on v. 12.

14. *Go, shew yourselves to the priests.* The answer of our Lord was a distinct test to the faith of the lepers. It was in fact the promise of a miracle, for it was only those who had been first cleansed who were told to go to the priests (Lev. xiv. 3). The fact that they all obeyed and went up to Jerusalem, to the Temple, shows that they all had great faith, and to this they owed their cure (*v.* 19).

16. *And this was a Samaritan.* On the Samaritans: see on ix. 52. The Samaritan here gives the example to the others, who were presumably Jews. As long as they were lepers, the Jews and Samaritans were together. When they were cleansed, the Samaritan would naturally separate himself from the others. That is of course no excuse for the nine omitting to return due thanks, after their visit to Jerusalem to offer sacrifice.

17 Samaritan. And Jesus answering, said: Were not ten
18 made clean? and where are the nine? There is no one
found to return and give glory to God, but this stranger.
19 And he said to him: Arise, go thy way; for thy faith hath
made thee whole.

Further Sayings of our Lord.

(VERS. 20-37.)

20 And being asked by the Pharisees: when the kingdom
of God should come? he answered them and said: The
21 kingdom of God cometh not with observation: neither
shall they say: Behold here, or behold there. For lo, the
22 kingdom of God is within you. And he said to his disciples: The days will come when you shall desire to see one
23 day of the son of man; and you shall not see it. And
they will say to you: See here, and see there. Go ye not
24 after, nor follow them: for as the lightning that lighteneth
from under heaven, shineth unto the parts that are under

18. *There is no one found to return and give glory to God.* Ingratitude is a failing specially antagonistic to the Christian spirit. See Eph. v. 20. Thus in this case the stranger, or Samaritan, by his natural instinct gave a lesson to Jews who should have been better instructed.

20. *When the kingdom of God should come.* On the meaning of the "Kingdom of God," see on xi. 2. The Pharisees in their question meant it in the sense of a triumphal kingdom, and establishment of power in this world. Their meaning seems in fact to be ironical. When was all this preaching to receive its fulfilment?

21. *The kingdom of God is within you*, i.e., that they were not to look for great manifestations from without, but to work at their own souls, that God might establish His kingdom over their hearts. The words ἐντὸς ὑμῶν might, however, mean "among you," and some have preferred this rendering as more suitable to the context, and an allusion to our Lord having already come to preach the kingdom.

22. *When you shall desire to see one day of the son of man.* The next verses are addressed to the disciples, and have no close connection with what has gone before. The meaning seems to be simply to point out what grace they were receiving daily, such as they might afterwards long for in vain.

23. *Go ye not after, nor follow them.* The warning here is against attending to false excitements or Messianic expectations. When our Lord is to come to judge us, He will come suddenly as lightning, and His presence will be equally apparent and universal.

heaven: so shall the son of man be in his day. But first 25 he must suffer many things, and be rejected by this generation. And as it came to pass in the days of Noe, 26 so shall it be also in the days of the son of man. They 27 did eat and drink, they married wives and were given in marriage, until the day that Noe entered into the ark: and the flood came and destroyed them all. Likewise as it 28 came to pass in the days of Lot: They did eat and drink, they bought and sold, they planted and built. And in the 29 day that Lot went out of Sodom, it rained fire and brimstone from heaven, and destroyed them all. Even thus 30 shall it be in the day when the son of man shall be revealed. In that hour he that shall be on the house-top, 31 and his goods in the house, let him not go down to take them away: and he that shall be in the field, in like manner let him not return back. Remember Lot's wife. 32 Whosoever shall seek to save his life, shall lose it: and 33 whosoever shall lose it, shall preserve it. I say to you: in 34 that night there shall be two men in one bed: the one shall be taken, and the other shall be left. Two women 35 shall be grinding together; the one shall be taken, and

25. *But first he must suffer many things.* The sense of these words seems to be that the fulfilment of the previous prediction is not to come yet, and that they need not look for the signs at present; for the passion and death of our Lord were to come first. Thus, as before, they were reminded that before our Lord's triumph must first come His suffering.

and be rejected by this generation, i.e., by the world and those who have power.

27. *They did eat and drink.* Our Lord is to come at the end suddenly, on a world engrossed in its own pursuits. The tense here is imperfect, "They were eating and were drinking." Cf. 2 Peter ii. 5, 6.

29. *It rained fire and brimstone.* See Gen. xix. 24.

31. *He that shall be on the house-top.* It was common in the East to sit on the house-top. The roof was generally flat: see on v. 19. These warnings concern in the first place the destruction of Jerusalem, which was the type of the day of judgment.

32. *Remember Lot's wife.* See Gen. xix. 26. She looked back, with longing, on her possessions and pleasures, and was punished immediately as an example to others.

33. *Whosoever shall seek to save his life.* See on ix. 24.

35. *Two women shall be grinding together.* See above, on v. 2. The grinding at a hand mill was done by women, and usually by

the other shall be left: two men shall be in the field; the one shall be taken, and the other shall be left. They answering say to him: Where, Lord? Who said to them: Wheresoever the body shall be, thither will the eagles also be gathered together.

two, who sat on the ground facing each other. Each held a handle by which the stone was turned, and the one who had her right hand free used it to put in the grain from time to time as required.

37. *Wheresoever the body shall be*, &c. This appears to have been a proverb, alluding to the fact that carcasses always attracted to them vultures, who devoured them. The word "Eagle" in Scripture frequently denotes the *Vulture fulvus* or griffin vulture. In the simile before us, it is usually supposed that the meaning is that all the elect will at once come to Christ at the day of judgment as naturally as vultures are attracted to a carcass.

CHAPTER XVIII.

The Unjust Judge.

(VERS. 1-8.)

AND he spoke also a parable to them, that we ought always to pray, and not to faint. Saying: There was a judge in a certain city, who feared not God, nor regarded man. And there was a certain widow in that city, and she came to him, saying: Avenge me of my adversary. And he would not for a long time. But afterwards he said within

1. *And he spoke also a parable to them.* The words "to them" show that our Lord was still addressing the same audience, and direct our attention to the connection with what has just gone before. The coming judgment should be a continual incentive to prayer. Cf. xxi. 36: "Praying at all times, that you may be accounted worthy to escape all these things that are to come."
that we ought always to pray and not to faint. This means to pray with perseverance and not lose courage if our answer seems delayed. The word ἐκκακεῖν is used in the same sense by St. Paul. See 2 Cor. iv. 1-16; Gal. vi. 9, &c. This and *v.* 9 are the only instances where the explanation of the scope of the parable precedes the parable itself. The explanation is, of course, not our Lord's, but St. Luke's.
2. *There was a judge in a certain city.* Very possibly this unjust judge was taken from real life.
3. *And there was a certain widow.* Of all people, a widow is the most helpless and defenceless against her enemies, and when mentioned in Scripture, this poverty and helplessness are commonly indicated. Hence they have a special right to the assistance of the law.
Avenge me of my adversary, i.e., "vindicate me" or "render me justice." The widow was apparently wronged, and was demanding justice.
4. *Although I fear not God.* The injustice of the judge is such that he himself admits it, as a matter of course.

5 himself: Although I fear not God, nor regard man, yet because this widow is troublesome to me, I will avenge her,
6 lest continually coming she weary me. And the Lord said:
7 Hear what the unjust judge saith. And will not God revenge his elect who cry to him day and night: and will
8 he have patience in their regard? I say to you that he will quickly revenge them. But yet the son of man when he cometh, shall he find, think you, faith on earth?

The Pharisee and Publican.

(VERS. 9–14.)

9 And to some who trusted in themselves as just, and
10 despised others, he spoke also this parable: Two men went up into the temple to pray: the one a Pharisee, and

5. *Lest continually coming she weary me.* Cf. xi. 5-8. The moral of both parables is the same. God desires us to pray as if we wished to conquer Him by importunity, and to drive Him to assist us.

7. *Will he have patience in their regard?* The whole sense of this phrase is changed in the A.V., chiefly by omitting the note of interrogation, and it reads "though he bear long with them." According to this, it means that though the answer to prayer seems long delayed, it will come at last. Our version, however, agrees better with the words which follow, "I say to you he will quickly revenge them." The answer to prayer often comes suddenly, and sooner than we had even hoped for.

8. *But yet the son of man when he cometh,* &c. The connection between these words and what has gone before is not at first sight evident. Perhaps our Lord meant to ask if He should at His coming find this confidence in prayer which was so necessary: see on *v.* 1.

9. *To some who trusted in themselves as just and despised others.* This description applied to all the Pharisees and to many others who had imbibed their spirit. Thus the parable was addressed especially to those amongst the Jews to whom the people naturally looked up as their religious guides and patterns. Like much of what has just preceded, this parable is placed in no particular context, and is only one of many miscellaneous sayings which St. Luke collects at this stage. We must, however, place it very near the end of our Lord's ministry, after the breach with the Pharisees was well established.

10. *The one a Pharisee, the other a publican.* No greater contrast could be imagined by the Jewish mind than between these two. The publicans were the outcast of the outcast, considered unworthy of the name of Jew: see on iii. 12.

the other a publican. The Pharisee standing prayed thus with himself: O God, I give thee thanks that I am not as the rest of men, extortioners, unjust, adulterers, as also is this publican. I fast twice in a week: I give tithes of all that I possess. And the publican standing afar off would not so much as lift up his eyes towards heaven; but struck his breast, saying: O God, be merciful to me a sinner. I say to you, this man went down into his house justified rather than the other: because every one that exalteth himself, shall be humbled; and he that humbleth himself, shall be exalted.

11. *The Pharisee standing prayed thus.* The usual posture for prayer among the Jews was standing, which practice still survives in some of our customs at the present day, such as standing on Sundays for the *Angelus*, the Antiphon of our Lady after Vespers, &c. Also it may be noted that standing is the usual posture in choir; and this is all a survival of the Jewish custom.

I give thee thanks that I am not as the rest of men. This pretended thanksgiving was in reality only self exaltation. There was no true prayer about it at all. The contempt expressed for the publican is evidence in itself of the Pharisee's absorption in himself and his excellences.

12. *I fast twice in a week.* Fasting in general was prescribed by the Scriptures (see e.g., Tobias xii. 8; Isa. lviii. 3; and Ecclus. xxxiv. 31), and our Lord had Himself promised that His own disciples should fast in due season. In the time of Zacharias, there were four fasts in the year established by custom (Zach. viii. 19) corresponding with our Ember weeks. The only fast in the written law was the annual Day of Atonement. The Pharisees interpreted the general command to fast (cf. v. 33), and in the oral law that had grown up, there was a fast twice a week, on Mondays and Thursdays.

I give tithes of all that I possess. See Deut. xiv. 22, 23. The precept was that tithes should be given of corn, wine and oil; and the firstborn of all herds and sheep. It would appear that the Pharisee here went further in giving tithes of everything he had, which they often did. See Matt. xxiii. 23.

13. *The publican standing afar off.* The publican also stood for prayer, but "far off," i.e., far off the Pharisee and far off the entrance into the Court of the Priests. But there is no reason to suppose that he remained in the Court of the Gentiles; presumably he was a Jew.

14. *This man went down into his house justified rather than the other,* i.e., this man was justified and the other was not.

every one that exalteth himself shall be humbled. Cf. xiv. 11, and elsewhere.

Children brought to Christ.

(Vers. 15-17.)

15 And they brought unto him also infants, that he might touch them. Which when the disciples saw, they rebuked
16 them. But Jesus calling them together, said: Suffer children to come to me, and forbid them not, for of such
17 is the kingdom of God. Amen I say to you: Whosoever shall not receive the kingdom of God as a child, shall not enter into it.

Evangelical Poverty.

(Vers. 18-30.)

18 And a certain ruler asked him, saying, Good master, what

15. *And they brought unto him also infants.* The expression used by St. Matthew (xix. 13), "That he should impose hands upon them and pray," suggests a regular recognized ceremony in presenting children to one who was looked on as a religious teacher.

Which when the disciples saw, they rebuked them. The disciples rebuked the parents, because of their supposed importunity, as if our Lord was so much occupied with healing the sick and teaching the people, that He had no time to attend to what appeared a useless ceremony.

16. *Suffer children to come to me.* Our Lord as usual used the opportunity to point some lesson which should reveal His spirit and character. He not only gave His time to them when asked, but even called them to Him, and "embracing them, and laying His hands upon them, He blessed them" (Mark x. 16).

of such is the kingdom of God. Among the qualities of children which made them specially typical of those who serve God, and caused them to be loved by our Lord, may be mentioned (1) their ready faith; (2) their docility; (3) their simplicity of speech and even of thought; (4) their natural humility and submission to authority; (5) their continual joyfulness, even in the midst of hardship and suffering.

18. *A certain ruler.* The word ἄρχων is quite vague in meaning. Possibly the man may have been a ruler of the synagogue; or he may have been any other kind of ruler. The other synoptists omit the word "ruler," and call him a "young man." There are evident traces of youth and its enthusiasm in his conduct. See Matt. xix. 16-24; Mark x. 17-27.

What shall I do to possess everlasting life? St. Mark says that the young man ran up and knelt before our Lord. This added to the context containing our Lord's answer, and the young man's failure to

shall I do to possess everlasting life? And Jesus said to 19
him: Why dost thou call me good? None is good but
God alone. Thou knowest the commandments: *Thou* 20
*shall not kill: Thou shalt not commit adultery: Thou
shalt not steal: Thou shalt not bear false witness: Honour
thy father and mother.* Who said: All these things have 21
I kept from my youth. Which when Jesus had heard, he 22
said to him: Yet one thing is wanting to thee: sell all
whatever thou hast, and give to the poor, and thou shalt
have treasure in heaven: and come, follow me. He 23
having heard these things, became sorrowful: for he was
very rich. And Jesus seeing him become sorrowful, said: 24
How hardly shall they that have riches enter into the king-

respond to it, suggest that this was an outburst of enthusiastic devotion which required to be checked, being in excess of his true feelings.

19. *None is good but God alone.* This answer is evidently meant to restrain the youth's enthusiasm. He had no idea of our Lord's Divine personality, and our Lord reminded him that no one is essentially and necessarily good but God Himself.

20. *Thou knowest the commandments.* This is again a repression of the young man's enthusiasm. It consists of an enumeration of the commandments; not of all ten, but of the second of the two divisions into which they are sometimes arranged—viz., those which concern our duties to our neighbour.

21. *All these things have I kept from my youth.* This answer seems expressive of some disappointment. He had known and kept the commandments always, and as a matter of course had expected some further advice than this. Hence he said, "What is yet wanting to me?" (Matt. xix. 20).

22. *Sell all whatever thou hast, and give to the poor.* St. Mark says (x. 21), "Jesus looking on him, loved him," and hence He called him to the highest vocation which is ever given, to share in the apostolic state by leaving all things to follow our Lord.

23. *He having heard these things became sorrowful.* St. Matthew says that he went away sad. It is clear that at that time he did not correspond with the grace given him. Many speculations have been made as to his ultimate end; but we are told nothing further about him in the Gospels.

24. *How hardly shall they that have riches enter into the kingdom of God.* The natural tendency of riches is to pride and self-indulgence, and forgetfulness of God, for a rich man naturally seeks his security in the human assistance which his riches can procure him. This is what is specially meant by a "trust" in riches (Prov. xi. 28). Poverty, on the other hand, should lead towards humility and self-denial, which is often a necessary self-denial, and likewise to a sense of dependence on Provi-

25 dom of God. For it is easier for a camel to pass through the eye of a needle, than for a rich man to enter into the
26 kingdom of God. And they that heard it said: Who then
27 can be saved? He said to them: The things that are
28 impossible with men, are possible with God. Then Peter said: Behold we have left all things, and have followed
29 thee. Who said to them: Amen I say to you, there is no man that hath left house, or parents, or brethren, or wife,
30 or children, for the kingdom of God's sake, who shall not receive much more in this present time, and in the world to come life everlasting.

dence, inasmuch as a man without means is at the mercy of what is apparently simple chance. Such is the natural tendency. Cf. vi. 20-25. Of course a rich man may counteract his natural tendency and become " poor in spirit " (Matt. v. 3), or a poor man may neglect his advantages and become discontented and morose. The latter may easily happen by the downward tendency of our nature; but the former wants a very special help of God's grace.

25. *It is easier for a camel to pass through the eye of a needle.* This seems to have been a proverb current at that time for denoting extreme impossibility. It has been explained by some that the name " needle's eye " was applied to the small city gateway for those on foot, through which a camel could not walk, or not without extreme difficulty, and without first being unladen. But there seems ground for thinking that this meaning of the expression is actually founded on the text before us, and is of later origin. The supposition that the word meant a rope or cable seems also unfounded. In the Talmud the simile of an elephant passing through the eye of a needle occurs in similar context; and also that of a camel dancing in a small corn measure.

26. *Who then can be saved?* Apparently the idea in the apostles' mind was that every one in this world is seeking after riches, and thus has much of the disadvantage our Lord was identifying with riches. The conversation is probably much abbreviated by the evangelist, and this makes the connection between different parts sometimes obscure.

27. *The things that are impossible with men.* God's grace is an actual necessity for salvation.

28. *Behold we have left all things.* St. Peter and the apostles had corresponded with the same vocation which the young man had refused; they had left all things and followed Christ; and though they had never had any great worldly possessions, the completeness of their sacrifice was none the less.

29. *There is no man that hath left house, or parents*, &c. See on iv. 38. This verse certainly leads us to suppose that St. Peter had left wife and home voluntarily, and of his own accord.

30. *Much more in this present time.* Our Lord here reminds us of a most important fact. True happiness, even in this world, depends on

Further Prophecy of the Passion.

(VERS. 31-34.)

Then Jesus took unto him the twelve, and said to them: 31 Behold we go up to Jerusalem, and all things shall be accomplished which were written by the prophets concern-

our conforming our life to the precepts of the Gospel. Self-control brings much more real comfort than self-indulgence. St. Mark adds the remarkable words "with persecutions," by which our Lord meant that whatever outward suffering we may be called on to undergo, there will be an inward peace which will be with us continually, even though we may not advert to it. Cf. John xiv. 27; Isa. xlviii. 22. Of course there are occasions when these words receive a rather different fulfilment, as, e.g., in the case of a martyr's death. In that case, the reward in this life is the grace of constancy to help him through his trial. And short of martyrdom, there are instances in which it is God's will that all human consolation should be for a time absent from us. At such times also the present reward is, as with the martyrs, a reward of grace to enable us to meet our trials.

31. *Behold we go up to Jerusalem.* With this verse we enter on our Lord's last journey to Jerusalem. The event which brought matters to a crisis was the raising of Lazarus. St. Luke, with the other synoptists, passes this over in silence, for reasons which we have already pointed out: see on x. 38. St. John gives a full account of it (xi. 1-44), and of a meeting of the chief priests and Pharisees afterwards (xi. 47-53), presided over by Caiphas, when they decided to put our Lord to death. St. Matthew, probably referring to the same meeting, says (xxvi. 5) that they likewise determined to avoid the festival day, for fear of a tumult. Finally, St. John says (xi. 56) that, expecting Him to come to the feast, they issued a standing order that "if any man knew where He was, he should tell, that they might apprehend Him," intending, no doubt, to keep Him in custody till the people had left the city, and He could be put to death quietly. Two or three weeks, if not more, must have intervened between the raising of Lazarus and the Pasch. The time was spent by our Lord in the neighbourhood of Ephrem (John xi. 54), and we must therefore assume that the journey towards Jerusalem began from there. The situation of Ephrem is not quite certain. St. John describes it as "in the country near the desert," which would apply to the wild region north-east of Jerusalem on either side of the Jordan. A probable opinion identifies it with Ophrah of the Old Testament, and if this be accepted, it would be about sixteen miles from Jerusalem. The road chosen by our Lord, however, down the Jordan valley and then through Jericho, would have been a good deal further: it was probably chosen because most of the journey would have been on the highway of the Galilean pilgrims going up to the feast.

32 ing the son of man. For he shall be delivered to the Gentiles, and shall be mocked, and scourged, and spit
33 upon: and after they have scourged him, they will put
34 him to death; and the third day he shall rise again. And they understood none of these things, and this word was hid from them, and they understood not the things that were said.

The Blind Man of Jericho.

(Vers. 35-43.)

35 Now it came to pass, when he drew nigh to Jericho, that a certain blind man sat by the way-side, begging.

32. *he shall be delivered to the Gentiles.* The prophecy of His passion and death was delivered by our Lord as they were on the way (Mark x. 32). It was more definite than the preceding ones (cf. ix. 22 and 44). For the first time our Lord talked of being delivered to the Gentiles, i.e., to Pontius Pilate; and He also mentioned some details of His passion, viz., the mocking and scourging.

35. *When he drew nigh to Jericho.* Jericho was an ancient and very flourishing city, frequently mentioned in the Old Testament, the first occasion being in Josue ii. 1, when spies were sent thither from Setim; and it was the first city to be taken by the Israelites. In the time of Herod the Great it rose to great prominence, as he built himself a palace there, in which, indeed, his death eventually took place. Afterwards the town was sacked and the palace burnt by a revolutionary mob; but the palace was rebuilt by Archelaus, who also founded a new town further down the plain, which he planted with palms. Jericho is connected by tradition with several gospel events. The mountain of our Lord's fast and temptation stood close beside it (see on iv. i.), and it is likewise said that our Lord's baptism took place at that part of the Jordan over against it: see on iii. 3. These are, however, merely traditions. The only incidents where it is directly mentioned, apart from the parable of the Good Samaritan, are the two which here follow —the cure of the blind man, and the conversion of Zaccheus.

a certain blind man sat by the way-side, begging. St. Matthew mentions two blind men just as he mentions two demoniacs in the country of the Gerasens, when the other evangelists only mention one (Matt. viii. 28-34; Mark v. 1-20; Luke viii. 26-39). Some have thought, however, that in this instance the two blind men were cured on separate occasions, one as our Lord entered Jericho, as told by St. Luke, and the other as He left it, told by St. Mark; and that St. Matthew really combines these two miracles into one narrative. The chief difficulty against this or any other hypothesis of two cures on

And when he heard the multitude passing by, he asked 36
what this meant. And they told him that Jesus of Naza- 37
reth was passing by. And he cried out, saying: Jesus, son 38
of David, have mercy on me. And they that went before, 39
rebuked him, that he should hold his peace. But he cried

successive days, is that it involves supposing that, after the disciples had been rebuked by our Lord for trying to hinder the approach of one blind man as He entered Jericho, they straightway repeated the offence the next day as He went out. Moreover, the cure of a blind man would make a great stir (John ix. 32), and it is recorded in each Gospel as though a well-known incident of our Lord's visit to Jericho. Many commentators, therefore, in order to identify the miracle told by St. Luke with that of the other synoptists, have supposed that it took place as our Lord left the old town of Jericho, and as He approached the new one founded by Archelaus; but there is no evidence that the new town was known to any one by the name of Jericho: its official title was that of its founder, Archelaus. Another hypothesis has been put forward by Cornelius à Lapide, and adopted by many later writers, to the effect that possibly the blind man with his companion first asked for their cure as our Lord went into Jericho, but did not obtain it till the next day, as He came out, when they were still sitting by the roadside and calling out as before. This would agree well enough with St. Matthew and St. Mark. To make it agree with St. Luke it would be only necessary to suppose that, after having begun the account of the blind man, he continues it till its finish, and then goes back to what took place during our Lord's stay in Jericho. But this is St. Luke's usual plan of writing, and follows indeed from his method of composition, taking each different incident from different records, either written or oral: see Introduction. The account of the blind man's cure may have been one document and that of Zaccheus another. It would seem, then, that this explanation is at least as good as any other, or as any that in the present state of our knowledge is likely to be forthcoming. A further positive argument in its favour can be urged from *v.* 39. See article on Father Coleridge's *Life of our Life* in the *Dublin Review* for April, 1877.

36. *When he heard the multitude passing by.* The caravan of those going up to the Pasch caused the multitude in the first instance; but evidently a special crowd had collected round our Lord.

38. *Jesus, son of David.* Son of David was the recognized title for the Messiah, and therefore this cry was a profession of faith in our Lord.

39. *And they that went before.* As the blind man did not begin to call out till he heard the multitude passing and had asked who was there, and as by that time "they that went before" must have passed away, this verse seems to imply definitely that they came upon him a second time, and that he was calling out even at the time that those in front were passing him. This would agree with the last suggestion made on *v.* 35.

40 out much more: Son of David, have mercy on me. And Jesus standing commanded him to be brought unto him.
41 And when he was come near, he asked him, saying: What wilt thou that I do to thee? But he said: Lord, that I
42 may see. And Jesus said to him: Receive thy sight; thy
43 faith hath made thee whole. And immediately he saw, and followed him, glorifying God. And all the people when they saw it, gave praise to God.

    41. *What wilt thou that I do to thee?* This question was no doubt partly for the bystanders, that they might see that the beggar was not simply asking for money.
    42. *Thy faith hath made thee whole.* Cf. viii. 48.

CHAPTER XIX.

Our Lord and Zaccheus.

(VERS. 1–10.)

AND entering in, he walked through Jericho. And behold there was a man named Zaccheus: who was the chief of the publicans, and he was rich. And he sought to see Jesus who he was, and he could not for the crowd, because he was low of stature. And running before, he climbed up into a sycamore tree that he might see him:

1. *He walked through Jericho*, i.e., He was walking through Jericho when Zaccheus met Him.
2. *A man named Zaccheus.* It has been conjectured by some that Zaccheus was the publican mentioned in the previous chapter, and a comparison has been made between the way in which he is mentioned and that in which the name of Mary Magdalen occurs. In her case, we have first an account of her conversion, no name being mentioned (vii. 37), and then in the following chapter she is mentioned by name as ministering to our Lord. In the case of Zaccheus it is of course only a conjecture. The Gospel tells us nothing about him except that he was very rich, as the chief of the tax-gatherers in so rich a city might well be.
3. *He sought to see Jesus.* Zaccheus's motive had no doubt a great admixture of mere curiosity; but there must also have been a feeling of longing for peace of conscience, and a confidence that from our Lord he could obtain it.
4. *He climbed up into a sycamore tree.* The sycamore tree (*Ficus Sycomorus*) is not now common in Palestine; but appears to have flourished in our Lord's time and before: see 1 Paral. xxvii. 28, where the fig-groves mentioned were of this species. The tree which we commonly call sycamore is a maple (*Acer Pseudoplatanus*), and has no affinity with this fig.

5 for he was to pass that way. And when Jesus was come to the place, looking up, he saw him, and said to him: Zaccheus, make haste and come down: for this day I 6 must abide in thy house. And he made haste and came 7 down, and received him with joy. And when all saw it, they murmured, saying that he was gone to be a guest 8 with a man that was a sinner. But Zaccheus standing said to the Lord: Behold, Lord, the half of my goods I give to the poor; and if I have wronged any man of any-9 thing, I restore him four-fold. Jesus said to him: This day is salvation come to this house: because he also is a 10 son of Abraham. For the son of man is come to seek and to save that which was lost.

5. *Zaccheus, make haste and come down.* Our Lord addressed Zaccheus by name, though apparently He had never seen him before. This fact Zaccheus would recognize as showing our Lord's knowledge of all things.

7. *When all saw it, they murmured.* The source of their murmuring was a sense of outrage, in the fact of our Lord visiting one who, by his profession, was considered outside the bounds of orthodoxy.

8. *The half of my goods I give to the poor.* Zaccheus here became, as Mary Magdalen had been, a model of penance. He made a public confession of his sins, and promised to give half his goods to the poor, as well as to make restitution to those whom he had wronged. The wrongs would have been by exacting too much in the execution of his calling. In many cases it would be impossible to undo the wrongs done, and it was no doubt to cover such cases that he gave half his goods to the poor. He thus took exactly the course that a modern theologian would insist on, but evidently he did so with generosity, and restored an amount which would far more than cover his misdeeds.

9. *This day is salvation come to this house.* Salvation came to the house in a twofold way. (1) By the presence of our Lord; (2) by the conversion of Zaccheus. And Zaccheus was not only a son of Abraham according to the flesh, but also a true and worthy son as shown by his faith and his generosity.

10. *To seek and to save that which was lost.* These words form a sort of answer to the people's murmuring related in verse 7. Our Lord justifies His conduct in mixing with this class of persons by the conversions which He effected.

Parable of the Pounds.

(VERS. 11–27.)

As they were hearing these things, he added and spoke a parable because he was nigh to Jerusalem, and because they thought that the kingdom of God should immediately be manifested. He said therefore: A certain nobleman went into a far country to receive for himself a kingdom, and to return. And calling his ten servants, he gave them

11. *They thought that the kingdom of God should immediately be manifested.* The longing for the establishment of the "Messianic Kingdom" was continually showing itself even among the apostles. That the multitudes should share this feeling was even more natural, for they had not had the constant restraining influence of our Lord's words. Now, therefore, that they were approaching Jerusalem with a great multitude, their hopes naturally began to rise, and they looked for the realization of their dreams.

12. *A certain nobleman went into a far country.* It has several times been suggested of particular parables, especially those in St. Luke's Gospel, that they may have been based on a true history, well known to our Lord's hearers. In the case of the parable of the pounds we can speak more confidently, for we are fortunately in possession of the facts on which it is founded; and although these facts are not reproduced with absolute accuracy in every little detail in the parable, the general outline is depicted with unmistakable plainness, and we can easily imagine how the attention of the people would have been attracted. Our Lord was just leaving Jericho. High up above the city stood the great palace of Archelaus: see on xviii. 35. This palace would naturally remind the people of him and his life, and they would remember how little more than thirty years before, he had, on the death of his father, Herod the Great, gone to Rome to obtain a kingdom. He returned appointed over Judea, though not with the title of *King* but only of "*Ethnarch*:" see on iii. 1, and cf. Matt. ii. 22. During his absence on his journey to Rome, there were great disturbances, as the Jews hated him; and on his return he rewarded those who had been faithful to him, many of whom he appointed governors of various cities. His enemies, on the other hand, he punished with great cruelty. Moreover, at one period the Jews were so infuriated against him that they sent an embassy of fifty to Augustus at Rome, to beg that he might be deposed, as in fact he subsequently was, about A.D. 6. All these events were within the memory of many, and the references of the parable would at once have been recognized.

13. *He gave them ten pounds.* The coin here named ($\mu\nu\tilde{\alpha}$), which we translate "pound," was worth about £3 6s. 8d. of our money. The meaning of the parable is pointed to in *v.* 11. The people

14 ten pounds, and said to them: Trade till I come. But his citizens hated him: and they sent an embassage after him,
15 saying: We will not have this man to reign over us. And it came to pass that he returned, having received the kingdom: and he commanded his servants to be called, to whom he had given the money; that he might know how
16 much every man had gained by trading. And the first came, saying: Lord, thy pound hath gained ten pounds.
17 And he said to him: Well done, thou good servant; because thou hast been faithful in a little, thou shalt have
18 power over ten cities. And the second came, saying:
19 Lord, thy pound hath gained five pounds. And he said
20 to him: Be thou also over five cities. And another came, saying: Lord, behold here is thy pound, which I have kept
21 laid up in a napkin: for I feared thee, because thou art an austere man: thou takest up what thou didst not lay down,

were becoming expectant of the establishment of the "Messianic Kingdom" at once, and our Lord wished to show them that there was to be no such immediate manifestation of His power, but that he was to be like one going into a far country, and that it would not be till the day of judgment that He would appear in majesty and glory. In the meantime their state must be like that of the servants of the parable. Their duty was to trade, that is to use their faculties for His greater glory, till He came.

16. *Thy pound hath gained me ten pounds.* There seems at first sight an essential difference between this parable and the better known one of the Talents. There, the more money each had entrusted to him, the more he produced at the end, as if in every case grace had fructified in the same proportion. Thus it brings forcibly before us the work which grace does in our souls. Here, however, each has the same initial amount, and the different results depend only on the use or misuse made thereof. Thus this parable brings out more forcibly the part which our free will has to play in corresponding with the grace we receive.

17. *Thou shalt have power over ten cities.* It will be seen that the rewards are proportional to the work done, as we know will be the case with us.

20. *And another came.* It was stated in *v.* 13 that there were ten servants, and it will be noticed that only three appear in the account of their judgment. These three must be therefore considered as samples of all the others. Some gained much, some little, some, like this one, nothing at all.

21. *Thou takest up what thou didst not lay down.* This was probably a current expression for to describe a grasping person.

and thou reapest that which thou didst not sow. He saith to him: Out of thy own mouth I judge thee, thou wicked servant. Thou knewest that I was an austere man, taking up what I laid not down, and reaping that which I did not sow: and why then didst thou not give my money into the bank, that at my coming I might have exacted it with usury? And he said to them that stood by: Take the pound away from him, and give it to him that hath the ten pounds. And they said to him: Lord, he hath ten pounds. But I say to you, that to every one that hath shall be given, and he shall abound: and from him that hath not, even that which he hath shall be taken from him. But as for those my enemies, who would not have me reign over them, bring them hither; and kill them before me.

Procession of Palms.

(VERS. 28–48.)

And having said these things, he went before, going up

22. *Out of thy own mouth I judge thee.* He had said that his master was severe; now he was, therefore, to be judged severely.

23. *Why then didst thou not give my money into the bank?* The answer of the king seems to place before the servant the level of an ordinary good life to which all are called, and which is therefore within the reach of all. This is compared to placing money out to interest at a bank. Those who traded aimed at something higher, and were therefore worthy of more special commendation.

24. *To them that stood by.* τοῖς παρεστῶσιν=to his attendants, who would carry out his orders.

25. *And they said to him.* Whether this is the interruption of the people, or the expostulation of the attendants in the parable, is uncertain. The sequence of the next two verses points to the latter meaning.

27. *As for these my enemies.* The parable ends with the punishment of the king's enemies, which formed part of the true history in the case of Archelaus, and was analogous to the fate of our Lord's enemies, the Jews.

28. *He went before, going up to Jerusalem.* Our Lord was now going to His passion and death, and He went in front, continually going forward and showing His anxiety for the time to arrive. Cf. Mark x. 32.

²⁹ to Jerusalem. And it came to pass, when he was come nigh to Bethphage and Bethania unto the mount called ³⁰ Olivet, he sent two of his disciples, saying : Go into the town which is over against you, at your entering into which, you shall find the colt of an ass tied, on which no man ever ³¹ hath sitten: loose him, and bring him hither. And if any man shall ask you : Why do you loose him ? you shall say thus unto him : Because the Lord hath need of his ser-

29. *When he was come nigh to Bethphage and Bethania.* Our Lord probably arrived at Bethany on the Saturday evening before Palm Sunday; this seems the most obvious meaning of St. John, xii. 1. For he speaks of the supper as if it were prepared on His arrival, and states that the next day was the day of Palms. St. Luke is silent as to the supper and the anointing of Christ, which led to the final determination of Judas to betray Him. The probable reason is that he had already related a very similar anointing, performed, according to the common Catholic belief, by the same person, and that he does not wish to repeat himself; and his silence as to Lazarus and his sisters has already been explained : see on x. 38.

The exact site of Bethphage is not known. A stone monument was discovered some years ago marking its spot near the summit of Mount Olivet, and the monument itself dated back to the time of the crusades. Though not decisive, this is interesting, as showing that in the Middle Ages there was a definite tradition as to its position.

From Bethany to Jerusalem was fifteen furlongs (John xi. 18) or about two miles, the former being on one side of Mount Olivet, and the latter on the other. Bethphage may have been between the two, unless, as some modern critics think, it was the name of a district which contained Bethany. The name Bethphage signifies "house of unripe figs." Bethany means "house of dates."

he sent two of his disciples. These are traditionally believed to have been Peter and John, the same two who were afterwards sent to prepare the Pasch (xxii. 8). The minute description given by St. Mark of the place where they found the colt suggests that St. Peter was an eyewitness, and therefore tends to confirm this tradition.

30. *You shall find the colt of an ass.* St. Matthew is the only evangelist who mentions (xxi. 2) the mother of the colt also, which he no doubt does in order to quote the prophecy which mentions both. If the disciples brought both, it is clear that the "colt on which no man ever hath sitten" was the one our Lord used. It was quite in keeping with Jewish traditions for unused animals to be put to sacred purposes. See Numb. xix. 2 ; 1 Kings vi. 7 ; and elsewhere.

31. *Because the Lord hath need of his service.* The use of the words "the Lord" indicates that the owner of the colt must have been a disciple, or at least a believer in our Lord. It would be enough for him therefore to know who had need of it, and he would let it go.

vice. And they that were sent went their way, and found 32 the colt standing, as he had said unto them. And as they 33 were loosing the colt, the owners thereof said to them: Why loose you the colt? But they said: Because the 34 Lord hath need of him. And they brought him to Jesus. 35 And casting their garments on the colt, they set Jesus thereon. And as he went, they spread their clothes under- 36 neath in the way. And when he was now coming near 37 the descent of mount Olivet, the whole multitude of his disciples began with joy to praise God with a loud voice, for all the mighty works they had seen, saying: Blessed 38 be the king who cometh in the name of the Lord, peace in heaven, and glory on high. And some of the Pharisees 39 from amongst the multitude said to him: Master, rebuke

35. *Casting their garments on the colt.* They cast their own chief or outer garments (ἱμάτια) on the animal, as though for a king.

they set Jesus thereon. This was the first time that our Lord had ever allowed anything of the nature of a popular demonstration in His favour, and the enthusiasm grew rapidly. It would have seemed to the people as if the "Messianic Kingdom" was at last to be established. The rumour must have reached Jerusalem, for many came to meet Him (John xii. 13, 18), and on His entry "the whole city was moved" (Matt. xxi. 10).

36. *As he went, they spread their clothes underneath.* This was the customary way of showing honour. From the other evangelists (Matt. xxi. 8; Mark xi. 8; John xii. 13) we see that they also carried branches of palms and other trees and spread them on the ground, which has led to the Church's ritual on Palm Sunday.

37. *When he was now coming near the descent of Mount Olivet.* The summit of the hill would be where Jerusalem comes suddenly into full view. Apparently, the sight of the holy city and the triumphal approach of the procession made the multitude so enthusiastic that the people burst forth into acclamations.

38. *Blessed be the king who cometh in the name of the Lord.* The account of the "procession of palms," as we now call it, is given in all four Gospels, and though the acclamations quoted in each are not the same, there is a general resemblance about them, such as would be expected in different summaries of what many people were crying out. They are all scriptural in form: cf., for example, Ps. cxvii. 26. It was customary for pilgrims going to and from Jerusalem to recite psalms or other portions of the Scripture, and they came to know many parts by heart. The "gradual psalms" were designed for that very purpose, and so-called because they were recited as people went up the steps of the temple. Naturally, now they chose such as would be suitable for the occasion of our Lord's solemn entry.

40 thy disciples. To whom he said: I say to you, that if
41 these shall hold their peace, the stones will cry out. And
when he drew near, seeing the city, he wept over it, say-
42 ing: If thou also hadst known, and that in this thy day,
the things that are to thy peace: but now they are hidden
43 from thy eyes. For the days shall come upon thee: and
thy enemies shall cast a trench about thee, and compass
44 thee round, and straighten thee on every side. And beat
thee flat to the ground, and thy children who are in thee:
and they shall not leave in thee a stone upon a stone: be-
45 cause thou hast not known the time of thy visitation. And
entering into the temple, he began to cast out them that

40. *If these shall hold their peace, the stones will cry out.* Some have seen a fulfilment of these words the following Friday, when our Lord's disciples were reduced to silence, and the earthquake and rending of the rocks gave testimony to Him.

41. *Seeing the city, he wept over it.* Cf. xxiii. 28: "Daughters of Jerusalem, weep not over me, but weep for yourselves and for your children:" see on v. 44.

43. *For the days shall come upon thee.* Our Lord proceeded to a definite prophecy of the destruction of Jerusalem. A further detailed prophecy is given in xxi. 5-24; and by the other synoptists.

44. *Because thou hast not known the time of thy visitation.* Our Lord wept because of the misfortunes which were to come on the city and its inhabitants; but He did not grieve over them as temporal calamities, but as the direct punishment for sin, and the sign of the final rejection of the Jews. Thus He gave as the reason, that they had not "known the time of [their] visitation"; i.e., of God's grace. This expression would have been quite in accordance with popular language: cf. vii. 16.

45. *And entering the temple.* This is the first occasion on which any of the synoptical Gospels record our Lord entering the Temple to teach during His public ministry. We know that it was not in fact at all the first time, for St. John gives many details of His visits to Jerusalem, to which indeed we find chance allusions in the synoptic Gospels: see on xiii. 34. For a description of the Temple, see chap. i. Our Lord, not being a Priest, would not have entered the temple itself. His teaching would have been in the two outer courts—of the Gentiles and of the Women. The exact place is described twice by St. John. Once (viii. 20) when He was in the treasury, which stood in the Court of the Women; and the other time (x. 23) when He walked in Solomon's porch, in the Court of the Gentiles. St. Mark (xii. 41) also alludes to His "sitting over against the treasury," and St. Luke (xxi. 1) implies the same. This was probably His most usual place for preaching.

sold therein and them that bought, saying to them: It is ⁴⁶
written: *My house is the house of prayer.* But you have
made it a den of thieves. And he was teaching daily in ⁴⁷
the temple. And the chief priests and the scribes and the
rulers of the people sought to destroy him: And they ⁴⁸
found not what to do to him. For all the people were very
attentive to hear him.

He began to cast out them that sold therein. The traffickers would have been in the outermost part, the Court of the Gentiles. Those familiar with places of modern pilgrimage are accustomed to see a trade in wax candles, rosaries, and other such objects which, however well conducted and free from grave scandal, nevertheless tends to grate on the feelings of those whose object is purely devotional. All this sort of traffic, even in the busiest of modern shrines, would be only a very faint shadow of that at Jerusalem at the time of a great feast, when the pilgrims were to be counted by tens of thousands, and each had to take part in the eating of a paschal lamb, and many offered other sacrifices of animals. St. John on a similar occasion describes (ii. 14) sellers of oxen, sheep and doves, and tables of money-changers, for many of the pilgrims came from foreign countries, and had to buy their "shekels" for temple offerings. This was at the first Pasch of the ministry, and our Lord made a scourge of small cords and drove them all out. On the occasion now before us, St. Matthew and St. Mark mention money-changers and sellers of doves; but not those of oxen or sheep. Possibly the effect of our Lord's former action had not altogether died away; but some of the abuses had revived, and accordingly He repeated it. We are told nothing this time of a scourge of cords: He may or may not have used one as before. In any case, it appears that His dignity and earnestness were a power which those with a guilty conscience could not withstand. From a comparison of the three synoptical Gospels, it appears certain that the cleansing of the temple took place on the Monday morning. St. Mark distinctly says (xi. 11) that on the Sunday, after viewing things round about, He retired to Bethany for the night; and the next day He came to Jerusalem, and drove the sellers out of the temple. St. Matthew appears at first sight to say otherwise, but his words can be understood in this sense without much difficulty. Moreover, it may be added, the trading would have been more in progress in the morning than in the evening. To cast the traders out early, when they were just ready for a day's business, would be at least more effective.

47. *And he was teaching daily in the temple.* St. Luke does not specify the exact sequence of days. All the information he gives is in this and the following verse, and in xxi. 37, 38. It is to the effect that our Lord taught "daily," or rather "by day" (καθ' ἡμέραν), in the Temple, and that at night He abode on Mount Olivet: that the people came to listen to Him early in the morning, and were very attentive to

His words ; and that the chief priests wished to put Him to death, but seemed unable to carry their wish into execution, because they feared the people. St. Mark gives more definite notes of time, and it has been customary, accordingly, to follow what appears to be his order in the division of the days of Holy Week. This would give it as follows :—

Sunday.—Procession of Palms. Our Lord retires in the evening to Bethany.

Monday.—Coming up from Bethany, our Lord curses the fig tree. Entering into the temple, He drives out the buyers and sellers. The people are attentive to His teaching. In the evening He retires again to Bethany, or to the Mount of Olives ; and passing the fig tree, the Apostles notice that it is dried up.

Tuesday.—The day of questions. Our Lord comes to Jerusalem as usual, and the various deputations come to Him. See chap. xx. At the end come the final denunciation of the Pharisees, and our Lord's last departure from the Temple.

Wednesday.—Probably is spent by our Lord at Bethany, or on the Mount of Olives with His disciples. On this day also, probably, Judas completes his bargain with the chief priests, and henceforth he seeks his opportunity to betray our Lord.

This arrangement, of course, cannot be considered as certain ; but it is a probable one, and can be accepted provisionally. If St. Mark really meant, as we suppose, to note every day as it occurred, his omission to assign anything to Wednesday must have been intentional. He passes on from the events of Tuesday, to the further note of time that "the feast of the Pasch and the Azymes was after two days" (xiv. 1), which, according to his usual method of calculating, means after two clear days. See Mark ix. 2, and cf. Luke ix. 28. In the case before us, the two days would be Wednesday and Thursday ; so that this confirms the supposition we are considering. We naturally conclude that our Lord spent Wednesday, the last full day before His passion, in the company of His disciples and friends, in or near Bethany, while very probably at that very time Judas was with the chief priests arranging plans for His betrayal : see on xxii. 3, 5.

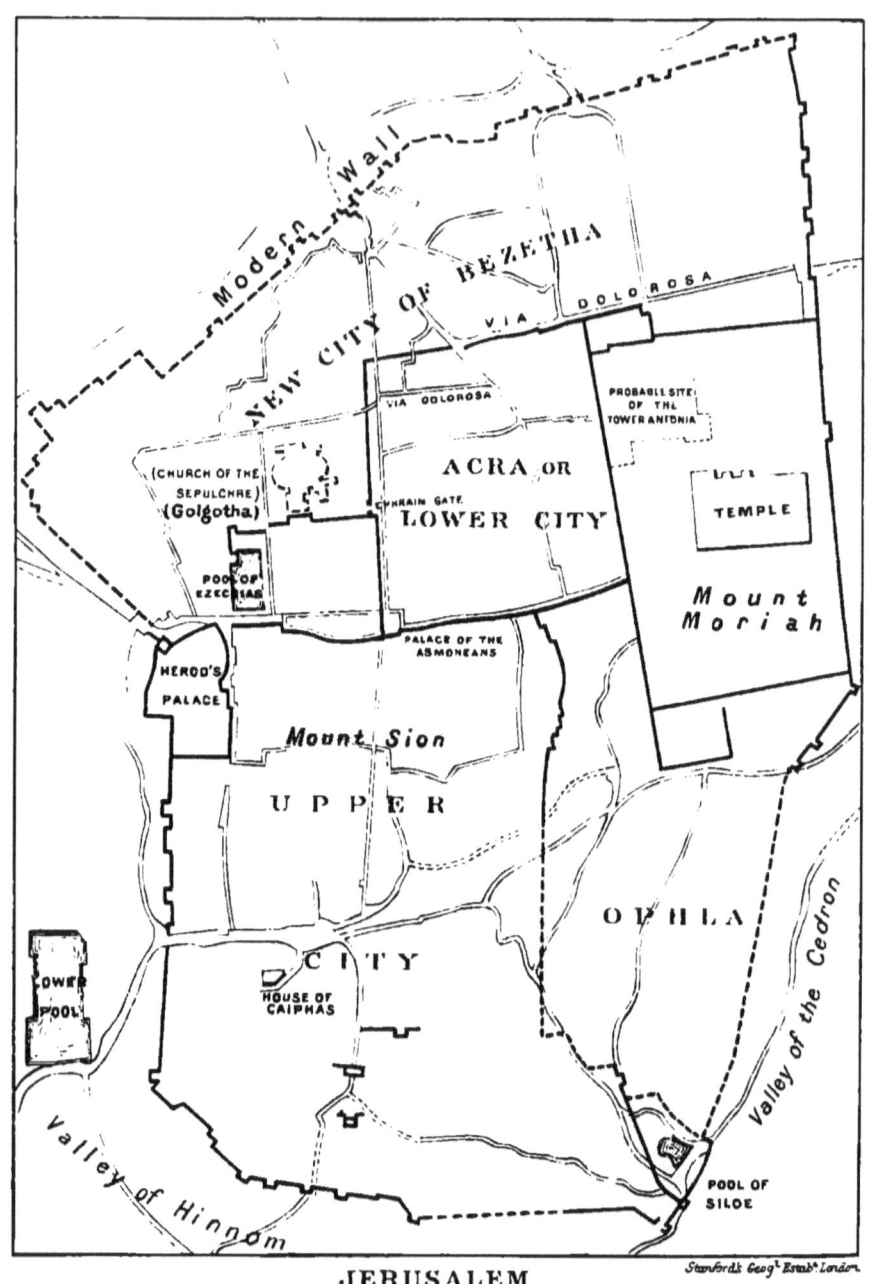
JERUSALEM

CHAPTER XX.

Question from the Sanhedrin.

(Vers. 1-8.)

AND it came to pass that on one of the days, as he was teaching the people in the temple and preaching the gospel, the chief priests and the scribes with the ancients met together. And spoke to him, saying: Tell us, by what authority dost thou do these things? or, Who

1. *On one of the days*, i.e., one of the days when our Lord taught by day in the Temple. St. Luke does not specify the date further than this, but implies that the various deputations described in this chapter all came the same day, which has therefore been commonly called the Day of Questions. According to the chronology suggested at the end of last chapter, based on St. Mark, this would have been Tuesday — Nisan 12.

and preaching the gospel. The word εὐαγγελιζομένου is more characteristic than διδάσκοντος, and, coming after it, implies something more; our Lord was not only teaching, but preaching the coming of the Messianic Kingdom.

The chief priests and the scribes with the ancients met together. The three classes here specified represent the various sections of the Sanhedrin or assembly of Jewish rulers. Hence this first deputation would have been regarded as official. The chief priests had already made up their minds to apprehend our Lord; the difficulty which stood in the way was the enthusiasm of the people in His favour, which would render it difficult to take Him without a popular outburst. Their first object, therefore, was to bring about His discredit among the people, and to turn them against Him. On the position and constitution of the Sanhedrin, see on xxii. 66.

2. *By what authority dost thou do these things?* The reference here is to the cleansing of the temple, which was an act of authority. On the previous occasion, when our Lord had acted similarly, at the first Pasch of His ministry, they had asked Him a like question (John ii.

3 is he that hath given thee this authority? And Jesus
answering, said to them: I will also ask you one thing.
4 Answer me: The baptism of John, was it from heaven, or
5 of men? But they thought within themselves, saying: If
we shall say, From heaven: he will say: Why then did
6 you not believe him? But if we say, Of men, the whole
people will stone us: for they are persuaded that John was
7 a prophet. And they answered that they knew not whence
8 it was. And Jesus said to them: Neither do I tell you by
what authority I do these things.

18), "What sign dost thou show unto us seeing thou dost these things?"
It was quite recognized that any one who claimed to be a prophet
should show some miraculous sign to authenticate his mission. Cf. xi. 16.
It has been conjectured that an additional reason why the chief priests
resented our Lord's action, was that by the expulsion of the buyers and
sellers much of their own illicit gains were stopped.

3. *I will also ask you one thing.* ἕνα λόγον, = one statement. On
the former occasion, our Lord answered by the prophecy "Destroy this
temple and in three days I will raise it up again" (John ii. 19), referring,
as we now see plainly enough, to His death and resurrection. Thus at
the time of the second cleansing His words were on the point of fulfilment. On this occasion, however, He did not repeat His former
answer, but instead proposed to them the question which follows.

4. *The baptism of John, was it from heaven?* The Scribes were
the religious teachers of the people. It was their special office, therefore, to decide between true and false prophets, and to say under which
category St. John was to be classed. The popular excitement at his
preaching, and the fact that he was the first great teacher after the lapse
of some three centuries, made the question a burning one among the
people, and one which the Scribes could not afford to ignore.

5. *But they thought within themselves,* &c. The dilemma in which
they found themselves is explained in full. Their own body had not
recognized St. John, at least not officially. Cf. vii. 30. The people, on
the other hand, were so enthusiastic in his favour, that the Scribes dared
not openly oppose them. Hence they were placed in a difficulty, and
knew not what to say; they were practically silenced. Nevertheless
our Lord's answer must not be taken as designed only to put them to
silence. There was a very positive meaning implied. St. John was
universally held as a prophet; so much so, that the Scribes could not
attempt to deny it. And St. John bore witness to our Lord in no
doubtful terms: therefore our Lord appealed to the authority of St.
John, in whom all believed.

6. *They are persuaded that John was a prophet.* Josephus bears
witness to the immense faith of the people in the Divine mission of
St. John.

8. *Neither do I tell you.* The answer of the Scribes had been a

Parable of the Vineyard and Husbandmen.

(VERS. 9-19.)

And he began to speak to the people this parable: A **9** certain man planted a vineyard, and let it out to husbandmen: and he was abroad for a long time. And at the **10** season he sent a servant to the husbandmen, that they should give him of the fruit of the vineyard. Who beating him sent him away empty. And again he sent another **11**

confession of incompetence in their own special function. Thus, our Lord would say, their inability to decide on so important and prominent a case as whether St. John was a true or false prophet, destroys any claim they might otherwise have to a direct answer from Him.

9. *A certain man planted a vineyard*, &c. Our Lord's final rupture with the Jewish rulers was now close at hand, and He spoke a series of parables which they recognized as applicable to themselves. St. Matthew gives three of them, viz., The two sons and the vineyard, the vineyard and husbandmen, and the wedding of the king's son. St. Luke gives only the second of the three. It was founded on the parable of Isa. v., where the Jewish Church was likened to a vineyard, for which everything had been done that was possible, and yet which bore no fruit but wild grapes. The judgment on the vineyard referred to the Babylonian captivity, and to the various details described have been attributed special meanings to represent the dealings of God with His chosen people. Our Lord's parable is a development of that of Isaias. St. Mark, who gives it more fully, mentions the very same details of what had been done for the vineyard as Isaias does—the hedge around it, the wine-vat, the watch-tower. There is, however, a new element in the husbandmen, to whose care the vineyard was entrusted. These might be taken to represent the religious leaders and teachers, to whose perversity was ultimately due the want of fruitfulness of the vineyard; or possibly the whole Jewish nation was intended, and the others who were to receive the vineyard in their stead were the Gentiles.

10. *He sent a servant.* By the servants are represented the prophets whom God sent from time to time. Cf. xi. 49, 50. There is considerable variation of detail in the three Gospels as to the treatment of the servants. According to St. Matthew, they beat one, killed another, and stoned a third. St. Mark says that they beat one and sent him away empty, wounded another and treated him reproachfully, and killed a third. He adds, however, that there were "many others, of whom some they beat and others they killed." No doubt our Lord spoke the parable at much greater length than that at which the evangelists give it, and that in summarizing it, different details have been selected by the three.

servant. But they beat him also, and treating him reproachfully, sent him away empty. And again he sent the third: and they wounded him also, and cast him out. 13 Then the lord of the vineyard said: What shall I do? I will send my beloved son: it may be when they see him, 14 they will reverence him. Whom when the husbandmen saw, they thought within themselves, saying: This is the 15 heir, let us kill him, that the inheritance may be ours. So casting him out of the vineyard, they killed him. What 16 therefore will the lord of the vineyard do to them? He will come, and will destroy these husbandmen, and will give the vineyard to others. Which they hearing, said to 17 him: God forbid. But he looking on them, said: What is this then that is written, *The stone which the builders* 18 *rejected, the same is become the head of the corner?* Whosoever shall fall upon that stone, shall be bruised: and

15. *What therefore will the lord of the vineyard do to them?* Here again there is some difference between the Gospels. According to St. Matthew, our Lord asked what the lord of the vineyard would do, and the priests answered Him in much the same words as St. Luke puts into the mouth of our Lord. Most probably our Lord repeated and solemnly confirmed their answer, and then proceeded to apply it.

God forbid. μὴ γένοιτο=let it not be so. This exclamation shows that they fully understood our Lord's meaning.

17. *What is this then that is written?* If they said "God forbid," that is, let this judgment not come, how were they to explain the following text?

The stone which the builders rejected. See Ps. cxvii. 22. Cf. Isa. xxviii. 16. Our Lord's meaning is explained more in full by St. Matthew, "Therefore I say to you that the kingdom of God shall be taken from you and shall be given to a nation yielding the fruits thereof."

18. *Whosoever shall fall upon that stone.* A person falling over a large stone would hurt himself; and so one who even through thoughtlessness opposes himself to God and His teaching will suffer thereby.

upon whomsoever it shall fall. This refers to those in open opposition to God and our Lord's preaching.

it will grind him to powder. The word is λικμήσει, and means originally to winnow; hence to separate the grain from the chaff; and hence to grind and scatter like chaff. Cf. Dan. ii. 34, where the stone cut out of a mountain without hands so destroys the statue representing the kingdoms opposed to Christ's rule, that the iron, clay, brass, silver, and gold become like the chaff on a summer's threshing floor, and are carried away by the wind.

upon whomsoever it shall fall, it will grind him to powder. And the chief priests and the scribes sought to lay hands on him the same hour; but they feared the people, for they knew that he spoke this parable to them.

Question of the Pharisees and Herodians.

(Vers. 20-26.)

And being upon the watch, they sent spies, who should feign themselves just, that they might take hold of him in his words, that they might deliver him up to the authority and power of the governor. And they asked him, saying: Master, we know that thou speakest and teachest rightly; and thou dost not respect any person, but teachest the way of God in truth. Is it lawful for us to give tribute to Cæsar,

19. *They knew that he spoke this parable to them.* "They knew" (ἔγνωσαν) means that the chief priests and scribes knew. Here it might mean also "the people knew," though in that case St. Luke would most probably have used the singular (ἔγνω) to agree with ὁ λαός; but in the corresponding passage of St. Matthew (xxi. 45) there is no ambiguity. Thus the meaning is that the chief priests and scribes recognized that the parable was aimed at them, and this made them fear the people, who had listened to it.

20. *They sent spies.* The "spies" mentioned by St. Luke are more definitely specified by the other two synoptists. They were a mixture of Pharisees and Herodians, the two parties who were ordinarily much at enmity with one another, and who were brought together, as once before (Mark iii. 6) by the single bond of union—hatred of our Lord. They were sent by the chief priests to ensnare Him, so that they (i.e. the priests) might find cause for delivering Him to Pilate, the governor. St. Luke states that their justice was *feigned*. Hence this introduction of themselves was hypocritical, as appears in the sequel. Their real object was the same as that of the former deputation.

22. *Is it lawful,* &c. The question asked was exactly that on which Herodians and Pharisees would have been at variance. Since the deposition of Archelaus, Judæa had been in fact a Roman province, but the stricter Jews regarded themselves as having an inalienable right to freedom, and the tribute, or capitation tax, was considered by the Scribes illegal. Herod, on the other hand, owed his power to the Romans, and not being himself a Jew, he did all he could to gain the favour of the Romans and to extinguish Jewish national aspirations. The Pharisees and Herodians, therefore, would naturally dispute whether the tribute should be paid, and they pretended to be referring such dispute to our Lord for settlement. The question was skilfully devised.

23 or no? But he considering their guile, said to them: Why
24 tempt you me? Shew me a penny. Whose image and inscription hath it? They answering said to him, Cæsar's.
25 And he said to them: Render therefore to Cæsar the things that are Cæsar's, and to God the things that are God's.
26 And they could not reprehend his word before the people: and wondering at his answer, they held their peace.

Question of the Sadducees.

(VERS. 27-40.)

27 And there came to him some of the Sadducees, who deny that there is any resurrection, and they asked him,

If our Lord answered in favour of the tribute, there would be a pretext for turning the people against Him, for many were very jealous of their nation's rights and their theoretical independence. If, on the other hand, our Lord were to answer against the tribute, as they would probably expect, the Roman authorities—Pilate and his assistants—would consider Him as fomenting insurrection, and could be easily induced to apprehend Him.

24. *Shew me a penny.* There were Roman coins coined specially for Judea, having the inscription but not the image of Cæsar. The one they showed, however, had his image, and must therefore have been a real Roman denarius. St. Mark implies that they had to fetch it. Possibly they obtained it from the temple money-changers, now no longer in the temple courts, but outside altogether.

25. *Render therefore to Cæsar*, &c. The doctrine here enunciated in brief has been since drawn out at length by Christian writers. The duty of a good citizen is to obey rightfully constituted authority within its own sphere; but when it clashes with duty to God, we are bound to resist it, even at the cost of our lives, as did the martyrs of the early Church. Our Lord's meaning, as addressed to His hearers, was, then, that the image of Cæsar and his inscription on their coins was an evidence to them of the establishment of the Roman rule; and as they profited by its protection, so they must obey it in things temporal, and pay their share of the cost of government. See Rom. xiii. 1-7; Titus iii. 1. It was in spiritual matters only that they were not under the Roman yoke; and their spiritual life belonged to God. Cf. Rom. xii. 1.

26. *They could not reprehend his word before the people.* Christ's answer had thus been in favour of paying the taxes, but it was accompanied with an explanation which carried conviction with it; so that "they could not reprehend his word before the people." Thus again the object of their questioning was not obtained.

27. *Some of the Sadducees.* The Sadducees as a party were as much

saying: Master, Moses wrote unto us, If any man's 28 brother die having a wife, and he leave no children, that his brother should take her to wife, and raise up seed unto his brother. There were therefore seven brethren: and 29 the first took a wife, and died without children. And the 30 next took her to wife, and he also died childless. And 31 the third took her. And in like manner all the seven, and they left no children, and died. Last of all the 32 woman died also. In the resurrection therefore, whose 33 wife of them shall she be? For *all* the seven had her

opposed to the Pharisees as were the Herodians. Herod himself was a Sadducee, as were the majority among the chief priests; but they had only a small following among the people, and were not looked up to as were the stricter Pharisees. The essential difference between the two parties turned on the "Oral Law" and "Traditions." The Pharisees, as we have already seen, set great store on numberless small laws which were traditional among them. Cf. Mark vii. 3–4. Some of these they maintained to have come down even from Moses. The Sadducees refused to recognize any of them. As a result, they did not believe in the resurrection after death—that is in a future life—maintaining that no such doctrine was taught in the Pentateuch; and though there are undoubted allusions to it in the Psalms, and in some of the Books of the Prophets, as well as in the Book of Job, they attached only a minor importance to these compared with the Books of Moses. Thus they also disbelieved in the existence of angels and spirits. Cf. Acts xxiii. 8. The result of their beliefs was that they lived a worldly and self-indulgent life, and were devoid of religious zeal. This accounts for their want of influence with the people, to whom the strictness of the Pharisees appealed as evidence of earnestness. But these same reasons prevented their coming so much into conflict with our Lord, who was continually speaking against the unreal and hypocritical religious observances of the Pharisees, joined as they were with the spirit of pride and self-assertion.

28. *If any man's brother die*, &c. The law about Levirate marriages (Deut. xxv.) has already been alluded to: see on iii. 23. The difficulty here raised may be compared with modern rationalistic difficulties against the resurrection of the body. It was probably one which was often used, and which had no doubt often puzzled the Pharisees or others.

29. *There were therefore seven brethren.* Seven being a mystical number, was frequently used by the Jews to represent any large number. Cf. xi. 26, xvii. 4: and Matt. xviii. 21, and elsewhere.

30. *And the next took her to wife.* It is said that Levirate marriages had become largely out of use. This case quoted is therefore of one who was unusually strict in keeping the law.

33. *Whose wife of them shall she be?* The question would have

34 to wife. And Jesus said to them: The children of this
35 world marry, and are given in marriage: but they that
shall be accounted worthy of that world and of the
resurrection from the dead, shall neither be married, nor
36 take wives. Neither can they die any more: for they are
equal to the angels, and are the children of God, being
37 the children of the resurrection. Now that the dead rise
again, Moses also shewed, at the bush, when he calleth
the Lord: *The God of Abraham, and the God of Isaac,*
38 *and the God of Jacob.* For he is not the God of the
39 dead, but of the living: for all live to him. And some
of the scribes answering, said to him: Master, thou hast
40 said well. And after that they durst not ask him any
more questions.

appeared to the common people a natural one; for clearly the woman could not have seven husbands in the next world.

34. *The children of this world marry.* Our Lord's answer is twofold. In the first part He draws a faint image of the joys of heaven and the dignity of the elect, who are immortal children of God, and shall be raised far above the cravings and aspirations of our human nature here below.

36. *They are equal to the angels.* In mentioning the angels, our Lord had no doubt further in view the scepticism of the Sadducees about their existence.

37. *That the dead rise again, Moses also shewed.* In His second answer, our Lord went further, and gave positive arguments against their tenets by quoting the Pentateuch itself. See Exod. iii. 6.

The God of Abraham. God would have ceased to be the God of Abraham if Abraham had ceased to exist; and hence, as he had been dead long before the time of Moses, and Moses quoted God as saying "I *am* the God of Abraham," he must have understood Abraham to have been still in existence after his death.

38. *All live to him.* At the time at which our Lord was speaking, the souls of the just were still detained in "*Limbo Patrum.*" Our Lord's words indicate a very real life there, and one that has a work to do, in forwarding God's interests by prayers and supplications, in the hope of the time when they were to see Him face to face.

39. *Master, thou hast said well.* Those Scribes who were Pharisaical would have had a certain satisfaction in the discomfiture of the Sadducees.

40. *After that they durst not ask him any more questions.* St. Matthew says (xxii. 34) that on learning the way in which the Sadducees had been answered, the Pharisees again returned to the attack, and it was no doubt after His answer to the "doctor of the law" that they finally abandoned questioning Him.

Final Rupture with the Jewish Rulers.

(VERS. 41-47.)

But he said to them: How say they that Christ is the son of David? And David himself saith in the book of psalms: *The Lord said to my Lord, sit thou on my right hand, till I make thy enemies thy footstool.* David then calleth him Lord: and how is he his son? And in the hearing of all the people, he said to his disciples: Beware of the scribes, who desire to walk in long robes, and love salutations in the market-place, and the first chairs in the synagogues, and the chief rooms at feasts: who devour the houses of widows, feigning long prayer. These shall receive greater damnation.

42. *The Lord said to my Lord.* The 109th Psalm was universally recognized as Messianic, and its author as David; but the full meaning of it was not at all understood, and the difficulty suggested by our Lord would require for its answer a knowledge of Christ's twofold generation—as God and as Man—which would be quite above anything which was then known.

45. *In the hearing of all the people.* As soon as they were reduced to silence, our Lord began His final denunciation of the Pharisees and Scribes, which formed His last public discourse in the Temple, and which we may look on as the last of His ministry; for the words recorded in the next chapter were addressed to His disciples. St. Luke gives this discourse briefly, but St. Matthew's account (chap. xxiii.), which is very full, shows that it closely resembled the denunciation at the Pharisee's house some weeks before, which St. Luke alone gives. See xi. 39-52. The only difference of importance was that the former occasion was more or less private, while now our Lord was speaking "in the hearing of all the people."

46. *Beware of the scribes.* There are three headings here in the indictment of the Jewish rulers: (1) pride; (2) avarice; (3) hypocrisy.

(1) Their pride was shown by fine dress, their desire for the salutations of the people, high places at feasts and the like.

(2) Their avarice was shown by their common practice of frequenting the houses of rich widows—the most defenceless of people—and accepting presents from them, for which Josephus says that they were notorious.

(3) Their hypocrisy was shown by their "feigned" prayers. They used to say certain long prayers daily. Cf. Mark vii. 6, (quoting Isa. xxix. 13: "This people honoureth me with their lips, but their heart is far from me."

47. *These shall receive greater damnation*, i.e., greater than those who did not profess the same religious zeal for the law. These words are strong enough, but if St. Matthew's account (xxiii. 14) be consulted, they appear even stronger in the context in which they are placed. In fact the final crisis had now arrived, and there was no further reason for reticence on our Lord's part. After such words, on so public an occasion, all His hearers must have felt that the rupture with the Jewish rulers was final. Our Lord left the Temple that day for the last time.

CHAPTER XXI.

The Widow's Mite.

(Vers. 1-4.)

AND looking on, he saw the rich men cast their gifts into the treasury. And he saw also a certain poor widow casting in two brass mites. And he said: Verily I say to you, that this poor widow hath cast in more than they all. For all these have of their abundance cast into the offerings of God: but she of her want, hath cast in all the living that she had.

1. *He saw the rich men cast their gifts into the treasury.* The "treasury" stood in the Court of the Women, in which, as we have seen, our Lord usually preached. There were thirteen trumpet-shaped caskets, or collecting boxes. Into these the people used to cast their offerings. On each was inscribed the special purpose on which the money collected therein would be spent. At the time of the feast, there was always a continual stream of donors passing by, and St. Mark says (xii. 41) that at this time "many that were rich cast in much."

2. *Two brass mites.* St. Mark also says that two mites make a farthing. The coin (λεπτόν) which we call a "mite," was the smallest one current. The "farthing" was the Roman quadrans, or quarter of an as, and equivalent to about half a farthing of English money. The "mite" was half of this, and the offering of two mites was the smallest one permissible.

3. *This poor widow hath cast in more than they all.* Our Lord's last words in the Temple were words of consolation. They show how God reads the heart and the intention, and values what is given by the self-denial entailed, and the motive for which it is done. The widow gave her whole subsistence, and did it from the best motive. She did not look upon her poverty as an excuse from the duty of giving, but rather as a help towards a good intention, inasmuch as there was less fear of the act being inspired by vain glory.

Prophecy of the Destruction of Jerusalem and of the Day of Judgment.

(Vers. 5-38.)

5 And some saying of the temple, that it was adorned
6 with goodly stones and gifts, he said: These things which you see, the days will come in which there shall not be left a stone upon a stone that shall not be thrown down.
7 And they asked him, saying: Master, when shall these things be: and what shall be the sign when they shall
8 begin to come to pass? Who said: Take heed you be not seduced; for many will come in my name, saying, I am he: and the time is at hand: go ye not therefore after

5. *Some saying of the temple*, &c. We learn from the other evangelists that the remark here given was made by the apostles on Mount Olivet. Our Lord was probably on His way to Bethany, where He was to spend the last day before His passion. The site where this was spoken was therefore near the place where He had wept over Jerusalem, and where He had delivered His first prophecy of its destruction (xix. 41-44). After the denunciation of the Priests and Pharisees, our Lord's disciples must have realized that there was now an end to their hopes of a Messianic kingdom, with its centre at Jerusalem, as they understood it, and the journey that evening would have suggested thoughts to them different from any before. Their remarks about the beauty of the Temple suggest the same idea, as though they thought that they were leaving Jerusalem rejected by the Jewish rulers.

adorned with goodly stones and gifts. The "gifts" by which the Temple was adorned were many and various. Some were given by kings. See 2 Mach. iii. 2-7. Among those of which we know may be mentioned the golden vine, with clusters "as large as a man," mentioned by Josephus as given by Herod; and the golden chain of Agrippa.

6. *There shall not be left a stone upon a stone.* Some of the stones of the Temple were of enormous size. The prophecy of its total destruction would have come on the apostles as a confirmation of their fears.

8. *Take heed you be not seduced.* The prophecy which follows is in parts difficult to understand. The difficulty arises from the fact that two distinct events are referred to, the one being a type of the other: namely, the destruction of Jerusalem, and the end of the world. In the minds of the apostles the two were closely connected: they seem to have had a definite idea that with the fall of Jerusalem, the world would come to an end. In examining our Lord's prophecy, we find a difficulty in determining to which of the two events any given part mainly refers: for in truth the whole refers in general to both: but in some parts the reference is more direct to one, in other parts to the other. Thus

them. And when you shall hear of wars and seditions, be 9
not terrified: these things must first come to pass, but the
end is not yet presently. Then he said to them: Nation 10
shall rise against nation, and kingdom against kingdom.
And there shall be great earthquakes in divers places, and 11
pestilences and famines, and terrors from heaven, and there
shall be great signs. But before all these things they will lay 12
their hands on you and persecute you, delivering you up to
the synagogues, and into prisons, dragging you before kings
and governors for my name's sake. And it shall happen 13
unto you for a testimony. Lay it up therefore in your 14

vv. 8–24 clearly refer in the first place to the history of apostolic times and the destruction of Jerusalem, and from *v.* 25 onwards the end of the world is the primary reference. But much throughout refers equally to both. In addition to these meanings, there seems also—especially in the last part—distinct allusion to the end of each man's life, and his own "particular judgment."

9. *When you shall hear of wars and seditions.* These signs were abundantly verified in apostolic times, and before the destruction of Jerusalem; and also the wars of nations, and the earthquakes, pestilences, and terrors from heaven. But the end was not at hand. οὐκ εὐθέως = not immediately.

10. *Nation shall rise against nation.* This seems a solemn and amplified reiteration of what has just gone before and has the same reference.

12. *They will lay their hands on you and persecute you.* Cf. John xv. 20 and xvi. 2, giving a similar warning delivered by our Lord two days later. It seems that before He parted from His apostles, He was anxious that they should realize fully what was in store for them, and what they were to suffer for His name. Of the complete fulfilment of these prophecies, we learn from the Acts of the Apostles and other sources.

13. *For a testimony*, i.e., a testimony of the truth of the gospel. The word is μαρτύριον; hence the word martyr, or one who testifies in the highest possible way, by laying down his life in token of his faith. According to tradition, all the apostles who listened to our Lord that evening ended their days by martyrdom, except only St. John and Judas Iscariot. St. John, however, was a martyr by desire, and bore as perfect witness as the others, when he was put into a cauldron of boiling oil at Rome outside the Latin Gate; and the fact that he did not die a martyr is only because he was miraculously preserved.

14. *Lay it up therefore in your hearts.* The meaning is that they were to take comfort now in our Lord's promise that whatever difficulties and persecutions they might have to face in the future, God would be with them and guide them with a special and particular providence. Cf. xii. 11 and Matt. x. 19, 20.

15 hearts, not to meditate before how you shall answer. For I will give you a mouth and wisdom, which all your adver-
16 saries shall not be able to resist and gainsay. And you shall be betrayed by your parents and brethren, and kinsmen and friends: and some of you they will put to death.
17 And you shall be hated by all men for my name's sake.
18
19 But a hair of your head shall not perish. In your patience
20 you shall possess your souls. And when you shall see Jerusalem compassed about with an army: then know
21 that the desolation thereof is at hand. Then let those who are in Judea flee to the mountains: and those who are in the midst thereof, depart out: and those who are in

15. *Wisdom which all your adversaries shall not be able to resist.* The power of truth is convincing, and the testimony of the early Christians convinced many even of their persecutors.

16. *You shall be betrayed by your parents and brethren.* Cf. Matt. x. 36: "A man's enemies shall be they of his own household."

some of you they will put to death. As has been just stated, according to tradition, all the apostles except St. John and Judas were martyred. These were, however, only "some of" those whom our Lord was then addressing. For although the first question, which led to the discourse was asked by four of the apostles apart (Matt. xxiv. 3), there is every reason to suppose that the discourse itself was delivered not only to these, but to all the apostles, and to other disciples who had followed our Lord from the Temple.

17. *You shall be hated by all men.* This has been a sign of the true Church throughout all history. Cf. Acts xxviii. 22: "Concerning this sect, we know that it is gainsayed everywhere." See also 1 Pet. ii. 12, iii. 16, iv. 14, 16.

18. *A hair of your head shall not perish.* This phrase is evidently intended figuratively. The meaning is that the apostles should suffer no true injury—not the slightest. That it is not to be taken literally is made clear by comparing it with *v.* 16.

19. *You shall possess your souls,* i.e., gain possession of them and work out salvation.

20. *When you shall see Jerusalem compassed about with an army.* The following verses refer directly to the Destruction of Jerusalem. The account given by St. Matthew is naturally more full. The word κυκλουμένην should be noted. It is the present participle, and denotes the compassing as in the act of taking place; and it is to be a sign of what is to follow, that the desolation thereof—or the Abomination of Desolation (Matt. xxiv. 15)—is at hand. Of course after the compassing was complete, escape would be impossible.

21. *In the midst thereof,* i.e., in Jerusalem, as contrasted with those "in the countries," who were warned not to enter it.

the countries, not enter into it. For these are the days of vengeance, that all things may be fulfilled that are written. But wo to them that are with child, and give suck in those days; for there shall be great distress in the land, and wrath upon this people. And they shall fall by the edge of the sword: and shall be led away captives into all nations: and Jerusalem shall be trodden down by the Gentiles: till the times of the nations be fulfilled. And there shall be signs in the sun, and in the moon, and in the stars: and upon the earth distress of nations, by reason of the confusion of the roaring of the sea and of the waves. Men withering away for fear, and expectation of what shall come upon the whole world. For the powers of heaven shall be moved: And then they shall see the son of man coming in a cloud with great power and majesty. But

23. *Wo to them that are with child.* This expression is of course not an imputation of blame, and is quite different in meaning from the woes of the Sermon on the Plain (vi. 24–26) and elsewhere. Here it simply denotes that as a fact those so placed will be in a pitiable position.

24. *And they shall fall by the edge of the sword.* It is said that over a million Jews perished in the siege of Jerusalem, and one hundred thousand others were led away captive. And to these must also be added the many massacres of Jews in different parts of the Empire. The fulfilment of the rest of the prophecy has also been complete. Jerusalem has been trodden under foot by many Gentile peoples, and this is to go on "till the time of the nations be fulfilled." The "time of the nations" means of course "of the Gentiles." The word is the same (ἐθνῶν) as that immediately above; our difference of rendering comes from the Vulgate. The "time of the Gentiles" must mean that for their evangelization, during which they receive the privileges originally intended for the Jews.

25. *And there shall be signs in the sun, and in the moon, and in the stars.* Our Lord is here speaking more directly of the day of judgment. The "signs in sun and moon and stars"—for in the Greek there is no article before each of these words—must probably be taken not too literally. They stand in general for astral phenomena, whether natural or otherwise; and of the precise manner of fulfilment we are as yet ignorant. Cf. Apoc. vi. 12, 13.

27. *And then they shall see the son of man.* Cf. Apoc. xiv. 14. The τότε is emphatic—"*then*" (and not before) "they shall see the Son of Man," &c.

28. *Look up and lift up your heads*, i.e., in the midst of all these signs of God's wrath there is motive for perfect hope, for the time of redemption is at hand.

when these things begin to come to pass, look up and lift up your heads: because your redemption is at hand. ²⁹ And he spoke to them a similitude. See the fig-tree, and ³⁰ all the trees: When they now shoot forth their fruit, you ³¹ know that summer is nigh. So you also when you shall see these things come to pass, know that the kingdom of ³² God is at hand. Amen I say to you, this generation shall ³³ not pass away, till all things be fulfilled. Heaven and earth shall pass away, but my words shall not pass away. ³⁴ And take heed to yourselves, lest perhaps your hearts be overcharged with surfeiting and drunkenness and the cares ³⁵ of this life: and that day come upon you suddenly. For as a snare shall it come upon all that sit upon the face of

29. *And he spoke to them a similitude.* This verse reads like a resumption after a pause or interval, and as it were the introduction of a new phase of the subject.

See the fig tree and all the trees. The fig tree would be familiar to Jewish, but not to Gentile, readers. Therefore St. Luke adds "and all the trees," which the other evangelists omit.

31. *Know that the kingdom of God is at hand*, i.e., the time when God is to come in majesty and to reign with absolute dominion over mankind, and all resistance to His will is to vanish for ever. Cf. on xi. 2.

32. *This generation shall not pass away.* "This generation" must mean primarily those who were alive at the time that our Lord spoke. The words, therefore, refer in the first place to the fall of Jerusalem, when many to whom our Lord had preached were still alive: cf. on ix. 27. If, however, we take "all things" to include everything to which the prophecy alluded, we should have to refer "this generation" to the Jewish race. Our Lord's meaning would then be that the race of the Jews would live to be witnesses of the *complete* fulfilment of His words.

33. *Heaven and earth shall pass away.* This is a figurative expression to show the extreme stability of our Lord's words. "Heaven and earth" stands for all creation (Gen. i. 1), and the meaning is that, though all creation should be destroyed, our Lord's words would remain and be fulfilled.

34. *And take heed to yourselves.* There seems a distinct application in this and the two following verses to what we call the particular judgment—God's coming to judge, not all mankind, but the individual soul. We are warned to be always ready for His coming.

35. *As a snare.* This life is not meant to be to us "as a snare." God wills the salvation of all, and has no wish to find a pretext for their condemnation. The meaning is simply that the suddenness of His

the whole earth. Watch ye therefore, praying at all times, 36 that you may be accounted worthy to escape all these things that are to come, and to stand before the son of man. And in the day-time he was teaching in the temple; 37 but at night going out, he abode in the mount of Olivet. And all the people came early in the morning to him in 38 the temple to hear him.

coming will be like that when a bird finds himself ensnared and in a trap.

36. *To escape all these things*, that is, to pass safely through the dangers and to be worthy to be brought before the Son of Man as His elect.

The parables of the ten virgins and of the talents and the detailed description of the day of judgment, which are given in the twenty-fifth chapter of St. Matthew, come at this stage, and probably formed the conclusion of our Lord's discourse on the Tuesday evening. We have no information of how He spent the Wednesday and the early part of Thursday, the time immediately before His passion. It is possible that He remained at Bethany with Martha and Mary. If, as we suppose, Judas went on Wednesday to the chief priests, it would seem to show that it was not a day of great activity in the ministry of our Lord.

37. *And in the day-time he was teaching in the temple*. This verse and the following one are evidently retrospective. The tense is the imperfect, and denotes a habit.

at night going out he abode on the Mount of Olivet. Many have supposed that our Lord went every night to Bethany, which was on Mount Olivet, and to the house of Martha and Mary; but this is not at all certain. We are told, indeed, definitely, that He went to Bethany on the Sunday night (Matt. xxi. 17; Mark xi. 11); but as to the other nights, we have only the words of St. Mark (xi. 19), that He went "out of the city," and those of St. Luke now before us, which might or might not mean Bethany. There is no doubt that many Galilean pilgrims would have camped out on Mount Olivet, as they could not possibly all find room within the city; and it appears from St. John (xviii. 2), and also from St. Luke (xxii. 39), that our Lord was accustomed to retire to the garden of Gethsemani, which was near the foot of Mount Olivet. And there seems some reason to suppose that He spent the night there more than once, for Judas naturally went straight there with the soldiers when he betrayed Him, and evidently looked on it as certain that he would find Him there. On Gethsemani itself, see on xxii. 39.

CHAPTER XXII.

Treachery of Judas.

(VERS. 1-6.)

NOW the feast of unleavened bread, which is called
2 the pasch, was at hand. And the chief priests and
the scribes sought how they might put Jesus to death : but

1. *The feast of unleavened bread.* St. Luke, writing for Gentiles, explains the meaning of "the feast of unleavened bread," that it was the Pasch or Passover: see on ii. 41. It opened on the 14th day of Nisan, on which the Paschal lambs were killed; and in the evening of which the Paschal suppers took place: see on *v.* 14. The following day, the 15th of Nisan, was the Feast itself, on which the same rules held as to abstaining from work as on the Sabbath. The festivities were prolonged throughout seven days, during which time all leaven was rigorously removed from the houses, and unleavened bread exclusively used. Hence the name of "the feast of unleavened bread." The question on what precise day the feast fell that year, is one of great difficulty, and one on which difference of opinion has always existed. The point raised is whether our Lord died on the feast day or the day before; which is the same as whether the feast day was on the Friday or Saturday, for all admit that He died on a Friday. There is no doubt that any one reading the synoptical Gospels only, would assume as a matter of course that the Last Supper was a paschal supper, and that our Lord suffered on the actual festival day. See Matt. xxvi. 17; Mark xiv. 12; Luke xxii. 7 and 15. Indeed, the decision of the chief priests not to put our Lord to death on the festival day would seem to be recorded by St. Matthew (xxvi. 5) and St. Mark (xiv. 2) without any reason, unless we understand them to be alluding to Providence having frustrated their design. If we turn to St. John, however, the evidence is, on the surface, all the other way. An exclusive reader of St. John would naturally infer that the feast day was on the Sabbath, for (1) he seems to say (xviii. 28) that on the Friday morning the Jews had not yet eaten their Pasch, but were about to

do so; (2) he says (xix. 14) that it was the Parasceve (i.e., day of preparation) of the Pasch; and (3) [*ibid. v.* 31] that the coming sabbath was "a great sabbath," which many understand to mean the feast day. The importance of the evidence from St. John is much enhanced by the fact that he wrote long after the others, and with a view to supplement them, and even to correct any false impressions that they might have been misunderstood to convey. And to this is added the argument that the feast day was ordered by the law (Deut. xvi. 8) to be kept as a Sabbath, and therefore if Friday was the feast day, the burial of our Lord would have been as illegal on Friday as on Saturday; and the whole history of His trial, condemnation and execution would have been a continued breach of the law. These considerations have induced many to seek to explain the words of the three synoptists in a sense different to what they bear at first sight. Some have supposed that our Lord anticipated the Pasch for Himself by virtue of His Divine authority; others have suggested that there might have been a custom, when the festival fell on a Friday, to postpone it to the Sabbath, in which case many of the Jews would have eaten their paschal meal on the Friday evening, while our Lord adhered to the proper day. Others again have thought that the Galileans kept their pasch a day earlier, or that there was some ambiguity as to which was the right day. These suggestions, though perhaps not impossible, cannot be considered satisfactory, and we have therefore preferred to adhere to the obvious meaning of the synoptists, and to seek some other explanation of the texts from St. John. A celebrated German Astronomer[1] has drawn out a list of days on which the feast would have fallen. If this list is taken as correct, it is decisive. In A.D. 30, the feast was on a Friday and this must have been the year that our Lord suffered. It did not occur on a Saturday, according to this list, till A.D. 33; nor on a Friday in any other possible year. Then we know that the observance of the feast had become relaxed, and it is probable that it would not have been regarded in the same light as a Sabbath, much in the same way that a holiday of obligation in England has come to be looked on less strictly than a Sunday, though the ecclesiastical law for both is identical. If we adopt this explanation, it remains only to say a few words on the meaning of the texts quoted from St. John. The first (xviii. 28) is the most difficult of explanation. The only possible supposition is that St. John spoke in general language, and in "eating the Pasch," he meant to include keeping all the Paschal festivities, especially the eating of certain voluntary sacrifices, called *Chagiga*, which the priests and Pharisees might have done ostentatiously. See Deut. xvi. 16; Exod. xxiii. 15. The second text (xix. 14) presents no great difficulty. Every Friday was a "parasceve," and St. Luke himself (xxiii. 54) calls the first Good Friday by that name. By "the parasceve of the Pasch," St. John may well have meant "Paschal Friday." In like manner, in the third text quoted (xix. 31) St. John may have only meant that it was a great Sabbath as being "Paschal Sabbath," or the

---

[1] See Didon's "Life of Christ," translated by C. Kegan Paul, vol. ii. p. 421.

3 they feared the people. And satan entered into Judas
4 who was surnamed Iscariot, one of the twelve. And he
went, and discoursed with the chief priests and the magis‑
5 trates, how he might betray him to them. And they were

Sabbath during the festal season. These are the explanations usually given by those who adopt this view, which has the balance of tradition in its favour. The further discussion of the texts belongs rather to a commentary on St. John.

2. *The chief priests and scribes sought how they might put Jesus to death.* This seems to allude to the council in the house of Caiphas, related by St. Matthew (xxvi. 3), which must have been held after the discomfiture of the priests in the temple, either on Tuesday evening or Wednesday. Two decisions were come to: first, to lay hold of Jesus "by some wile" (Mark xiv. 1) and kill Him; secondly, to avoid the festival day for fear of a tumult among the people. This might be expected from any uprising in our Lord's favour on the part of the Galilean pilgrims, among whom most of His disciples were, and who were present in great numbers at the feast.

3. *Satan entered into Judas.* In these words St. Luke describes the final fall of the apostle. St. John uses the same expression (xiii. 27). At the time of his call, about two years before, Judas no doubt believed in our Lord, and during the mission of the apostles (ix. 1–10) he may have even worked miracles in His name. But his fall was not sudden. Already at the time of the Pasch, a year before, our Lord said that one of the twelve "is a devil," referring of course to him (John vi. 71). All the apostles had had ambitious ideas, and had looked forward to a temporal kingdom, to be founded by our Lord: but in the mind of Judas such ideas had held a more prominent place than with the others, and while their aspirations became gradually spiritualized, his were more and more directed to material advantage. Thus all the time he kept the purse for our Lord's followers, he was dishonest (John xii. 6). By now, he must have made up his mind to leave our Lord; for he could never have hoped to be received by the others again after his treachery. His selling his Master was thus the last chance of making some profit before he left Him.

4. *He went and discoursed with the chief priests.* This must have been on the Wednesday; for it was evidently after the council in the court of Caiphas.

5. *And covenanted to give him money.* We know from St. Matthew that the money was actually paid before our Lord's apprehension. Possibly it was only paid on the Thursday night, when he came to them to say that an opportunity had come, and led them out to Gethsemani; for after paying him the money, they would hardly have let him out of their sight till he had kept his promise. The amount paid was (Matt. xxvi. 15) thirty pieces of silver, equivalent in our money to about £3 10s. It was the price of a slave. An ordinary day's wage was

glad, and covenanted to give him money. And he promised. And he sought opportunity to betray him in the absence of the multitude.

Preparation for the Paschal Supper.

(VERS. 7–13.)

And the day of the unleavened bread came, on which it was necessary that the pasch should be killed. And he sent Peter and John, saying: Go and prepare for us the pasch, that we may eat. But they said: Where wilt thou

one denarius, and a piece of silver would have been worth four denarii. Thus the price was worth about 120 days' wages of a labouring man.

6. *He sought opportunity to betray him in the absence of the multitude.* The betrayal must needs have occupied some time, in order to get together those who were to carry it out. It was impossible in the day time, while so many Galileans and other disciples of our Lord were in Jerusalem. The only chance was to find Him in the evening, "in the absence of the multitude," or else to intercept Him outside the city, on some day when He did not come to Jerusalem. Our Lord appears to have kept His future movements from Judas's knowledge, probably for this very reason, so that it appeared as though His enemies would have to wait some little time for a convenient opportunity. Probably they expected to effect their purpose after the feast; but in the event, matters were hurried on by force of circumstances which were not foreseen.

7. *And the day of the unleavened bread came.* The 13th of Nisan was the day when all leaven was removed from the houses, and was burnt in the open air. The following day, therefore, or the 14th of Nisan, would have been known as "the day of the unleavened bread." In the afternoon of that day the lambs were killed; and after sunset the pasch was eaten. This therefore seems to be the day here described, and it was the fifth day of the week, or Thursday. And it cannot be supposed, without straining the meaning of the words, that St. Luke was alluding to the Jewish day beginning at sunset on Thursday evening as "the day of the unleavened bread"; for the plain meaning is that the time came for killing and eating the pasch, and that this was accordingly done.

8. *And he sent Peter and John.* Our Lord kept secret from the apostles, up to the last, the place where the paschal supper was to be, no doubt for the same reason as before. It would have been a favourable occasion for His apprehension, and if Judas had known, plans could have been concerted for it to take place in the evening when the city was quiet. Possibly Judas was one of those who asked our Lord where the pasch was to be prepared (Matt. xxvi. 17; Mark xiv. 12). Our Lord

¹⁰ that we prepare? And he said to them: Behold, as you go into the city, there shall meet you a man carrying a pitcher of water: follow him into the house where he ¹¹ entereth in: and you shall say to the good man of the house: The master saith to thee: Where is the guest-chamber, where I may eat the pasch with my disciples? ¹² And he will shew you a large dining-room furnished: and ¹³ there prepare. And they going, found as he said to them, and made ready the pasch.

answered by sending not Judas, as would have been naturally expected, but Peter and John. Probably Judas would have recognized in this a warning to himself, as though our Lord was aware of what he was planning.

10. *There shall meet you a man carrying a pitcher of water.* The description of the two apostles meeting a man with a pitcher of water showed a knowledge more than human, and rendered it impossible for any one who did not accompany them to have any idea where they were to go. There would have been probably little difficulty in finding in Jerusalem, many who would have been glad to lend their house to our Lord for the paschal supper. It was quite customary to entertain guests for this purpose, and of the large number of pilgrims from all parts, a considerable proportion would have to find houses which they could enter as guests. The number who partook of the meal was not less than ten, and sometimes as many as forty or fifty. See Exod. xii. 4.

11. *And you shall say to the good man of the house.* The "good man of the house" was no doubt a disciple of our Lord.

12. *And he will shew you a large dining-room.* The word (ἀνάγαιον) translated dining-room would be more properly rendered an upper-room, and would have been a large room on the first floor, such as was commonly used for occasions of this kind. It is believed to be the same upper-chamber into which the apostles retired after the Ascension (Acts i. 13), and which therefore witnessed the Descent of the Holy Ghost, and much of the early life of the first Christian community.

13. *And made ready the pasch.* The ceremonies to be observed, both in the preparation and the eating of the paschal supper, are given in the twelfth chapter of the book of Exodus. The description there given refers primarily to the first paschal supper, on the night of the deliverance of the Israelites from Egypt. But much of what is put down was clearly meant for future occasions, and would have been impossible to observe on the first occasion; as, for instance, that the day following should be kept as a feast. On the other hand, many of the rules there put down had become obsolete by our Lord's time. The lambs were never kept four days (*v.* 6), nor was the door post sprinkled with blood (*v.* 7); and the directions for eating the pasch standing as if ready for a journey was likewise obsolete. The rule for cooking with

The Last Supper.

(VERS. 14–38.)

And when the hour was come, he sat down and the 14 twelve apostles with him. And he said to them: With 15 desire I have desired to eat this pasch with you before I suffer. For I say to you, that from this time I will not 16 eat it till it be fulfilled in the kingdom of God. And 17 having taken the chalice, he gave thanks, and said: Take,

lettuce was observed, and traditions had grown up as to the same. The lambs were allowed to be slaughtered earlier in the afternoon, instead of " between the two evenings " (i.e., between sunset and dark), a provision that had become necessary in consequence of the very large number that took part in the feast in later times. For a similar reason, they were allowed to be slaughtered by any one not ceremonially unclean (cf. 2 Paral. xxx. 17), and the fat and blood were given to the priests, who that night had to burn all the fat and sprinkle the blood on the altar. The court of the temple was then carefully cleansed. In the meantime, the owners of the lambs took them to their homes, where they roasted them whole, and seasoned them with wild lettuce, eating together with them only unleavened bread, exactly as prescribed in Exodus (xii. 8–10). They were all eaten that night, that is after the 15th of Nisan had legally begun, and anything left had to be burnt before morning. It may be remarked that all these preparations must have been made by the "good man of the house," and at his expense, for otherwise Judas would have had to assist in the arrangements.

14. *He sat down and the twelve apostles with him.* In our Lord's time the pasch was eaten in the same manner as any other meal, and the guests would *recline:* see on vii. 38. The Greek word (ἀνέπεσεν) is indeed best rendered "reclined." Cf. John xiii. 23. The position of St. John himself, there described, would have been natural only if all were reclining.

15. *With desire I have desired.* This is a Hebraism, very common in the Septuagint, denoting an earnest desire.

to eat this pasch. The obvious meaning of this expression implies that it was a true paschal supper, and if so, the next day must have been the feast.

16. *Till it be fulfilled in the kingdom of God.* The fulfilment in the kingdom of God referred to here and in *v.* 18 seems to be the institution of the Eucharist: see on *v.* 18.

17. *Having taken the chalice.* Passing round the chalice was part of the ritual commonly observed, though not in the written law. The head of the house first solemnly blessed with the words "Blessed art thou, O Lord, who hast created the fruit of the vine." Then he partook of it himself, and passed it to the others. A similar performance took place a second, a third, and sometimes even a fourth time, with

18 and divide *it* among you. For I say to you, that I will not drink of the fruit of the vine, till the kingdom of God 19 come. And taking bread, he gave thanks, and brake; and gave to them, saying: This is my body which is given

various traditional ceremonies. We cannot be quite sure whether the passing of the chalice here mentioned by St. Luke is to be identified with the first or with one of the others; but it seems most probable to suppose that it was the first, and that the last was used for the institution of the Eucharist.

18. *I will not drink of the fruit of the vine till the kingdom of God come.* See on v. 16. St. Luke is here drawing out the parallel between the Paschal Supper and the Eucharist; hence he records our Lord's words pointing out the eating of the pasch and the drinking of the chalice as respectively typical of the two species in the Blessed Sacrament. This double type is not drawn out by the other synoptists. The similar words given by St. Matthew (xxvi. 29) were used *after* its institution, alluding to His passion and death as the fulfilment of the Eucharistic sacrifice.

19. *And taking bread,* &c. Having given the double type, St. Luke proceeds to give its double fulfilment. This would be an explanation of his inverting the order of events, should we wish to identify the warning given to Judas in v. 21 with that recorded by St. Matthew (xxvi. 21) and St. Mark (xiv. 17), which was before the institution of the Eucharist. We cannot, however, be sure that they *do* refer to the same remark of our Lord. There is nothing improbable in His giving two, or more than two, separate warnings to Judas; and the context seems by no means the same in the two cases.

We have in all four accounts of the institution of the Blessed Eucharist—Matt. xxvi. 26-29; Mark xiv. 22-25; Luke xxii. 19, 20; 1 Cor. xi. 23-25. The one given by St. Luke is almost word for word the same as that of St. Paul, and this is a striking illustration of the effect of St. Paul's influence on his mind. Probably he derived his information on this particular point from St. Paul, who had himself learnt it by revelation (1 Cor. xi. 23). The following are the two side by side:

St. Luke xxii. 19, 20.

And taking bread, he gave thanks, and brake; and gave to them, saying: This is my body which is given for you. Do this for a commemoration of me. In like manner the chalice also, after he had supped, saying: This is the chalice, the new testament in my blood, which shall be shed for you.

St. Paul, 1 Cor. xi. 23-25.

[The Lord Jesus] took bread, and giving thanks, broke, and said: Take ye, and eat: this is my body, which shall be delivered for you: this do for the commemoration of me. In like manner also the chalice, after he had supped, saying: This chalice is the new testament in my blood: this do ye, as often as you shall drink, in commemoration of me.

for you. Do this for a commemoration of me. In like 20
manner the chalice also, after he had supped, saying:
This is the chalice, the new testament in my blood, which
shall be shed for you. But yet behold, the hand of him 21
that betrayeth me is with me on the table. And the son 22
of man indeed goeth, according to that which is determined : but yet wo to that man by whom he shall be
betrayed. And they began to inquire among themselves 23
which of them it was that should do this thing. And there 24
was also a strife amongst them, which of them should seem

In the original Greek the resemblance is even closer.

It may be noted that St. Matthew and St. Mark both describe the institution of the first part of the Eucharist as during the progress of the supper, while St. Luke and St. Paul say that the second part was "after he had supped." Many grave authors, among them St. Thomas Aquinas, have concluded that the consecration of the bread was separated from that of the wine by a considerable interval. Such a supposition is, however, so foreign to our usual ideas, that we hesitate to adopt it unless obliged to do so. And it really seems hardly necessary to attach so strict a meaning to the words of St. Matthew, "while they were at supper," or to the corresponding words of St. Mark. It does not seem a great stretch of meaning to take this simply as "while they were at table," or "at the end of supper." The words "In like manner," which both St. Luke and St. Paul give, may very probably be meant to call attention to the fact of both consecrations taking place after supper. The specification "after supper" for the chalice was necessary, since, as has been stated, according to the ceremonial the chalice was passed round four times, and this one must probably be identified with the fourth or after supper cup.

21. *The hand of him that betrayeth me is with me on the table.* It has already been questioned whether this is the same warning as is recorded in the other Gospels. The words describing the inquiry among the apostles as to who it should be rather point to its being the same. Possibly St. Luke puts it here to lead up to the conversation which follows : see on *v.* 24.

St. John tells us (xiii. 27) that our Lord pointed out Judas as the traitor, and said to him, "That which thou dost, do quickly." Judas would have, therefore, recognized the necessity of acting at once if at all, and would have insisted on this to the chief priests ; for now that our Lord knew his intention, he would certainly have to leave the band of apostles, and hence he would not have another opportunity.

24. *There was also a strife amongst them, which of them should seem to be greater.* This was an old contention among the apostles. Cf. Matt. xviii. 1 ; Mark ix. 33. It was part of their idea of the Messianic kingdom in which they hoped for high positions. The dis-

25 to be greater. And he said to them: The kings of the gentiles lord it over them; and they that have power over 26 them, are called beneficent. But you not so: but he that is the greater among you, let him become as the younger: 27 and he that is the leader, as he that serveth. For which is greater, he that sitteth at table or he that serveth? Is not he that sitteth at table? but I am in the midst of you 28 as he that serveth: and you are they who have continued 29 with me in my temptations. And I dispose to you, as my 30 Father hath disposed to me, a kingdom: that you may eat and drink at my table in my kingdom: and may sit 31 upon thrones judging the twelve tribes of Israel. And the Lord said: Simon, Simon, behold Satan hath desired to 32 have you that he may sift you as wheat. But I have prayed for thee that thy faith fail not: and thou being

pute in this case seems to have arisen out of the discussion as to who was to be the unfaithful one, and perhaps this furnishes an additional reason for St. Luke placing the warning to Judas here, if we suppose it to be out of its place.

25. *The kings of the Gentiles*, &c. Cf. Matt. xx. 25; Mark x. 42. The title Beneficent or Benefactor was considered by the ancients a great distinction. Thus, for example, Ptolemy III., bore the name of "Euergetes" or Benefactor.

27. *I am in the midst of you as he that serveth.* Our Lord appears to refer here to the act of service which He had just performed in the washing of the apostles' feet. See John xiii. 16.

29. *I dispose to you*, &c. The promise is that of pre-eminence in the celestial kingdom prepared for all (Matt. xxv. 34).

30. *And may sit upon thrones judging the twelve tribes of Israel.* Cf. Matt. xix. 28. No mention is made in this case of the number of thrones, perhaps because of the defection of Judas, whose place was not filled till afterwards.

31. *And the Lord said.* These words are probably an interpolation, though found in several good MSS. It would seem as if the apparent break in the sense led to their insertion.

Simon, Simon, &c. Our Lord was clearly addressing St. Peter as the representative of the apostolic band. The words, "Satan hath desired to have *you* (plural) that he may sift *you* as wheat," indicate a great trial to come on all the apostles, which was to separate them as wheat from chaff (Matt. iii. 12; Luke iii. 17). Satan had already gained Judas; he was to have St. Peter for a time; and in a sense all the apostles except St. John.

32. *But I have prayed for thee.* Our Lord's prayer was for St. Peter himself, who was to take His place after He was gone. In the

once converted, confirm thy brethren. Who said to him: 33 Lord, I am ready to go with thee both into prison and to death. And he said: I say to thee, Peter, the cock shall 34 not crow this day, till thou thrice deniest that thou knowest me. And he said to them: When I sent you 35 without purse and scrip and shoes, did you want anything? But they said: Nothing. Then said he unto them: But 36 now he that hath a purse, let him take it, and likewise a scrip: and he that hath not, let him sell his coat, and buy a sword. For I say unto you, that this that is written, 37 must yet be fulfilled in me, *And with the wicked was he reckoned.* For the things concerning me have an end. But they said: Lord, behold here *are* two swords. And 38 he said to them: It is enough.

event we see how after the resurrection St. Peter's faith became the mainstay of that of the other apostles, and even St. Thomas was eventually "confirmed."

34. *The cock shall not crow this day,* &c. This seems to be the same warning as that recorded by St. John (xiii. 38), but possibly different from that of Matt. xxvi. 34 and Mark xiv. 30. It is quite likely that our Lord warned St. Peter more than once. In St. Mark's account the prophecy is "before the cock crow twice," and two distinct crowings are described. St. Peter, who directed St. Mark, would naturally remember every such detail with great exactness. The cock crew about midnight, but the time known as "cock-crow" was about dawn: see on *v.* 58.

35. *When I sent you without purse and scrip and shoes, did you want anything?* Our Lord was here preparing the apostles for His being taken away from them, and called their attention to the first time they went forth alone and away from Him, which was their training for the future; and God's providence was with them, so that they wanted nothing.

36. *Let him sell his coat and buy a sword.* These words indicate only in general that they must be ready to defend themselves, as they would henceforth be alone in the world.

37. *And with the wicked was he reckoned.* Our Lord added the reason, quoting words from Isa. liii. 12, which were a prophecy of His passion; and added words which meant that His life on earth was nearly finished.

38. *Here are two swords.* As so often before, the apostles took our Lord's words more literally than they were meant. St. Peter had one of the swords (John xviii. 10), and was very possibly the speaker.

It is enough. This seems equivalent to a little rebuke. The apostles had misunderstood our Lord, and the answer was meant to

The Agony in the Garden.

(VERS. 39-46.)

³⁹ And going out he went according to his custom to the mount of Olives. And his disciples also followed him. ⁴⁰ And when he was come to the place, he said to them: ⁴¹ Pray, lest you enter into temptation. And he was withdrawn away from them a stone's cast; and kneeling down ⁴² he prayed, saying: Father, if thou wilt, remove this chalice from me: But yet not my will, but thine be ⁴³ done. And there appeared to him an Angel from heaven, strengthening him. And being in an agony, he prayed

stop the subject. The meaning, "two swords are enough," though supported by Venerable Bede and others, seems hardly a likely one.

39. *He went according to his custom to the mount of Olives.* The name Gethsemani (meaning "oil-press") is given by the other synoptists for the place to which our Lord retired. St. Matthew calls it (xxvi. 36) simply a place; St. Mark says (xiv. 32) it was a farm; St. John (xviii. 1) calls it a garden, and says it was across the brook of Cedron. It is thought to have been about half a mile outside the city walls, and some have conjectured that it belonged to the family of Martha and Mary, from the privacy which our Lord seems to have had there, and from the fact that it was on the way to Bethany. Gardens and orchards abounded outside the city walls. For the meaning of "according to his custom," see on xxi. 37.

40. *Pray, lest you enter into temptation.* St. Luke writes his account of the agony in the garden as if with the sole view of supplementing the other two synoptical Gospels. He adds several important details, but omits others which had been already chronicled. Thus from St. Matthew and St. Mark we learn that our Lord first took His three favourite apostles—Peter, James, and John—apart from the others; and these words, "Pray, lest you enter into temptation," were probably addressed to these three only. The words given by the other evangelists are "Stay you here and watch with me," as if their watching was to be a special solace to Him at that hour.

41. *He was withdrawn.* These words express a similar sentiment, as if even to be taken this short distance from His apostles was a wrench to Him. The detail that He prayed *kneeling* is peculiar to St. Luke.

42. *Father, if thou wilt*, &c. St. Luke does not divide the agony into three parts, as the others do, but the details he gives in the two following verses are peculiar to his Gospel, and give an addition to the picture of our Lord's suffering which is necessary for completeness.

43. *There appeared to him an Angel.* The answer to our Lord's prayer was not the passing away of the chalice, but the comfort and

the longer. And his sweat became as drops of blood trickling down upon the ground. And when he rose up from praying, and was come to his disciples, he found them sleeping for sorrow. And he said to them: Why sleep you? arise, pray, lest you enter into temptation.

The Betrayal.

(VERS. 47–53.)

As he was yet speaking, behold a multitude: and he that was called Judas, one of the twelve, went before them, and drew near to Jesus for to kiss him. And Jesus said to him: Judas, dost thou betray the son of man with a

strength brought by the ministry of the angel. The word *agony* denotes an intense struggle. The fear of His coming passion was the least part of it. The chief cause of His suffering was the sinfulness and ingratitude of men, and the comparatively small fruit of the Redemption, which was placed before His mind.

he prayed the longer. This is hardly an adequate translation of the Greek word ἐκτενέστερον. "More persistently" would be better. The A.V. gives "more earnestly." Either of these agrees somewhat better with the general sense.

44. *His sweat became as drops of blood.* This has always been taken to mean an actual sweat of blood, which it is said is a phenomenon not wholly unknown in cases of very violent emotion.

46. *Why sleep you?* The words here were addressed to the apostles at the end of the first or second period of the agony. At the end of the third period our Lord's words were, "Sleep ye now and take your rest" (Matt. xxvi. 45), that is, for all the good they might then do by praying with Him; for He added, "Arise, let us go; behold he is at hand that shall betray me."

47. *Behold a multitude.* To ascertain the exact composition of the "multitude" here described, we must carefully compare the four Gospels. We find that it included some of the "chief priests and magistrates of the temple" (*v.* 52), with their servants, including the ordinary Levitical guards of the temple (John xviii. 3), and some Pharisees (*ibid.*), Scribes, and ancients of the people (Mark xiv. 43; Matt. xxvi. 47), as well as a detachment of Roman soldiers, with their tribune in command (John xviii. 12); and they came out "with lanterns and torches and weapons." We conclude that when Judas went to the chief priests, they thought it advisable first to communicate with Pilate, in order to have some soldiers at their disposal. They would have represented the necessity of apprehending one whom they would describe as a false Messiah, and an inciter of the people, and therefore

49 kiss? And they that were about him, seeing what would follow, said to him: Lord, shall we strike with the sword? 50 And one of them struck the servant of the high-priest, and 51 cut off his right ear. But Jesus answering, said: Suffer ye thus far. And when he had touched his ear, he healed 52 him. And Jesus said to the chief priests, and magistrates of the temple, and the ancients that were come unto him: Are you come out, as it were against a thief, with swords 53 and clubs? When I was daily with you in the temple, you did not stretch forth your hands against me: but this is your hour, and the power of darkness.

dangerous to the peace of the nation. Many of the chief priests and elders accompanied the soldiers, to see that the arrest was duly carried out. Judas agreed on the signal which was to identify our Lord, the ordinary kiss of salutation between disciple and Master (Mark xiv. 44), and he walked in front of them, as St. Luke says, as if unconnected with them. Our Lord came out to meet the multitude (John xviii. 4), but whether this was before or after the traitor's kiss is uncertain.

49. *Shall we strike with the sword?* See on v. 38.

50. *And one of them struck the servant of the high-priest.* This was St. Peter, and the servant's name was Malchus, as we know from St. John (xviii. 10), who was acquainted with the household of the high priest. The synoptists are throughout reticent about giving names, for reasons already alluded to.

51. *Suffer ye thus far.* The sense of these words is not clear. Possibly they were addressed to those who had just apprehended our Lord, and it may have been equivalent to "Suffer me to move sufficiently to touch the servant's ear and cure it"; or they may have been a plea on behalf of the apostles, and equivalent to a request that their outburst of anger should be excused; or they may have been addressed to the apostles as a rebuke for what is described in v. 50, which our Lord remedied by the miracle which follows.

And when he had touched his ear, he healed him. All the evangelists mention the cutting off of the servant's ear: St. Luke alone records what has been termed the surgical miracle, the healing of it. He alone also tells us that it was the *right* ear.

52. *As it were against a thief,* i.e., one of the *Sicarii,* or bandits, who infested the country at that time.

53. *This is your hour, and the power of darkness.* These words have a twofold signification, relating, in the first place, to the possibility, humanly speaking, of our Lord's arrest in the night-time when they were afraid to touch Him in the day; and, secondly, to the activity of the evil spirits, who are designated by the word darkness. The full sense may be thus paraphrased: "You have come out in tumult with swords and clubs to seize Me as if I were a robber. Yet I was much

Denials of St. Peter.

(VERS. 54-62.)

And apprehending him, they led him to the high-priest's 54
house. But Peter followed afar off. And when they had 55
kindled a fire in the midst of the hall, and were sitting
about it, Peter was in the midst of them. Whom when a 56
certain servant-maid had seen sitting at the light, and had
earnestly beheld him, she said: This man also was with
him. But he denied him, saying: Woman, I know him 57

more in your power in the Temple, and you were afraid to take Me; nor
would your swords and clubs help you now were it not God's will and
the hour of your strength, when the powers of darkness are set free
against Me."

54. *They led him to the high-priest's house.* From St. John (xviii. 13)
we learn that they did not take our Lord straight to the house of Caiphas,
but first to Annas his father-in-law (see on iii. 2), and Annas having interrogated Him, sent Him in turn to Caiphas. It seems at first sight
as if St. John means to describe the first denial of St. Peter as in the
house of Annas, while the other evangelists describe all three in that of
Caiphas. Some have, therefore, thought that the two houses abutted
on each other, and had one common courtyard, where the denials took
place. But it is not necessary to understand St. John in this sense.
He is avowedly supplementing former accounts, and we might understand his words, for example, something as follows: "There are two
things to add. One is about our Lord. He was taken to Annas first,
before being taken to Caiphas, &c. The other thing to add is about St.
Peter, and how he gained access to the house of the high priest, &c."
This would make St. John's meaning consistent with his here alluding
to the house of Caiphas.

But Peter followed afar off. His motive was, according to St.
Matthew (xxvi. 58), "That he might see the end."

55. *When they had kindled a fire.* A night in April may be very
cold in Jerusalem. Cf. John xviii. 18.

Peter was in the midst of them. He had obtained access to the high
priest's house through the portress, whom St. John knew (John xviii.
15, 16). Thus St. John must also have been inside with the others.
He was, however, not so well known as a companion of Christ, and
apparently escaped observation; while St. Peter, who was always in
the front when our Lord was with the people, attracted the attention of
several.

56. *A certain servant-maid.* This maid was the portress (John xviii.
17), but it appears from this verse that she did not accuse St. Peter of
being a disciple till some time after he had come in, when he was sitting
by the fire.

58 not. And after a little while another seeing him, said: Thou also art one of them. But Peter said: O man, I
59 am not. And after the space as it were of one hour, another certain man affirmed, saying: Of a truth, this man
60 was also with him: for he is also a Galilean. And Peter said: Man, I know not what thou sayest. And im-
61 mediately as he was yet speaking, the cock crew. And the Lord turning looked on Peter. And Peter remembered the word of the Lord, as he had said: Before the
62 cock crow, thou shalt deny me thrice. And Peter going out wept bitterly.

Christ in the House of Caiphas.

(VERS. 63–65.)

63 And the men that held him, mocked him, and struck
64 him. And they blindfolded him, and smote his face. And they asked him, saying: Prophesy, who is it that struck
65 thee. And blaspheming, many other things they said against him.

58. *Another seeing him.* ἕτερος = another *man*. The first denial is given similarly in each of the Gospels. In order to reconcile the four accounts of the other two, it is necessary to suppose that on each of these occasions St. Peter denied our Lord more than once, which is most easily conceived. The three denials do not, therefore, mean three single answers to questions, but three occasions when St. Peter, in answer to several, asserted that he did not know our Lord. The first or midnight cock-crow intervened between the first and second denials, as we learn from St. Peter himself, through St. Mark's Gospel: see on v. 34.

59. *Another certain man.* This man was a kinsman of Malchus (John xviii. 26); but others joined in the accusation (Matt. xxvi. 73; Mark xiv. 70). St. Peter's Galilean accent directed their attention to him.

61. *The Lord turning looked on Peter.* St. Luke alone records our Lord's look towards the fallen apostle. He must have been at that moment led across the court, after His derision; for the day was beginning to dawn, when His formal trial took place. We have, therefore, here another instance of St. Luke's custom of following out a subject to the end, and then returning to what happened in the meantime.

63. *And the men that held him, mocked him,* &c. The insults here described occupied the time between the preliminary rial in the house

Trial before the Sanhedrin.

(VERS. 66-71.)

And as soon as it was day, the ancients of the people, 66 and the chief priests, and scribes came together, and they brought him into their council, saying: If thou be the Christ, tell us. And he said to them: If I shall tell you, 67 you will not believe me: and if I shall also ask you, 68

of the high priest, and the assembly of the Sanhedrin at daybreak. They thus took place during the time that St. Peter was in the house of Caiaphas, as explained above. St. Matthew (xxvi. 67, 68) and St. Mark (xiv. 65) give further details. The servants of the chief priests, interpreting the will of their masters, treated our Lord with extraordinary barbarity. Some of the details prophesied by Isaias (e.g., l. 6), are not, however, mentioned in the Gospels.

66. *They brought him into their council.* The council of the chief priests and Scribes was called the Sanhedrin (= συνέδριον), and probably represented directly the seventy elders whom Moses associated with himself in the government of the Israelites. See Numb. xi. 16. Whether they numbered seventy or seventy-two is uncertain; see on x. 1. The Romans allowed the Jews a fair measure of self-government, and the powers of the Sanhedrin were extensive. It was the supreme court of justice and carried out all its own sentences, with the sole exception of capital punishment (John xviii. 31). In the time of our Lord, the Pharisees formed the predominant party in the Sanhedrin; but the Sadducees were an important minority, and included many of the chief priests, including Annas and Caiaphas and their following.

This trial of our Lord before the Sanhedrin is alluded to by St. Matthew (xxvii. 1) and St. Mark (xv. 1); but the details of it are given by St. Luke only. To understand the course pursued, we have to refer back to the other synoptic Gospels. We find that an informal meeting was held at the house of Caiaphas, in order to prepare the evidence for the trial, which could not legally be held before daybreak. The first plan was to suborn "false witnesses," which does not necessarily imply that they invented fresh stories, but that they perverted the meaning of what our Lord had actually said. In the event, they were so mutually contradictory that their stories only led to confusion; and, ultimately, Caiaphas fell back on our Lord's own declaration that He was Christ, which he termed blasphemy. On the occasion of the formal trial, therefore, no witnesses were called; but our Lord was asked at once for a declaration of His Divinity.

67. *If I shall tell you, you will not believe me.* Our Lord's answer was a gentle rebuke. They did not really want to know the truth nor to believe it. They had apprehended Him and would not let Him go till they had completed their purpose and put an end to His life.

(a) you will not answer me, nor let me go. But hereafter the son of man shall be sitting on the right hand of the power
70 of God. Then said they all: Art thou then the Son of
71 God? Who said: You say that I am. And they said: What need we any farther testimony? For we ourselves have heard it from his own mouth.

69. *Hereafter the son of man shall be sitting on the right hand of the power of God.* In these words our Lord repeated His former assertion, however, as they desired, and (*v.* 70) said in so many words that He was the Son of God—for that is the force of the phrase, "You say that I am."

71. *What need we any farther testimony?* Again the answer satisfied His accusers, and once more they asked each other, "What need we any farther testimony?" So far as they were concerned, therefore, they were ready to condemn our Lord to death. It remained only to obtain the authority of the Roman governor, to which they then proceeded.

CHAPTER XXIII.

Christ before Pilate.

(VERS. 1-7.)

AND the whole multitude of them rising up, led him to Pilate. And they began to accuse him, saying: We ² have found this man perverting our nation, and forbidding

1. *The whole multitude.* In Greek the words are ἅπαν τὸ πλῆθος. They mean evidently to include all the members of the Sanhedrin and the servants or others who were present; but not any indiscriminate crowd from the town. By comparison with the other Gospels, it becomes clear that at that early hour the crowd had not yet come together.

led him to Pilate. Though Pilate commonly lived at Cæsarea, he used to come to Jerusalem for the chief Festivals, and was accordingly there at this time. He had the choice of two large palaces to live in, both of which had been built by Herod the Great, on a scale of great magnificence, and had in due course passed into possession of the Roman governor. One of these was on Mount Sion, at the northwest corner of the upper city, and was known as Herod's palace; and this would have been the ordinary residence of the Roman governor. At the time of the Pasch, however, it was important for him to be in the vicinity of the Temple, in case any sudden tumult should break out which would require immediate action to suppress. At such time, therefore, Pilate took up his quarters in Herod's other great palace, known as the Prætorium—for so the residence of the Roman governor was called, even though he was not a Prætor—and it was used as judgment hall and barracks as well. It probably formed part of the fortress of Antonia, adjoining the Temple buildings on the north side, and separated from the Court of the Gentiles by a large paved place called *Lithostrotos*, or in Hebrew *Gabbatha* (John xix. 13), where the official judgment seat stood.

2. *And they began to accuse him.* Probably the chief priests did

to give tribute to Cæsar, and saying that he is Christ the
3 king. And Pilate asked him, saying: Art thou the king of

not anticipate much difficulty in procuring a condemnation from Pilate, who had already sent them Roman soldiers to apprehend our Lord : see on xxii. 47. In this they were disappointed. Pilate saw that their zeal against our Lord was caused by envy (Matt. xxvii. 18 ; Mark xv. 10), and determined to examine into the matter himself. As an educated Roman, he had a strong sense of justice, while at the same time he had a sovereign contempt for the chief priests and their followers. Being only a Procurator, he had no quæstor under him and accordingly had to conduct any inquiry himself. Thus St. John tells us (xviii. 29) that he came out himself to ask "What accusation bring you against this man?"

We have found this man perverting our nation. It was evidently useless for the chief priests to give the accusation on the strength of which the Sanhedrin had condemned our Lord : Pilate would only have answered, as Gallio did when St. Paul was brought before him : "If they be questions of . . . your law, look you to it : I will not be judge of such things." (Acts xviii. 15). Accordingly, they made out a political offence. They accused our Lord of perverting the nation, and mentioned two specific charges : (1) that He forbade the paying of tribute to Cæsar ; and (2) that He was proclaiming Himself king. All these accusations went together, and were meant to persuade Pilate that our Lord was plotting for the overthrow of the Roman power in Judea, and with some success, for He was "perverting the nation." The falsity of that part of their accusation which related to the tribute was very marked, as only three days before, He had been preaching the exact contrary: see on xx. 25. The part about proclaiming Himself king was equally false in the sense in which it was meant, for He had always consistently avoided any public demonstration in His favour, with the sole exception of the Procession of Palms, which no one could have seriously called a plot to make Him king. See John vi. 15.

3. *Art thou the king of the Jews?* A more detailed account of the conversation between our Lord and Pilate is given by St. John (xviii. 33-38), which should be carefully consulted ; otherwise what is given here will be hardly intelligible. There is an evident touch of irony in Pilate's question to our Lord, and he no doubt asked it with undisguised contempt for the nation which could have a claimant such as this to be its king.

Thou sayest it, i.e., it is as thou sayest : see on xxii. 70. This simple answer would, however, not have been enough to convince Pilate of our Lord's innocence. On referring to St. John, we find a further account. Our Lord added, "My kingdom is not of this world . . . my kingdom is not from hence." Pilate easily saw that He was not claiming any sort of earthly kingdom or any that would conflict with Roman authority.

the Jews? But he answering, said: Thou sayest it. And Pilate said to the chief priests and to the multitude: I find no cause in this man. But they were more earnest, saying: He stirreth up the people, teaching throughout all Judea, beginning from Galilee to this place. But Pilate hearing Galilee, asked if the man were of Galilee? And when he understood that he was of Herod's jurisdiction, he sent him away to Herod, who was also himself at Jerusalem in those days.

4. *And to the multitude.* This is the first mention of the presence of a crowd properly so-called, the Greek word being ὄχλοις. See on *v.* 1. The procession of the Sanhedrin and others through the town would gradually attract a crowd, which, standing in front of the Prætorium, would increase as the day advanced. The people took an important part in what followed. The chief priests seem to have had little difficulty in gaining them over to their side. They no doubt represented themselves as fighting a great battle for their religion in demanding our Lord's death. They must have put some such idea forcibly before them in order to gain them over, for only three days before many of them were listening to our Lord in the Temple, and "very attentive to hear him" (xix. 48). It is possible that our Lord's final denunciation of the Jewish rulers (Matt. xxiii.) would have set many of the people against Him, at least those of them who were zealous Pharisees, and these would have the greatest influence among the people.

5. *Throughout all Judea.* The context shows that by Judea is here meant the whole Jewish kingdom over which Herod the Great had been king. It included therefore Galilee and Perea: see on iv. 44. It is very probable that the chief priests mentioned the name Galilee knowing of the enmity between Pilate and Herod, and thinking that Pilate would be more inclined to put our Lord to death on that account.

6. *He sent him away to Herod.* The verb ἀνέπεμψεν is the same as that used in *v.* 11 which we render "sent back." Our Lord having been originally under Herod's jurisdiction in Galilee, sending Him to Herod would have that force. Pilate did so simply because he was in a difficulty. There is no sign that he did it as an act of civility or with a view to pacifying Herod, though, as it turned out, it had that effect. Herod was at Jerusalem, as Pilate was, on account of the feast. He commonly lived at Tiberias, which town he had himself founded: see on v. 1. When at Jerusalem, he lived in the old Asmonæan palace, which had belonged to his father before he built the two new ones alluded to above. It was situated in the valley between Mount Sion and Mount Moriah, and at no great distance from the Prætorium.

Christ before Herod.

(VERS. 8-12.)

8 And Herod seeing Jesus, was very glad, for he was desirous of a long time to see him, because he had heard many things of him : and he hoped to see some sign
9 wrought by him. And he questioned him in many words.
10 But he answered him nothing. And the chief priests and
11 the scribes stood by, earnestly accusing him. And Herod with his army set him at nought : and mocked him, putting on him a white garment, and sent him back to Pilate.
12 And Herod and Pilate were made friends that same day : for before they were enemies one to another.

8. *He was desirous of a long time to see him.* St. Luke has previously mentioned (ix. 9) Herod's desire to see our Lord. It appears that it arose from mere curiosity and craving for excitement. Our Lord was reported to work many miracles and to do great wonders. Herod supposed that He would do some at his bidding, for the amusement of himself and his courtiers. The whole incident is peculiar to this Gospel.

9. *But he answered him nothing.* The αὐτὸς δὲ is emphatic. Our Lord's silence is put in contrast with Herod's voluminous questioning, and the continued accusations of His enemies mentioned in the next verse.

11. *And Herod with his army set him at nought.* Herod's vexation at not seeing any miracles, and not even hearing our Lord's voice, showed itself in contempt. His vexation was shared by his "army," which must have been a guard of honour who had accompanied him to Jerusalem. They "set him at nought," that is, thought him of no account, and treated Him not as a criminal, but as a fool—a fanatical enthusiast.

putting on him a white garment. The A.V. has a "gorgeous robe," which is more in accordance with the Greek—ἐσθῆτα λαμπράν. It was no doubt meant as a sort of mockery of His royalty. As a fact, the royal robe of state (e.g., that of Agrippa and that of Archelaus) was silvery or *white*.

12. *For before they were enemies one to another.* There is no record of the cause of the enmity between Pilate and Herod ; but the governors of adjacent provinces, peopled by the same race, would easily have had occasion to fall out, especially as one was directly the representative of the Roman Government, and the other only indirectly subject to it. The presence of the Galileans in such numbers in Jerusalem at the times of the feasts would furnish very probable occasions. Possibly the quarrel may have been connected with the massacre of Galileans recorded in xiii. 1. Herod's refusal to condemn our Lord was equiva-

Before Pilate the Second Time.

(VERS. 13-25.)

And Pilate calling together the chief priests, and the magistrates, and the people, said to them: You have presented unto me this man, as one that perverteth the people, and behold I, having examined him before you, find no cause in this man in those things wherein you accuse him. No, nor Herod neither. For I sent you to him, and behold nothing worthy of death is done to him. I will chastise him therefore, and release him. Now of necessity he was to release unto them one upon the feast-

lent to a declaration of His innocence, so that when they had dragged Him back to the Prætorium, Pilate found himself in exactly the same difficulty as before. It does not appear, therefore, that he had much to thank Herod for. Herod, on the other hand, had to thank Pilate for the opportunity of seeing our Lord, for which he had so long wished. The fact then that they were made friends that day therefore points to the enmity having been on Herod's side, which would indeed, in any case, appear the more probable.

13. *Pilate calling together the chief priests.* Pilate, as has been stated, now found himself in the same difficulty as before. His sense of justice prompted him to dismiss our Lord; his want of courage made him seek for some *via media* to avoid the displeasure of the Jews. So he once more called " the chief priests and the magistrates and the people " (see on xxii. 52), to ask them further questions and to discuss the affair again. This was quite in keeping with his general character and want of courage. He had already convinced himself of our Lord's innocence, and no further discussion should have been needed.

14. *I, having examined him before you.* They had accused our Lord of making certain claims to royalty, inconsistent with the Roman government of the province. His own repudiation of any such claims in the sense meant, was a complete refutation of the charge ; and this repudiation had been made publicly at His judicial examination, before all the people.

16. *I will chastise him.* Here Pilate began the concessions which eventually led him to condemn our Lord to death. While protesting His innocence, he offered, in order to pacify the Jews, to inflict the awful punishment of scourging. This punishment was illegal for Roman citizens, but in common use for slaves, who often died under its torture. The instrument used was a leathern thong with hard knobs at its extremity, and called by Horace (Satires, I. iii. 119), the *horribile flagellum*. Scourging was a punishment familiar to the Jews, and could even be inflicted by the officers of the synagogue (see on xii. 11), but the number of blows was limited to forty (Deut. xxv. 3). St.

18 day. But the whole multitude together cried out, saying: 19 Away with this man, and release unto us Barabbas. Who for a certain sedition made in the city, and for a murder, 20 was cast into prison. And Pilate again spoke to them, 21 desiring to release Jesus. But they cried again, saying:

Paul went through this punishment no less than five times (2 Cor. xi. 24). In our Lord's case, however, being a Roman scourging, there was no limit put to the number of blows.

17. *Now of necessity he was to release unto them one upon the feast day.* There is no record of this custom except in the Gospels, but it is quite in accordance with Roman usage, and though this verse of St. Luke is of doubtful authenticity, the corresponding ones in the other Gospels are undoubtedly genuine, so that there is no doubt of the fact. St. Mark seems to say (xv. 8) that the multitude spontaneously clamoured for the annual release of a prisoner. The mere fact of a crowd being collected outside the Prætorium on the feast day would have put them in mind of it, and their clamours would again have suggested to Pilate a possibility of getting out of his difficulty. So he brought the worst criminal he could find, *a notorious prisoner* (Matt. xxvii. 16), guilty of sedition and murder, and put him side by side with our Lord.

18. *The whole multitude together cried out.* This is the first direct mention of the multitude being openly hostile to our Lord: see above on v. 4. There were probably very many gathered together by this time, for on such occasions a crowd grows rapidly.

release unto us Barabbas. The word Barabbas means "son of Abbas," and Abbas itself signifies "father." It is therefore not certain that it was a proper name at all, and in any case, it is only a patronymic. Origen alludes to a curious reading in St. Matthew (xxvii. 16, 17) in which Pilate offers the people their choice between Jesus Barabbas and Jesus who is called the Christ. The name Jesus was of course very common, and there is no intrinsic improbability in Barabbas bearing that name; but the reading is not supported in any of the good MSS.

21. *Crucify him, crucify him.* Crucifixion was a common punishment of the Romans and other ancient nations, and was no doubt familiar to the Jews since they had been under the Empire, though their own law only provided for suspending the bodies *after* death (Deut. xxi. 22). It was universally considered the most horrible form of punishment, and all Roman citizens were exempt from it. Hence while St. Peter was crucified, St. Paul, being a Roman citizen, was beheaded. The Romans always fastened their victims to the cross by nails, and often also by cords. The wounds so made, however, were not fatal, and people often lived on the cross for a long time, and eventually died mainly of starvation. It is said that such was the suffering of those hanging on a cross, that they would often call out to

Crucify him, crucify him. And he said to them the third 22
time: Why, what evil hath this man done? I find no
cause of death in him: I will chastise him therefore, and
let him go. But they were instant with loud voices 23
requiring that he might be crucified: and their voices prevailed. And Pilate gave sentence that it should be as they 24
required. And he released unto them him who for murder 25
and sedition had been cast into prison, whom they had
desired: but Jesus he delivered up to their will.

The Way of the Cross.

(VERS. 26–32.)

And as they led him away, they laid hold of one Simon 26
of Cyrene, coming from the country: and they laid the

the bystanders, beseeching them to put an end to their agony by killing them. A case is recorded of three who were crucified being taken down, at the request of Josephus, and by order of the Emperor, when still alive; but only one of the three survived.

22. *He said to them the third time.* "The third time" again denotes Pilate's great anxiety to release our Lord; yet he had not the courage simply to exert his authority, and again therefore he suggested the alternative of scourging. The message from his wife (Matt. xxvii. 19) must be placed about here or perhaps a little earlier.

23. *Their voices prevailed.* St. Luke does not mention that the scourging actually took place. The verses of St. John's Gospel (xix. 1–16) should therefore be inserted here. They describe the scourging and crowning with thorns, and the second derision of Christ, this time at the hands of the Roman soldiers; and the well-known scene when Pilate brought our Lord forth with the words "*Ecce homo*," or "*Behold the man.*"

26. *As they led him away.* The exact course of the "Way of the Cross," or the "Via Dolorosa," is not quite free from uncertainty. The traditional route corresponds nearly with that marked in Dr. William Smith's well-known *Ancient Atlas*. If, as we have supposed (see on v. 1), the *Lithostrotos* was on the south side of the Prætorium, the procession may have started from within the Temple enclosure. It would then have gone out by the gate at the north-east corner, passed north of Fort Antonia, and after turning down through the lower town, again moved upwards to the west, and so out through the gate of Ephraim. The total length would have been less than a mile. Calvary itself was but a short distance outside the old walls, and within the new wall which Herod Agrippa built round the suburb on Mount Bezetha: see on v. 33. The crosses would have been made of any wood which was most plentiful, and microscopic examinations of some of the relics of the true cross show

27 cross on him to carry after Jesus. And there followed him a great multitude of people, and of women who bewailed

it to have been made of pine, or some kind of fir. Our Lord's cross would not have differed in size or shape from those of the two thieves. When the three crosses were found by St. Helena, A.D. 326, it required a miracle to distinguish our Lord's from the others. They were probably all of the ordinary Roman shape, or *Crux Immissa*, and not as some pictures have them, the T-shape, or *Crux Commissa*. Their height cannot be actually determined; but while our Lord was probably raised above the heads of the surrounding people, He must have been sufficiently near them to address our Lady and St. John without difficulty. The largest relic of the true cross now extant is kept at Rome, in the church of Santa Croce. There are very many smaller relics all over the world, the majority of which are undoubtedly genuine.

they laid hold of one Simon of Cyrene. St. John is the only evangelist who says (xix. 17) that our Lord bore His own cross. The other three all mention Simon of Cyrene as having carried it. He met the procession by chance on the way, and it would seem that the Jews were afraid of our Lord's strength not lasting long enough for them to complete the crucifixion. In pictures of the stations of the cross, our Lord always appears carrying His cross, even after the fifth station which represents the arrival of Simon of Cyrene. Our tradition is certainly that He carried it to the end; and the verse in St. John seems to require this meaning. It is quite possible that the Cyrenian only assisted Him by carrying the part of it which was behind. This accords with Christian tradition, and is not at variance with the text of the Gospels. Cyrene was a flourishing city in Africa, of which a considerable proportion of the population were Jews. Simon was very probably coming to Jerusalem for the Pasch, as many from his city did (Acts ii. 10), and if belated, he would travel even on the festival day itself, so as to reach Jerusalem before it was over. The expression "coming from the country" need not denote anything more than "being on his journey." On the other hand, the Cyrenians had a synagogue of their own at Jerusalem (Acts vi. 9), and hence some of them must have resided there, and Simon may have been one of these. In that case he must have been out in the country on a journey of some kind, probably within the limits prescribed for a Sabbath day, and now on his way back. We know little or nothing of Simon himself. St. Mark tells us that he was "the father of Alexander and Rufus," as if they were well-known Christians at the time when he wrote. Possibly they may be identical with those mentioned in Acts xix. 33 and Rom. xvi. 13. Some have also thought that Simon himself may be identical with Simon Niger, who is mentioned in company with Lucius of Cyrene in Acts xiii. 1.

27. *There followed him a great multitude.* The procession to Calvary would have been headed by a centurion (see *v.* 47) on horseback, followed by four soldiers; and then by our Lord and the two thieves afterwards mentioned, each bearing his own cross. The title mentioned in *v.* 38 may have been already attached to the cross, or may

and lamented him. But Jesus turning to them, said: 28 Daughters of Jerusalem, weep not over me, but weep for yourselves, and for your children. For behold the 29 days shall come, wherein they will say: Blessed are the barren, and the wombs that have not borne, and the paps that have not given suck. Then shall they begin to say to 30 the mountains: Fall upon us: and to the hills: Cover us. For if in the green wood they do these things, what shall 31 be done in the dry? And there were also two other 32 malefactors led with him to be put to death.

have been carried separately. It was usual to write the criminal's "cause" on each gibbet. Apparently in their eagerness to carry out the crucifixion, the chief priests overlooked the writing on the title till the cross had been erected with our Lord on it. See note on v. 38.

and of women who bewailed and lamented him. It is quite clear that the "ministering women" and those who "had followed Him from Galilee" are not here alluded to. St. Luke means to describe ordinary Jewish women, who were present by chance, and followed with the crowd, and were moved to tears by the sight of our Lord in the power of His enemies and going through such sufferings. Some of them may easily have listened to Him in the temple but a few days before, as well as very probably on other occasions: but they do not appear to have been of His regular disciples or followers. Of the incidents of the Way of the Cross which are rendered familiar to us by the fourteen "stations," the majority are only traditional. There is nothing in the Gospels about the three falls, nor about Veronica's veil. The meeting with our Lady is indirectly mentioned by St. John, as he says (xix. 25) that she "stood by the cross of Jesus." The only incidents mentioned in so many words are the arrival of Simon of Cyrene described above, and our Lord's words to the women of Jerusalem which now follow, and are peculiar to this Gospel.

28. *Weep not over me.* This is the last recorded sermon of our Lord. It was of course not meant as in any sense a rebuke to the women for their wailing. The meaning is that they had really more cause to weep for themselves, because of the judgment that was to come on them, and that He was willing and even longingly anxious to suffer, if by His passion He could save them.

weep for yourselves and for your children. Some of those who actually heard these words might not have been more than sixty or seventy years old when the fulfilment came at the fall of Jerusalem; while their children would have been in the prime of life.

29. *Behold the day shall come,* &c. Cf. xxi. 23.

31. *If in the green wood they do these things, what shall be done in the dry?* This was probably a well-known expression and somewhat similar in meaning to 1 Pet. iv. 18, "If the just man shall scarcely be saved, where shall the ungodly and the sinner appear?"

The Crucifixion.

(VERS. 33-38.)

33 And when they were come to the place which is called
Calvary, they crucified him there: and the robbers, one
34 on the right and the other on the left. And Jesus said:
Father, forgive them, for they know not what they do. But

33. *To the place which is called Calvary.* The word κρανίον, which, following the Vulgate, we translate as Calvary, means a skull, and is the translation of the Hebrew word Golgotha. The R.V., therefore renders the passage, "the place which is called the Skull." Its position is almost certainly that which tradition assigns to it, within the walls of the present Church of the Holy Sepulchre, which dates back to the time of Constantine. It is not called a *mount* in Scripture, but only a *place*; but very possibly it was a somewhat elevated spot, such as would naturally be chosen for the execution of criminals. Various reasons have been suggested for the name Golgotha, the most probable one being that the shape of the hill resembled a skull. The tradition of Adam being buried there is quite untrustworthy. The skull and cross-bones usually represented at the foot of a crucifix are only allegorical, representing Christ's triumph over death.

they crucified him. Authorities are not agreed as to the manner in which the crucifixion was carried out. The more common tradition, perpetuated in the Stations of the Cross, represents our Lord as crucified on the ground, and the cross afterwards raised. Whether three or four nails were used is also uncertain; if the latter, the small wedge-shaped block which is seen on many crucifixes is probably correct.

34. It has already been remarked that St. John's Gospel appears to have been written especially to supplement St. Luke; and it is noteworthy that of the seven last words of our Lord, six occur in these two Gospels only, viz., three (first, second and seventh) in St. Luke, and three (third, fifth and sixth) in St. John. St. Matthew and St. Mark both record the fourth word only. The following is a list of the seven words:—

1. "Father, forgive them, for they know not what they do" (Luke xxiii. 34).
2. "Amen I say to thee, this day thou shall be with me in paradise" (Luke xxiii. 43).
3. "Woman behold thy son." "Behold thy mother" (John xix. 26, 27).
4. "My God, my God, why hast thou forsaken me?" (Matt. xxvii. 46; Mark xv. 34).
5. "I thirst" (John xix. 28).
6. "It is consummated" (John xix. 30).
7. "Father, into thy hands I commend my spirit" (Luke xxiii. 46).

they dividing his garments, cast lots. And the people stood 35
beholding, and the rulers with them derided him, saying:
He saved others, let him save himself, if he be Christ, the
elect of God. And the soldiers also mocked him, coming 36
to him, and offering him vinegar, and saying: If thou be 37

The first two words were spoken within a few minutes of noon; the
last four at about three o'clock. The exact time of the third word is
uncertain. It could not have been quite at the beginning of the three
hours, as our Lady and St. John would not have been close to the cross
at that time. It must have been some time after the dispersion of the
crowd, and after the chief priests had gone.

And Jesus said. The imperfect tense may indicate continued action,
and many have thought that the prayer of our Lord was repeated continually as the process of crucifixion proceeded.

Father forgive them, for they know not what they do. The last
phrase is an extenuation of their guilt. The soldiers certainly knew
nothing of our Lord's Divinity, but they must have been aware of His
innocence. The prayer was not only for those physically engaged in
the work of Crucifixion, but also for the chief priests and rulers under
whose orders it was being done; see on xii. 48; and Acts iii. 17.
St. Stephen, the first martyr, repeated a similar prayer at his death.
" Lord, lay not this sin to their charge" (Acts vii. 59).

But they dividing his garments cast lots. The dividing of our Lord's
garments is alluded to by each of the four evangelists and is given in
full detail by St. John (xix. 23, 24). The four executioners would have
taken them as perquisites. The over-garment (ἱμάτιον), or *tallith*, they
tore into four parts, one for each soldier. The word (χιτών) which we
translate *coat*, was the *cetoneth* or under-garment. Being without
seam, the soldiers cast lots for it (John xix. 24). Tradition asserts
that it was recovered by Christians soon after our Lord's death,
and it is now shown in the Cathedral at Treves, in Germany.

35. *And the rulers with them derided him.* It seems from St.
Matthew (xxvii. 39, 40) and St. Mark (xv. 29, 30) that many of
the people joined in blaspheming; but of course the rulers and chief
priests were the leaders.

36. *And the soldiers also mocked him.* It was the duty of the four
soldiers to stay and watch our Lord (Matt. xxvii. 36) till the end, and
they naturally joined in the spirit of the rulers.

offering him vinegar. If this is the same incident as that recorded
by the other evangelists, it was towards the end of the time during which
our Lord was hanging on the cross. The vinegar, or sour wine, was the
drink of the Roman soldiers, and hence a jar of it lay by the cross (John
xix. 29). Our Lord had refused to take the wine given at the beginning
of the Crucifixion, for being an anæsthetic, it would have mitigated His
suffering, and it was commonly given to criminals for that purpose. He
did not, however, refuse the vinegar, which would not have had that
effect, but would have completed His suffering by adding that of the taste.

38 the king of the Jews, save thyself. And there was also a superscription written over him in letters of Greek, and Latin, and Hebrew: THIS IS THE KING OF THE JEWS.

The Penitent Thief.

(VERS. 39-43.)

39 And one of those robbers who were hanged, blasphemed

38. *And there was also a superscription.* The title of the cross had been written by Pilate at the time of the condemnation: see on v. 27. St. Mark calls it "the inscription of his cause"; and St. Matthew uses a similar expression. It is well known that the four Gospels give the inscription in slightly different form. They give it as follows:—

St. Matthew xxvii. 37. "THIS IS JESUS THE KING OF THE JEWS."
St. Mark xv. 26. "THE KING OF THE JEWS."
St. Luke xxiii. 38. "THIS IS THE KING OF THE JEWS."
St. John xix. 19. "JESUS OF NAZARETH, THE KING OF THE JEWS."

Many conjectures have been made to reconcile the four forms, one being that the inscriptions in the three different languages were not quite the same, and that three of the evangelists take those of the different languages, while the fourth evangelist is summarizing them. It seems, however, more natural to suppose that the first three evangelists were each summarizing the inscription, and that St. John supplements the others by giving it in full. In either form it would have been equally distasteful to the chief priests, and we see in it a sign of Pilate's annoyance which he showed in satire. He had said to them, "Behold your king," "Shall I crucify your king?" and the like. Now he put up His *cause* on the cross. "the King of the Jews." It has been pointed out that the title must have been carried in the procession from the Prætorium, but apparently the chief priests were so anxious to have the crucifixion accomplished, that they failed to observe it at the time. Their subsequent protest and Pilate's answer are given by St. John (xix. 21, 22).

39. *One of those robbers who were hanged, blasphemed him.* St. Matthew says (xxvii. 44) "And the self-same thing (i.e., "let God deliver him if he will have him") the *thieves* also, that were crucified with him, reproached him with"; and St. Mark (xv. 32) speaks similarly. Some have therefore supposed that at first both of the robbers spoke against our Lord, and that it was a little later on that one was converted. Others have drawn a distinction between "reproached" (ὠνείδιζον), the word used by St. Matthew and St. Mark, and "blasphemed" (ἐβλασφήμει) used by St. Luke, and have suggested that both robbers began by reproaching our Lord, but that while one was converted, the other went from bad to worse, till he actually blasphemed Him. It is, however, simpler to suppose, with St. Augustine and others of the Fathers, that the plural was used by St. Matthew and St. Mark only in

him, saying: If thou be Christ, save thyself, and us. But 40 the other answering, rebuked him, saying: Neither dost thou fear God, seeing thou art under the same condemnation? And we indeed justly, for we receive the due 41 reward of our deeds: but this man hath done no evil. And he said to Jesus: Lord, remember me when thou shalt 42 come into thy kingdom. And Jesus said to him: Amen 43 I say to thee, this day thou shalt be with me in paradise.

a general sense, and that in reality only one of the thieves reviled our Lord. Cf. Matt. xxvi. 8: "And the disciples seeing it, had indignation," whereas we know from St. John (xii. 4) that only one of them, namely Judas, was indignant.

40. *Neither dost thou fear God, seeing thou art under the same condemnation?* The precise sense of these words is not clear. Possibly the good thief was referring to condemnation or judgment, which follows death. This agrees well with the context, and the meaning would be, that whereas the Scribes and Pharisees were so moved with envy and passion that they had for the time lost all fear of God, those who are condemned to appear before Him would naturally have this fear; and that while our Lord had done nothing wrong, the thieves on the other hand would be justly afraid.

42. *He said to Jesus: Lord, remember me.* The true reading here is probably, "He said, Jesus remember me." The word Ἰησοῦ seems to have been mistaken as the dative and κυρίε to have been interpolated; but our reading has found its way into all the chief English versions except the Revised.

when thou shalt come into thy kingdom. The reading "*into* thy kingdom" is clearly wrong: it is in the dative, ἐν τῇ βασιλείᾳ σου, "*in* thy kingdom." Christ had often spoken of coming again in His kingdom, or in power and glory, and the good thief seems to be alluding to this.

43. *This day thou shalt be with me in paradise.* Our Lord did not enter heaven till Ascension day, some six weeks after this. On His death, He went to the abode which we now call Limbo Patrum, where the souls of the just who died before that time were waiting. This must be the place He alludes to as paradise. The word itself is of Persian origin, and means a garden. It is used throughout the Septuagint Version for the Garden of Eden; but it was also in popular use as denoting "Abraham's bosom," or the abode of the just, as distinguished from Gehenna, the abode of the wicked: see on xvi. 22. It was never used in precisely the sense we now use it, of heaven where those who are there enjoy the Beatific vision; for the Jews had no clear idea of the details of the future state, and certainly could have made no distinction between Limbo Patrum and heaven.

It is noticeable that this is the only instance recorded in the Bible of a good death after a bad life. The good thief was almost certainly a

Death of our Lord.

(VERS. 44-49.)

44 And it was almost the sixth hour; and there was dark-

Jew—otherwise he would not have understood the expression "paradise." His traditional name is Dismas, and he is honoured as a Saint in many countries. Recently a Mass and Office in his honour have been added to the Calendar in the diocese of Westminster.

44. *And it was almost the sixth hour.* This is the first definite note of time since xxii. 66, when daybreak was denoted. Six hours had therefore elapsed since then, and it was close on midday. St. Mark, who throughout Holy week gives particulars as to time which the others omit, here also tells us more. He says that it was the third hour when the Crucifixion took place; but that the darkness began when the sixth hour had come. The ancients divided their day into four chief divisions, the first hour, third hour, sixth hour and ninth hour. The remains of this division still survive in the titles of the "Little Hours" of the Breviary. It must be remembered that the notes of time were then very vague. There was nothing to guide people as to the hour of the day except the position of the sun, which could only furnish a very rough idea. Thus any more minute divisions would hardly have been possible. All the time between the first and third hour would be called the "first hour"; and so with the others. Thus when St. Mark says that it was the third hour when our Lord was crucified, it is only necessary to suppose that the sun had not yet reached its middle position in the heavens, and noon had not yet arrived. If, moreover, he intended to designate the whole act of crucifixion, beginning from the time when the procession set forth from the Prætorium, it would not be straining his words to suppose them to mean that this took place at about half-past ten, and that our Lord was hanging on the cross by half-past eleven. The difficulty comes when we turn to St. John, for he says (xix. 14) that it was "about the sixth hour" when our Lord stood before Pilate. The common answer given, that it was after eleven, and that St. John in saying "about the sixth hour" does not mean to imply any more exact information than this would involve, can be accepted only if no better explanation is forthcoming. It would involve the whole of the way of the cross and crucifixion being compressed into little more than half an hour; and at last would not agree very well with the natural meaning of St. Mark. Some have supposed that St John was using a different method of reckoning hours, similar to our own, namely from midnight and midday respectively. There is some evidence of this reckoning having been used in Asia Minor, and it is not impossible that St. John might have adopted it. But if so, we should be only answering one difficulty by propounding another; for the latest hour for our Lord's condemnation would then be about 8 a.m.; and this would leave very little time for all the events since the Sanhedrin

ness over all the earth until the ninth hour. And the sun 45
was darkened; and the veil of the temple was rent in the
midst. And Jesus crying with a loud voice, said: Father, 46
into thy hands I commend my spirit. And saying this he
gave up the ghost. Now the centurion seeing what was 47
done, glorified God, saying: Indeed this was a just man.
And all the multitude of them that were come together to 48
that sight, and saw the things that were done, returned

met at daybreak. A third solution is that the word "sixth" in St. John
ought to be "third," the two symbols (Γ = 3, ϛ = 6) being very like each
other in manuscript, and one having been mistaken for the other by one
of the earliest copyists, under the vague impression gathered from the
other Gospels, that the sixth hour was the one to be prominently mentioned in connection with the Crucifixion. This is far the easiest answer;
and the reading "third" is supported by a few ancient MSS.; but
there is no trace of it in any of the early Uncials. If we reject this
solution, therefore, we must fall back on one of the others till a better
is forthcoming.

there was darkness over all the earth. This should rather be over
all the land—'Εφ' ὅλην τὴν γῆν. There is no reason to think that it
extended beyond Judea, and it is difficult to suppose that it did so,
without much more definite records of so extraordinary a phenomenon
having survived. The two or three allusions sometimes quoted are
from obscure writers, and of doubtful date; and very probably refer
to some ordinary eclipse. The darkness here mentioned could not
have been an eclipse, as being Paschal week, the moon was at its full.
It was clearly a miraculous sign.

45. *The veil of the temple was rent in the midst.* The veil of the
temple was in the "Holy Place," and divided off the "Holy of Holies:"
see on i. 9. Its rending was significant of the end of the old dispensation and the beginning of the new. See Heb. x. 19, 20. There was
also an outer veil in front of the Holy Place; but it is always believed
that the inner one was that which was rent.

47. *The centurion.* See on v. 27. He had been in command of
the soldiers who carried out the crucifixion.

Indeed this was a just man. The conversion of the centurion may be
considered the first answer to our Lord's prayer in v. 34. St. Matthew
(xxvii. 54), and St. Mark (xv. 39), both give his words as "Indeed this
was the Son of God." In the mouth of a pagan, the words "Son of
God" would not mean anything very definite, and there is not much
difference between the two expressions; but it is quite possible that he
used both successively.

48. *All the multitude.* The people must have gradually dispersed
as soon as the crucifixion was accomplished; otherwise indeed our
Lady and St. John could not have come close to the cross. There
were, therefore, probably very few people present at our Lord's

⁴⁹ striking their breasts. And all his acquaintance, and the women that had followed him from Galilee, stood afar off beholding these things.

Burial of our Lord.

(VERS. 50-56.)

⁵⁰ And behold there was a man named Joseph, who was
⁵¹ a counsellor, a good and a just man : (the same had not consented to their counsel and doings,) of Arimathea, a city of Judea, who also himself looked for the kingdom
⁵² of God. This man went to Pilate, and begged the body of

death. But all would have noticed the darkness and the earthquakes and other signs mentioned by the evangelists.

49. *All his acquaintance.* The Greek word is γνωστοί. St. Luke probably means to designate all those who were in any sense disciples, possibly including the apostles themselves.

the women that had followed him from Galilee. See viii. 2, 3. Most of them would not have ventured near the cross before the arrival of Joseph and Nicodemus. We know, however, that our Lady, Mary Magdalen, Mary of Alpheus, and most probably Salome also, stood close to the cross while our Lord was hanging on it still alive. See John xix. 25.

50. *There was a man named Joseph.* This is the only occasion on which he is mentioned.

a counsellor, i.e., a member of the Sanhedrin.

51. *The same had not consented to their counsel and doings.* From this it follows that the condemnation of our Lord was not unanimous. St. Mark, in saying (xiv. 64) that they "all condemned him to be guilty of death," may be speaking generally, and mean that practically all of them did so ; or possibly Joseph had left the council before that time. Most probably Nicodemus had also dissented ; and he likewise took part in our Lord's burial (John xix. 39).

of Arimathea, a city of Judea. Nothing further is known for certain about Arimathea beyond what St. Luke tells us, viz., that it was a city of Judea. The other evangelists do not tell us even this, so that it must have been a city well known to the Jews. Some have conjectured that it was the same as Ramath, the birthplace of the prophet Samuel (1 Kings i. 19).

52. *This man went to Pilate,* &c. The Jewish law (Deut. xxi. 23) forbade the bodies of victims to be left on the gibbet for more than a single day. But, as has already been noted, it was supposed that they would be hung thereon after death instead of before. The Romans often left the bodies hanging to be the prey of vultures. Moreover, in most cases the victims did not die on the day on which they were crucified. In the case of our Lord and the two thieves, as the Sabbath

Jesus. And taking him down, he wrapped him in fine linen, 53
and laid him in a sepulchre that was hewed in stone, wherein
never yet any man had been laid. And it was the day of
the Parasceve, and the sabbath drew on. And the women 54
that were come with him from Galilee, following after, saw 55
the sepulchre, and how his body was laid. And returning, 56
they prepared spices and ointments: and on the sabbath-
day they rested according to the commandment.

was approaching, the Jews obtained from Pilate an order for their legs
to be broken, which was a common way of accelerating death. See
John xix. 31. Our Lord being already dead, the soldiers did not
break His bones, but they opened His side with a lance, which St.
John himself saw (John xix. 35). When Joseph of Arimathea came to
Pilate, the latter wondered that our Lord should be already dead
(Mark xv. 44), and sent for the centurion. Understanding from him
that it was so, he gave Joseph the body.

53. *He wrapped him in fine linen.* Joseph had bought the σινδών,
or winding sheet, that day (Mark xv. 46). A prominent feature in the
ceremonies used before a Jewish burial was the anointing of the corpse.
Nicodemus had brought unguents with him (John xix. 39), but owing to
the late hour and the approach of the Sabbath, everything had to be
done very hurriedly and incompletely.

and laid him in a sepulchre that was hewed in stone. The sepulchre
was in a garden close to the place of crucifixion (John xix. 41), and had
been lately hewn, so that it was new. St. Matthew says (xxvii. 60)
that it belonged to Joseph of Arimathea, and it has been supposed that
it had been intended for himself.

54. *The day of the Parasceve,* i.e., the day of preparation. Every
Friday was known by this name, but this was a special parasceve.

the sabbath drew on. ἐπέφωσκεν = lit. *dawned.* Our translation
expresses the idea meant by St. Luke better than the Greek word, for
the Sabbath began not at dawn, but at sunset, and the time denoted here
is late in the afternoon.

55. *Following after.* The holy women followed the funeral. Thus
among those who assisted at our Lord's burial, we know that there
were present our Lady, St. John, Joseph, Nicodemus, Mary of
Alpheus, Mary Magdalen, and Salome.

56. *And returning, they prepared spices and ointments.* It appears
from this that they reached their homes before sunset, and in time to
get the spices ready before the legal Sabbath began.

on the sabbath-day they rested. These words are put in antithesis
to the opening ones of the next chapter, which should read, "*but* on
the first day of the week," &c. The holy women would have been
permitted by the law to go to the tomb any time after sunset on the
Saturday, when the Sabbath was legally over; but it was useless to
be there before daylight; so they waited till it was towards morning,
and timed themselves so as to arrive at the sepulchre at sunrise.

CHAPTER XXIV.

The Resurrection.

(Vers. 1–12.)

A<small>ND</small> on the first *day* of the week very early in the morning, they came to the sepulchre, bringing the 2 spices which they had prepared. And they found the

1. *Very early in the morning.* There is some difficulty here as to the time. St. Luke says it was "very early," and "before it was light" (*v.* 22); St. John that it was "yet dark"; while St. Mark says "the sun being now risen." The difficulty, however, exists not only in harmonizing St. Mark with the others, but also with himself, for he describes the time as λίαν πρωΐ, which we translate as "very early," and which it is commonly conceded cannot easily be applied to the time after sunrise. On the only other occasion when he uses these words (i. 35), he evidently refers to a very early hour. Probably therefore when he says, "the sun being now risen," he must mean only that dawn had begun to be visible. Thus the hour was shortly before sunrise.

they came to the sepulchre, i.e., the women just alluded to, who had followed our Lord from Galilee. There is no reason to suppose that they all arrived together. St. John seems to say (xx. 1) that Mary Magdalen was there before the others, and "while it was yet dark," but his language does not necessarily imply that she came alone, and in the next verse the use of the first person plural shows at least that she did not leave the tomb till some others had arrived. Being festival time the gates of the city may have been left open all night; or else very probably some of the women, including Mary Magdalen, came from Bethany. The three synoptists each mention Mary of James as accompanying her. St. Mark adds the name of Salome, St. Luke that of Joanna; and he says there were others besides those named: see on *v.* 10.

2. *They found the stone rolled back.* The expression, "the stone," (-ὸν λίθον) is remarkable, as St. Luke has not mentioned any stone. He

stone rolled back from the sepulchre. And going in, 3
they found not the body of the Lord Jesus. And it came 4
to pass, as they were astonished in their mind at this,

seems to assume its existence as well known. To close a grave of this sort with a stone was quite customary : cf. John xi. 38. It is also remarkable that the holy women had not anticipated the difficulty of how to roll it back, or at least they had not allowed it to deter them from going to the sepulchre. Probably in any case they would have been able to find some one to move it for them. A greater obstacle in their way was the presence of the guards (Matt. xxvii. 66). Possibly they did not know that they were there. In the event, the earthquake and the appearance of the angel had the effect of making the guards "as dead men" (Matt. xxviii. 4). The Resurrection had taken place long before the arrival of the women. The only note of time which we have is in St. Mark (xvi. 9), where the word used is πρωί, and denotes an early hour, but is not definite. It is indeed less marked than the λίαν πρωί alluded to above. According to our commonly received tradition, the Resurrection took place a considerable time before sunrise.

4. *As they were astonished.* ἐν τῷ ἀιαπορεῖσθαι = as they were perplexed. The word denotes complete bewilderment.

two men stood by them in shining apparel. The different accounts here present considerable apparent divergencies. St. Matthew and St. Mark mention only one angel; St. Luke mentions two. St. Matthew says the angel was outside, St. Mark and St. Luke that he was inside. Very probably there were several apparitions. As each newcomer arrived, she would enter the sepulchre in order to verify with her own eyes the absence of the sacred body, and the angels would have appeared at least several times. The general drift of their announcement was the same in all cases, but St. Matthew and St. Luke each records what suits the purposes of his own work. There were two great objects which our Lord had in His manifestations after the Resurrection. St. Matthew dwells chiefly on one; St. Luke chiefly on the other. The first was to authenticate the fact of the Resurrection beyond possibility of doubt. This was done by the great Galilean manifestation, the only one made by appointment; and all St. Matthew's last chapter leads up to and describes this. It was necessary that it should take place in Galilee, or at least that it should be far away, for if it had taken place in the neighbourhood of Jerusalem, it would have assumed a public character inconsistent with God's designs. See St. Peter's words (Acts x. 40, 41): "Him God raised up the third day, and gave him to be made manifest, not to all the people, but to witnesses preordained by God, even to us, who did eat and drink with him after he arose again from the dead." The truth of the Resurrection rests not on the few fragmentary records we have of the various apparitions, but on the fact testified by St. Paul (1 Cor. xv.) and known as a certain historical fact, that it was universally accepted and believed by the Christian body. St. Matthew therefore records both the promise of a

19

5 behold two men stood by them in shining apparel. And as they were afraid and bowed down their countenance towards the ground, they said unto them: Why seek you 6 the living with the dead? He is not here, but is risen. Remember how he spoke unto you, when he was yet in 7 Galilee, saying: The son of man must be delivered into the hands of sinful men, and be crucified, and the third 8 day rise again. And they remembered his words. And 9 going back from the sepulchre, they told all these things 10 to the eleven, and to all the rest. And it was Mary Magdalen, and Joanna, and Mary of James, and the other women that were with them, who told these things

great manifestation in Galilee and its fulfilment ; and he also alludes to some of the early apparitions in Jerusalem, which were necessary as preliminary evidence, without which the disciples would never have been induced to take so long a journey in the expectation of seeing our Lord. St. Matthew ends his Gospel with the account of Christ's commission to the apostles given before all the Church. St. Luke, on the other hand, keeps in view the other great object of our Lord's apparitions, namely, that of instructing the apostles in what they had been unable to understand before His death. He says nothing of the promise of a Galilean manifestation, nor of its taking place. If we had nothing but this Gospel to guide us, we should even think that our Lord appeared only in or near Jerusalem. From St. Luke's words in the Acts (i. 3), it appears that during a great part of the forty days, His appearances to the apostles were frequent. This was probably after the Galilean manifestation, and is summed up in *v.* 45 of this chapter. All that St. Luke tells, whether in his Gospel or in the Acts, has reference to the effect on the minds of the apostles and their instruction by our Lord.

7. *The son of man must be delivered into the hands of sinful men and be crucified.* Cf. ix. 22. We have no record of our Lord predicting the manner of His death till Matt. xx. 19, when He was in Judea. But there are evident allusions to it in St. Luke : e.g. ix. 23. If our Lord did prophecy it in detail, His words about carrying the cross after Him would have been all the more intelligible to His hearers.

10. *And it was Mary Magdalen,* &c. The words here do not mean that the women named came to the apostles all together. There were many others who are not named (Mark xv. 41), and they may have arrived singly, or in groups, each to tell her own tale. From St. John (xx. 1) we learn that Mary Magdalen at least arrived alone, and before any of the others. Joanna was the wife of Herod's steward : see on viii. 3. Mary of James is described by St. Matthew (xxviii. 1) as " the other Mary," which is a considerable confirmation of the common Catholic belief concerning the identity of Mary Magdalen with

to the apostles. And these words seemed to them as idle tales: and they did not believe them. But Peter rising up ran to the sepulchre; and stooping down, he saw the linen cloths laid by themselves, and went away wondering in himself at that which was come to pass.

The Two Disciples going to Emmaus.

(VERS. 13-32.)

And behold, two of them went the same day to a town which was sixty furlongs from Jerusalem, named Mary of Bethany, for if there had been two well-known Marys besides our Lady, the appellation, "the other Mary," would not have been applicable to either. Indeed, the absolute silence of the Gospels in regard of Mary of Bethany from the time that she anointed our Lord is, to say the least, a presumptive evidence for identifying her with Magdalen. We can hardly imagine her to have been absent from Calvary during the Crucifixion, living as she did within two miles; or to have been present without being mentioned, at least by St. John.

who told all these things to the eleven. There is really no discrepancy between this and Mark xvi. 8. The meaning is easy to see. The first thought of the holy women would have been to publish the resurrection to every one, and to tell especially our Lord's enemies, the chief priests and those who had put Him to death. But "fear" restrained them. They had nothing to fear from the apostles, however, and naturally told them all they knew.

11. *As idle tales.* λῆρος = nonsense. As a medical word it used to be applied to the wanderings of a delirious person, and no doubt St. Luke used it in the sense familiar to himself as a doctor.

12. *Peter rising up ran to the sepulchre.* See John xx. 3-10. It appears also from St. Luke's words in *v.* 24, that St. Peter did not go alone: we learn from St. John that he himself accompanied him. There is no record of the details of our Lord's appearance to St. Peter; but we know from *v.* 34 that it took place on Easter Sunday, and it is alluded to by St. Paul (1 Cor. xv. 5). The appearance to Mary Magdalen is described by St. John (xx. 11-18), and alluded to by St. Mark (xvi. 9). Thus she was the first of the holy women to see Him, as St. Peter was the first of the apostles. Our Lord also appeared to the other women during the day (Matt. xxviii. 9), and to the apostles and disciples in the evening (*infra, vv.* 33 and 36).

13. *A town which was sixty furlongs from Jerusalem, named Emmaus.* The situation of Emmaus has been, and is still, the subject of much controversy. The specification that it was sixty furlongs—or between six and seven miles—from Jerusalem ought, it would appear,

14 Emmaus. And they talked together of all these things
15 which had happened. And it came to pass, that while
they talked and reasoned with themselves, Jesus himself

to be a considerable guide in helping us to determine its position, and Josephus mentions a hamlet called Ammaous at just that distance, where Titus founded a colony of veterans. This seems so far almost decisive. Nevertheless, we have to face a tradition which existed without dispute for more than a thousand years, identifying the Emmaus of St. Luke with a town formerly called Emmaus, on the ruins of which a fortified city was built under Heliogabalus, in the first half of the third century, and named Nicopolis, which is nearly twenty miles from Jerusalem. Eusebius considers it certainly the same, St. Jerome accepts it without question; and it was commonly received till the fourteenth century. Even now it finds many supporters. The difficulty about the distance from Jerusalem has been partially met by supposing that "sixty furlongs" is a misreading for "one hundred and sixty furlongs"; i.e., that the word ἑκατόν has been omitted. Several of the minor MSS. have the word, and when on the discovery of the Sinaitic Codex it was found that it also had this reading, considerable weight was added to the opinion. But St. Jerome himself, in the Vulgate, gives "sixty furlongs," which shows that he at least thought that reading certain; for he would not otherwise have given one which was fatal to his theory. Moreover, it is quite easy to suppose that early copyists inserted the word ἑκατόν, in consequence of the prevalent belief identifying the spot with Nicopolis, whereas it is difficult to account for its disappearance if it was originally there. A little consideration, however, will show that on other grounds the tradition as to Nicopolis is hardly tenable. A distance of twenty miles would take at least five or six hours to walk, and even leaving for the moment the detail that it was towards evening (vv. 29 and 33) before the disciples started back on their return journey, and taking the rest as it stands, we see that the whole day's walk would have been some forty miles, which could not have occupied less than twelve hours; and if the two returned in reasonable time—as we know they did, for the apostles had not yet had their evening meal (v. 43)—it follows that they must have set out originally at about six or seven in the morning; and this would not have given them time to learn such details about the events of Easter morning as they knew and discoursed about on the way. Moreover, it is very difficult to suppose that our Lord walked with them expounding the Scriptures for so long a time as five or six hours; and the conversation certainly appears to have opened before they were far from Jerusalem. We have, therefore, to seek for another site. Several are mentioned. A village called El Kubeibeh is sometimes pointed to as being just sixty furlongs from Jerusalem, to the north-west; others identify it with a village called Kolonieh, on the road to Jaffa, though it is not much more than forty furlongs from Jerusalem. The name suggests that it was once colonized, and it is

also drawing near went with them. But their eyes were 16 held that they should not know him. And he said to 17 them: What are these discourses that you hold one with another as you walk, and are sad? And the one of them, 18 whose name was Cleophas, answering, said to him: Art thou only a stranger in Jerusalem, and hast not known the things that have been done there in these days? To 19 whom he said: What things? And they said: Concerning Jesus of Nazareth, who was a prophet, mighty in work

supposed that if this is the place alluded to by Josephus, the name Ammaous gave place to the present one on that account. There is, however, not enough known to arrive at any certainty, or even high degree of probability, in the matter.

16. *Their eyes were held that they should not know him.* There was evidently a great change in our Lord's glorified body which prevented recognition at first. Cf. John xx. 14, and xxi. 4. It was not, however, such a change as to prevent those who knew Him from arriving at absolute certainty as to His indentity when they looked at His features and heard His voice. Cf. John xx. 16. It should also be remembered that the two disciples here mentioned were not among His most intimate followers, and would not have known Him as the apostles did.

18. *One of them, whose name was Cleophas.* This is not the same word in Greek as that in John xix. 25, which the Vulgate also translates as Cleophas. The latter is of Aramaic origin, and is derived from the same word as Alpheus, and represents the same person as in Matt. x. 3 and Mark ii. 14. Here the word is Κλεόπας, which is short for Κλεόπατρος, and is of Greek origin. It is possible that it is meant for the same person as the other, but not very likely. He must have been St. Luke's informant, and his name is probably given for that reason. The supposition that St. Luke himself was the second one is most unlikely; for it rests only on pure conjecture, and is not easily reconcilable with his own words (i. 1-4), which imply that he had never seen our Lord. Moreover, throughout the Acts, when recounting anything at which he was present, he invariably used the first person plural; and there is no reason to suppose that he would not have done the same here, had he been present. We have no information as to who the second one was, nor is there any reliable tradition.

Art thou only a stranger. This rendering cannot be correct for μόνος παροικεῖς. "Art thou a stranger all alone" would represent the meaning better.

19. *Concerning Jesus of Nazareth.* The words which follow are of great interest, as showing the extent to which the faith of the ordinary disciples had reached at the end of our Lord's ministry. They recognized Him as a prophet and "a man mighty in word and work": but were still far from the knowledge of what even the apostles only

20 and word before God and all the people. And how our chief priests and princes delivered him to be condemned
21 to death, and crucified him. But we hoped that it was he that should have redeemed Israel : and now besides all this, to-day is the third day since these things were done.
22 Yea, and certain women, also of our company affrighted
23 us, who before it was light were at the sepulchre. And not finding his body, came, saying that they had also seen
24 a vision of angels, who say that he is alive. And some of our people went to the sepulchre : and found it so as the
25 women had said, but him they found not. Then he said to them : O foolish, and slow of heart to believe in all
26 things which the prophets have spoken. Ought not Christ to have suffered these things, and so to enter into his
27 glory ? And beginning at Moses and all the prophets, he expounded to them in all the scriptures the things that

partially realized, but what St. Peter expressed in the words, "Thou art Christ, the Son of the living God" (Matt. xvi. 16).

21. *We hoped*, i.e., we were hoping. The death of our Lord had appeared to frustrate these hopes ; but there was still a glimmer left, as they remembered that He had spoken of His death as about to take place, and of a resurrection to follow.

to-day is the third day. Our Lord's prophecies had always ended with foretelling His resurrection on the third day. Evidently these two disciples remembered this, though very confusedly. Cf. John xx. 9 : " As yet they knew not the scripture, that he must rise again from the dead." Nevertheless the fact of all the strange things reported that morning, added to the fact that it *was* the third day, made them anxious, and gave them some hope.

24. *Some of our people.* These we know to have been St. Peter and St. John (xx. 3–10). As St. Luke has only mentioned the former, the use of the plural here is remarkable. It shows that he was aware that St. Peter had not gone alone : see on *v.* 12.

him they found not. Thus so far, the hopes which had revived had not been realized.

25. *O foolish, and slow of heart to believe.* Our Lord's reproach to them was hardly as strongly expressed as our translation makes it— ἀνόητοι may be better rendered " unintelligent."

26. *Ought not Christ to have suffered*, i.e., was it not so ordained by God ? Cf. Matt. xxvi. 54.

27. *He expounded to them in all the scriptures the things that were concerning him.* The Messianic character of the prophecies of the Old Testament is evident on the surface. Their perfect fulfilment in our Lord required to be pointed out and expounded. See, for example,

were concerning him. And they drew nigh to the town 28 whither they were going : and he made as though he would go farther. But they constrained him, saying : Stay with 29 us, because it is towards evening, and the day is now far spent. And he went in with them. And it came to pass, 30 whilst he was at table with them, he took bread, and blessed and brake, and gave to them. And their eyes 31 were opened, and they knew him : and he vanished out of their sight. And they said one to the other : Was not our 32 heart burning within us, whilst he spoke in the way, and opened to us the scriptures?

Isa. liii., which to us is so plain that it has sometimes been called a fifth gospel of the Passion ; yet none of the Jews before the time of our Lord recognized its true meaning.

28. *They drew nigh to the town whither they were going.* The duration of the conversation between our Lord and the two disciples is not given. He may perhaps have done sufficient expounding in half an hour or a little more ; and this would agree with the supposition we have made : see on *v.* 13. To suppose that He talked for four or five hours—as we should have to do if Emmaus were twenty miles off—would make this apparition very much out of proportion to all the others.

he made as though he would go farther. This translation agrees with the A.V. and also with the R.V. The original Rheims was "he made semblance to go further," which is taken from the Vulgate, *se finxit longius ire.* It does not appear, however, that any pretence or simulation is indicated, and it is probable that He would actually have left them if they had not prayed Him to stop.

30. *He took bread, and blessed and brake, and gave to them.* Many Catholic commentators recognize here a repetition of the Eucharistic sacrament as instituted by our Lord three days before. The close analogy between the wording here and in xxii. 19, points in this direction ; and moreover it has been remarked that the "breaking of bread" was the term used in the Apostolic Church to designate the Mass, and it is used in that sense by St. Luke in the Acts (ii. 42, xx. 7, &c.), so that its use here (see *infra v.* 35) is significant. Against this we have to set the intrinsic improbability of our Lord repeating the Holy Communion, and the fact that as these two had not been present at the Last Supper, it would not have been to them a reason for immediate recognition. It has also been pointed out that the transition from Aorist to Imperfect in the words "He blessed and brake (*aor.*) and gave (*imp.*) to them" agrees with the account of the distribution of the multiplied loaves, but not with any account of the Holy Communion. It is indeed hardly credible that our Lord should have given Holy Communion to these two and not to the apostles the same evening ; and the description in *v.* 43, though somewhat similar to that here, evidently does *not* refer to Holy Communion.

Apparitions to the Eleven.

(VERS. 33-49.)

33 And rising up the same hour they went back to Jerusalem: and they found the eleven gathered together, and
34 those that were with them, saying: The Lord is risen
35 indeed, and hath appeared to Simon. And they told what things were done in the way: and how they knew
36 him in the breaking of bread. Now whilst they were speaking these things, Jesus stood in the midst of them, and saith to them: Peace be to you; it is I, fear not.
37 But they being troubled and frighted, supposed that they
38 saw a spirit. And he said to them: Why are you troubled,
39 and why do thoughts arise in your hearts? See my hands and feet, that it is I myself; handle, and see: for a spirit hath not flesh and bones, as you see me to have.

33. *They found the eleven gathered together.* These words have sometimes raised a difficulty, since we know that only ten of the apostles were present; for Judas was dead and St. Thomas was absent (John xx. 24): but it is surely most natural to suppose that after the death of Judas, "the eleven" was the expression ordinarily used to designate the apostles, just as before they had been called "the twelve." Cf. Mark xiv. 17, when two were already in the supper room, and yet our Lord is said to have arrived "with the twelve."

and those that were with them. We learn definitely from this verse that the apostles had been collected together since their dispersion, and not only the apostles, but also other disciples, here described as "those that were with them." Cleophas and his companion had apparently been of their number, for they knew exactly where to find them. They were probably in the same "upper chamber" where the Last Supper had taken place.

34. *And hath appeared to Simon.* See on v. 12. We have no account of this apparition, but it is alluded to by St. Paul (1. Cor. xv. 5), the fact of its being mentioned only by these two can hardly be accidental, considering the intimate relations in which they stood to one another.

35. *They knew him in the breaking of bread.* See on v. 30.

36. *Jesus stood in the midst of them.* These words suggest a sudden apparition. St. John (xx. 19) is more precise, and tells us that the doors were "shut," i.e., fastened, for fear of the Jews.

37. *They being troubled and frighted.* The little addition from St. John explains this verse, for it gives the reason why they took Him for a spirit, viz., that He stood in the midst, the doors being shut.

And when he had said this, he shewed them his hands 40
and feet. But while they yet believed not and wondered 41
for joy, he said: Have you here anything to eat. And 42
they offered him a piece of a broiled fish, and a honey-
comb. And when he had eaten before them, taking the 43
remains he gave to them. And he said to them: These 44
are the words which I spoke to you while I was yet with
you, and all things must needs be fulfilled, which are
written in the law of Moses, and in the prophets, and in
the psalms, concerning me. Then he opened their under- 45

40. *He shewed them his hands and feet.* The signs of our Lord's identity were His wounds, which He showed them His hands and feet; and St. John adds also His side. These were now, of course, not really wounds: and, in general, the marks of the Passion were entirely removed from our Lord's glorified Body. But He seems to have kept His five wounds visible and palpable, now as signs of His glory, and the work He had done on earth. It is quite probable that Thomas had not rejoined the apostles in the upper chamber at all since our Lord's death, and it was not till they talked to him about the Resurrection that they could induce him to do so. His natural despondency of mind has already been alluded to: see on vi. 15.

41. *Have you here anything to eat?* Our Lord's glorified Body was in no need of food. Our Lord proposed to eat before them as a proof of the reality of His human nature after the Resurrection. See Acts x. 41.

44. *These are the words*, i.e., this is the fulfilment of the words, &c. See John xvi. 16, *seq.*, and also elsewhere.

in the law of Moses, and in the prophets, and in the psalms. This is the only place in the whole New Testament where the Scriptures are divided into three parts. The usual division was simply the law and prophets: see on iv. 15. The Psalms would, of course, in that case, fall under the latter of these divisions.

45. *Then he opened their understanding.* At first sight it would appear that St. Luke means to describe our Lord as ascending into heaven on Easter Sunday. That he did not so intend is evident from the third verse of the Acts, where he himself tells us of the forty days interval, of the length of which we have no other record. A little closer inspection of his Gospel will show independently that such could not have been his meaning; for when the disciples first arrived at Emmaus, he says that it was "towards evening," and the day was "far spent." And, after that, we have to place the supper at Emmaus, the return of the disciples to Jerusalem, and the apparition of our Lord to the apostles. Thus it would be in the middle of the night before they could have been at Bethany. Some have thought that between verses 49 and 50 an interval

46 standing, that they might understand the scriptures. And he said to them : Thus it is written, and thus it behoved Christ to suffer, and to rise again from the dead the third 47 day. And that penance and the remission of sins should be preached in his name unto all nations, beginning at 48 Jerusalem. And you are witnesses of these things. And 49 I send the promise of my Father upon you : but stay you in the city, till you be endued with power from on high.

of forty days is supposed to elapse. This, however, would introduce a new difficulty, as it would place our Lord's instructions to them to remain in Jerusalem on Easter Sunday, which would be inconsistent with the account of the arrangement for the Galilean manifestation given by St. Matthew. Others put the interval between verses 43 and 44, which is a possible supposition. But it seems simpler to suppose that v. 45 covers the interval. We should then paraphrase it thus : " At that time He began a course of instruction on the references to Himself in the Scriptures, and He continued to expound it to them at intervals, when He visited them during the next forty days. Then, at the final interview, He summed up what He had told them, saying, 'Thus it is written,' &c. (v. 46)." This also agrees better with the general scope of this chapter.

47. *And that penance and the remission of sins should be preached in his name.* Here the virtue of penance and God's forgivingness are mentioned as the chief characteristics of Christianity. On the word μετάνοια, see on iii. 3.

unto all nations. St. Luke here gives the summing up of Christian teaching, as delivered by our Lord at the very end of His time on earth, when the apostles were able more fully to understand it. Hence, writing for Gentiles, he naturally points to the universality of the Redemption, and the fact that the Gospel was to be preached "unto all nations."

beginning at Jerusalem. The apostles' labours naturally began at Jerusalem, and were first directed to the conversion of the Jews. The instructions of our Lord in this respect must have been very much fuller than the words here indicate, and probably our Lord told them some definite period that must elapse before their dispersion. Hence, even at a time when there was great persecution, so that the faithful in general were scattered through Judea and Samaria, the apostles remained in Jerusalem (Acts viii. 1).

48. *And you are witnesses of these things.* One of the chief parts of the apostolic office was to be an authorised witness of the Resurrection : see on vi. 13 ; and Acts i. 22.

49. *Stay you in the city.* See Acts i. 4. The meaning that they were to stay in Jerusalem for the coming of the Holy Ghost, was evidently quite understood by the apostles.

The Ascension.

(VERS. 50-53.)

And he led them out as far as Bethania: and lifting up ⁵⁰ his hands he blessed them. And it came to pass, whilst ⁵¹ he blessed them, he departed from them, and was carried up to heaven. And they adoring went back into Jerusalem ⁵² with great joy. And they were always in the temple prais- ⁵³ ing and blessing God. Amen.

50. *And he led them out.* This is the only instance recorded of our Lord walking through the streets of Jerusalem after His resurrection. We cannot doubt but that in some way He was unrecognizable, or at least unrecognized, by those whom He met. From Acts i. 6 it would appear that he was accompanied by others besides the apostles.

as far as Bethania. ἕως πρὸς Βηθανίαν, should be rather "towards Bethany," to the summit of Mount Olivet. See Acts i. 12, where the place of the Ascension is described as distant from Jerusalem "a Sabbath day's journey," i.e., less than a mile. Bethany itself was nearly two miles away.

51. *Whilst he blessed them, he departed from them.* In the Acts (i. 9) St. Luke says "a cloud received Him out of their sight." St. Mark adds (xvi. 19) that He "sitteth at the right hand of God." The meaning is clear, and whether the words which follow—"and was carried up to heaven"—are genuine or not, about which there is a slight doubt, it is certain that they really express St. Luke's meaning. Our Lord entered heaven that day as Man, and with Him all the souls of the just who had died before that time and had been waiting in Limbo. They entered heaven that day as the first-fruits of the Redemption.

52. *But they adoring,* i.e., adoring *Him.* Their faith in Christ as God was much more vivid after the Resurrection than it had been before. Cf. Matt. xxviii. 17.

with great joy. The apostles evidently recognized that this was a final parting from our Lord, which makes their joy remarkable. It shows that they realized the greatness of the work before them, and the holiness of their vocation. With such thoughts filling their minds, they would feel joy that the time had come for them to begin their work.

53. *And they were always in the temple, praising and blessing God.* St. Luke ends his Gospel with these few words about the early ministry of the apostles, details of which he was to give in his second treatise, which we now call the Acts of the Apostles. It is worthy of remark that each of the three synoptists ends his Gospel by recording in some shape the apostolic commission; and very appropriately so, for the announcement and explanation of it was in truth the main object for which the Gospels themselves were written.

Amen. This word is probably an addition, being absent in several of the earliest MSS.

INDEX.

Jericho, 137, 208, 213
Jerome, St., xix, 144
Jerusalem, 6, 124, 134, 171, 174, 218, 232-5, 274
Joachim, St., 5, 12
John the Baptist, St., 5, 15, 17, 20, 40-6, 92, 113, 143, 222
John the Evangelist, St., 65, 79, 119, 248
Jonas, 150
Jordan, 40
Joseph, St., 11, 31, 36
Juda, 14
Judas the Gaulonite, 11, 23
Judas Iscariot, 50, 240, 244, 249
Jude, St. (= Thaddeus), 80
Judea, 14, 61, 91, 183, 257

KINGDOM, various meanings of, 143, 198, 213

LAST SUPPER, 238
Law, the, 55
Lawyer, 135
Lazarus, 3, 138
Lazarus, the beggar, 192
Limbo Patrum, 228, 269, 283
Lithostrotos, 255, 261
Lectionaria, xv.
Legion, 107
Leprosy, 66
Levi (= St. Matthew), 70
Levirate marriages, 49, 227
Lord, the, 129
Lord's Prayer, 142
Luke, St., Life of, ix-xi
  ,, his Gospel, xliv-lxvii

MAGDALA, 95
Magnificat, the, xlviii, 15
Mammon, 189
Marcion, Gospel of, xii, 2
Mary of Cleophas, 104
Mary Magdalen, 3, 96, 98, 139, 275
Mary of Bethany, 96, 139, 275
Mary, the Blessed Virgin, xlviii, 11, 24, 27, 30, 34, 50, 104, 263, &c.

Mass, xlix, 55
" Master," 65
Matthew, St. (= Levi), 70,
MacMahon, Rev. B., xxxviii
Messiah, 44
Messianic Age, 177, 213, 217, 278
Millstone, 195
Mote, 56
Muratorian Fragment, xii
Murray's Bible, xl
Mustard Seed, 170

NAAMAN, 58
Naim, 90
Nazareth, 11, 32, 56, 58
Nazarites, 8
Needle's eye, 206
Newman, Cardinal, xxxv
Nicodemus, 270
Ninive, 150
Nunc Dimittis, the, xlviii, 29

OINTMENTS, 96
Olivet, 216, 237
Oral Law, 42, 152, 154, 203, 227

PARABLES, 100
Paradise, 207
Paragraph Bibles, xxiii
Paralytic, healing of the, 68
Parasceve, 239
Pasch, 33, 74, 238
Paschal Supper, 242-5
Paul, St., xlviii, 166, 244
Penny, 138, 226
Pentecost, 33
Peter, St., 60, 76, 78, 111, 116-7, 119, 152, 163, 173, 177, 191, 195, 197, 202, 216, 225, 229, 239, 241, 246, 251, 275, 278, 280
Pharisees, 22, 42, 75, 113, 170, 176, 183, 253
Philip, St., 80
Philip the Tetrarch, 38
Philip, husband of Herodias, 38
Phylactery, 34, 136

Pilate, 37, 166, 249, 255, 259, 261, 266, 270
Possession by devils, 59
Pound, 213
Prætorium, 255
Prayer, lv, 145, 201
Procurators, 39
Prophet, 20
Psalms, gradual, 217
Psalter, versions of, xx, xxvii
Publicans, 43, 202
Purification, 27
Purim, 33, 74
Purgatory, 165, 193

QUARANTINE, MOUNT, 51
Quirinus, 23

RABBI, 136
Resurrection, the, 273
Resurrection after death, 227
Revised Version, xxx
Roman Rule, 5, 22, 88, 166, 225, 253
Ruler of the Synagogue, 55

SABA, QUEEN OF, 150
Sabbath, 74, 75, 76, 169, 175, 271
Samaritans, 125, 137
Sanctification of the male first-born, 26
Sanhedrin, 136, 221, 253
Sarepta, 57
Satan, 134
Saviour, 26
Scandal, 195
Scapegoat, 33
Scourging, 259
Scribes, 69, 135, 253
Scrip, 113
Septuagint, x, xlvii
Seventy-two, the, 130
Shekel, 29, 219
Siloe, 167
Simeon, 28
Simon, *see* Peter
Simon the leper, 97
Simon of Cyrene, 262

Son of Man, 69, 117, 122, 127
Supersubstantial, 144
Supper, The Last, 238
Syer's Bible, xxxix
Synagogue, 55, 135, 153, 158

TABERNACLES, FEAST OF, 33, 167
Tatian's Diatesseron, lvii
Temple, the, 6, 27, 33, 136, 218, 219, 232, 269
Temptation, the, 51
Tetrarchies, the, 38
Text of the Gospel, xii-xliii
Textual criticism, xv
Thabor, Mount, 119
Theophilus, xlvi, 4
Thief, the penitent, 267
Thomas, St., 80
Tiberius Cæsar, 37
Tithes, 203
Title on the Cross, 266
Traditions, xiii
Transfiguration, the, 119
Treasury, the, 218, 231
Trent, Council of, xxi, xxiv
Trinity, Blessed, 9, 46, 134
Troy's Bible, xxxix

UNCIALS, iii, xv
Unleavened Bread, feast of, 238, 241
Urevangelion, 1

VIRGINITY, VOW OF, 13
Vulgate, *see* Text

WAY OF THE CROSS, 261-4
"White Garment," 258
Wiseman, Cardinal, xvii, xxxv, xxxviii
Writing Table, 18
Wycliffe's Bible, xxix

ZACCHEUS, 211
Zacharias, 154
Zachary, 5, 8, 10, 18-20.
Zealots, 43, 80
Zebedee, 65

INDEX.

ABEL, 154
Adoptionist Heresy, 47
Agony in the Garden, 248
Analysis of St. Luke's Gospel, lxii–lxvi
Ancyra Marble, the, 22
Andrew, St., 64, 79
Anna, lv, 30
Annas, 39, 251
Anne, St., 5, 12
Antonia, Fort, 255, 261
Apocryphal Gospels, the, 1, 2
Apostles, the, 77, 112, 117, 233, 240
Apostolic office, 77
Aramaic, 26, 144
Archelaus, 31, 38, 208, 213
Arimathea, 270
Ascension, the, 283
Augustine, St., his Gospel Harmony, lvii
Authority of the four Gospels, xlviii
Authorised Version, the, xxx

BAAL, 147
Baptism, character of St. John's, 42
Baptism of our Lord, 46
Barabbas, 260
Barrels of oil, 189
Bartholomew, St. (= Nathanael), 80
Baskets, 116
Beatitudes, the, liii, 82
Beelzebub, 147
Benedictus, the, xlviii, 19
Bethany, 216, 237, 283

Bethlehem, 24
Bethphage, 216
Bethsaida, 64, 79, 133
Bethsaida Julias, 114
Blasphemy against the Holy Ghost, 158
Blood, sweat of, 249
Bramston's Bible, xxxix
"Breaking of Bread," the, 279
Brethren of the Lord, 80, 104
Burial, Jewish, 90

CÆSAREA, xi, xiv, 3, 255
Caiphas, 39, 240, 251, 253
Calvary, 261, 264
Canon of the Mass, 49
Canticles, xlviii
Capharnaum, 58, 70, 89
Catacombs, 64, 115
Centurion, 88, 262, 269
Census, 22, 23
Chagiga, 239
Chapters of the Bible, origin of, xxii
Circumcision, 18, 27
Clementine edition of the Vulgate, xxv
Cleophas, 277
Codices of the New Testament, xiii
Communion of Saints, 183
Confession of St. Peter, 116
Corozain, 132
Cotton's "Rhemes and Doway," xxviii, xxxviii
Cross, 262, 266
Cross, doctrine of the, 117
Crucifixion, 260, 264

Cubit, 160
Cursives, xiii
Cyrene, 262
Cyrinus, 22

"Daily Bread," 144
David, 75
Denarius, 157, 226
Denvir's Bible, xl
Desert, 21
Devil, the, 51
Devils, possession by, 59
Diatesseron, Tatian's, lvii
Disciples, call of the, 64
Divinity of our Lord, 35, 117, 129, 254
Divisions of the New Testament, xiv, xxii
Doctors of the Law, 68

Eagle, 200
"Eleven," the, 280
Elias, 9
Elizabeth, St., 5, 8, 10, 14, 15
Emmaus, 275
Epiphany, 31
Ephrem, 207
Essenes, the, 9
Eucharist, institution of, 244
Excommunication, Jewish, 169
Exorcism, 148
Extreme unction, 137

Farthing, 157
Fasting, 71, 203
Feasts, Jewish, 33, 238
Feeding of Five Thousand, 114
First-born, 24, 28
Flight into Egypt, 31
Free-will, 182

Gabbatha, 254
Gabriel, 10
Galileans, massacre of, 166, 258
Galilee, 11, 54, 61, 257, 273
Galilee, Sea of, 63
Gallican Psalter, xx, xxiv, xxvii
Gasquet's "Old English Bible," xxix

Gehenna, 157, 193
Genealogy of our Lord, liii, 47
Generation, this, 236
Genesareth, lake of, 63
Gentiles, lii
Gentiles, Court of the, 6, 219
Gerasens, country of the, 106
Gethsemani, 237, 248
Golgotha, 264
Gospel, nature of, xlvi, lviii
Gospel Harmony, lvii-lxii
Groat, 184

Hades, 193
Hail Mary, 12, 15
Haydock's Bible, xxxix
Hebrew Poetry, 8, 25
Hebron, 10
Hell, 157, 193
Hellenists, xlvii
Hermas, Shepherd of, 2
Hermon, 119
Herod the Great, 5, 23, 31, 37
Herod, Antipas, 38, 45, 100, 113, 173, 257
Herod Archelaus, 31, 38, 208, 213
Herodians, 77, 173, 225
Herodias, 38, 45
Hexapla, xvii, xx
High Priesthood, 39
Holy Ghost, 9, 13, 46, 134
Holy of Holies, the, 7, 269
Holy Week, Sequence of Events, 219
Hospitality among Jews, 113, 242
Houses, Eastern, 68, 199
Hypocrite, 164

Idumeans, 5
Incense, 7
Inscription, 226, 267
Institution of Eucharist, 244

Jairus, 109
James, St. (the less), 9, 80
James, St. (the greater) 65, 79, 119, 248

www.ingramcontent.com/pod-product-compliance
Lightning Source LLC
Chambersburg PA
CBHW031427230426
43668CB00007B/471